Contemporary Financial Reporting:
A Casebook

Contemporary Financial Reporting: A Casebook

DAVID A. WILSON

Arthur Young and Company
The University of
Texas at Austin

JOHN SHANK

The Ohio State University

DENNIS FROLIN

Harvard University

Prentice-Hall, Inc., Englewood Cliffs, New Jersey 07632

Library of Congress Cataloging in Publication Data

Wilson, David A.
    Contemporary financial reporting.

    1. Accounting—Problems, exercises, etc.
2. Accounting—Case studies. I. Shank, John K.,
joint author. II. Frolin, Dennis, joint author.
III. Title.
HF5661.W54   657   78-21862
ISBN 0-13-170332-3

Editorial/production supervision by Linda Stewart
Interior design by Robert Smith
Cover design by Linda Conway
Manufacturing buyer: Phil Galea

Printed in the United States of America

10 9 8 7 6 5 4 3

Prentice-Hall International, Inc., *London*
Prentice-Hall of Australia Pty. Limited, *Sydney*
Prentice-Hall of Canada, Ltd., *Toronto*
Prentice-Hall of India Private Limited, *New Delhi*
Prentice-Hall of Japan, Inc., *Tokyo*
Prentice-Hall of Southeast Asia Pte. Ltd., *Singapore*
Whitehall Books Limited, *Wellington, New Zealand*

Contents

Preface

Dramatic changes have occurred in recent years in the corporate financial reporting environment. The volume and velocity of changes in and modifications to those accounting principles which are accorded the status of "generally accepted" place demands on the accounting student of the late 1970's which would have been incomprehensible a decade ago. Further, scarce evidence exists which would suggest a deceleration in the rate of issue of new pronouncements.

These changes in the countenance of financial accounting may well demand the development of alternative pedagogical modes to the conventional accounting curriculum. The use of case material is one such alternative. Unfortunately, the location and identification of good case material is an arduous task for any faculty member. This difficulty is compounded for those of us who are not affiliated with those few business schools which dedicate substantial energies to case method instruction. While there are, indeed, bibliographies of case material available, there is scarce information given as to the quality of a specific case as a teaching instrument or of its pedagogical appeal. Further, teaching commentaries are often buried in the files of the original case writer.

The cases included in this book have been used in classrooms at The Ohio State University, Harvard University, The University of Texas at Austin, Northwestern University and the University of Pennsylvania as well as in numerous executive education programs in the United States, Canada and Europe. The case material is organized in a structure parallel to that of most accounting texts, dealing initially with questions of revenue recognition and subsequently with asset valuation, the accounting for liabilities and shareholder's equity and finally addressing some of the unique contemporary problems of corporate financial reporting.

The book may be used alone in the classroom, as a supplement to one of the more conventional financial accounting texts, or together with selected readings in a "contemporary topics" course.

To the many students who, over the past years, participated in the development and revision of the case material, to Ellen Robinson for so patiently tolerating our revisions and diligently executing them, to Lori Neill and Becky Copeland for their tireless assistance with the galley and page proof, and to Ron Ledwith and Elinor Paige for their constant encouragement and support, we extend our thanks. Unfortunately, we cannot transmit to them responsibility for any remaining errors, we assume that responsibility ourselves.

David A. Wilson
John K. Shank
Dennis P. Frolin

August 1978
Houston, Texas

PART I

Revenue Recognition

Foxes
in Spring

*If you haven't learned to love it by 1979, we'll buy it back at the
original price.*

The above statement appeared as the prominent headline in a Limited
Editions, Inc., advertisement placed in a monthly magazine catering to a select,
high-income readership. Its intent is to announce the company's new porcelain
figurine, "Foxes in Spring," which would be offered in limited quantities at a
price of $2,000. Limited Editions' idea is to offer literally "a beautiful invest-
ment opportunity" with capital gains potential to a wealthy investor. By guaran-
teeing that production would be limited, the figurines could immediately attain
status similar to an antique.

The guarantee offered by Limited was quite simple:

> *Subject to being in its original condition, we guarantee to repurchase
> any of our "Foxes in Spring" figurines at the original price of $2,000
> at any time after five years from the date of purchase.*[1]

The guarantee was not restricted to the original purchaser and hence was trans-
ferable from one party to another. The only other return provision allowed a
purchaser to receive an 80 percent refund of the purchase price if the figurine
was returned within three months from the date of purchase.

The figurines are offered for sale in only one extremely reputable store in
each of ten large American cities. These stores were individually identified in

---

This case was written by Dennis P. Frolin as a basis for class discussion rather than to illustrate either effective or ineffective handling of an administrative situation.
Copyright © 1976 by the President and Fellows of Harvard College. Distributed by the Intercollegiate Case Clearing House, Soldiers Field, Boston, Mass. 02163. All rights reserved to the
contributors. Printed in the U.S.A.

[1] As printed in the advertisement.

the advertisement. Each of the ten was provided with one "Foxes in Spring" figurine to be used for display. It was informally understood that Limited Editions would not ask for the return of the figurine. The stores otherwise have no inventory. When a customer signs a "subscription request" the store forwards it to Limited. The "subscription" was an indication of interest but carried no contractual obligation on the part of the buyer. Limited would fill the subscription by shipping directly to the customer. Upon notification of shipment, the retail store would then bill the customer. Upon collection, the store deducted its 10 percent commission and forwarded the net amount of $1,800 to Limited. If a figurine was returned in the first three months, Limited simply sent an 80 percent refund ($1,600) to the customer. Limited did not request a refund of the 10 percent sales commission from the retail store.

Production of "Foxes in Spring" was strictly limited to 500 pieces. The design of the figurine and the mold from which it would be produced were created by an artist for a fee of $50,000. This fee was paid in 1974. Production was contracted out to a reputable company which agreed to run batches of 100 pieces upon instructions from Limited. When a batch was produced, each figurine was then hand painted and finished by skilled workers. Due to the extremely high quality standards demanded by Limited, the early batches cost substantially more to produce, paint, and finish than did the later batches. Production cost data is summarized in Exhibit 1.

Limited Editions was incorporated as a separate legal entity in June 1974. The stock was sold for $10,000. The stock is 50 percent owned by a small, diversified, over-the-counter company engaged in a variety of businesses and 50 percent owned by a small number of self-proclaimed "venture capitalists" who play no active role in managing the company. The "venture capitalists" readily admit that their interest in Limited Editions, Inc., was in part nurtured

Exhibit 1. Batch Production Data

BATCH	DATE	UNITS	COST	AVERAGE COST PER UNIT
1	July 1974	100	$100,000	$1000
2	September 1974	100	80,000	800
3	October 1974	100	60,000	600
4	December 1974*	100	40,000	400
5	March 1975†	100	20,000	200

*The manufacturer was paid for the December shipment in January 1975.
†As of December 31, 1974, Limited Editions was not really sure what the last batch of 100 figurines would cost. The $20,000 ultimately paid would have been a reasonable estimate as of December 31, 1974.

by the widely publicized success stories of companies like The Franklin Mint[2] that have capitalized on the public's recent interest in "collector items" as an investment hedge against inflation. Both the management and owners of Limited Editions hope to build the company into a leader in this new, unexploited figurine market. Encouraged by the apparent success of the company's first figurine, management was already laying detailed plans for a number of future offerings.

Design and production began in July 1974; promotion in September; and sales in October. Summary of activities is presented in Exhibit 2. The bulk of 1974 sales appeared to be related to the year-end Christmas season. Of the 290 figurines shipped to customers in 1974, 100 were to shareholders (or members of their families), or to management employees (or members of their families). Since these sales were not made through a retail dealer, the full $2,000 purchase price was received in cash by Limited Editions. Of the 190 pieces shipped to non-related parties, cash had been received by year end from the retailer for 140 pieces; 50 pieces were uncollected; none of the 190 pieces were returned in 1974 but 20 of them were returned early in 1975, some after the three-month return period had expired. Each of the 20 customers promptly received a $1,600 cash refund.

Promotional and advertising costs of $25,000 were paid in 1974. Limited planned to do no further advertising of "Foxes in Spring" in 1975. General and Administrative expenses for 1974 were $50,000 and all these expenses were paid in cash before year end. It was expected that these costs would continue at roughly the same level in future years.

Exhibit 2. Summary of Activities for the Year Ended December 31, 1974

	1974
Figurines produced	400
Figurine subscriptions received	320
Figurines shipped to customers	290
Figurines sent to retailers for display	10
Figurines returned	0
Figurines in inventory	100
Figurines for which cash was collected by December 31, 1974	240
Figurines shipped but not paid for by December 31, 1974	50

[2] The Franklin Mint, traded on the New York Stock Exchange, is recognized as one of the leading producers of limited edition collectibles. Its issues include commemorative and art medals in silver and gold, sculptures in pewter and bronze, deluxe leather bound books, and works of art in fine crystal.

1. (a) To prepare financial statements for 1974 for Limited Editions, you must make accounting policy decisions in several areas. List the areas requiring an accounting policy decision. For each such decision, describe what approach you would take and explain why you choose that approach. *Ignore income tax considerations.*

   (b) Based on the accounting policies you recommend in part (a), prepare an income statement for 1974 and a balance sheet as of December 31, 1974 for Limited Editions. *Ignore income tax considerations.*

2. Assume that Limited Editions will use the "cash basis" for federal income tax purposes so that *taxable* income is $87,000.* Assuming a 50% tax rate, the tax due is $43,500. Assume that this amount will be paid in 1975. Revise your balance sheet and income statement from Question 1 to allow for income taxes.

3. Prepare a statement of sources and uses of cash for Limited Editions for 1974 (the first line of your statement should be net income after taxes for 1974 as shown in Question 2).

---

*Calculation of taxable profit:

Collections		$452,000
Cash Payments:		
to Artist	$ 50,000	
Promotion & Advertising	25,000	
Gen'l. & Admin. Expenses	50,000	
Paid to Manufacturer	240,000	365,000
Taxable Profit		$ 87,000

MacDonald's Farm

Dennis Grey, an assistant vice president dealing with consumer credit at a large New York bank, was opening his mail in his office high above the street at No. 23 Wall. Among the letters was notification from a lawyer that the estate of his recently deceased uncle, Jeremiah MacDonald, had been settled, leaving Dennis as the owner of a 2,000 acre wheat farm in east central Iowa. As a result of this letter and a subsequent telephone conversation, Mr. Grey obtained certain information about the operations of the farm in 1972 and its financial position at the end of that year. The lawyer who furnished the data had stated that the numbers were, in some instances, approximate. Mr. MacDonald's managers "weren't great bookkeepers," according to the lawyer.

Dennis had taken a course in agribusiness at a leading Eastern business school and, despite the distance between New York and Iowa, he was interested in retaining ownership of the farm if he could determine its profitability. During the last ten years of his life, Jeremiah MacDonald had hired professional managers to run his farm while he remained in semi-retirement in Florida.

Keeping the farm as an investment was particularly interesting to Dennis for the following reasons:

1. Recent grain deals with Communist countries had increased present farm commodity prices substantially; many experts believed these prices would remain high for the next several years.
2. While the number of small farms had decreased markedly in the last 20

This case was written by Jonathan Brown, Research Assistant, under the supervision of Assistant Professor John K. Shank as the basis for class discussion rather than to illustrate either effective or ineffective handling of an administrative situation.

years, large farms such as MacDonald's, using mechanization and new hybrid seed varieties, could be extremely profitable.

3. The value of good farmland in Iowa was appreciating at about 10 to 15 percent a year. Also, a proposed shopping center would border on 100 acres of the farm. Such developments, if actually built, usually increase the value of frontage property by several times.

Looking over the data on revenues and expenses, Dennis discovered that there was no number for total revenues for the year or for the beginning or ending inventory. The lawyer's letter explained that there was some doubt in his mind about when revenue for the farm should be recognized and about the appropriate way to value the grain inventory. There are at least three alternative stages in the wheat growing cycle at which revenue could be counted.

First, the *production method* could be used. Since wheat has a daily valuation on the Chicago Commodity Exchange, any unsold inventory as of December 31 could be valued at market price very objectively. In this way, revenue can be counted for all wheat produced in a given year, regardless of whether it is sold or not. A decision not to sell this wheat before December 31 is based on speculation about future wheat price increases.

Second, the *sale method* could be used. This would recognize revenue when the grain is purchased from the farm by the grain elevator operator in the neighboring town. In this instance, the owner of the grain elevator had just sold control to a Kansas City company with no previous experience in running such a facility. The manager of the MacDonald Farm had expressed some concern about selling to an unknown operator.

Third, the *collection method* could be used. Under this approach revenue is counted when the cash is actually received by the farm from the grain elevator operator. Full collection often takes several months because a grain elevator operator might keep wheat for a considerable time in the hope that prices would rise so he could sell at a greater profit.

The following data for 1972 were obtained from the lawyer:

INVENTORY

Beginning inventory	0 bushels
1972 wheat production	210,000 bushels
Sold to grain elevator	180,000 bushels
Ending inventory	30,000 bushels

PRICES

The average price per bushel for wheat sold to the grain elevator operator in 1972 was $2.20. The price per bushel at the time of the wheat harvest was $2.10. The closing price per bushel at December 31, 1972, was $2.28.

ACCOUNTS RECEIVABLE

At year end, the proceeds from 20,000 bushels had not yet been received from the elevator operator. The average sales price of this wheat had been $2.22 per bushel. There were no uncollected proceeds at December 31, 1971.

CASH

Also at year end, the farm had a checking account balance of $5,800 and a savings account totalling $15,000.

LAND

The original cost of the land was $250,000. It was appraised for estate tax purposes at $700 per acre, or $1,400,000.

BUILDINGS AND MACHINERY

Buildings and machinery with an original cost of $275,000 and accumulated depreciation of $200,000 are employed on the farm. The depreciation expense for 1972 would be $19,000. New equipment costing $25,000 had been bought during the year.

CURRENT LIABILITIES

The farm has notes payable and accounts payable totalling $22,000.

OWNERS' EQUITY

Common stock has a par value of $5,000 plus additional paid-in capital of $300,000. The lawyer had no idea of the amount of retained earnings, if any, but he did say, "If they're there they must be pretty old, because old Gerry withdrew most of the earnings in the last few years in order to continue the life style to which he had become accustomed in Florida."

Mr. Grey also learned that "the only string attached" to his uncle's gift was that any 1972 income in excess of the withdrawals already made was to be turned over to Mrs. Ruth Dorrance, a widow who had kept house for Mr. MacDonald in Florida.

1972 EXPENSES FOR THE MACDONALD FARM

A. VARIABLE COSTS PER BUSHEL

(assuming a yield per acre of 100 bushels which was the average over the past five years)

Seed	$.035
Fertilizer and chemicals	$.210
Machinery costs, fuel, and repairs	$.065
Part-time labor and other costs	$.025
Variable cost per bushel	$.335

B. ANNUAL COSTS NOT RELATED TO THE VOLUME OF PRODUCTION

Salaries and wages	$45,000
Insurance	4,000
Taxes other than income taxes*	15,000
Other expenses	30,000
Total	$94,000
Depreciation in 1972	$19,000

*This figure excludes income taxes, since the business was taxed as a sole proprietorship.

1. It should not be difficult to visualize the funds flow results of the 1972 operations. After having estimated them, consider the results of the three methods of recognizing revenue upon all the accounts that would be affected. Under the production method, the unsold wheat can be entered in an account, "Inventory at sale value."

2. It will be more difficult to estimate the balance sheet for December 31, 1972, but try to do so.

3. Estimating the amount of Mr. MacDonald's withdrawals in 1972 requires assumptions about the 1971 balance sheet (why?). Make reasonable assumptions, and try it.

4. If it appears that a balance of 1972 income is due Mrs. Dorrance, where will the money come from to pay her?

5. Should Dennis Grey keep the farm as an investment? As a general guideline, Mr. Grey felt that a good investment should return 15 to 20 percent a year (before taxes).

Great Southwest Corporation (C)

On June 30, 1969, Great Southwest Corporation (GSC) sold its amusement park in Dallas, called Six Flags Over Texas, to a group of private investors. The purchase price was $40 million. The terms were $1.5 million down and the balance over 35 years with interest at 6½ percent. The note receivable of $38.5 million was to be paid off in 35 annual payments of $2.8 million. (The present value of 35 annual payments of $2.8 million discounted at 6½ percent interest is $38.5 million.) The note was secured only by the amusement park. GSC signed an agreement with the new owners whereby GSC would continue to operate the park for an annual management fee.

The amusement park had been carried on the books of GSC at a gross cost of $14.2 million, offset partially by accumulated depreciation of $4.8 million. GSC paid a 5 percent commission ($2 million) to a real estate firm for finding a buyer for the park. You may assume that any gain on the sale would be taxed to GSC at the rate of 25 percent, which then applied to "capital gains."

The new owners allocated the $40 million purchase price as follows:

Land	$ 5. million
Buildings and equipment	25. million
Non-competition agreement with GSC for 10 years	8. million
License to use the "Six Flags Over Texas" name— unlimited life	2. million
Total	$40. million

This case was prepared by Associate Professor John K. Shank as the basis for class discussion rather than to illustrate the effective or ineffective handling of an administrative situation.

1. Should GSC recognize the full profit on the sale of this amusement park in 1969? What factors would you consider in deciding when to recognize the gain?
2. Assuming the gain were to be recognized in 1969, how would you compute the gain? What is the amount of the gain, after taxes?
3. How would your answer to question 2 change if the sale had taken place in 1972 (after adoption of the imputed interest accounting principle)? You may use an interest rate of 9 percent for purposes of this question.
4. Should the accounting treatment by the new owners regarding the "non-competition agreement" influence the way the sale transaction is recorded by GSC?

Teltronics
Services Inc.

"The irony of life is that what one person thinks is conservative another feels is downright misleading," said Ed Beagan, Chairman of the Board and President of Teltronics. "We want to tell our financial story as it is, show the Ericsson Corporation that we are profitable, the banks that we are solvent, and reflect to prospective clients that we will continue to be in business in spite of the fact that a number of large companies have dropped out of the interconnect business. Everyone seems to believe that accounting for long-term leases on the operating basis is the conservative approach, but I don't think that this method accurately portrays the operations of this company and I think it deludes our present investors."

Ed Beagan made the above comment in late July during an Executive Committee meeting devoted to determining the way in which the company would report its earnings for the first half of 1974. Although the selection of an accounting method for the interim report would not preclude the use of alternative methods at year end, the Executive Committee felt strongly that switching methods six months from now would damage the company's credibility in the investment community.

BACKGROUND ON THE COMPANY

Teltronics Services was incorporated in late 1971 and began operating in 1972. It provides business telephone systems to organizations in the greater New York

This case was prepared by professors Neil C. Churchill and Dennis P. Frolin as a basis for class discussion rather than to illustrate either effective or ineffective handling of an administrative situation.

metropolitan area. Teltronics' product line included telephone switching equipment called PABX's (Private Automatic Branch Exchange) located on the customer's premises and connected to AT&T's trunk lines, telephone instruments, and telephone-type intercom systems.

The Industry

The industry in which Teltronics operates is known as the interconnect market, which was given its start by the landmark Federal Communications Commission's Carterfone decision in 1968. This ruling required AT&T to permit private telephone equipment to be attached to operating telephone companies' circuits. Since that decision, the interconnect business has grown from 59 systems in 1970 to 2,935 in 1973 and is estimated by the New York State Public Service Commission to grow to 5,000 systems in 1974 and to 63,000 by 1984.

The potential of the interconnect market attracted many firms, but the small initial size of the market and the inappropriate strategies used to deal with it caused such firms as Litton, Norelco, G.E., Plessy, Arcata, and Teleprompter to withdraw after sustaining losses from $1 million to $40 million. At present Teltronics has over 45 percent of the metropolitan New York interconnect market. The balance is distributed as follows: 14 percent to ITT, which is down nationwide from 15 to 2 offices; 8 percent to Stromberg-Carlson, which has closed over 20 offices; and 32 percent to some 20 small companies.

Of the factors contributing to the failure of so many firms, Ed Beagan believes the following to be the most significant:

- Direction of initial sales effort to the Fortune 500 companies, which put the firms in head-to-head competition with AT&T without first demonstrating the credibility of their product through smaller systems in companies where AT&T's influence is less pervasive.
- The relatively small size of the initial market could only support one or two firms.
- Attempting to sell nationwide at standard prices in a country where local tariffs make individual pricing policies mandatory.
- Installing a variety of equipment in a dispersed geographical area, which makes the high level of service that must be provided very difficult and very, very expensive.
- The disinclination of equipment manufacturers who sell primarily to independent telephone companies to compete aggressively and thus jeopardize a significantly larger market for their products.
- The undercapitalization of small firms that limited their ability to finance customer systems and the tendency of larger firms to utilize ex-telephone company personnel who were less than familiar with rough-and-tumble competitive situations.
- Differing union wage structures which, for some companies, resulted in installation and service rates double those of others.

Teltronics viewed the interconnect market as a classic situation in which penetration would initially occur in small- to medium-sized firms and then move to the Fortune 500. That this was indeed true has been borne out by Teltronics' average sale, increasing from $8,000 in 1972 to $15,000 in 1973 and $22,000 in the first half of 1974. This increase in size coupled with a growth in the number of systems installed has produced a 50 percent annual growth rate in sales in Teltronics' four-year history.

The second major strategy was financial. Teltronics was formed with the realization of the need to go public as soon as possible in order to have the capital necessary to offer a lease program which, in Ed Beagan's words, "is essential for successful marketing of telephone equipment. A lease program effectively counters the Telephone Company's argument to customers that 'interconnect companies will sell you the equipment and then walk away.' However lease programs require substantial capital because of the investment required in equipment and installation and the delayed return of cash in the form of rental payments spread, in Teltronics' leases, over three to nearly ten years."

To implement its financial strategy, Teltronics looked to the financial markets. In July 1972 it received an offer from a New York Stock Exchange member firm to make a $1 million private placement. Teltronics turned it down but accepted a $100,000, three-year convertible note[1] with a firm letter of intent for a subsequent public offering. In January 1973, the company sold 200,000 shares of common stock to the public at $10 a share, netting $1,670,000. These funds and the close connections the company has maintained with the banking community—four of the six company officers were formerly employed in financial positions—allowed Teltronics to maintain a cash balance of nearly $500,000. "A customer often has a vision—often implanted by a Telephone Company salesperson—that interconnect firms are going to sell the equipment and disappear. When they see a half million in cash on the balance sheet, the sale is half made." In 1972 and 1973 the company entered into an arrangement with the Chemical Bank of New York to "sell" them customer leases at "prime plus 2½ percent" with a minimum of requirements—a restricted recourse cash fund amounting to 3 percent of the aggregate unpaid balance of these contracts. This amounted to an effective interest rate of about 11 percent a year in 1974.

In personnel, Teltronics has recruited only successful Telephone salespersons for marketing, and its technical people are recruited primarily from the computer industry because of both their technical expertise—which is relevant to the modern equipment Teltronics installs—and the mental attitude toward their job that the computer industry engenders and that by and large the telephone industry fails to produce. Teltronics' installation personnel are represented

---

[1] The convertible notes carry a 7 percent coupon and mature in August 1975. The conversion price is $5.00.

by the Communications Workers of America—the same union representing Telephone Company personnel.

Teltronics' market area has been restricted to metropolitan New York. Teltronics' management estimates that 20 percent of the world's PABX equipment is located within 75 miles of New York City, 98 percent supplied by AT&T. New York telephone rates are presently 40 percent higher than telephone rates in all other states. Thus any ultimate expansion will depend on rate increases in other areas—which Teltronics' management estimates to be five to ten years away.

Teltronics' relationship with the L. M. Ericsson Company of Sweden provides it with a strong product line and increased financial strength. Ericsson's worldwide sales in 1973 were $1.2 billion, with $204 million in private exchanges and telephone instruments. Less than 2 percent of Ericsson's sales are in the United States. Teltronics serves as Ericsson's PABX marketing arm in the New York metropolitan area. The closeness of this relationship is exemplified by Ericsson's agreeing to guarantee a forthcoming Teltronics five-year bank loan to fund its rental program. The Ericsson product line is complete, ranging from small telephone systems to huge computer-controlled switching systems. In Europe, Ericsson's computer switch dominates the market against such competition as IBM's 3750 Telephone System. Ericsson's downtime is estimated to be two hours every 40 years versus the weekly interruptions accepted in conventional computer-based systems. Though higher priced, 20 percent above competition, Teltronics believes Ericsson's superior quality overcomes any market resistance the price may produce and accounts for Ericsson's being the second largest telephone equipment manufacturer in the world—next only to Western Electric.

PRESENT SITUATION

The Market

Teltronics offers equipment to customers for purchase or for lease. The leasing terms normally range from three to ten years with the provision that the customer has the right to buy the equipment at the end of the lease at its current market value. In an environment of constantly increasing rates charged by New York Telephone—an average rate increase over the last five years of 10 percent a year—the equipment has actually been increasing in value. As Paul Dominick, Vice President Operations stated, "The telephone business is a peculiar one. Our old equipment goes up in value each year. It takes 40 years to wear out and, as the cost to manufacture it steadily increases with Ma Bell continually receiving rate increases, we can keep releasing most of what we have for the next 25 or so years."

Teltronics installs the equipment free, generally including one year's free service, and offers service on a low fixed-rate contract or a time-and-materials basis for the life of the lease. As Melvin Silverstein, Vice President Marketing, put it, "We are happy to use our service contract as a loss leader; the installing equipment is the key to this business and you'd be amazed how well customers respond to a guaranteed rental rate and essentially free service." The reliability of the equipment is attested to by the fact that maintenance expenses run some 2 percent of operating expense.

Customer choice between outright purchase and leasing (rental) has been changing (see Exhibit 1). The current shift toward leasing has been due in part to Teltronics' sales efforts, in part the nature of the economy, but it is also attributable to the larger systems Teltronics is now selling. "It is much easier for the communications manager to get top-level approval—or to even avoid going to the top altogether—on a telephone equipment rental contract than for a capital expenditure. After all, companies have to have telephone service and they always rented it. If you ask a manager what his phone system is worth he has a hard time deciding even a ballpark number. 'We get it from Ma Bell free, don't we?' is a typical response. We are flexible, however, and we will try to accommodate the customer in any way that is appropriate—cash purchase, lease funding, investment tax credit, depreciation—you name it."

The Economics

Teltronics' rates for telephone equipment are approximately 20 percent under those of the New York Telephone Co. In spite of the flexibility in the terms available, most customers either purchase for cash or take a lease, now tending toward five years in length, that provides for a series of monthly payments with an extra one in the first month and another in the last. Thus a five-year lease would have 59 equal payments plus a double payment in the first month and an extra one at the end. Teltronics uses a 16-plus percent interest rate to calculate the monthly payments which, with the two extra payments, approximates the 18 percent interest charged by banks to finance competitors' interconnect installations. This rate is caused both by the high current interest charges and the drop outs experienced in the interconnect business. Using

Exhibit 1. *Nature of Equipment Placements*

YEAR	OUTRIGHT "CASH" SALE	LEASE PLACEMENTS RETAINED	LEASE PLACEMENTS SOLD TO BANKS
1972	20%	—	80%
1973	30%	10%	60%
1974 (1st half)	40%	25%	35%
1975 (est.)	40%	40%	20%
1979 (est.)	33%	67%	—
1981 (est.)	25%	75%	—

interest tables, the monthly factor for five years is 0.0245. This times the cash selling price yields the monthly payment.[2] For a system with a cash selling price of \$32,000 and a five-year lease (see Exhibit 2), the comparative rate would be \$784 per month (.0245 × \$32,000) versus \$940 per month for the New York Telephone Co. The average cost of sales to Teltronics has been 55 percent including installation.[3] Teltronics pays a sales commission of 10 percent of the cash sales price. The \$32,000 system cited above, if sold for cash, would produce a direct contribution of \$11,200 calculated as follows:

Sales revenue		\$32,000
Cost of sales		
Equipment	\$15,000	
Installation	2,600	17,600
Sales commission		3,200
Direct contribution		\$11,200

In 1973 Teltronics increased its sales to \$1,549,000 from \$1,061,000 in 1972. During the year the company's owners became divided over whether or not Teltronics should go into manufacturing. The issue was resolved at a stockholders' meeting with a subsequent buyout of the former president. In 1973 Teltronics experienced an operating loss due in part to the dissension that existed, and in part to the write-off of the manufacturing project's study costs (see Exhibits 3 and 4 for the 1973 financial statements). The stock, issued at \$10 had fluctuated between \$9.50 and \$11 per share until June 1973 when the underwriting firm was suspended from the New York Stock Exchange. This resulted in the release of a substantial number of Teltronics' shares onto a relatively thin and, in general, a declining market. As a result, the stock dropped to \$3 within 10 days and has stayed between \$1.75 and \$3 ever since. In July 1974, a class action lawsuit was filed by a group of stockholders to recover the \$10 purchase price of their stock. Teltronics Services, Inc., sees no merit in the action and believes it has good and meritorious defenses to the claims asserted against it.

The 1973 customer installations were mostly in the form of leases which Teltronics turned around and "sold" to Chemical Bank at an average of 9¾

---

[2] The factor is calculated as that number which equates a stream of rental payments at the end of each month for 5 years with the present lump sum cash price at an interest rate of 16.34 percent.

[3] The average cost of equipment has been going down—45 percent (excluding installation fee) in 1974 and 30 percent estimated in a few years. This is because Teltronics has been selling both new and used equipment. While Teltronics is currently acquiring very little used equipment, the company is anticipating reacquiring equipment through conversions of customers to larger systems and reinstalling this equipment elsewhere at essentially zero cost.

Exhibit 2. *Typical Contract*

Cash Sales Price $32,000
    Cost of Equipment $15,000
    Cost of Installation   2,600

Lease Terms:

         $32,000 X .0245 = $784 per month for 5 years

Cash Flow: Contract effective January 1, 1974.*

YEAR	JAN-UARY	FEB-RUARY	MARCH		DECEM-BER	TOTAL PAYMENTS
1974	$1,568	$784	$784	. . .	$ 784	$10,192
1975	784	784	784	. . .	784	9,408
1976	784	784	784	. . .	784	9,408
1977	784	784	784	. . .	784	9,408
1978	784	784	784	. . .	1,568	10,192
Total						$48,608

*Rents are received on the first day of each month.

Present value of cash stream to equal cash price of $32,000 is about 18 3/4%.

Cost of equipment, installation, and selling commission ($3,200) is recovered in 2 years and 2 months.

Exhibit 3. *Consolidated Statement of Operations, Year Ended December 31, 1973 (in thousands except per share data)*

Sales revenues	$1,570
Cost of goods sold	863
Total gross margin	$ 707
Selling, general, and administrative expense	934
Non-recurring write offs	133
Profit before income tax (loss)	$ (360)
Income taxes	
Federal	(70)
State and local	(29)
Net income (loss)	$ (261)
Earnings per share	($.47)

Exhibit 4. *Consolidated Balance Sheet, December 31, 1973 (in thousands)*

Cash and certificates of deposit	$ 868
Accounts receivable (net of estimated losses)	105
Inventory	489
Property and equipment	
leased to customers (net)	69
operating (net)	49
Other assets	22
Total	$1,602
Notes payable	$ 5
Accounts payable and accrued liabilities	79
Customer deposits	38
7% convertible notes payable	100
Common stock and capital in excess of par	1,748
Retained earnings (deficit)	(168)
Less treasury stock at cost	(200)
Total	$1,602

percent interest annually and the provision of the 3 percent recourse account. These advantageous terms were due to Teltronics' solid financial position and a history of many lease placements with essentially a no-default record. Chemical discounted the lease payments and put the money in Teltronics' bank account. Teltronics recorded the cash received from the bank as sales revenue in the same way it did cash from customers. If in the Exhibit 2 example a lease were signed and then sold to the bank, sales revenue would be recorded at $38,685 and the direct contribution is $17,885 as calculated below:

Sales revenue (discounted at .008125	
per month)	$38,685
Cost of sales	
Equipment	15,000
Installation	2,600
Sales commission	3,200
	$17,885

The few leases not "sold" were accounted for on a monthly operating basis. In addition, customers are continually adding instruments and features to systems they have purchased or leased. Each year this business totals approximately 10 percent of the installed equipment base and produces a 40 percent profit on sales.

The First Six Months of 1974

In the first half of 1974, Teltronics increased the number of placements and the dollar value of each over the same 1973 period. While the number sold for cash increased, Teltronics also began to increase the number of leases it held and thus to reduce from 60 to 35 percent the number of leases sold to Chemical Bank. In effect, Teltronics was using its own cash and its general credit to finance its sales, and this was expected to continue as Teltronics' financial structure increases its capacity to finance the leases and as Chemical Bank has indicated a rate increase by the end of the year. This shift in the nature of the sales arrangement and the prediction of its future trend—see Exhibit 1—called for a reconsideration of the method for recording "lease placements."

THE EXECUTIVE COMMITTEE MEETING

In preparation for the Executive Committee Meeting, Robert Chanda, Vice President Finance, projected that equipment placements, priced on a cash sales basis, would be about $2 million in 1974—better than a 50 percent increase over 1973—divided between cash sales, retained leases, and leases sold to Chemical on a 40-30-30 basis. When asked what he forecasted Teltronics' profit would be, Bob Chanda replied, "That depends."—An answer which required the following explanation:

> *There is no problem when we record a cash sale. We show the cash price as revenue, the costs of equipment, installation, and sales commission as expenses and the difference is a profit contribution—and we get the cash.*
>
> *In the past, when we signed a customer to a lease, we would take it to Chemical Bank and get cash for it. Thus we have always recorded as sales revenue the cash the lease provided without having to worry about interest income. Then we deducted the equipment and commission costs and showed a profit—one higher than cash sales because of the 16 to 19% interest rate built into our leases. When we kept an occasional lease, we used the operating method. In the past this problem just wasn't worth worrying about.*
>
> *This year we are beginning to keep as many leases as we sell to the bank and we will be keeping all of them in a few years. Thus Ed [the Chairman and President] wanted us to review the way we record profit on the leases we keep since we don't immediately get much in the way of cash.*
>
> *One way to do this is to record profit on the so-called* operating method *in which we would show only the lease payments we receive each year as revenue, write off the sales commission as expense, and depreciate the cost of equipment and installation over its useful life.*

A second way is known as the financial method. *This method treats a lease essentially as a sale. With the finance method you determine the selling price by calculating the present value of the lease payments. We could make the sales revenue on a lease equal to the cash sales price by discounting the lease at the 18¾% rate we charge our customers. Then we would treat all costs as we do with a cash sale and would show the same operating profit whether we leased or sold—and our "financial profit" would show the 18¾% interest revenue.*

The third alternative is also the financial method *but doing what we do now—discounting the lease at the 11% bank rate. With this method, the sales revenue on a leased placement is greater than on a cash sale. If you look at the first sheet in front of you (Exhibit 5), you will see for our lease example the profit pattern we would report if it was a cash sale and if it was a lease under each accounting alternative.*

Following Bob Chanda's explanation of the financial alternatives, a rather heated discussion ensued:

Sal Lo Bianco *(Vice President, Leasing) The Way I look at it is that we are in two businesses: marketing and banking. We make a profit on both and we have the market savvy and the cash to do both. I can't see why we should get one marketing profit on a sale and another one on a lease. My salespeople get the same 10%. The critical element in this business is installing our equipment. How it is financed is a secondary consideration. We check the customer's credit and if it is O.K., we will make any deal he wants in order to make a sale. If we think rental is the only way to overcome his skepticism to non-Bell equipment, we will rent to him and I'll write the lease to best suit the customer's objectives. To me a sale is a sale and I say, show the same profit on every transaction.*

Paul Dominick *(Vice President Operations) I don't agree, Sal. There is something different about a lease. The customer doesn't own the equipment—we do—and it is good for 20 or more years. Further we don't get the cash the first year so how can we take the profit. Let's use the operating method but depreciate the leases we keep over 25 years. In five years we know we are going to get back a perfectly usable, solid telephone system which you tell me, Sal, we can lease out at at least 75 percent of a new one—and that could be 125 percent of the old price. I think our business is renting out equipment for 3- to 10-year periods; let's show our profit that way—and you can't call me conservative since my method will show more total profit in five years than yours will. You know, our present accounting method is too conservative for the people who invested in our company.*

Ed Beagan *(Chairman and President) One thing, Bob, about the financial method is that you never lose sight of sales on an annual basis. With the operating method there is a guaranteed income stream, and thus people can*

Exhibit 5. Alternative Accounting for Leases

Cash sales price	$32,000
Cost (including installation of $2,600)	17,600
Sales commission	3,200

	1974	1975	1976	1977	1978	Total
			Cash Sale			
Revenue	$32,000	—	—	—	—	$32,000
Cost of equipment	17,600	—	—	—	—	17,600
Commission	3,200	—	—	—	—	3,200
Profit before taxes	$11,200	0	0	0	0	$11,200
			Operating Lease			
Revenue	$10,192	$9,408	$9,408	$9,408	$10,192	$48,608
Cost of equipment						
Depreciated over 10 yr. incl. installation	1,760	1,760	1,760	1,760	1,760	8,800
Commission	3,200	—	—	—	—	3,200
Profit before taxes	$ 5,232	$7,648	$7,648	$7,648	$ 8,432	$36,608
			Financial Lease ($18\frac{3}{4}\%$)			
Revenue	$32,000	—	—	—	—	$32,000
Cost of equipment	17,600	—	—	—	—	17,600
Commission	3,200	—	—	—	—	3,200
Interest income	5,318	$4,535	$3,538	$2,337	$ 880	$16,608
Profit before taxes	$16,518	$4,535	$3,538	$2,337	$ 880	$27,808
			Financial Lease (11%)			
Revenue	$37,631	—	—	—	—	$37,631
Cost of Equipment	17,600	—	—	—	—	17,600
Commission	3,200	—	—	—	—	3,200
Interest income	3,684	$3,022	$2,282	$1,458	$ 531	10,977
Profit before taxes	$20,515	$3,022	$2,282	$1,458	$ 531	$27,808

rest on previous efforts and it takes you a while to see the slowdown. You see it right away when you present value the lease.

Bob, what does the accounting profession have to say about lease accounting? IBM and others surely face this problem.

Bob Chanda *In a way, Ed, our problem is to decide if we are in the equipment or the banking business. The accounting rules offer some basic guidelines to help decide but in the end we have to choose—along with our auditors. Generally we should look at the nature of our leasing activity, the terms of the lease relative to its useful life, the renewal and purchase options of the lease, the probability that these options will be exercised and the risks and rewards of ownership. This last factor relates to who "really" worries about the equipment. For example, if the equipment became totally obsolete, who is stuck with it; or, if a major repair became necessary, who pays the bill; or if the rates that Ma Bell charges for this sort of equipment were doubled, who benefits from the rate increase?*

If we want to treat these leases on a financing basis, the accounting profession has set down some minimum criteria to be met; these include the following:

1. Collectibility of rents must be highly certain.
2. Any future costs that have to be incurred with regard to the leased equipment must be known or accurately estimated.
3. And at least one of the following conditions must hold:
   a) Title of the equipment transfers to the lessee at the end of the lease.
   b) The lease term runs the full economic life of the equipment.
   c) A "favorably" priced option to purchase or renew exists— so that it is highly likely to be exercised.
   d) The present value of the rent payments is greater than usual selling price or the fair value of the equipment.

As to the interest rate used to generate the sales revenue, it is often suggested that the rate normally used by the person leasing the equipment is appropriate.

Sal Lo Bianco *That would be the 18% we charge them.*

Melvin Silverstein *(Vice President, Marketing) Oh come on Sal, you know the only reason we can charge 18% is that Ma Bell charges so much and has so conditioned people to believe that telephone rental is the only way to go. Prime plus a few points depending on their credit rating would be a better estimate.*

I like 11%, it is near prime and it makes Teltronics' profits look the best. We use the fact that we are a public company in our sales presentations. Customers in this industry have seen enough 'red ink.' Our customers are sophisticated; yet, I am afraid they would not be able to perceive that Teltronics is running an efficient organization · if its profits are way down as they would be under the operating method. I don't think our sales people have the expertise necessary to explain the differing effects of accounting. Let's show our profits on the fi-nancial basis and use 11%. Isn't that the rate at which we sell our leases to the bank? Don't we want to be consistent and isn't that what our auditors keep talking about?

Paul Dominick

I don't know what accountants talk about but I think our investors and even our customers should be sophisticated enough to realize the possible distortions that can occur in reporting on an operating basis. I don't want to go too far by comparing Teltronics to IBM, but wouldn't we face exactly the opposite problem that IBM has been warning its shareholders about for years if we use the financing method? When the placement mix shifts at IBM from leasing to outright cash sales, they record a large chunk of profits immediately—the full gross margin to be precise—and thus "lose" the future rental profits they would other-wise have. Every year they've been warning the shareholders that out-right sales make the company look highly profitable now, but should not be expected to continue at that level particularly if the mix shifts back to leasing. Our problem will be just reversed if we decide to use the present value method of reporting. Because of the interest rate dif-ferential between what we charge and what we use for discounting, every time we sign a lease we will record more immediate profit than if we sold it outright. Thus a shift from leasing hurts our current year profits while at IBM it boosts it. Which is fair? Sounds to me like one of us would have an inaccurate accounting method.

Bob Chanda

I have made up some projected financials under four methods for 1974. Maybe it's time for me to hand them out (Exhibit 6). You will notice that I kept our accounting for cash sales constant. The only difference is in the way we handle the leases. The income statements are based on the same assumptions underlying the cash flow figures on the next page (Exhibit 7) and reflect the fact that 35 percent of the leases we will retain have come in during the first six months—the rest will come in from now until December. As for our cash flows in future years, they will be increased by 1975 sales and so on. We haven't had enough unsold leases in the past to make any difference. I personally believe we should adopt the operating method for all *leases—the stock market is really lousy right now, so good earnings won't help us and bad earnings won't hurt us. If we adopt the operating method, we will have built up a nice "kicker" which can help us out in future years and it hasn't cost us a thing.*

IBM and Teltronics are two different animals. We are four years old in a brand-new industry which did not exist a few years ago and is characterized by a high dropout rate and dominated by the most widely known government-sanctioned monopoly in North America. We serve as a marketing arm of a billion-dollar foreign telephone manufacturer. How much profit would we make if a couple of lessees

Exhibit 6. *Estimated Profit for 1974 (in thousands)*

	OPERATING METHOD		FINANCIAL METHOD	
	ALL LEASES (A)	RETAINED LEASES (B)	$18^3/_4\%$ (C)	11% (D)
Sales Revenue				
Cash Sales	$ 800	$ 800	$ 800	$ 800
Retained Leases	70	70	610	770
Sold Leases	70	770	610	770
Total Sales Revenue	$ 940	$1,640	$2,020	$2,340
Cost of Sales				
Cash Sales	$ 440	$ 440	$ 440	$ 440
Retained Leases	33	33	330	330
Sold Leases	33	330	330	330
Total Cost of Sales	$ 506	$ 803	$1,100	$1,100
Sales Gross Margin	$ 434	$ 837	$ 920	$1,240
Financial Profit				
From Banks*	—	30	190	30
Interest Income	—	—	47	25
Total Gross Margin	$ 434	$ 867	$1,157	$1,295
Less:				
Sales Commissions	200	200	200	200
General & Admin Expense	650	650	650	650
Net Profit Before Taxes	$ (416)	$ 17	$ 307	$ 445
Income Taxes				
Federal	$ (170)	$ 7	$ 125	$ 182
State & Local	(62)	3	46	67
	$ (184)	$ 7	$ 136	$ 196
Earnings Per Share	$ (.37)	$ .01	$ .28	$ .40

*The difference in present value of the leases sold to the bank calculated at Tel-tronics' rate, $18^3/_4\%$ or 11%, and the bank rate—which averaged $9^3/_4\%$.

Exhibit 7. Estimated Cash Flow from 1974 Equipment Placements (in thousands)

YEAR	CASH SALES	LEASES KEPT	LEASES SOLD
1974	$ 800	$ 70	$ 800
1975		150	
1976		140	
1977		135	
1978		130	
1979		120	
1980		120	
1981		120	
1982		100	
1983		80	

decide they like Ma Bell better than us? Sure, we can sue for collection but all that would bring us would be legal bills and headaches. As long as that lease is in force we bear the risk of ownership. It's not at all like making a sale. I really think we can prove that the operating method is best, given what happened to other companies in this industry. And besides, think of the future.

Paul Dominick   *Wait a minute, Bob. I want operating but not on the leases we sell Chemical. We haven't any defaults on our leases to speak of and on the one or two we have had, the equipment was worth more than the balance of the contract. Besides, if the customer has two bills to pay— the IRS and the telephone—guess which one he will pick. He will pay us and call up the IRS to discuss the problem. Chemical gets its cash from our customers and they gave us ours. I say it would be a real crime to hide that money from profits. We are in a cash flow business—let's record the profits when we get the money.*

Sal Lo Bianco   *Bob, the operating method is just too conservative. I like the thinking behind the numbers in column C. They show our profits when we earn them, when we put the equipment in, and that is the story of our business. The gross profit is due to operations and it doesn't change with differing financial terms; the financial profit is shown separately where it should be.*

Mel Silverstein   *Well, I like the financial method too, but one thing I don't like about your proposal, Sal, is all the financial profit it shows. I say use the prices we charge as the sales revenue and show Ericsson we are great equipment salesmen and not just efficient bankers. If we didn't have a price list, you couldn't use the 18 percent but would take the rate at which we borrow to produce the sales figure—that's what column D shows and that is what is right.*

27

Ed Beagan

Bob, I think these income statements, the cash flow streams, and the examples of what happens in each year are helping us to put the problem in the proper perspective. I don't think the operating method fairly reflects this company for its current accounting period because it doesn't show the future effects of today's transactions—the company's sales. In effect future stockholders will be buying earnings subsidized by previous losses. That's not even conservative—that is unfair. The present stockholders are also deluded into making decisions based on a distorted picture of operations. Bob, I appreciate your strategic view; Mel, I understand your wanting to see figures that reflect sales efforts and, Sal and Paul, I understand your concerns for cash and for equipment placements. What we want to do is to show this business as it is. Now let's take a look at the options again and see how they match up to the way we really operate Teltronics.

QUESTIONS

1. Which revenue recognition method should Teltronics adopt?
2. What criteria should be considered in selecting this method?
3. How well does the method you selected meet these criteria?

Data Consultants, Inc.

In the summer of 1973, John Wilson, an investor in a variety of small companies, had an option to purchase a controlling interest in Data Consultants, Inc.

Data Consultants, Inc. (DCI) was a small, closely held company engaged actively in several related fields. The company conducted business and industry surveys, developed special computer programs, and offered various management services such as information planning, guidance in mathematical techniques, and marketing research. The customers of the company included both government agencies and commercial firms. The results of the operations of the company for the fiscal year ended July 31, 1973, are shown in Exhibit 1. The balance sheet appears in Exhibit 2.

Beginning in the fall of 1972, DCI had implemented a new strategy, designed to reduce the fluctuations in its level of activity and provide a better basis for long-term, profitable growth. Although the company had been profitable in each of the last several years, profits had been somewhat erratic because most of the company's projects were of relatively short duration (two to three months), with the result that sales volume was erratic and unpredictable. The new strategy was to seek longer term projects which might run for 18 to 30 months, thus permitting a more stable work flow, better work force planning and, management hoped, eventually higher profits. By July 31, 1973, a major shift in the nature of the company's projects had been achieved; nearly three-quarters of the activity in the month of July had been on long-term projects.

This case was prepared by Associate Professor John K. Shank as the basis for class discussion rather than to illustrate either the effective or ineffective handling of an administrative situation.

Exhibit 1. *Statement of Earnings* for the Year Ended July 31, 1973*

Revenues		$12,100,000
Costs and expenses		
Research and development	$3,200,000	
Sales and marketing	2,900,000	
Contract installation expenses	8,250,000	
Service costs	1,300,000	
Administrative expenses	950,000	
Depreciation	700,000	17,300,000
Operating loss		(5,200,000)
Gain on sale of marketable securities		1,300,000
Net loss before taxes		$(3,900,000)

*Statement prepared on a modified cash basis such that

1. Revenue is recognized only when actually received in cash.
2. All expenses (except depreciation) are recognized when paid in cash.

Exhibit 2. *Comparative Balance Sheet*

		JULY 31	
		1973*	1972
Assets			
Cash		$ 1,800,000	$ 3,100,000
Marketable securities		3,600,000	6,800,000
Property and equipment			
Land, buildings and equipment	$8,000,000		
Less accumulated depreciation	2,000,000	6,000,000	5,700,000
		$11,400,000	$15,600,000
Liabilities and Equity			
Equipment notes payable		$ 1,700,000	$ 2,000,000
Common stock and paid in capital		3,200,000	3,200,000
Retained earnings		6,500,000	10,400,000
		$11,400,000	$15,600,000

*Before consideration of tax loss carryback.

Mr. Wilson did not contemplate any further basic changes in the company's way of doing business. However, he was not satisfied with the financial data provided to the Board of Directors. Also, he felt the company's reports to the shareholders were inadequate; first, the accounts of the company were maintained on a modified cash basis rather than an accrual basis, which sought to match revenues and related costs; and second, the company had used its independent public accountant primarily to prepare tax returns, rather than to assist in the preparation of financial reports for stockholders.

Mr. Wilson wanted to review the company's general accounting policies before he exercised his option to purchase the stock. Accordingly, he arranged a meeting to discuss this matter with the company's auditors, his personal auditors, and an executive from another business in which he had an interest.

AUGUST 24 MEETING

The meeting to discuss the accounting policies of DCI was held on Friday, August 24, 1973. Prior to the meeting, Mr. Wilson had received the statements shown in Exhibits 1 and 2 from Fred Kneads, the controller of DCI. Three other men were at the meeting in addition to Wilson and Kneads: Jeff Davis of the Fraser Construction Company, Price Anderson of the CPA firm of Anderson, Mitchell and Company (the firm frequently used by Mr. Wilson) and Peter Bird, present auditor of DCI. John Wilson was the controlling shareholder of Fraser Construction.

Wilson   *This morning I'd like to discuss the accounting policies of DCI. Of course, if necessary, I hope you will make suggestions as to possible changes in the company's accounting policies. Has Fred (Kneads) provided you with copies of the company's latest financial statements?* (All nod in agreement.) *Naturally, I am quite disturbed with the net operating loss of over $5 million for the year ended July 31, 1973, for two reasons: First, the contracts obtained by the company during fiscal 1973 are up 30 percent over last year and management seems to think they were profitable, but the statements indicate a large loss; second, although I can't put my finger on it, I don't think the present set of statements are adequate for my needs.*

I'd like to pass around an agenda which I think will help us focus this discussion.

Mr. Wilson's Agenda

1. *How does Data Consultants, Inc., make a profit:*
   by developing a product?
   by finding customers and signing a contract?
   by performing work on a contract?

by completing a contract?
by billing a customer?
by being paid by a customer?
2. *When should the company recognize sales revenue?*
3. *When should the company recognize expenses?*
4. *What accounting policies best reflect our conclusions on these questions?*

Fred, could you describe briefly the results of the operations of the company during fiscal 1973 (see Exhibit 1) and give us your thoughts on the first item on the agenda.

Kneads   *Gladly, John. First, the company statements of profit and loss have always been drawn up on a modified cash basis. That is, all our expenses are recorded when they are paid out and all our revenue arises when our customers pay us for the services we provide. An exception is expenditures for fixed assets. The depreciation expense on our statements is the same as we are allowed for tax purposes. That way, you see, we do not anticipate revenue which we may not be able to collect, and the statement reflects very closely the change in our flow of cash during the year. Also, it is essentially the same as the statement we submit to the tax authorities.*

Wilson   *Fred, I've always believed a company's financial statements should reflect the basic economics of the business. Why don't you start by telling us how DCI makes a profit?*

Kneads   *Surely, let me show how by describing a typical series of events from start to finish. Since many of our new contracts are linked with new computer software packages developed in our research department, I will start there. Furthermore, to give you a sense of the time element let me break the year into four equal periods. During period 1, we pay the wages of our research staff and the expenses for the computer time and supplies they use in their work. They may complete a project in one quarter or it may take several quarters. Upon completion, the new development or technique is turned over to our sales engineers who attempt to match the capabilities of our new program with the needs of a customer. Sometimes, of course, the customer describes his needs to us first and the program or technique is developed specifically for that customer. Let's assume that the customer is found in period 4 and a contract is completed by period 6. At this point we have either integrated the program to run on the customer's equipment or trained the customer's staff in the use of the technique. For the first six periods then (or about a year and a half) we, out of our own pocket, paid for developing, selling, and delivery.*

Normally, after the customer is satisfied that our service or program is functioning satisfactorily, we bill him some time during the initial period of use. Usually, customers pay the amount of the contract over the next two quarters in accordance with our terms of pay-

ment. If we mail the invoice in the sixth period, we frequently receive half of the amount in the seventh period and half in the eighth. Also, our service department handles inquiries from the customer for four periods after installation for which we do not charge any fee. Thus, most of our contracts last for about ten periods, or two and one-half years, from initial development to final services. Some contracts are only a few months long, but we're now ten months into another contract which we expect will run for two more years.

To sum up, gentlemen, our cash outflow is spread fairly evenly over the life of our contracts, and our cash inflow usually is received in two parts at the end of the contract.

To answer your question directly, Mr. Wilson, I guess we make a profit when we receive more money during a month than we pay out.

Wilson *Price, you have been very patient, but I can see that you are itching to make some comments, so the podium is yours.*

Anderson *Thanks, John. I have some ideas and I'd like to express them in the form of a revised statement for the company for 1973. As you know, I've had the company's 1973 statement for a day or so now, and with Fred's help I revised the statements. Now, I'd like to distribute copies of them to you. (*Mr. Anderson distributes a statement which has been recast and is shown as the first column of Exhibit 3.*) Of course, John, these are rough drafts subject to refinement, but I think they'll help to express my ideas.*

Wilson *Fantastic, Price. The loss of $3.9 million is now a profit of $1.6 million. That's better! (*All laugh*). Perhaps you could tell me where you buy your pencils.*

Anderson *Let me assure you, John, it isn't just a sharp pencil (*smiling*). Fortunately, Fred maintained records of his accumulated costs by contracts, portion of contracts completed, including information on payments received and estimates of the percentage completion on each contract. With this information, Fred and I were able to revise the financial statements using the following underlying assumptions:*

1. *Accrual—that is, matching costs and revenues—instead of merely showing the net cash flow from operations*
2. *Revenue recorded when billed to customer*
3. *Costs deferred—now shown as assets rather than expenses—for contracts not completed*

John, these assumptions can be taken as replies to the first three questions on your agenda. I'd like to comment on each assumption.

First, I used the accrual method to estimate the results of operations rather than the modified cash basis. Let me explain it this way. If all contracts had been completed during the accounting period, all bills paid and all invoices collected, there'd be no difference between

Exhibit 3. *Alternative Earnings Statements* for the Year Ended July 31, 1973*

	COMPLETED CONTRACT BASIS	PERCENTAGE OF COST COMPLETION BASIS	ECONOMIC EARNINGS BASIS
Contract Income:			
Billings on completed contracts	$16,400,000	$16,400,000	$16,400,000
Related installation costs	7,050,000	7,050,000	7,050,000
	9,350,000	9,350,000	9,350,000
Plus earnings recognized on open contracts	—	1,500,000	1,000,000
	9,350,000	10,850,000	10,350,000
Other operating expenses:			
Research and development	3,200,000	3,200,000	} 5,000,000
Sales and marketing	2,900,000	2,900,000	
Service costs	1,300,000	1,300,000	1,300,000
Administrative expenses	950,000	950,000	950,000
Depreciation expense	700,000	700,000	700,000
	9,050,000	9,050,000	7,950,000
Operating earnings	300,000	1,800,000	2,400,000
Gain on temporary investments	1,300,000	1,300,000	2,100,000
Net earnings before taxes	$ 1,600,000	$ 3,100,000	$ 4,500,000

*See Exhibits 4 and 5 for an explanation of the three alternative methods and for additional information related to the calculations.

the cash profit and the accounting accrual profit. But if, on the other hand, you spend money on a contract one period and collect the fee in the second period, you show a cash loss in the first, a cash profit in the second, and have no reasonable estimate of the results of operations for either period. Therefore, in general, the new statements reflect the accrual basis of accounting rather than the modified cash basis. I might add that during the fiscal year ended July 31, 1972, the year before last, the cash profit was approximately equal to the accounting profit. This occurred because most of the projects were of short duration. They were started, completed, and customers' payments were received, all during fiscal 1972.

At the beginning of this last accounting period (fiscal 1973), according to our calculations, there were neither accounts receivable nor uncompleted contracts of any significant amount. Note that at the end of fiscal 1973 accounts receivable on contracts completed or partially completed and deferred costs totalled over $5 million. This reflects the company's new policy of seeking larger and longer term contracts.

I understand that the company is attempting to work out a new form of contract which would make some provision for advance and progress payments on longer term contracts. Of course, the adoption of the "accrual basis" does not mean we don't have to prepare cash budgets. Also, to complete the picture a statement summarizing the sources and uses of funds for the year should be prepared.

Second, revenue has been recorded at the time the customer was billed, rather than when his payments are received. Previously only a memorandum file of accounts receivable was maintained. It seemed to me that you "make your profit" when you complete the contract and bill the customer.

Third, costs incurred on the uncompleted unbilled portion of contracts are deferred to the time period when the revenue will be recognized. Development costs not clearly associated directly with specific uncompleted contracts are included in cost of service. That is, they are written off during this accounting period.

Let me sum up by telling you what my intentions were. I tried to accumulate costs and revenues as they were incurred and earned, respectively; that is, I tried to match together costs and related revenues.

Wilson   *Jeff, would you like to comment on Price's remarks?*

Davis   *Well, let me describe the accounting policy we follow at Fraser Construction for revenue recognition and the matching of costs and revenues. We have a similar problem. Perhaps our experience may suggest a better way to deal with the questions raised in your agenda. Somewhere in my briefcase here . . . I have a Fraser annual report with me and . . . if I can find it, I'd like to read directly from the* Notes to the Financial Statements *. . . ah, here it is.*

Note C—Unbilled Costs and Profits Included in Sales: The company follows the procedure reflecting, on a percentage-of-completion basis, the costs incurred and related profits on fixed-price contracts with progress payment provisions as sales in the month in which such costs are incurred. Included herein are unbilled costs and related profits of $1,000,000 in excess of progress billing of $1,900,000 at November 30, 1972, and unbilled costs and related profits of $500,000 in excess of progress billings of $700,000 at November 30, 1971. In addition, costs on cost-plus-fixed-fee government contracts amounting to $100,000 in 1972 and $150,000 in 1971 are included.

In other words, Price, we take into account not only progress billings which are "legally enforceable" claims as you refer to them, but also the value of work completed but not billed. It seems to me our accounting policy provides a pretty good matching of costs and revenues.

I guess you can argue that our policy is not as "conservative," but the policy is based on competent business judgment which has been substantiated over the years; and the amounts involved are material. Also, our annual report is signed by the auditors.

The auditors agreed to that accounting policy years ago and I guess it's really up to them to decide such things as a company's accounting policy anyway.

Wilson I couldn't disagree more. This matter of setting accounting policy is very important to me and I think it demands the involvement of all our managers and the auditors in the discussion . . . but, management has the final word on accounting policy.

Now, from my understanding thus far, it seems to me that all three proposals have some shortcomings in terms of really reflecting the economics of business. Without going into a criticism of your proposals, let me just suggest another. First, while it's true that we probably earn a part of the ultimate profit each day as work on a project progresses, it seems to me that we earn because of the work that our people do, not just because costs are incurred. In the early stages of many projects there are substantial costs for computer time which we purchase from service bureaus. I don't think we make a profit on buying that service; our profit is more related to the idea of value added by the work of our staff. Second, we incur major costs for product development and marketing, the sole purpose of which is ultimately to produce contract revenue and profit. I don't see how any of your proposals match these costs with revenue. Finally, although no one has mentioned it yet, the company had a quite successful year in the management of its temporary investments—more successful than it first appears. Wouldn't our statements be more informative if we recognized the fact that, as of the end of the year, we've got a gain of $800,000 in the securities that we're holding? After all, if we didn't make that money this year, when did we make it?

My problem, of course, is that I'm not an accountant, so I don't know whether my ideas conform to the generally accepted principles. But that's why we've got two CPA's at this meeting. I may be wrong in my suggestions, in the sense that they're not the best way to measure what happened. I'm anxious to hear such arguments. I may also be wrong in the sense that my suggestions are not permissible. If so, I'd like to know about it, but I'd also like to know why the traditional principles are set up the way they are, so I can rethink my ideas. What do you say?

QUESTIONS

1. For this question, please confine your discussion to the determination of pre-tax net income. Exhibits 3, 4, and 5 present and explain income statements reflecting the accounting policies suggested, respectively, by Messrs. Anderson, Davis, and Wilson. The company also has the alternative of continuing to use the modified cash basis, as shown in Exhibit 1.

Exhibit 4. *Explanation of the Alternative Accounting Methods*

COMPLETED CONTRACT METHOD

1. Expense all development and marketing costs as incurred.
2. Expense all service and administrative costs as incurred.
3. Defer contract installation costs until contracts are completed and billings are rendered.
4. Recognize revenues when billings are rendered.
5. Recognize securities gains or losses only when realized.

PERCENTAGE OF COST COMPLETION METHOD

1. Expense all development and marketing costs as incurred.
2. Expense all service and administrative costs as incurred.
3. Recognize expected contract income (contract billings less contract installation costs) on the basis of percentage of installation costs incurred to total expected installation costs.
4. Recognize securities profits or losses when realized.

ECONOMIC EARNINGS METHOD

1. Expense all service and administrative costs as incurred.
2. Defer development and marketing costs for the year. Charge to contracts on the basis of the ratio of contract amount to total value of contracts awarded. In subsequent years, development and marketing expenses for the year will equal beginning of the year deferral plus actual costs for the year less ending deferral.
3. Recognize expected contract income on the basis of percentage of "Value Added" on the contracts (determined from independent estimates).
4. Recognize securities gains or losses at year end whether or not the securities are actually sold.

(a) Of these four alternatives, which one would you recommend to Mr. Wilson as the most appropriate for DCI? Why?

(b) If you think that some other combination of accounting policies would be better than any of the four, describe your proposal and support it.

2. Please revise the balance sheet in Exhibit 2 to make it consistent with the method of income determination that you selected in question 1(a) above. The revised balance sheet should also reflect the effects of federal income taxes. You may assume that:

(a) The appropriate tax rate is 50 percent on operating income and 30 percent on capital gains.

(b) The company will continue to use the modified cash basis for determining taxable income.

(c) The company's tax-basis loss for fiscal 1973 can be used to claim a refund of taxes paid in prior years. The amount of the refund to be received is $1,950,000 (50 percent of the net loss of $3,900,000).

3. (a) Using the revised balance sheet from question 2 and your income statement from question 1, prepare a Funds Flow Statement (all financial resources) for DCI for the year ended July 31, 1973.

   (b) How and why would this statement differ from one prepared directly from Exhibits 1 and 2?

Exhibit 5. *Additional Information*

A. *For Percentage Completion Calculations*

OPEN CONTRACTS AT 7–31–73

Contract Amount	Billings To Date	Costs Incurred To Date	Anticipated Costs To Complete	Total Expected Profit
$3,600,000		$1,200,000	$400,000	$2,000,000

a. % of Expected Total Costs Incurred to Date   75%
b. "Value Added" Percentage (Independent Estimate)   50%

B. *Deferred Marketing and Development Costs*

$$\left(\frac{\text{Value of Open Contracts at Year End}}{\text{Total Value of Contracts for the Year}}\right) \times \begin{matrix}\text{Total Development}\\\text{and Marketing}\\\text{Expenses for the}\\\text{Year}\end{matrix} = \begin{matrix}\text{Deferred}\\\text{Development}\\\text{and}\\\text{Marketing}\\\text{Expense at}\\\text{Year End}\end{matrix}$$

$$\left(\frac{\$3,600,000}{\$16,400,000 + \$3,600,000}\right) \times \$6,100,000 = \$1,100,000$$

C. *Security Trading Profits*

	COST	MARKET PRICE	GAIN*
1. Securities sold during the year	$3,200,000	$4,500,000	$1,300,000
2. Securities still held at year end	3,600,000	4,400,000	800,000

*These securities have been held by DCI for eighteen months; thus, any gains are taxable at the capital gains rate.

Rocky Mountain Construction Company

During a meeting of the Board of Directors of the Rocky Mountain Construction Company in early February 1960, Mr. Benthall, President and chief operating officer, expressed his concern over an operating statement which had been presented at the meeting (see Exhibit 1). A discussion of this statement ensued in which several of the directors and officers present took opposing views concerning the proper presentation of income for the land development department of the company. The company's statements were not only used by management for evaluation of company operations, but were also sent to the company's stockholders. Furthermore, Mr. Benthall realized that the company's statements were going to be presented either to a potential investor or to a commercial bank in the near future in order to raise the capital necessitated by the company's recent expansion into the field of land development.

As a result of the confusion and uncertainty created at the board meeting and because of the importance of correct financial statements, Mr. Benthall contacted Mr. Reardon, a member of the staff of a management consulting firm located in Denver, Colorado. He asked Mr. Reardon to evaluate each of the opposing viewpoints presented at the board meeting and to recommend to him the best method of preparing the statement under discussion. He then explained to Mr. Reardon the events which had led up to his present request.

Case material of the Harvard Graduate School of Business Administration is prepared as a basis for class discussion. Cases are not designed to present illustrations of either effective or ineffective handling of administrative problems.

Copyright © 1960 by the President and Fellows of Harvard College. Revised 1969. Distributed by the Intercollegiate Case Clearing House, Soldiers Field, Boston, Mass. 02163. All rights reserved to the contributors. Printed in the U.S.A.

Exhibit 1. *Modified* Cash Operating Statement for the Year Ending December 31, 1959*

Sales Revenue:

Plot Number	Amount Received		
1	$632,000		
3	158,945		

Total Sales Revenue		$790,945	
Other Income:			
Purchase option on Plot Number 9		5,000	
Total Income for Period			$795,945
Less Cost of Sales:			
Original Purchase Price of Land		$500,000	
Land Development Costs to Dec. 31, 1959 (see Exhibit 3)		299,564	
Total Land Costs			$799,564

Operating Expenses:

Advertising	$ 475	
Commissions to Outside Brokers	665	
Park Dedication and Press Conferences	1,140	
Purchase of Signs and Office Equipment	6,226	
Inspection Fees	928	
Legal and Accounting	7,850	
(Includes Legal Fee, Title Fee, and Insurance Premium Incurred on Original Land Purchase)		
Photographs and Renderings	2,113	
Salaries—Salesmen	12,695	
Salaries—Office	6,620	
Salaries—Engineering	3,113	
Salaries—Gen. Manager Land Department	10,000	
Sales Commissions	3,480	
Taxes	5,315	
Direct Operating Expense		60,620
Expense Allocation (from the Construction Department)**		8,533
Total Expenses for Period		$868,717
Net Cash Loss for Year Ending December 31, 1959		$ 72,772

*All operating expenses have been computed on an accrual basis and thus include not only cash expenditures made during 1959 but also include those expenses due but not paid as of December 31, 1959.

**Allocated on the basis of each department's total sales revenue. This includes heat, light, and power, rent on the office building, telephone and telegraph, and other joint expenses.

Mr. Benthall and his two sons had incorporated the Rocky Mountain Construction Company in 1946 as a small masonry and general home improvements construction organization located in Boulder, Colorado. The company had grown rapidly during its first few years and had expanded its operations into residential home construction and small plant construction. As additional financing became necessary, Mr. Benthall had sold stock to several local Boulder businessmen, but he and his sons retained ownership of 65 percent of the stock and desired to maintain a controlling interest in the company if possible. However, the need for cash was so pressing, that Mr. Benthall and his sons had agreed to seek additional equity investors, if this was the only alternative. The company's net profits before taxes had been in excess of $50,000 every year since 1951, and had reached $70,000 for the year ending December 31, 1958. The company was expecting annual profits of $75,000 from its construction operations during the next few years.

Up until 1959, the company had primarily built private homes, and had constructed small manufacturing plants in the Boulder-Denver area. The industrial growth of Boulder was quite rapid between 1946 and 1958, and continued rapid growth of this area was expected. The population of Boulder, located 30 miles from Denver via a turnpike, had increased from 20,000 in 1950 to close to 40,000 in 1958, and the number of industrial plants in the city had increased more than fourfold. Many national companies had indicated their interest in building local branch plants and offices in Boulder because of its ideal geographical location and pleasant living conditions at the foot of the Rocky Mountains.

In late 1958, Mr. Benthall and his sons decided that the development of an industrial park in Boulder would probably be a profitable venture in view of the area's growth expectations. After consulting with local real estate agencies, they decided that the purchase of fully improved, subdivided land would be economically unsound, and therefore decided to establish a land development department in the company which was to develop raw land into plots suitable for industrial plant construction. If this operation proved to be profitable, they planned further industrial land development undertakings of this same nature in the Denver-Boulder area.

The company purchased a tract of land, 2,768,709 square feet or 65 acres, adjoining Route 119, a major highway leading into Boulder, and began planning Boulder Industrial Park. They hired an accountant to maintain all financial records and act as office manager for the new department with the responsibility of carrying out the plans indicated by Mr. Benthall. The accountant, David Rowan, was a former classmate of Mr. Benthall's elder son, Cameron. For the past six years he has been associated with a small regional CPA firm in the Denver area.

41

In mid-December 1958, a purchase price of $500,000 for the land was agreed upon, and an architect was hired to draw up plans for the proposed industrial park (see Exhibit 2). Legal fees, title transfer fees, and title insurance premiums of $3,909.00 were also expended on the project at that time.

During 1959, the company began to develop the raw farmland into tracts suitable for the construction of industrial plants. Some of the work was performed by the land development department itself, and other phases of the work were subcontracted to specialists.

After the initial phase of surveying and laying corner markers, general excavation was started. The land was first cleared of trees, brush, rocks, and old farm buildings, and, in some spots, geological deposits of peat moss had to be removed and filled with gravel or other solid fill. Grading or leveling was the second step in the land improvement program. Next came the installation of temporary haul roads and storm ditches or drains. Once this work had

Exhibit 2
ROCKY MOUNTAIN CONSTRUCTION COMPANY
Land Development Department
Land Layout for Boulder Industrial Park

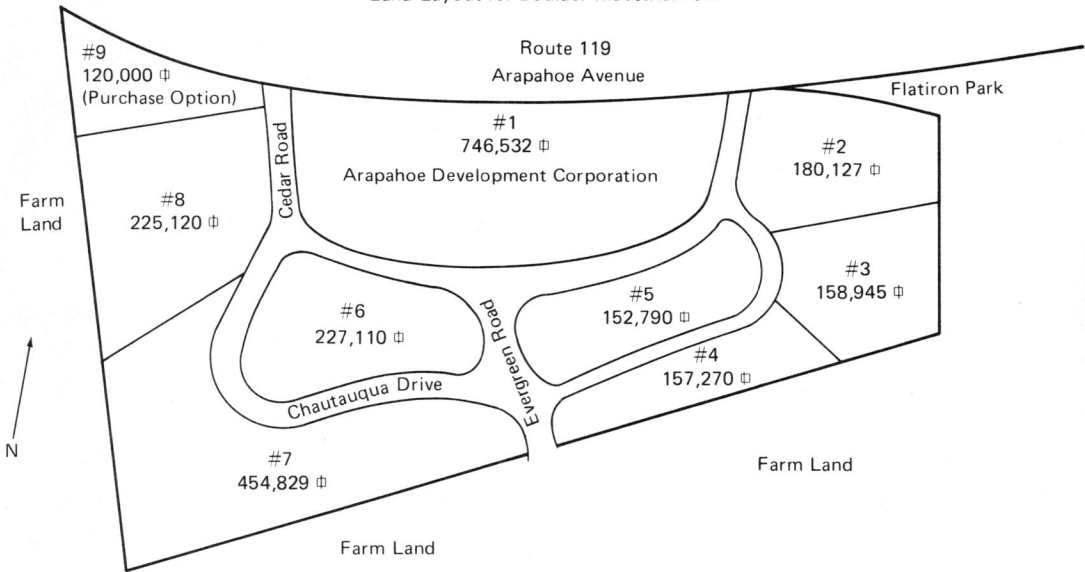

Land	Area	
Total	Area	2,768,709
Roads		315,986
Total Area Available for Sale		2,452,723

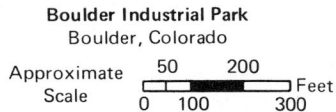

Boulder Industrial Park
Boulder, Colorado

Approximate Scale

⏚ Square Feet

Jan. 1, 1960

been completed, permanent access roads, storm drains, sewers, and water mains were installed in the industrial park. As of December 31, 1959, certain of these operations had been fully completed, while others were only partially completed. Nearly $300,000 had been spent on these operations during 1959. Exhibit 3 lists the total improvement costs incurred as of December 31, 1959, for each of the major land development phases, as well as the required cost to complete each improvement phase as estimated by the individual project or operation superintendent or contractor. The first column (labor) lists the labor cost of those operations performed directly by the land development department itself, while the second column (invoice) lists not only the cost of materials, but also the cost of that work which had been subcontracted. The third column accumulates the total cost of land improvement to December 31, 1959. The last three columns list the estimated costs of completing this land development project.

Two parcels of land were completed and disposed of during 1959 as indicated in Exhibit 4. One was sold to a development corporation for a shopping center site, while the other was transferred to the construction department for construction of a plant which would then be sold or leased by the company to an industrial concern desiring to locate in the Boulder area.

In order to summarize the operations for the year 1959, Mr. Rowen, accountant and office manager of the land development department, prepared an operating statement, reproduced as Exhibit 1, for the land development department and presented it to Mr. Benthall and the Board of Directors for approval at their February meeting. It was because of the ensuing discussion that Mr. Benthall felt he had to consult with Mr. Reardon in order to clear up the confusion created at the meeting.

Exhibit 3. Improvement Costs to December 31, 1959

ACCOUNT CLASSIFICATION	ACTUAL COST TO DATE			ESTIMATED TO FINISH		
	Labor	*Invoice*	*Total*	*Labor*	*Invoice*	*Total*
500 SITE WORK*						
8 Pile Driving						
10 Temporary Lights						
11 Clearing	2,406	9,037	11,443			
12 Unclassified Excavation	769	709	1,478			
13 Earth Excavation	34	101	135			
14 Peat Excavation	536	8,131	8,667			
15 Rock Excavation	9,208	19,060	28,268			
16 Temporary Storm Ditches						
17 Temporary Site Work						
18 Temporary (Haul) Roads						
19 Gravel Borrow	2,351	32,493	34,844			
Total	15,304	69,531	84,835	0	0	0

Exhibit 3. *(continued)*

ACCOUNT CLASSIFICATION	ACTUAL COST TO DATE			ESTIMATED TO FINISH		
	Labor	*Invoice*	*Total*	*Labor*	*Invoice*	*Total*
520 ROADS						
21 Unclassified Excavation	1,037	2,736	3,773			
22 Earth Excavation	2,034	4,908	6,942			
23 Peat Excavation	68	4,050	4,118			
24 Rock Excavation	2,319	35,680	37,999			
25 Gravel Borrow	677	15,229	15,906	562	32,438	33,000
26 Finish Roadwork—Subcontr.	49	37	86			
30 Granite Curbing	795	4,914	5,709			
32 Loam, Spread & Seed	985	965	1,950	2,400	3,290	5,690
33 Maintenance	293	311	604			
Total	8,257	68,830	77,087	2,962	35,728	38,690
540 STORM DRAINS						
40 10″ R. C. Pipe	2,511	2,882	5,393			
41 18″ R. C. Pipe	305	1,051	1,356			
42 24″ R. C. Pipe	1,122	3,723	4,845			
43 Manholes: Incl. Castings	1,004	1,150	2,154			
44 Catchbasins	2,085	1,749	3,834			
46 21″ R. C. Pipe	32	62	94	11,320	16,860	28,180
47 15″ R. C. Pipe	339	1,544	1,883			
48 30″ R. C. Pipe	864	3,605	4,469			
Total	8,262	15,766	24,028	11,320	16,860	28,180
550 SEWERAGE						
50 8″ Sewer	1,209	5,731	6,940			
51 10″ Sewer	1,907	14,371	16,278	8,617	17,682	26,299
52 Forced Main						
53 Manholes: Incl. Castings	2,607	3,448	6,055			
54 Adjust to Line & Grade	94		94			
55 Pumping Station					22,680	22,680
56 Maintenance of Utilities	392		392	2,436		2,436
57 12″ Sewer		1,542	1,542	3,860	4,120	7,980
58 Exploration for 10″						
Total	6,209	25,092	31,301	14,913	44,482	59,395
560 WATER MAINS						
61 10″ C. I. Pipe	2,567	19,463	22,030	3,110	30,245	33,355
62 12″ C. I. Pipe		295	295		4,820	4,820
63 Hydrants	125	230	355	6,500	15,977	22,477
64 8″ C. I. Pipe	1,072	3,689	4,761	3,700	7,400	11,100
Total	3,764	23,677	27,441	13,310	58,442	71,752
570 OPEN DRAINAGE DITCH	5,609	28,706	34,315	0	0	0
580 ENGINEERING	2,204	6,508	8,712	620	1,416	2,036

Exhibit 3. *(continued)*

ACCOUNT CLASSIFICATION		ACTUAL COST TO DATE			ESTIMATED TO FINISH		
		Labor	Invoice	Total	Labor	Invoice	Total
590	INDIRECT GENERAL						
	CONDITIONS†	5,942	5,903	11,845	4,812	6,237	11,049
	GRAND TOTALS	55,551	244,013	299,564	47,937	163,165	211,102

*Includes site work chargeable directly to specific plots.
†Includes field supervision, watchman's salary, temporary toilets, rain gear and field telephone.

GENERAL MEETING OF ROCKY MOUNTAIN'S
BOARD OF DIRECTORS

Roy Benthall   *Our next item of business is the operating statement of the land development department as prepared by Mr. Rowen, the department's accountant (Exhibit 1). As Mr. Rowen has explained it to me, this statement is essentially a cash statement, with certain normal accruals and deferrals. Our problem now is to decide how to adjust this statement, if at all, to arrive at the department's profit or loss for the year. I'd be very loath to accept this statement as it is, because combining this department's $73,000 loss with the construction department's 1959 profit of $68,000 would result in a net loss for the year of $5,000. Not only will our present shareholders be quite concerned over this loss, but the probability of selling additional stock or of obtaining a bank loan would be substantially reduced by the presentation of such a statement.*

Frank Reed   *(Director of Rocky Mountain and owner of Ledgewood Realty Co.) Well, of course, it doesn't make any sense at all to use cash flow as a measure of profit or loss; that completely ignores the fact that the department has a large inventory of partially improved plots on hand as of the end of the year. The cash statement deducts from sales income the total cost of the entire tract and all the land development costs to date. Some of these costs should be deferred as the cost of land that is still available for sale. If certain land costs are deferred, the department will show a profit rather than a loss for 1959.*

Roy Benthall   *That's one of the suggestions Mr. Rowen made, Frank, but two points about that approach bother me. First, what happens to these deferred costs if our expected future sales don't materialize? We might not sell all of those plots for two or three years yet, even though we have spent the money. And second, how do you propose to allocate the total land costs to the plots which were sold? Mr. Rowen couldn't keep track of the costs by individual plots, and as you know the plots are at various stages of completion.*

Exhibit 4. Land Development Department SALES STATUS REPORT, December 31, 1959

PLOT NUM-BER	SQUARE FOOTAGE		ANTICIPATED SALES PRICE (AT START OF DEVELOPMENT)			SOLD TO	PRICE RECEIVED	COMMENTS
	Feet	*%*	*Per Foot*	*Total Price*	*%*			
1	746,532	30.5	$1.70	$1,270,000	36.2	Arapahoe Development Corporation	$632,000	First plot sold. Sold at discount since the proposed shopping center is expected to increase other land values.
2	180,127	7.3	1.50	270,000	7.7			
3	158,945	6.5	1.20	190,000	5.4	Rocky Mountain Construction Company	158,945	All land used by the construction department is priced at a set rate of $1 per square foot.
4	157,270	6.5	1.30	200,000	5.7	Rocky Mountain expects to use this plot for plant construction at some future time.		
5	152,790	6.2	1.40	215,000	6.1			
6	227,110	9.2	1.40	320,000	9.1			
7	454,829	18.5	1.20	550,000	15.6			
8	255,120	10.4	1.20	310,000	8.8			
9	120,000	4.9	1.60	190,000	5.4	Arapahoe Development Corporation	170,000	Sold purchase option for $5,000. Option must be exercised by January 1, 1962, its expiration date.
Totals	2,452,723	100.0%		$3,515,000	100.0%			

46

James Hickman   *(Director of Rocky Mountain and Vice President of Construction Contracting) Roy, I think that Frank is making a mistake when he only looks at individual plots. I think we should consider the Park as a complete entity in itself, and recognize income from it based on the percentage of completion method used in our construction operation. From the figures Mr. Rowen gave you (Exhibit 3), you can estimate the completed cost of the development. You could then reestimate the total income which you expect to receive from the development based on sales to date. Then the profit recognized this year would be the percentage of estimated total profit that incurred costs to date bear to estimated total costs. And furthermore, such a statement would show a higher profit than the one which Frank proposes, and thus the earnings per share figure this year would reflect the true profit which the company earned during the year. This would provide a healthy income statement which could be used to sell some stock or obtain a bank loan. This method would also eliminate the necessity of trying to assign costs to individual plots.*

Roy Benthall   *Jim, I like your idea of the high earnings figure. . . .*

Frank Reed   *Now just a second, Roy! Don't let Jim confuse you by his slippery methods of pulling a big profit out of the clear blue! That land hasn't been sold yet and you can't recognize profit on your inventory just because you would like to have a pretty income statement. The only profit we are entitled to show is that profit which we made on actual sales during 1959. Why, Jim's method would have us showing income this year on plots which may not be sold for two years! That just isn't good accounting. And not only that, but think of the additional income tax you would have to pay under his method. You would be paying tax this year on cash income which you wouldn't be receiving until next year or the year after.*

Bill Collins   *(Rocky Mountain stockholder) You're right, Frank, that Jim's method would show a higher profit figure, but this is not allowed by the tax authorities. The tax code clearly specifies the method of accounting that land development companies are required to use in computing taxable income, thus leaving us little leeway in preparing our published statements. The Prentice-Hall Tax Service states in ¶31.207(5), "Where a tract of land is acquired as unit for lump sum consideration and is subsequently sold in parcels, total cost must be allocated among parcels and a basis for each lot sold determined." This rule implies that there will be an individual gain or loss on every lot sold and not that the taxpayer shall wait until the capital on the entire tract has been recovered through sales receipts before any taxable income is to be returned. Development costs, including future development costs, may be included in computing gain or loss on sale of lots. Cost apportionment must be made equitably and not ratably, that is, on market price rather than a square-foot basis, since front lots would ordinarily bear a greater portion of the cost than those in the rear of the development.*

Bob Allen   *(Director of Rocky Mountain and Executive Vice President of the First National Bank of Boulder) You are probably right on the tax regulations, Bill, but that doesn't mean we have to prepare our published statements in accordance with the tax code. We can prepare them in any manner we desire, and I can't agree with you, Jim, or with the tax code, Bill, when you propose a recognition of profits which may never materialize. Your methods assume that all the land will eventually be sold, and at a profit. However, I think Jim started out on the right track when he said you had to look at the Park as one complete entity, not as nine separate units. I don't think you should show any profit until you have fully recovered all your costs, because, in reality, you just plain don't make a profit on this development until you have sold enough land to recover all your costs! Then the rest is gravy. I think that all income and all expense from the development should be deferred until the entire project is finished and then you can decide how much profit you made. You aren't grabbing in the dark for estimated this and estimated that, as your method does, Jim. You know, for a fact, exactly how much you made on the project. This is the method my bank uses in recasting submitted corporate statements, since it doesn't want to loan money to a company on the basis of unearned profits which may never be realized. As you know, Roy, there is considerable risk that actual future costs will not be the same as estimated costs, and this is* particularly *true in the construction business, and heaven only knows how far off your estimated sales prices might be!*

Cameron Benthall   *(Mr. Benthall's eldest son and Executive Vice President of Rocky Mountain) I can understand that bankers need to be conservative, Bob, but we're talking about preparing a statement for our stockholders, and for that purpose I'm in total disagreement with your approach. The plain fact is that we went into this deal knowing that it was risky, but that if we won, we'd win big—maybe a couple of million dollars. Well, we've won. That is to say, now that Arapahoe has come in, a lot of the risk is gone. We didn't do as well as we expected on plot number one, but we'll do better than expected on the others, now that the Park is an established success. I think we will make two million bucks; no, I think we* have *made it already. You can be sure the city of Boulder isn't blinded by conservative accounting. They've just quadrupled the assessed valuation, now that it's developed land. I think we have an obligation to inform our stockholders as to just how well we've done. If anybody else wants to buy stock now, they're going to have to pay a price based on the current value of this Park, not just a pro rata share of the original cost of the plots we haven't sold yet.*

Bradley Benthall   *(Mr. Benthall's youngest son and General Construction Manager) Gee, Cam, you and Bob really are worlds apart. Your method would show a huge profit—all the profit, really—this year, and none the next. Bob's would show no profit for two or three years, and our chance of selling stock would be nil if we presented such a statement to pro-*

spective stockholders. I think a combination of methods is what we really need. I agree with Bill when he says we must recognize the profit we made on the plots which were sold in 1959. The land costs could be allocated to these plots on the basis of expected market price, just as the tax regulations require. Further, I think that these plots should also bear some portion of the general operating expenses which will be incurred during the next two years, the time we anticipate it will take to completely dispose of all the plots. It seems likely to me that these expenses will remain relatively constant during the life of the development, regardless of the percent of completion or degree of sales saturation. Finally, I think estimated profit should be recognized on those plots which are held under a sales option contract or intended for use by the construction department. It appears likely that these options will be taken up, since land prices are constantly increasing. All costs not allocated to the plots sold in 1959, or under option, should be deferred until future years. This method would provide the most realistic reporting of earnings. The consistent use of this method will provide our stockholders and potential investors with stable revenue and earnings figures on which year-to-year operating comparisons can be based. I think this is something we should consider before we choose a method of reporting income.

Roy Benthall   *It seems to me that the objective of a good income statement should be to match costs and revenues during a given period of time and only then can the true profitability of a firm be judged. I am not sure which of your proposed methods would do this, so I suggest we adjourn until such time as I can gather together the results which would be reported under each of your methods. We will then meet and discuss the merits of each one and decide at that time which one best fulfills our needs relative to internal reporting, external reporting, and tax reporting.*

QUESTIONS

1. Using the originally anticipated market prices listed in Exhibit 4, prepare profit and loss statements for the land development department for 1959 using the following accounting principles:
   (a) The percentage of completion method, as suggested by Mr. James Hickman in the case, and
   (b) The cost allocation method, and related proposals, suggested by Mr. Bradley Benthall.
2. Applying either of these two methods requires a set of assumptions and decisions about how to handle certain items. Identify these items and appraise the relative importance of each in terms of its impact on the profit calculation.
3. Which of the four major proposals (the two above, plus Mr. Allen's and Mr. Cameron Benthall's) would you recommend that Rocky Mountain adopt for reporting to its stockholders?

O. M. Scott
and Sons (C)

The following news report appeared in the February 1969 issue of the *Journal of Accountancy* published by the American Institute of Certified Public Accountants.

Auditors Report Exception to GAAP in Publicly[1] *Owned Company*

> *Ernst & Ernst, auditors of The O.M. Scott & Sons Company, took exception to an accounting practice used by Scott in reporting the results of its operations for the year ended September 30, 1968. From its "income before revenue reserve and federal income taxes" of $7,940,101, Scott deducted a "revenue reserve provision for revenue allocable to future periods" of $443,000 to arrive at "income before federal taxes." This "revenue reserve" appeared as a separate liability classification between current and long-term liabilities on the balance sheet with reference to note (d) which revealed the following:*
>
> > *Provision for revenue allocable to future periods: The special revenue reserve provides adjustment of earnings due to dealer inventory carryover being at a level which might reduce Company sales in*

This case was prepared by Assistant Professor John K. Shank as the basis for class discussion rather than to illustrate either effective or ineffective handling of an administrative situation.

Copyright © 1970 by the President and Fellows of Harvard College. Distributed by the Intercollegiate Case Clearing House, Soldiers Field, Boston, Mass., 02163. All rights reserved to the contributors. Printed in the U.S.A.

[1]*Note to students:* The publicly owned stock of the company is fully participating non-voting common.

fiscal 1969. The effect of this statistically determined adjustment is to reduce earnings for the current year $0.14 per share of Common Stock.

The income statement indicated that "earnings per share applicable to common stock" was $2.36 after the adjustment. The chairman and president discussed the revenue reserve in their letter, noting that "neither the auditors nor the Internal Revenue Service accept this particular method of accounting at this time." This is not surprising since adjusting earnings in this conservative fashion is an unusual accounting treatment. Nevertheless, management believes it is in keeping with the economic realities of the company's unique business endeavor and that it is sound, valid and proper for Scott's business.

Ernst & Ernst took exception in the opinion paragraph of their report, as follows:

In our opinion, except for the revenue reserve which is at variance with generally accepted accounting principles, and the effect of which was to reduce net income as explained in note (d), the accompanying balance sheet, statements of income and retained earnings, and source and application of funds present fairly the consolidated financial position of the O.M. Scott & Sons Company and its subsidiaries at September 30, 1968, and the consolidated results of their operations and consolidated source and application of funds for the year then ended, in conformity with generally accepted accounting principles applied on a basis consistent, except for the aforementioned change, with that of the preceding year.

Such an exception is rare for publicly traded companies. None of the annual reports of the 600 companies analyzed in the 1968 edition of Accounting Trends & Techniques *contained a qualification as to generally accepted accounting principles.*

The SEC and the stock exchanges do not normally accept reports to which the auditor has taken exception. As O.M. Scott & Sons Company is traded over the counter, it is not subject to review by a stock exchange. However, Scott is subject to SEC jurisdiction and must file its audited financial statements on Form 10K with the Commission within 120 days after its fiscal year end.

BACKGROUND

The decision by Scott's management to initiate the "revenue reserve" in 1968 had its origins in the company's deeply rooted consumer orientation. Scott had a long history of strong commitment to the ultimate satisfaction of consumers even though their customer was legally the retail outlet. One of the most striking examples of their belief in the consumer and their concern with his acceptance of Scott's products was their unique money-back guarantee. In their own words:

If for any reason you are not satisfied with results after using this product, you are entitled to get your money back. Simply send us evidence of purchase and we will mail you a refund check promptly.

They were also well-known for their magazine, *Lawn Care,* which was distributed monthly to over two million homeowners and which, according to the *Wall Street Journal,* had a readership as good as *Time* or *Life.* Another example of their consumer orientation was the Scott Neighborhood List Program, under which the company communicated directly with over five million individually selected "lawn-owners" throughout the country by means of direct mail advertising. The purpose of the program was to promote neighborhood level acceptance of Scott's as "the grass people."

To put real teeth into this philosophy, the company stressed recruiting service-oriented dealers and used retail price maintenance to insure them the "fair return" necessary to support a full-scale customer service program. The success of this program was acknowledged by a U.S. District Court in 1969 when it found the company not guilty of "fixing" prices under the Sherman Act. Quoting from the opinion of the court:

. . . The manufacturer produced premium products and felt that the success of its business depended on service-oriented dealers who would inform and instruct the consumer on proper use of the products, as well as making instructional material available to dealers and consumers; a "fair return" on resale was deemed desirable to insure that dealers gave the service. The firm designated a retail price on its products that would provide the profit, attempted to choose independent type dealers who would provide the service, and kept the retail price before dealers and consumers through advertising, order forms and other literature. . . . The firm very carefully chose, to the extent that it was able, dealers that it believed would be service-oriented and who could find it in their own self-interest to sell at the designated price; . . .

The company's efforts in the period 1957–1961 to translate this consumer orientation into a higher level of sales and profits are described in the original Scott case. It focuses upon the financing problems associated with the program in 1960 and 1961 to build a national distribution network and to ensure that dealers were adequately stocked with Scott's products. As shown in the case, the big increases in sales to dealers in 1960 and 1961 were not matched by corresponding increases in dealer sales to consumers (move-through). Dealer inventories at the end of 1961 were over $28 million as compared to estimated total move-through for the year of about $30 million. In the subsequent two years, although move-through continued to grow steadily, the company reported accounting losses as returned excess merchandise was written off and dealer inventories and accounts receivable were worked down to lower levels. In discussing these years, Paul Williams, Chairman of the Board, had said: "Contrary to our expectations, providing floor stock financing to enable our dealers to carry inventory in depth was not the right answer to lack of available merchandise." Although the means adopted to implement the national distribution strategy led to what he called "the traumatic loss years of 1962 and 1963," Williams is convinced that the desired longer term results were achieved. As he says, "When the new competitors—mainly giants in chemicals, drugs and oil—went after our dealers in the early 1960s with attractive consignment offers, fat discounts, and generous advertising allowances, they made little progress because they found the dealers' floor and warehouse space already occupied with Scott's products."

Given this firmly established national dealer network, the company was still faced with the problem of providing adequate but not excessive dealer inventories while insuring firm commitment by the dealers to move the merchandise. They phased out the trust receipts floor stock financing program over the years 1962–1965 and returned to their previous unconditional sale agreement with normal seasonal dating terms. At the same time, the company undertook a joint effort with the Operations Research Staff of its public accounting firm to develop a statistical sampling program to monitor dealer inventories and move-through and to forecast consumer sales. At a minimum, they felt such a system would enable them to prevent the extreme pipeline overloading they experienced in 1961. Ideally, it would also enable them eventually to scientifically control the level of dealer inventories in terms of demand fluctuations, to smooth their own production schedules, and to monitor the company's success in generating consumer sales, which they had always felt to be the real criterion of their performance.

Although direct involvement with the consuming public had characterized Scott's marketing and research efforts since the founding of the company in the 1860s, it took the severe problems of the early 1960s to trigger a formal effort to relate this orientation to the problems of production/inventory control and the evaluation of overall firm performance. The move-through measurement and forecasting system represented such an effort.

THE MOVE-THROUGH SYSTEM

In considering the measurement of move-through, the Scott's/Ernst & Ernst project team quickly determined that it would not be feasible to poll all of the 15,000 individual dealers to obtain "complete enumeration" data. Some kind of sampling plan was required. After much experimentation and testing, it was determined that four panels of about 150 dealers each, with one panel sampled each week and each panel sampled once a month, would provide a large enough data base to allow the estimation of total sales, sales by product groups, sales by metropolitan market area and of dealer inventories by product group at an acceptable level of statistical reliability. The reports issued as a result of the move-through sampling program focused upon inventory status by product groups and by marketing regions, upon trends in move-through by product groups, and upon the relationships among trends in inventory level, move-through, and dealer shipments by marketing region. Each of these reports was updated monthly from October through February, and then weekly from March through September. The years 1963 to 1968 were devoted to refining the various calculational aspects of this comprehensive statistical sampling system and building the confidence of the management group in the reliability of its output. The system was used from the beginning as an aid in internal decision making and performance evaluation, but the company had much more confidence in the system with each year's additional experience.

Jack Cantu, Director of Marketing, outlined three areas in which he had used the system in 1968 to help him make significant decisions. The first related to a customer who placed an order in excess of his established credit limit. By reviewing the trend of move-through in the market area served by this dealer, Mr. Cantu was able to determine that there was sufficient justification for raising his credit limit even though the increase represented a substantial jump in terms of actual past shipments. The second type of use of the system was typified by a large customer who was objecting to the seasonal dating payment terms which Scott applied to all customers. The dealer felt that he should be compensated with special payment terms for his large preseason orders which are clearly advantageous to Scott in terms of production planning. Based on this complaint, the company considered a change to payment terms based on move-through, which would be very appealing to many dealers because of its close relationship to dealer cash flow. Although this approach was ultimately rejected by top management, the company was only willing to consider using such a basis for setting payment terms because it was able to measure move- through accurately.

The third and most dramatic use of the system involved a large number of dealer orders in June of 1968, which the company decided were based on excessive optimism about continuing demand conditions. Weather conditions had been excellent that spring and the sales of all Scott's products, particularly Turf-Builder and Turf-Builder Plus 2, were well beyond dealer expectations. With this level of demand fresh in their minds, many of the dealers were very optimistic in placing orders for the fall season. Based on its measurement of projected fall move-through for these products and of existing dealer inventories, the company was placed in a difficult position. On the one hand, it did not want to create a situation in which dealers were overstocked. As in 1961, this could lead to significant revenue recognition problems and could also have a detrimental impact on dealer morale. On the other hand, not filling the orders would mean denying some salesmen the commissions which they had worked to earn, and could also prove very embarrassing if the subsequent demand bore out the dealers' optimism. There was adequate production capacity available to fill all the orders. After much discussion, management decided it was confident enough of its move-through estimates to stick with its judgment and scale down the orders from the dealers.

Although the move-through system was not yet being used formally in the product–inventory control area in 1968, it did have one other major use apart from the kinds of marketing decisions mentioned above. That year the company began using it as a basis for adjusting net shipments to dealers in arriving at a more meaningful measure of sales revenue. In line with the long-standing emphasis on their relationship with the consumer, management decided to incorporate their ability to measure consumer acceptance of Scott's products into a measure of overall performance of the firm, thereby eliminating their previous reliance on dealer shipments alone.

THE REVENUE RESERVE

The "revenue reserve provision for revenue allocable to future periods" item first appeared in the nine-month interim report issued as of June 30, 1968. This report is shown as Exhibit 1. Excerpts from the 1968 Annual Report are reproduced as Exhibit 2. Shortly after the issuance of the Annual Report, an article by Robert Metz in the *New York Times* (Exhibit 3) pointed out the nature of the revenue reserve and the accountants' exception to it. Wall Street reaction to the issue was mixed, however, and many security analysts approved of the reserve. As a result of the article, the SEC requested an advance copy of the Annual Report so they would be familiar with it if they received any inquiries before the 10K report was filed. The 10K itself was filed on January 25, 1969. During the following two months, the company and the SEC were in frequent contact as they debated what the SEC should do about the accountants' exception. The SEC was willing to let the accounting treatment stand only if Ernst & Ernst would withdraw its exception with respect to "generally accepted accounting principles." The accounting firm felt it was not able to do this because there was no authoritative support for such accounting treatment with respect to what were acknowledged as legally binding sales transactions.

Finally, in early April the SEC informed the company that they would have to change their accounting methods in reporting to stockholders in 1969 so as to enable the accountants to give a "clean opinion." With respect to 1968, the Annual Report would not have to be changed since it had already been released. However, the financial statements in the 1968 10K report had to be amended to enable the accountants to certify them without exception. Mr. Leon Herron, President of the company, informed the partner-in-charge of the audit for Ernst & Ernst that Scott intended to continue using this reserve concept for internal reporting purposes no matter what eventually resulted with respect to the published reports.

QUESTIONS

1. Do you think that the "revenue reserve" established by O. M. Scott & Sons, Inc. results in a fairer reporting of the results of operations for the year ended September 30, 1968?
2. How should O. M. Scott & Sons, Inc. disclose the revenue reserve in its 1969 annual report?
3. Do you concur with the position taken by the auditors in their report on the financial statements for the 1968 fiscal year?

Exhibit 1. *The O.M. Scott & Sons Company (B)*

The O M SCOTT & SONS COMPANY *and Subsidiaries*
Marysville, Ohio 43040

Interim Statement of Consolidated Operations

Scotts.

Unaudited and subject to adjustments at end of fiscal year (September 30).

	Nine Months Ended June 30		
	1968	*1967*	*1966*
Net sales	$52,358,091	$41,500,346	$35,752,988
Income before taxes and revenue reserve	7,837,276	4,709,650	3,480,212
Revenue reserve—provision for revenue allocable to future periods (a)	720,000	– 0 –	– 0 –
Tax provision	3,674,303	2,356,829	1,706,894
Net income	3,442,973	2,352,821	1,773,318
Earnings per share on Common Stock (b)	$2.23	$1.52	$1.13

(a) Special revenue reserve to provide for year-end adjustment of earnings in the event dealer inventory carryover is above a level which might reduce company sales in the succeeding year. The effect of this statistically determined adjustment is to reduce stated earnings for the current period 23¢ per share.

(b) After preferred dividends and based on shares outstanding June 30 each year.

The Board of Directors of The O M Scott and Sons Company has declared a dividend of 10¢ per share on its common stock, payable September 20 to holders of record at the close of business August 30, 1968.

To our stockholders:

FOR the 9 months ended June 30, the company's net sales increased $10,857,745 or 26%. Net income increase amounted to $1,090,152 or 46%.

These favorable results were due, in part, to the sales momentum generated by excellent weather conditions over most of the country in late March and early April. In addition, we believe that our stepped-up advertising and promotional efforts are increasingly effective.

As you realize, a large proportion of the company's seasonal products must be shipped to retailers well ahead of consumer buying periods. Accordingly, the company has set up a revenue reserve to cushion the effect of an abnormal dealer carryover which might curtail order writing, hence sales, for next spring. The net income shown in this Interim Report reflects such reserve adjustment, which may be greater or less at fiscal year-end.

Sincerely

Chairman

President

August 10, 1968

Exhibit 2. The O.M. Scott & Sons Company (B)

To our Stockholders, Associates and Dealers:

YOUR MANAGEMENT is pleased to report another record year in both sales and earnings. *Earnings* for the year ended September 30, 1968, reached an all-time high of $2.36 per share (despite an 18¢ per share surtax charge) and were 46.6% over the year earlier.

Net earnings on common stock equity at the beginning of the year were 25.8% compared to 20.4% the year earlier, the previous record. *Income before taxes* was $7,497,101 in the fiscal year just ended. The previous high, achieved in 1967, was $4,813,710. In ratio to sales, both pre-tax and after-tax earnings were at all-time highs.

Sales in the current year were $59,817,693, an increase of 23% over the previous year.

In the past 5 years, on a compounded basis, our average annual increase in sales was 18%, while our average annual increase in earnings per share was 66%. Calculated in the same manner, over the past 20-year span, sales were up 13% per year, earnings 14%.

Results exceeded expectations

This year our organizational strength was tested as never before. It proved equal to the task of meeting the unprecedented surge of consumer buying in late March and April. This demand exceeded our expectations as well as those of our dealers who had taken in much bigger pre-season stocks than we anticipated. In general, we were able to rebuild retail stocks within a few days after weekend depletions.

Although favorable weather conditions over much of the country were an important factor in greater consumer buying, we feel that unified effort in marketing, production and distribution was also a vital element. Certainly our enlarged advertising program was made more effective by the success of our field sales people in gaining the cooperation of retailers in local area-wide promotions. This would have been meaningless, however, had not production and distribution been able to deliver reorders promptly.

Advertising expenditures increased

Results of the year's operations lead us to believe that our advertising and promotion efforts, as well as those of our dealers, are reaching more effectively the special markets which we serve. Our strong growth in sales has enabled us to invest more substantially in the total field of advertising. Dollars expended in 1968 were more than three times what they were five years ago.

Financial comments

Short-term bank borrowings were utilized from December to May to a maximum of $8 million. Adequate lines of bank credit on favorable terms have been arranged for the coming year. The company is free of long-term debt except for mortgage obligations of a subsidiary on property leased to the company.

The net book value of our property at the year end was $6,809,156 compared to $5,495,144 a year earlier. In 1968, as in the past several years, capital expenditures were readily financed from general corporate funds. No change is anticipated for the coming year although increased bank borrowings may be needed.

Capital disbursements

As announced a year ago, we are in the process of completing a new facility that will add greatly to our capacity to produce fertilizers, both straight and in various combinations. These products will include unique polymer formulations, fully patented. While they will have certain manufacturing advantages over our present patented *Trionized* products, they will by no means replace them. We are, however, rapidly reaching total capacity in our present Turf Builder plant. If advisable, this plant could be converted to the new process though the likelihood of so doing is some years in the future.

The new plant is expected to be in production in mid 1969 but none of its products will reach consumers until fiscal 1970. Together with certain increased

Exhibit 2. *(continued)*

warehousing and shipping facilities and other equipment, our total capital expenditures in the coming fiscal year are likely to be in the area of $6 million. Even so, this will not require new equity financing nor seriously affect our working capital.

Voting trust established

To further strengthen Scotts future as an independent company in a specialized business, the owners of its closely-held Class B common stock (the voting stock) have placed their shares in a voting trust with Charles B Mills, Paul C Williams, John W Christensen and F Leon Herron, Jr as trustees, voting on an equal basis. These trustees will elect the directors and exercise all voting rights. The trust continues until July 15, 1978, and is subject to extension upon vote of the beneficiaries.

Revenue reserve inaugurated

For the year, our net shipments increased 23% over the year earlier. This was the highest ratio increase in 10 years. During the year, the ratio increase in consumer purchases of Scotts was even higher; in fact, the highest since we started the statistical program to measure move-through five years ago.

In spite of the big increase in sales, accounts receivable at year end were less than 17% of sales, the lowest ratio in 10 years. Past due receivables were at an historic low of less than 1% of sales. Receivables at September 30 were substantially collected at mid-November.

During the past five years, the company has carried on an effective, country-wide sampling program to determine the move-through of its products from retailers to consumers. This is done on a weekly basis during the active retailing season from March until November. The procedures followed, as well as the statistical calculations, are checked regularly by specialists affiliated with the company's independent auditors.

On the basis of the information obtained as of June 30, management decided to report the company's nine months earnings after setting up a revenue reserve against the possibility that dealer inventories might curb their buying in future periods.

At year end, inventories of Scotts products in the hands of our retailers were likely lower in relation to consumer purchases than any time in our history. Despite this lower ratio, total dealer inventories increased during the year. When such increases occur, management feels that reported earnings should be adjusted to more nearly reflect consumer purchases during the year.

Accordingly, the revenue reserve established at year end and shown in this report defers earnings on the difference between our reported net sales (adjusted for increase in retail outlets) and the total of products actually purchased by consumers during the year, calculated at Scotts billing prices. The effect was to reduce earnings 14¢ per share.

In the future, the revenue reserve will be adjusted upward or downward, at nine months and year end, to reflect the relationship between consumer purchases and the company's net sales.

Neither the auditors nor the Internal Revenue Service accept this particular method of accounting at this time. This is not surprising since adjusting earnings in this conservative fashion is an unusual accounting treatment. Nevertheless, management believes it is in keeping with the economic realities of the company's unique business endeavor and that it is sound, valid and proper for Scotts business.

Sales patterns in 1968

As in the past, sales and earnings increases were basically generated within our traditional business, and primarily in veteran products. This year, however, we did introduce larger size packages in some lines. These met with surprisingly good reception, particularly the new triple size of Turf Builder. During the year there were selective price increases but these were partly offset by lower realized prices in consumer purchases of the larger, more economical sizes.

Resources employed

Gratifying as our return on equity was, we are not satisfied with it since one of the most valuable of our corporate resources is not capitalized on our books. We refer to the priceless value of our name

Exhibit 2. *(continued)*

with the consuming public and the business momentum generated in our first hundred years. Each day adds to our responsibility for developing earnings commensurate with our total resources.

Another unrecorded resource of incalculable value is the interest, enthusiasm and dedication of the people of Scotts. Now numbering over 1,000 and varying in service from one year to 45 years, they are tied closely to our headquarters at Marysville whether they live in this farming community or in sales districts throughout the country.

The founders of Scotts, and their followers, have had deep concern for the people of Scotts as well as for the users of the company's products. Long before the advent of today's broad social legislation, the company provided family benefits in disability payments, hospitalization, life insurance and non-contributory pensions. In addition, all the people of Scotts, with two years service or more, benefit from a generous profit-sharing program set up more than a quarter of a century ago.

Wide variations in age and length of service are represented in company management. In senior management, the age spread is from 47 to 64 years; the years of service from 3 to 42. In divisional management, the age spread is 34 to 54 years; the years of service from 5 to 31.

☆   ☆   ☆

The Scotts name and the people of Scotts are indeed important in an evaluation of our position and in setting our goals for future accomplishment.

Paul L. Williams
CHAIRMAN

F. Leon Herron
PRESIDENT

November 30, 1968

Exhibit 2. *(continued)*

THE O M SCOTT & SONS COMPANY

Statements of Consolidated Income and Retained Earnings

INCOME

	YEARS ENDED SEPTEMBER 30,	
	1968	1967
NET SALES	$59,817,693	$48,352,858
COST OF SALES AND OPERATING EXPENSES		
Cost of goods sold including processing, warehousing, delivering, and merchandising	$43,577,763	$36,757,169
General and administrative and research and development expenses	7,405,243	5,780,402
Provision for depreciation	811,637	745,991
Interest charges — net of interest income	82,949	255,586
	$51,877,592	$43,539,148
INCOME BEFORE REVENUE RESERVE AND FEDERAL INCOME TAXES	$ 7,940,101	$ 4,813,710
REVENUE RESERVE		
Provision for revenue allocable to future periods	443,000	–0–
INCOME BEFORE FEDERAL INCOME TAXES	$ 7,497,101	$ 4,813,710
FEDERAL INCOME TAXES		
Provision for the year	$ 4,237,478	$ 2,613,271
Income taxes paid or provided allocable to future years	(416,890)	(307,354)
	$ 3,820,588	$ 2,305,917
NET INCOME	$ 3,676,513	$ 2,507,793
EARNINGS PER SHARE APPLICABLE TO COMMON STOCK	$2.36	$1.61

RETAINED EARNINGS

Balance at beginning of the year	$ 8,003,173	$ 5,888,046
Net income for the year	3,676,513	2,507,793
	$11,679,686	$ 8,395,839
Deduct cash dividends paid:		
On Preferred Stock at $5.00 per share	$ 88,671	$ 92,630
On Common Stock at $0.40 per share ($0.20 per share in 1967)	603,008	300,036
	$ 691,679	$ 392,666
Balance at end of the year	$10,988,007	$ 8,003,173

Notes to consolidated financial statements appear on page 12.

Exhibit 2. *(continued)*

Consolidated Source and Application of Funds

	YEARS ENDED SEPTEMBER 30,	
SOURCE OF FUNDS	1968	1967
Net income for the year	$ 3,676,513	$ 2,507,793
Provision for depreciation	811,637	745,991
Revenue reserve — provision for income allocable to future periods	443,000	–0–
Sale of Common Stock	532,370	–0–
	$ 5,463,520	$ 3,253,784
APPLICATION OF FUNDS		
Increase in working capital	$ 1,645,232	$ 1,428,463
Long-term debt reduction	311,000	509,281
Capital expenditures — net	2,125,649	504,454
Purchases of Preferred and Common Stock	110,455	117,021
Cash dividends	691,679	392,666
Increase in other assets and deferred charges	579,505	301,899
	$ 5,463,520	$ 3,253,784

Board of Directors
The O M Scott & Sons Company
Marysville, Ohio

We have examined the consolidated balance sheet of The O M Scott & Sons Company and its subsidiaries as of September 30, 1968, and the related statements of consolidated income and retained earnings and consolidated source and application of funds for the year then ended. Our examination was made in accordance with generally accepted auditing standards, and accordingly included such tests of the accounting records and such other auditing procedures as we considered necessary in the circumstances.

In our opinion, except for the revenue reserve which is at variance with generally accepted accounting principles, and the effect of which was to reduce net income as explained in note (d), the accompanying balance sheet, statements of income and retained earnings, and source and application of funds present fairly the consolidated financial position of The O M Scott & Sons Company and its subsidiaries at September 30, 1968, and the consolidated results of their operations and consolidated source and application of funds for the year then ended, in conformity with generally accepted accounting principles applied on a basis consistent, except for the aforementioned change, with that of the preceding year.

Dayton, Ohio
November 18, 1968

Ernst & Ernst

Exhibit 2. *(continued)*

25 Year Summary

BALANCE SHEET HIGHLIGHTS

Year (a)	Working Capital	Property & Equipment (Net)	Long-Term Debt	Preferred Stock	Common Stockholders' Investment
1968	$12,345,834	$6,809,156	$ 1,342,000	$1,726,300	$17,390,553
1967	10,700,602	5,495,144	1,653,000	1,809,800	13,900,304
1966	9,272,139	5,736,681	2,162,281	1,901,500	11,810,498
1965	10,952,618	4,988,909	4,521,500	2,038,100	10,213,665
1964	10,615,806	4,770,684	4,975,234	2,193,700	8,742,721
1963	19,822,930	5,278,356	15,423,847	2,246,200	8,281,792
1962	21,251,237	5,768,492	15,792,896	2,246,000	9,543,885
1961	20,585,939	6,123,119	16,170,383	2,254,300	9,355,762
1960	14,907,449	6,316,286	13,649,500	2,347,500	8,120,674
1959	6,457,822	6,153,230	6,939,765	2,392,500	4,754,364
1958	5,552,031	1,789,507	2,059,716	2,432,200	3,255,104
1957	3,022,066	1,709,576	2,186,724	1,757,200	2,341,924
1956 (b)	1,999,063	3,035,682	1,711,298	1,811,400	1,941,506
1955	1,822,700	1,394,818	463,177	1,832,200	1,473,575
1954	1,637,253	848,128	525,172	827,200	1,452,810
1953	1,551,074	931,680	602,593	847,200	1,295,707
1952	1,519,171	411,126	659,317	354,700	1,199,874
1951	1,478,268	338,128	705,087	362,200	1,000,483
1950	1,482,055	318,035	739,972	369,700	935,853
1949	928,238	329,186	383,500	377,200	719,247
1948	815,168	263,924	449,500	233,700	614,173
1947	700,250	143,388	266,500	242,200	483,414
1946	742,129	115,455	284,000	250,000	440,572
1945	598,922	99,234	200,000	250,000	358,036
1944	527,957	96,905	191,760	175,000	318,791

Notes: *(a) Fiscal year: Ended September 30, 1968-1956; ended November 30, 1955-1944.*
(b) Period of 10 months. Fiscal year changed.

Exhibit 2. *(continued)*

THE O M SCOTT & SONS COMPANY • MARYSVILLE, OHIO

founded by O M Scott 1868 • incorporated 1914

SALES, EARNINGS, DIVIDENDS, EMPLOYEES

Year (a)	Net Sales	Income Before Taxes on Income	Net Income	Common Stock Earnings Per Share (c)	Common Stock Cash Dividends Per Share (c)	Employees at Year End
1968	$59,817,693	$ 7,497,101	$ 3,676,513	$2.36	$.40	1,067
1967	48,352,858	4,813,710	2,507,793	1.61	.20	947
1966	41,733,939	3,578,679	2,012,200	1.27	.20	864
1965	36,240,323	2,821,674	1,685,137	1.05	.05	777
1964	30,108,786	968,010	573,177	.31	–0–	690
1963	26,135,832	(2,226,250)	(999,340)	(.74)	.10	808
1962	28,817,154	(2,987,302)	(1,522,302)	(1.09)	.10	950
1961	42,637,180	3,236,575	1,570,626	.99	.10	949
1960	36,856,310	2,259,112	1,114,351	1.15	–0–	938
1959	30,197,730	2,558,179	1,196,538	1.00	–0–	913
1958	23,400,208	1,952,745	901,090	.68	–0–	739
1957	18,675,926	894,807	451,287	.31	–0–	639
1956 (b)	12,494,961	712,149	322,449	.23	–0–	494
1955	11,465,759	361,078	211,078	.28	.02	315
1954	10,385,136	459,428	259,428	.25	.02	302
1953	9,445,803	324,023	169,023	.15	.03	262
1952	8,149,120	308,633	141,633	.14	.02	212
1951	7,745,005	231,378	116,378	.12	.05	186
1950	7,459,174	397,093	200,093	.23	.10	183
1949	5,434,587	199,431	123,431	.17	.06	163
1948	4,407,180	123,665	71,665	.10	.06	159
1947	3,847,265	128,286	77,286	.14	.10	156
1946	3,622,499	134,901	78,901	.15	.06	132
1945	2,703,169	70,043	30,043	.05	.03	152
1944	2,277,135	54,959	32,959	.07	.04	103

( ) *Indicates loss*

(c) *Basis of shares outstanding at the end of each fiscal year, adjusted for all stock dividends and splits.*

Exhibit 3. MARKETPLACE: Profits Listed in Offbeat Way
     by Robert Metz

The company that improved the scenery but ruins the weekends for many a suburban crabgrass fighter, O. M. Scott & Sons, has adopted an offbeat accounting method in the name of fiscal conservatism.

In the annual report just out, the chairman and the president of the Marysville, Ohio, company indicate they distrust the excellent results they have been enjoying in the rooted-outdoor carpeting business.

On the theory that Scott grass dealers have perhaps overbought—total dealer inventories increased during the year—the company has reported earnings less a "revenue reserve" against the "possibility that dealer inventories might curb their buying in future periods."

The auditors, Ernst & Ernst, signed the report but took exception to this novel approach that clipped 14 cents a share from per-share results and tended to level off an earnings peak.

For the year ended last September 30, the company takes a $443,000 revenue reserve "allocable to future periods," thus trimming earnings that would otherwise be reported to a mere $7,497,101 or $2.36 a share. This is still a whopping increase over the $4,813,710, or $1.61 a share, earned in the previous 12 months. There was no similar reserve in the 1967 fiscal year.

Scott's note to stockholders said the company planned to watch dealer inventories carefully and adjust earnings to "more nearly reflect consumer purchases during the year."

The company notes that the Internal Revenue Service has objected, as have the auditors, and says: "This is not surprising since adjusting earnings in this conservative fashion is an unusual accounting treatment. Nevertheless, management believes it is in keeping with the economic realities of the company's unique business endeavor and it is sound, valid and proper for Scott's business."

Like as not, the Securities and Exchange Commission will look askance when the company files its annual report on form 10-K, which is due soon.

However, the flashy annual report is already out and the letter to stockholders is dated November 30. One thing is sure, if O. M. Scott were a listed company, it could not deviate from accepted principles in this manner. This suggests the over-the-counter stock is not slated for listing in the foreseeable future.

This, incidentally, is not the first time this company has raised eyebrows in the business community. Some years ago, the company took a tack that brought quite a different result. It based profits on goods shipped to dealers under "trust receipts," a device Scott used to provide needed dealer financing.

In some sophisticated circles there was a feeling that Scott, by reporting its earnings on the basis of these receipts—whether the goods were sold or not—had distorted its actual results.

Earnings in 1958, two years before the plan went into effect, were 69 cents a share and they jumped to $1.15 a share in 1959, still a year before the change. They were $1.21 in 1960 and 99 cents a share in 1961.

PART II

Asset
Valuation

Chrysler Corporation: The 1970 Accounting Change

In late February 1971, Larry Polk, a recent graduate of the Harvard Business School and an analyst with a medium-sized mutual fund, made an appointment to discuss with one of his former professors the letter to stockholders which his firm had recently received from Chrysler.

The letter, addressed "To Our Shareholders," was a multilith copy of a typewritten three-page letter from Lynn Townsend, Chairman, and John Riccardo, President of Chrysler, together with a typewritten copy of the financial statements of both Chrysler Corporation (and consolidated subsidiaries) and Chrysler Realty Corporation, as audited by Touche Ross & Co. Both the letter and the auditor's opinion were dated February 9, 1971.

The first three paragraphs of the letter outlined the essential communication to the stockholders:

> Sales of Chrysler Corporation and consolidated subsidiaries throughout the world in 1970 totaled $7.0 billion, compared with $7.1 billion in 1969. Operations for the year resulted in a net loss of $7.6 million or $0.16 a share, compared with net earnings of $99.0 million or $2.09 a share in 1969.
>
> Net earnings for 1969 are restated to reflect a retroactive change in the company's method of valuing inventories, from a LIFO (last-in, first-out) to a FIFO (first-in, first-out)) cost basis, as explained in the notes to financial statements. The LIFO method reduces inventory values and earnings in periods of rising costs. The rate of inflation in costs in 1970 and for the projected short-term future is so high that

Rev. 4/73. Copyright © 1973 by the President and Fellows of Harvard College. Distributed by the Intercollegiate Case Clearing House, Soldiers Field, Boston, Mass. 20163. All rights reserved to the contributors. Printed in the U.S.A.

significant understatements of inventory values and earnings result. The use of the LIFO method in 1970 would have reduced inventory amounts at December 31, 1970, by approximately $150 million and did reduce inventory amounts reported at December 31, 1969, by approximately $110 million. Also, the use of the LIFO method in 1970 would have increased the loss for the year by approximately $20.0 million, and its use in 1969 reduced the earnings as reported for that year by $10.2 million. The other three U.S. automobile manufacturers have consistently used the FIFO method. Therefore the reported loss for 1970 and the restated profit for 1969 are on a comparable basis as to inventory valuation with the other three companies. Prior years' earnings have been restated to make them comparable.

Results of operations for the first three quarters of 1970 were previously reported on the LIFO method of valuing inventories. The restated results, on the FIFO method of valuing inventories, for the four quarters of 1970 are as follows:

	NET EARNINGS (LOSS) (MILLIONS)	EARNINGS (LOSS) PER SHARE
1st Quarter	$(27.4)	$(0.57)
2nd Quarter	10.1	0.21
3rd Quarter	2.1	0.05
4th Quarter	7.6	0.15
1970	$(7.6)	$(0.16)

The letter stressed the economic conditions that had led to the losses for Chrysler. The total sales of the company's passenger cars, trucks, and tractors, both domestic and overseas, had increased slightly in 1970. However, the management stated:

. . . the United States economy during 1970 experienced a combination of inflation and recession, high employment, high interest rates and restricted growth. Consumer confidence was weakened by economic and social problems at home, and by serious crises in the Middle East and Southeast Asia. A major strike in the automotive industry cut North American vehicle production and added to the consumer's lack of confidence. As a result, United States automobile industry sales for the year reached their lowest point since 1962.

The letter pointed out that these economic factors were reflected in the company's financial statements, and further revealed that there was a drop in North American factory sales of 64,339 cars and trucks, as well as a shifting in consumer demand toward smaller, less expensive automobiles, resulting in a less profitable product mix. Further, the company had experienced increased costs not recoverable through increased selling prices.

The company's response to the economic pressures was described as review and reduction of operating expense and capital expenditures, realignment of the organization to produce a more direct system of operational controls, and improvements in the marketing and product programs, both short and long term.

The letter stressed that "Chrysler Corporation has operated at a profit for the nine-month period since April 1, 1970."

COMPETITIVE SITUATION

Chrysler, ranked third among U.S. auto manufacturers, was not the only major auto company to find 1970 a difficult year. General Motors had experienced a 23 percent drop in sales; 1970 sales were $18.8 billion in contrast to $24.3 billion in 1969. Consequently, profits fell from 1969's $1.7 billion to $670 million. This represented a decline in net income as a percentage of sales to 3.2 percent from the usual level of 7 percent. Earnings per share of $2.09 failed to cover a dividend reduced to $3.40 from the prior $4.30 level. The 1969 earnings per share had been $5.95. General Motors attributed the decline in company sales and profit partially to U.S. inflation and, particularly, to the strike which had halted production for more than ten weeks primarily in the fourth quarter of the calendar year. Stock prices reflected the company's problems; from a high of $72 in 1968 the stock had fallen to $26 in February. (See Exhibit 6.)

Ford Motor Co. had fared better in the inflationary economy. Fourth-quarter introduction of the Pinto had reversed the trend of declining retail car sales, and total sales for 1970 were $15 billion, a slight increase over 1969's sales of $14.8 billion. The impact of inflation could be viewed in corporate profits, which had fallen to $516 million from 1969's $547 million. The annual dividend was held at $2.40 in both years; 1969 earnings per share had been $5.03, and, 1970, $4.77 (selected statistics for the three major auto companies are included in Exhibit 5).

ACCOUNTING POLICIES

The accounting policies of the three companies were generally considered to be conservative by security analysts. All three companies expensed research and development costs as incurred. All deferred the investment tax credit over the life of the equipment which gave rise to the credit. GM and Chrysler used accelerated depreciation for all fixed assets; Ford followed a similar policy for 78 percent of its plant and equipment accounts.

Due to union contracts, pension costs were major expenses of all major auto manufacturers. All three companies funded current pension provisions costs; past service costs were amortized over 30 years.

Up until 1970, the primary differences in accounting were in the treatment of goodwill and inventory. Chrysler alone was on LIFO; the others used FIFO or lower of cost or market. Neither Ford nor Chrysler amortized goodwill; GM amortized goodwill over 20 years.

CHRYSLER'S PROBLEMS, 1970

Beyond the general inflation and labor problems common to all auto manufacturers, Chrysler Corporation had a number of other problems in 1970. Among these were:

1. Unexpectedly low fourth-quarter sales. Profits were $7.6 million, rather than $20 million expected by security analysts. Typically, the fourth quarter was the profit setter for auto companies.
2. Net loss of $7.9 million on overseas sales of $1.6 billion. In 1969 Chrysler had earned $19 million on $1.5 billion sales.
3. A substantial change in sales by product lines. Compact cars accounted for 34 percent of Chrysler sales in 1970.
4. A drop in U.S. factory sales of nearly 100,000 units in 1970.
5. Due to lower 1969 profits and 1970 losses, pressure on working capital, especially cash.

THE ACOUNTING CHANGE

In Mr. Polk's conference, two key issues in the 1970 accounting change were pointed out, namely, the change in inventory valuation policy and the allocation of income taxes. These were described in footnotes to the financial statements:

Inventories—Accounting Change

> *Inventories are stated at the lower of cost or market. For the period January 1, 1957, through December 31, 1969, the last-in, first-out (LIFO) method of inventory valuation had been used for approximately 60 percent of the consolidated inventory. The cost of the remaining 40 percent of inventories was determined using the first-in, first-out (FIFO) or average cost methods. Effective January 1, 1970, the FIFO method of inventory valuation has been adopted for inventories previously valued using the LIFO method. This results in a more uniform valuation method throughout the Corporation and its consolidated subsidiaries and makes the financial statements with respect to inventory valuation comparable with those of the other United States automobile manufacturers. As a result of adopting FIFO in*

1970, the net loss reported is less than it would have been on a LIFO basis by approximately $20.0 million, or $0.40 a share. Inventory amounts at December 31, 1969 and 1970 are stated higher by approximately $110.0 million and $150.0 million, respectively, than they would have been had the LIFO method been continued.

The Corporation has retroactively adjusted financial statements of prior years for this change. Accordingly, the 1969 financial statements have been restated resulting in an increase in Net Earnings of $10.2 million; also Net Earnings Retained for Use in the Business at December 31, 1969 and 1968 have been increased by $53.5 million and $43.3 million, respectively.

For United States income tax purposes the adjustment to inventory amounts will be taken into taxable income ratably over 20 years commencing January 1, 1971.

Taxes on Income

Taxes on income as shown in the consolidated statement of net earnings include the following:

	1970	1969
Currently payable:		
United States taxes [credit]	$[81,800,000]	$50,000,000
Other countries	44,300,000	36,300,000
Deferred taxes	16,100,000	[6,000,000]
As previously reported		80,300,000
Adjustment in deferred taxes for change in inventory valuation		11,400,000
Total taxes on income [credit]	$[21,400,000]	$91,700,000

The change in inventory valuation resulted in a reduction in income taxes allocable to the following year of approximately $56.0 million at December 31, 1969.

Reductions in taxes resulting from the investment credit provisions of the Internal Revenue Code are being taken into income over the estimated lives of the related assets. The amounts of such credits which were reflected in net earnings were $6,300,000 in 1970 and $5,400,000 in 1969.

The change in inventory valuation method was made as of January 1, 1970; thus it included a retroactive adjustment to Chrysler's 1969 retained earnings. The Chrysler financial statements are shown in Exhibits 1 (Net Earnings), 2 (Retained Earnings), 3 (Source and Application of Funds), and 4 (Balance Sheet).

From this information, it was suggested that Mr. Polk could estimate Chrysler's 1970:

1. Pre-tax loss
2. Loss reported to the IRS
3. The benefit of changing inventory valuation methods

FIRST QUARTER, 1971

On April 19, 1971, Chrysler management reported that the company had earned $.22 a share, as compared with a net loss of $.57 a year earlier. A condensed financial report is included as Exhibit 7.

QUESTIONS

1. Why did Chrysler change accounting methods?
2. What was the cost to Chrysler of using a LIFO inventory method in 1970? in 1969? in 1965?
3. What was the cost to Chrysler of changing from LIFO to FIFO?
4. Approximate Chrysler's reported income for federal tax purposes. What does it tell you?

Exhibit 1. Chrysler Corporation: The 1970 Accounting Change

CONSOLIDATED STATEMENT OF NET EARNINGS Chrysler Corporation and Consolidated Subsidiaries

Year ended December 31	1970	1969*
Net sales	$ 6,999,675,655	$ 7,052,184,678
Equity in net earnings (loss) of unconsolidated subsidiaries	(6,210,013)	(6,286,309)
Other income and deductions	(19,962,022)	23,261,424
	6,973,503,620	7,069,159,793
Cost of products sold, other than items below	6,103,250,974	5,966,732,377
Depreciation of plant and equipment	176,758,139	170,305,745
Amortization of special tools	172,568,348	167,194,002
Selling and administrative expenses	386,041,866	431,706,851
Pension and retirement plans	121,406,136	114,577,630
Interest on long-term debt	46,998,713	31,702,530
Taxes on income (credit)	(21,400,000)	91,700,000
	6,985,624,176	6,973,919,135
NET EARNINGS (LOSS) INCLUDING MINORITY INTEREST	(12,120,556)	95,240,658
Minority interest in net loss of consolidated subsidiaries	4,517,536	3,730,564
NET EARNINGS (LOSS)	$(7,603,020)	$ 98,971,222
Average number of shares of Common Stock outstanding during the year	48,693,200	47,390,561
Net earnings (loss) a share	$(0.16)	$2.09

*Restated to reflect the change made in 1970 in accounting for inventories and to conform to 1970 classifications. The 1969 net earnings and net earnings a share, as previously reported, were $88.8 million and $1.87 respectively. See Inventories—Accounting Change note.

Exhibit 2. Chrysler Corporation: The 1970 Accounting Change

CONSOLIDATED STATEMENT OF ADDITIONAL PAID-IN CAPITAL
Chrysler Corporation and Consolidated Subsidiaries

Year ended December 31	1970	1969
Balance at beginning of year..	$ 455,739,253	$ 421,184,933
Excess of market price over par value of newly issued shares of Common Stock sold to the thrift-stock ownership programs (1,556,843 in 1970; 927,276 in 1969)	28,281,685	33,796,320
Excess of option price over par value of shares of Common Stock issued under the stock option plans (none in 1970; 25,172 in 1969)	–	758,000
Balance at end of year...	$ 484,020,938	$ 455,739,253

CONSOLIDATED STATEMENT OF NET EARNINGS RETAINED FOR USE IN THE BUSINESS

Year ended December 31	1970	1969*
Balance at beginning of year..	$1,399,028,028	$1,351,453,762
Adjustment (for the years 1957 through 1968)		43,309,750
As restated		1,394,763,512
Net loss	(7,603,020)	
Net earnings as restated..		98,971,222
	1,391,425,008	1,493,734,734
Cash dividends paid ($0.60 a share in 1970 and $2.00 a share in 1969)	29,193,336	94,706,706
Balance at end of year	$1,362,231,672	$1,399,028,028

*Restated to reflect the change made in 1970 in accounting for inventories.

Exhibit 3. *Chrysler Corporation: The 1970 Accounting Change*

CONSOLIDATED SOURCE AND APPLICATION OF WORKING CAPITAL
Chrysler Corporation and Consolidated Subsidiaries

Year ended December 31	1970	1969*
Additions to working capital:		
From operations:		
Net earnings (loss)	$(7,603,020)	$ 98,971,222
Depreciation	176,758,139	170,305,745
Amortization of special tools..	172,568,348	167,194,002
Decrease (increase) in income taxes allocable—noncurrent	10,163,405	(9,242,610)
Proceeds from long-term borrowing	241,550,761	91,062,485
Proceeds from sale of common stock...................................	38,011,954	40,507,120
Retirement of property, plant and equipment	14,856,466	23,414,707
TOTAL ADDITIONS	646,306,053	582,212,671
Dispositions of working capital:		
Cash dividends paid	29,193,336	94,706,706
Increase in investments and advances.................................	107,570,466	32,587,326
Expenditures for property, plant and equipment........................	173,792,798	374,534,311
Expenditures for special tools..	241,745,805	271,761,847
Payments on long-term borrowing	37,449,055	39,391,567
Decrease in other liabilities	19,896,695	6,877,073
Other	3,712,747	2,231,075
TOTAL DISPOSITIONS	613,360,902	822,089,905
INCREASE (DECREASE) IN WORKING CAPITAL DURING THE YEAR	$ 32,945,151	$(239,877,234)

*Restated to reflect the change made in 1970 in accounting for inventories and to conform to 1970 classifications.

Exhibit 4. Chrysler Corporation: The 1970 Accounting Change

LIABILITIES AND SHAREHOLDERS' INVESTMENT December 31	1970	1969*
Current Liabilities:		
Accounts payable and accrued expenses.................................	$1,095,984,194	$1,116,607,970
Short-term debt	374,186,273	477,442,371
Payments due within one year on long-term debt	34,572,552	39,825,038
Taxes on income	43,136,332	9,969,436
TOTAL CURRENT LIABILITIES	1,547,879,351	1,643,844,815
Other Liabilities:		
Deferred incentive compensation	2,726,641	7,493,823
Other employee benefit plans...	63,462,301	55,575,476
Deferred investment tax credit...	21,774,580	25,598,022
Unrealized profits on sales to unconsolidated subsidiaries...................	49,280,076	47,336,034
Other noncurrent liabilities	68,733,595	89,870,533
TOTAL OTHER LIABILITIES	205,977,193	225,873,888
Long-Term Debt:		
Notes and debentures payable..	671,053,172	466,951,466
Convertible sinking fund debentures....................................	119,999,000	119,999,000
TOTAL LONG-TERM DEBT	791,052,172	586,950,466
International Operations Reserve...	35,500,000	35,500,000
Minority Interest in Net Assets of Consolidated Subsidiaries....................	79,742,516	95,149,271
Shareholders' Investment:		
Represented by		
Common Stock — par value $6.25 a share:		
Authorized 80,000,000 shares; issued and outstanding 49,498,979 shares at December 31, 1970 and 47,942,136 shares at December 31, 1969...........	309,368,619	299,638,350
Additional paid-in capital...	484,020,938	455,739,253
Net earnings retained for use in the business...........................	1,362,231,672	1,399,028,028
TOTAL SHAREHOLDERS' INVESTMENT	2,155,621,229	2,154,405,631
TOTAL LIABILITIES AND SHAREHOLDERS' INVESTMENT	$4,815,772,461	$4,741,724,071

*Restated to reflect the change made in 1970 in accounting for inventories.

Exhibit 4. (continued)

CONSOLIDATED BALANCE SHEET Chrysler Corporation and Consolidated Subsidiaries

ASSETS December 31	1970	1969*
Current Assets:		
Cash	$ 95,807,393	$ 78,768,440
Marketable securities — at cost and accrued interest	60,607,134	230,562,926
Accounts receivable (less allowance for doubtful accounts: 1970–$15,700,000; 1969–$13,400,000)	438,852,496	477,880,423
Refundable United States taxes on income	80,000,000	—
Inventories (See Inventories-Accounting Change note)	1,390,681,228	1,335,198,128
Prepaid insurance, taxes and other expenses	83,299,833	80,087,753
Income taxes allocable to the following year	17,415,554	27,186,281
TOTAL CURRENT ASSETS	2,166,663,638	2,229,683,951
Investments and Other Assets:		
Investments in and advances to associated companies outside the United States	24,907,266	15,496,619
Investments in and advances to unconsolidated subsidiaries	675,212,687	577,052,868
Income taxes allocable — noncurrent	22,301,845	32,465,250
Other noncurrent assets	44,971,952	55,814,937
TOTAL INVESTMENTS AND OTHER ASSETS	767,393,750	680,829,674
Property, Plant and Equipment:		
Land, buildings, machinery and equipment	2,949,256,417	2,825,623,645
Less accumulated depreciation	1,593,482,362	1,451,750,556
	1,355,774,055	1,373,873,089
Unamortized special tools	447,449,636	379,153,112
NET PROPERTY, PLANT AND EQUIPMENT	1,803,223,691	1,753,026,201
Cost of Investments in Consolidated Subsidiaries in Excess of Equity	78,491,382	78,184,245
TOTAL ASSETS	$4,815,772,461	$4,741,724,071

*Restated to reflect the change made in 1970 in accounting for inventories.

Exhibit 5. Selected Statistics, Major Auto Manufacturers (in millions of dollars, except as noted)

	1970	1969	1968	1967	1966	1965
Ford Motor Co.						
Sales	$14,979.9	$14,755.6	$10,515.7	$12,240.0	$11,536.8	$9,670.8
Net income before tax	1,006.2	1,115.1	1,291.3	133.5	1,183.1	1,319.1
Tax provision	479.8	554.4	656.5	44.5	555.9	610.2
Net income	515.7	546.5	626.6	84.1	621.0	703.0
Capital expenditure	563.6	553.5	462.4	661.1	692.5	629.1
Depreciation (special tools)	413.6	385.2	366.1	344.7	307.9	267.5
Expenditure (special tools)	483.5	424.3	416.9	374.8	358.9	366.6
Amortization	409.9	418.5	382.1	331.3	322.5	267.4
Balance Sheet						
Deferred tax and ITC	216.0	169.9	111.0	109.2	74.0	57.3
Prepaid tax	317.2	246.4	220.2	227.7	167.5	142.9
Earnings per share } dollars	4.77	5.03	5.73	.77	5.63	6.33
Dividends	2.40	2.40	2.40	2.40	2.40	2.10
Net income/sales	3.5%	3.8%	4.5%	0.8%	5.1%	6.2%
General Motors						
Sales	$18,752.4	$22,295.1	$22,755.4	$20,026.3	$20,208.5	$20,734.0
Net income before tax	169.4	1,743.3				
Tax provision	609.1	1,710.7				
Net income			1,731.9	1,627.3	1,793.4	2,125.6
Capital expenditure	1,134.2	1,043.8	860.2	912.6	1,188.1	1,322.0
Depreciation (special tools)	841.5	765.8	729.1	712.6	654.1	556.7
Expenditure (special tools)	1,148.6	863.1	865.8	881.2	890.8	729.8
Amortization	677.3	891.8	853.1	839.6	860.8	744.7
Balance Sheet						
Deferred tax and ITC	133.8	162.9	N.A.	N.A.	N.A.	N.A.
Prepaid tax	—	—	N.A.	N.A.	N.A.	N.A.
Earnings per share } dollars	2.09	5.95	6.02	5.66	6.24	7.41
Dividends	3.40	4.30	4.30	3.80	4.53	5.25
Net income/sales	3.2%	7.0%	7.6%	8.1%	8.9%	10.3%

*Chrysler**

	$7,000	$7,052	$7,445	$6,213	$5,650	$5,300
Sales	$7,000	$7,052	$7,445	$6,213	$5,650	$5,300
Net income before tax and minority interest	165	165	611	367	356	448
Tax provision	(21)	80	321	169	164	213
Net income	(8)	89	291	200	189	233
Capital expenditure	174	375	217	191	306	292
Depreciation (special tools)	177	170	162	153	130	102
Expenditure (special tools)	242	272	205	201	200	157
Amortization	173	167	187	161	173	148
Balance Sheet						
Deferred taxes and ITC		25.6†	23.9†	35.4†	50.1	38.4
Prepaid tax		83.7	85.2	67.0	40.5	35.4
Inventory reserve	—	20	24	6	10	12
Earnings per share ⎱ (dollars)	(.16)	1.87	6.23	4.35	4.16	5.44
Dividends ⎰	.60	2.00	2.00	2.00	2.00	1.25
Net income/sales	(.2)%	1.2%	3.9%	3.2%	3.4%	4.4%

*As reported on a LIFO basis, except for 1970 which is on FIFO.

†ITC only. Other deferred taxes not separately stated.

Exhibit 6. Selected Auto Manufacturers' Stock Prices and Price Earnings Ratios, 1965–1970

	FORD		GENERAL MOTORS		CHRYSLER	
	Stock Price Range	P/E Ratio	Stock Price Range	P/E Ratio	Stock Price Range	P/E Ratio
1970	56–37	8.5	81–59	33.9	35–16	—
1969	54–40	9.7	83–65	12.5	57–31	24.2
1968	60–48	9.5	89–72	13.5	72–48	9.8
1967	55–39	9.4	89–67	13.9	57–31	10.2
1966	57–38	9.9	108–65	13.9	61–29	,11.0
1965	62–50	10.1	113–91	13.8	62–41	10.1

Exhibit 7. Consolidated Statement of Net Earnings
Three months ended March 31, 1971 and 1970 (in millions of dollars)

	1971	1970*
Net sales	$ 1,846.4	$ 1,511.4
Equity in net earnings (loss) of unconsolidated subsidiaries	(.7)	(7.2)
Other income and deductions	(5.0)	(6.1)
	1,840.7	1,498.1
Cost of products sold, other than items below	1,580.0	1,331.3
Depreciation of plant and equipment	43.8	46.1
Amortization of special tools	46.1	42.9
Selling and administrative expenses	96.2	103.5
Pension and retirement plans	39.2	29.9
Interest on long-term debt	12.8	8.7
Taxes on income (credit)	11.3	(32.1)
	1,829.4	1,530.3
Net earnings (loss) including minority interest	11.3	(32.2)
Minority interest in net (income) loss of consolidated subsidiaries	(.5)	4.8
Net earnings (loss)	$ 10.8	$(27.4)
Average number of shares of common stock outstanding during the period (in thousands)	49,673	48,106
Net earnings (loss) a share	$0.22	$(0.57)

Exhibit 7. Consolidated Statement of Net Earnings
Three months ended March 31, 1971 and 1970 (in millions of dollars) (continued)

Condensed Consolidated Balance Sheet—March 31, 1971 and 1970 (in millions of dollars)

Assets

	1971	1970
Cash and marketable securities	$ 195.6	$ 414.4
Accounts receivable	550.3	555.9
Inventories	1,352.0	1,290.5
Prepaid expenses	78.5	152.7
Income taxes allocable to the following year	16.3	12.8
Total Current Assets	2,192.7	2,426.3
Investments and other assets	780.4	689.3
Property, plant and equipment	2,975.7	2,860.5
Less accumulated depreciation	1,633.9	1,490.9
	1,341.8	1,369.6
Unamortized special tools	440.1	398.6
Net property, plant and equipment	1,781.9	1,768.2
Cost of investments in consolidated subsidiaries in excess of equity	78.5	78.5
Total Assets	$4,833.5	$4,962.3

Liabilities and Shareholders' Investment

	1971	1970
Accounts payable	$ 734.9	$ 662.0
Accrued expenses	430.2	411.3
Short-term debt	328.8	641.5
Payments due within one year on long-term debt	31.9	31.7
Taxes on income	37.2	—
Total Current Liabilities	1,563.0	1,746.5
Other liabilities	211.7	183.4
Long-term debt		
Notes and debentures payable	654.5	657.2
Convertible sinking fund debentures	120.0	120.0
International operations reserve	35.5	35.5
Minority interest in net assets of consolidated subsidiaries	80.2	90.3
Shareholders' investment		
Common stock—par value $6.25 a share (outstanding shares at March 31, 1971—49,858,287 and 1970—48,279,144)	311.6	301.8
Additional paid-in capital	491.4	463.2
Net earnings retained	1,365.6	1,364.4
Total Shareholders' Investment	2,168.6	2,129.4
Total Liabilities and Shareholders' Investment	$4,833.5	$4,962.3

*1970 has been restated to reflect the change in accounting for inventories. Accordingly, the net loss for the first quarter of 1970 is restated at $27.4 million or $0.57 a share, compared to the previously reported net loss of $29.4 million or $0.61 a share.

CPC
International, Inc.

The Notes to the financial statements in the 1973 Annual Report for CPC International, Inc. (a food products company) included the following item:

Effective with the year ended December 31, 1973, the company adopted in the United States the last-in, first-out, method of inventory valuation for certain basic raw agricultural commodities used. Prior to 1973 such inventories had been valued on the first-in, first-out method. This change was made because management believes that the last-in, first-out method (which charges current earnings with current costs) minimizes the inflation-induced inventory profit in respect to these inventories and thus more clearly reflects the results of operations. The effect of the change was to reduce inventories by approximately $16,500,000 and net income by approximately $8,600,000 ($.36 per share). There is no cumulative effect of the change on prior periods since the December 31, 1972 inventory as previously reported in the opening inventory under the last-in, first-out method.

REQUIRED

1. Based on the information in this note, estimate the marginal tax rate that CPC used in its calculations. Is this different from the statutory rate? If so, what might be a reason for this? *Show your computations.*

2. Based on the information in this note and the accompanying financial statements for 1973, estimate the amounts that would have been shown for the following items *assuming that CPC had continued to use FIFO:*

This case was prepared by Professor Thomas H. Williams, The University of Wisconsin—Madison, as a basis for classroom discussion rather than to illustrate the effective or ineffective handling of an administrative situation.

(a) Cost of sales (1973)

(b) Provision for taxes on income (1973)

(c) Net income (1973)

(d) Inventory, December 31, 1972

(e) Inventory, December 31, 1973

(f) Income taxes payable, December 31, 1973

(g) Retained earnings, December 31, 1973.

3. Estimate the average number of shares of common stock that were outstanding during 1973. How many shares of common stock were outstanding at the end of 1973?

4. In the footnote CPC gives one reason for changing to LIFO. Give another reason the company may have had for making the change.

5. CPC characterizes LIFO as a method which "charges current earnings with current costs." What is the effect of the method on the valuation of inventories in the balance sheet? Is there a valuation model which assigns "current costs" both to cost of sales and inventory? If so, which one?

Exhibit 1. Consolidated Statement of Income and Retained Earnings For the Years Ended December 31, 1973 and 1972

	1973	1972
Net sales	$1,874,302,075	$1,549,581,549
Other income	15,437,237	10,115,821
	1,889,739,312	1,559,697,370
Cost of sales	1,372,791,776	1,106,780,601
Marketing, administrative, and general expenses	341,386,267	300,759,444
Interest expense	26,300,244	25,921,310
	1,740,478,287	1,433,461,355
Income from continuing operations before income taxes and extraordinary items	149,261,025	126,236,015
Provision for taxes on income	71,530,653	60,175,608
	77,730,372	66,060,407
Minority shareholders' interest	2,237,755	1,786,852
Income from continuing operations before extraordinary items	75,492,617	64,273,555
Income from divested and discontinued operations (net of income taxes)	—	2,114,336
Income before extraordinary items	75,492,617	66,387,891
Extraordinary items (net of income taxes)	—	20,234,288
Net income for the year	75,492,617	86,622,179
Retained earnings at beginning of year	356,588,687	310,605,144
Additions and adjustments from capital transactions	(155,683)	28,779
Cash dividends declared: (1973) $1.791 per share; (1972) $1.717 per share	(42,364,218)	(40,667,415)
Retained earnings at end of year	$ 389,561,403	$ 356,588,687

Exhibit 1. *(continued)*

Earnings per share based on average shares outstanding		
Income from continuing operations before extra- ordinary items	$3.19	$2.71
Income from divested and discontinued operations (net of income taxes)	—	.09
Income before extraordinary items	3.19	2.80
Extraordinary items (net of income taxes)	—	.85
Earnings per share	$3.19	$3.65

Exhibit 2. *Consolidated Balance Sheet as of December 31, 1973 and 1972*

Assets		
Current Assets		
Cash	$ 30,256,549	$ 25,626,883
Temporary investments at cost which approximates market	35,980,136	52,998,855
Notes and accounts receivable less reserves of $4,163,519 for 1973 and $3,481,822 for 1972	250,658,828	204,038,090
Inventories	316,839,607	250,478,306
Prepaid expenses	6,145,228	5,469,409
Total Current Assets	639,980,348	538,611,543
Investments in and advances to unconsolidated subsidiaries and affiliates	18,610,955	16,509,358
Plants and properties, at cost		
Buildings	206,894,934	203,233,478
Machinery and equipment	692,678,443	654,074,147
	899,573,377	857,307,625
Less accumulated depreciation	441,913,416	417,967,280
	457,659,961	439,340,345
Land	21,238,486	21,364,720
	478,898,447	460,705,065
Other assets and deferred items	18,357,275	22,117,810
Goodwill, patents, and trademarks	45,073,751	45,619,283
	$1,200,820,776	$1,083,563,059

Exhibit 2. *(continued)*

	1973	1972
Liabilities		
Current Liabilities		
Notes and drafts payable	$ 111,926,837	$ 90,104,404
Accounts payable and accrued items	207,418,558	142,337,023
Income taxes	40,467,056	57,317,180
Dividends payable	10,990,713	10,464,379
Total Current Liabilities	370,803,164	300,222,986
Noncurrent liabilities	88,831,880	67,111,916
Long-term debt	166,914,093	175,337,121
Deferred taxes on income	25,378,825	24,203,054
Minority shareholders' interest	6,569,952	6,698,229
Shareholders' Equity		
Preferred stock, par value $1.00; authorized 3,500,000 shares, none issued	—	—
Common stock, par value $.50; authorized 30,000,000 shares, issued 1973 and 1972— 23,923,124 shares	11,961,562	11,961,562
Capital in excess of par value of stock	148,124,663	148,124,663
Retained earnings	389,561,403	356,588,687
	549,647,628	516,674,912
Less common stock in treasury, at cost, 207,722 shares in 1973 and 183,459 shares in 1972	7,314,766	6,685,159
Total Shareholders' Equity	542,332,862	509,989,753
	$1,200,820,776	$1,083,563,059

Control Data
Corporation (D)

In the spring of 1965, the management of Control Data Corporation was considering a revision in the company's depreciation policies for the computers which it manufactured and rented to customers. The company defined its principal product as computer "systems": one or more electronic data-processing machines plus related peripheral equipment and coded operating instructions which were combined from a set of basic components in such a way as to satisfy the computational requirements of the customer. Such systems were offered for outright sale, or the customer could elect to lease the system from the company for a monthly rental fee.

Rental of data-processing equipment was a well-established industrial practice. The acknowledged industry leader, International Business Machines Corporation (IBM), had originally offered its punched-card and electro-mechanical calculating equipment only on a rental basis. During the early 1950s, antitrust action by the federal government forced IBM to establish selling prices for its products. The industry, however, had long been characterized by rapid technological change, a trend that was accelerated by the development of the electronic computer. Thus, many customers continued to prefer the flexibility of renting such equipment; when new and better machines became available the rental customer could return his old equipment to the manufacturer without penalty and replace it with the latest model, perhaps from a different manufacturer.

Control Data Corporation (CDC), organized in July 1957, had originally

This case was made possible by the cooperation of Control Data Corporation. It was prepared by Professor Richard F. Vancil as the basis for class discussion rather than to illustrate either effective or ineffective handling of an administrative situation.

Exhibit 1. *Seven Year Financial Summary* (In thousands except for per share data)

	1958	1959	1960	1961	1962	1963	1964†
Profit and Loss Data							
Net sales	$625	$4,588	$9,442	$18,062	$32,128	$44,861	$105,452
Rentals and service income	–	–	222	1,721	8,905	18,249	25,618
Total revenues	$625	$4,588	$9,665	$19,783	$41,034	$63,111	$131,071
Research and development expenditures—company sponsored	50	16	355	1,707	2,615	5,129	12,323
Earnings before income taxes	(114)	418	1,306	2,197	3,532	8,004	15,215
Net earnings after income taxes	(114)	283	551	842	1,542	3,064	6,018
Earnings per share of common stock after preferred stock dividends§	(.04)	.07	.12	.16	.26	.50	.84
Depreciation of property, plant, and equipment	31	53	235	1,377	5,181	8,852	13,614
Balance Sheet Data							
Current assets	$857	$2,092	$6,037	$14,336	$26,536	$47,326	$102,926
Current liabilities	473	470	3,526	8,884	16,760	22,149	38,452
Net working capital	384	1,621	2,510	5,451	9,775	25,177	64,474
Current ratio	1.8	4.4	1.7	1.6	1.6	2.1	2.7
Net property, plant, and equipment	295	251	1,809	4,586	12,959	21,382	33,105
Long-term debt	100	75	33	71	35	19,535	38,470
Stockholders' equity	650	1,828	4,318	9,793	23,390	29,468	61,252
Other Information							
Thousands of shares of common stock outstanding§	2,992	3,531	4,358	5,040	5,796	6,065	7,208
Total building occupancy (thousands of sq. ft.)	32	75	110	238	455	735	1,465
Expenditures for property, plant, and equipment	$326	$26	$1,643	$4,161	$13,756	$18,363	$29,754

Source: Annual Report for 1965.

*As reported in annual reports pertaining to the respective periods except for 1964, which has been adjusted to reflect retroactively acquisitions since June 30, 1964, accounted for as poolings of interests.

†Operating results for 1964 as reported for that year were:

Net sales $95,820,961
Rentals and service income 25,618,729
Total Revenues $121,439,690

Net earnings $6,072,921
Earnings per share of common stock $0.88 (as per footnote below)

§Adjusted for 3-for-1 stock split in September 1961 and 3-for-2 stock split in September 1964.

concentrated on the design of very large-scale electronic computers developed under contract for the federal government. During the early years, most of its systems were sold outright. CDC was a successful company almost from the start (see Exhibit 1), and grew at a rapid rate as it developed new models to serve industrial and commercial customers. A listing of the company's principal product lines, as of mid-1965, is shown in the table below.

			MAIN MEMORY CHARACTERISTICS	
Series Designation	*Model Number*	*Date of First Delivery*	*Memory Cycle Time (millionths of a second)*	*Maximum Character Storage*
	160	May 1960	6.4	8,192
Under 2000	160-A	July 1961	6.4	65,536
	1604	January 1960	6.4	262,144
	3100	January 1965	1.75	131,072
Lower 3000	3200	May 1964	1.75	131,072
	3400	November 1964	1.5	262,144
Upper 3000	3600	June 1963	1.5	2,097,152
	6600	September 1964	1.0	1,310,720
	8090	July 1964	6.4	65,536

The model numbers refer to the computer system. The system included a central processing unit (main frame); main memory; a variety of peripheral equipment, such as printers, readers, and auxiliary storage devices; and sets of instructions (software) to direct the system in its solution of a problem. Application programs were developed for the solution of particular problems or the accomplishment of specific data-processing tasks.

Beginning in 1960, the company adopted the traditional practice of offering to rent its computer systems to customers. For the fiscal year ended June 30, 1964, CDC reported that 40 percent of the systems installed during that year were on a rental basis. As may be seen in Exhibit 2, rental and service income for that year was only 21 percent of total revenue, because the first year's rental income was only a fraction of the revenue that was recognized if the system were sold. A condensed balance sheet as of June 30, 1964, is shown in Exhibit 3.

Company officials expected that the trend toward renting would continue, and believed that the depreciation policy adopted in 1960 ought to be reviewed to make sure that it was still appropriate under the changing circumstances. An accurate determination of annual profit was regarded as particularly critical by CDC officials; the common stock of the company had been listed on the New

Exhibit 2. Consolidated Statement of Earnings—Years Ended June 30, 1964 and 1963 (amounts in thousands)

	1964	1963
Net sales	$95,820	$47,845
Rentals and service income	25,618	18,302
	121,439	66,147
Cost of sales, rentals and service	70,117	42,690
Gross profit	51,322	23,456
Selling, administrative, and general expenses	22,499	9,502
Research and development expenses	12,123	5,625
	34,623	15,128
Operating profit	16,698	8,328
Other income	219	138
	16,918	8,466
Interest and other deductions	1,795	962
Earnings before taxes	15,122	7,503
Federal, state, and foreign income taxes, est.	9,050	4,830
Net earnings	$6,072	$2,672
Net earnings per share of common stock (after preferred stock dividends)*	$1.32	$0.64
Depreciation and amortization of fixed and intangible assets included in costs and expenses	$13,513	$8,991

Source: Annual Report for 1964.

*Net earnings per share of common stock have been calculated to include the shares issued in the several pooling of interest acquisitions and to reflect retroactively to September 1, 1962, the conversion since June 20, 1963, of the 4¼ percent convertible subordinated debentures.

York Stock Exchange in March 1963, and had traded as high as $75.00 per share[1] that year. In early 1965, the stock was trading in the mid-$50's.

DEPRECIATION POLICY

For computer systems rented to its customers, CDC followed the practice of depreciating the cost of the equipment over four years using a modified double-declining balance method. The equipment was assumed to have no salvage value

[1] Adjusted to reflect the 3-for-1 stock split in September 1961 and the 3-for-2 split in September 1964.

Exhibit 3. *Condensed Consolidated Balance Sheet As of June 30, 1964 and 1963 (amounts in thousands)*

	1964	1963
Assets		
Current Assets		
Cash	$4,426	$2,068
Receivables	45,969	22,692
Inventories	47,675	24,129
Prepaid expenses and deposits	882	89
Total Current Assets	98,953	48,979
Investments and other assets	1,023	2,590
Property, plant, and equipment at cost		
Land, buildings, and improvements	7,101	3,099
Machinery, equipment, and rental machines	47,574	33,666
Construction in progress	648	283
	55,323	37,050
Less allowance for depreciation and amortization	23,548	15,157
Net Property and Plant Equipment	31,775	21,893
Deferred charges	1,301	307
Total Assets	$133,054	$73,770
Liabilities		
Current Liabilities		
Notes payable to banks	$3,200	$10,368
Current maturities of long-term debt	1,355	1,010
Customer advances and accounts payable	14,499	5,340
Accrued taxes and other accrued liabilities	16,705	6,360
Total Current Liabilities	35,861	23,080
Long-Term Debt, less current maturities		
Equipment purchase contracts	2,210	4,535
$3\frac{3}{4}$% convertible subordinated debentures	35,000	
$4\frac{1}{4}$% convertible subordinated debentures		15,000
Other mortgages and notes	98	10
Total Long-Term Debt	37,309	19,545
Reserve for product and service warranties	172	186
Minority interest in foreign subsidiary	92	

Stockholders' equity:		
Cumulative preferred stock		325
Common stock	2,309	2,050
Additional paid-in capital	46,259	23,584
Retained earnings	12,381	6,330
	60,951	32,290
Deduct cost of treasury stock	1,332	1,332
Total Stockholders' Equity	59,618	30,958
Total Liabilities and Equity	$133,054	$73,770

Source: Annual Report for 1964.

at the end of four years. Thus, in the first twelve months on rental, 50 percent of the cost of the equipment was charged as depreciation expense (double the 25 percent rate that would result from straight-line depreciation). One-twelfth of this amount was recorded for each month of the taxable year after the equipment was first accepted by a customer. In the second twelve months, 50 percent of the unrecovered cost (25 percent of the original cost) was taken as depreciation. For the third and fourth years, the company then switched to straight-line depreciation; one-eighth of the original cost was written off each year. Idle equipment, returned by the original customer and not yet sold or rented to another customer, continued to be depreciated even though it produced no revenue. Salvage value was ignored because of the uncertainty concerning the economically useful life of the equipment in the face of rapid technological change. The company's depreciation policy was used for calculating taxable income, and was also used in determining income reported to stockholders.

PRICES AND GROSS MARGIN

Sales and rental prices in the industry were determined by competitive interplay among the major computer manufacturers. Many well-known companies shared a part of the electronic data-processing industry. The market shares, based on the selling value of installed equipment, were estimated by one firm of security analysts in a report made available to the investing public in January 1965 as follows:

International Business Machines	72.0%
Sperry Rand	8.7
Control Data	4.5
Radio Corporation of America	2.9
Honeywell	2.5
Burroughs	2.4
National Cash Register	2.2
General Electric	2.1
All Others	2.7
	100.0%

The price for a CDC system was the sum of the list prices for the various pieces of equipment required, and list prices were revised from time to time. A major price reduction was announced by the company in 1964. The table below illustrates the impact of that change for three of the most popular CDC systems.

	PRICE OF AVERAGE INSTALLATION		RENTAL PER MONTH	
Model	Before July 1 1964	After July 1 1964	Before July 1 1964	After July 1 1964
3200	$700,000	$500,000	$15,000	$12,000
3600	$2,400,000	$2,300,000	$60,000	$41,000
6600	$7,900,000	$6,900,000	$197,000	$116,000

Despite these price reductions, Mr. William C. Norris, President of CDC, was able to report at the seventh annual stockholders' meeting in September 1964, that, "Today the rate of gross profit on our computer systems is greater than any time in the history of Control Data . . . even though we are also at the same time offering more computing per dollar to our customers through reduced selling prices. These reductions in selling prices have come about because of a number of reasons, the principal one being the reduction in manufacturing costs, particularly in the cost of components."

The cost of components was an important factor in CDC's profitability. Management believed that the company's primary competitive advantage lay in its ability to design the most advanced computer systems. Major emphasis was also placed on the distribution function, particularly systems engineering, to tailor a system composed of CDC equipment to meet the user's need. CDC's production operation in 1965 was primarily one of assembling components into completed units. The company prepared specifications for each piece of equipment and contracted for the production of various components with other manufacturers. Purchased materials and components accounted for about 90 percent of the manufacturing costs.

THE CONTROLLER'S OPINION

Mr. B. R. Eng, Controller of CDC, was one member of management who believed that a change in depreciation policy was necessary, despite the difficulties that might arise in explaining such a change to the investment community. Expressing his view on the situation in mid-1965, Mr. Eng said, "When a company makes a change in accounting practices it means that either the practices it *was* using were wrong, or *conditions* have changed and the former practices are no longer correct and must be changed. It is the latter situation in which we find ourselves. There was nothing wrong with the accounting practices we have been following, but conditions have changed.

"It all stems from an unavoidable conflict in the application of accounting principles—the conflict between the principle of conservatism and the principle of the proper matching of costs against related revenues. Conservatism demands that you not anticipate income but that you do anticipate all losses; thus, it encourages charging off costs as incurred if there is any doubt about recovering those costs in the future. But the proper matching of costs against revenues demands that costs and expenses not be charged off as incurred, but that they be deferred and applied against the revenues to which such costs and expenses relate.

"The fundamental objective is the proper determination of income. If you're too conservative, you understate current income and overstate future income, which is wrong. If you are not conservative enough, you overstate current income and understate future income, which is also wrong. So the application of the principle of conservatism must, of necessity, be a matter of judgment. Of course, the greater the risk, the greater the degree of conservatism to be applied.

"The computer business is a fast moving, highly competitive business. When Control Data Corporation started its operations eight years ago the risk was tremendous. But we have learned a great deal in the past eight years, and we've gained a lot more confidence. The risks which Control Data faced in its formative years demanded ultra-conservative accounting practices.

"But an even more significant change has occurred that has demanded the more realistic application of the principles of conservatism and the matching of costs against related revenues. I'm referring to the significant increase in our lease business. Approximately 55 percent of the orders booked by the Company in fiscal year 1965 were lease orders, compared with 40 percent in fiscal year 1964, and this upward trend appears to be continuing.

94

"This problem is not unique with Control Data. Many other companies are encountering the same problem and are doing something about it. One of those companies depreciates its leased equipment over a five-year period, another uses six years, and the third uses five to eight years for its various classes of leased equipment."

ASSIGNMENT

1. Evaluate alternative depreciation policies for CDC's leased equipment. Which combination of depreciable life and depreciation method do you believe would provide the best matching of equipment cost against rental income? It may be assumed that, on the average, the total manufacturing cost of a piece of CDC equipment is approximately 50 percent of the listed selling price for commercial and industrial customers.
2. Should CDC change its depreciation policy? If so, what policy should be adopted? How should this change be explained to stockholders?

Loews
Corporation (A)

Loews Corporation, formed in Delaware in November 1969, operates principally as a holding company controlling more than 100 wholly owned subsidiaries.[1] In addition it manages a large portfolio of securities, primarily common stocks. This case focuses on the financial accounting aspects of the portfolio.

BACKGROUND

Through its subsidiaries, Loews operates hotels, exhibits motion pictures through theatre ownership, develops residential real estate, and manufactures and sells tobacco products.

Loews operates 11 hotels and motels in the United States, Canada, Europe, and the Caribbean; and also provides management and other services for hotel operations in various countries. Its hotels are classified principally as "luxury" accommodations, and include the Regency in New York, the Churchill in London, and Le Concorde in Quebec City.

It operates 84 motion picture theatres located in 30 cities in 15 states.

This case was prepared by Dennis P. Frolin and James F. Smith as a basis for class discussion rather than to illustrate either effective or ineffective handling of an administrative situation.

Copyright © 1975 by the President and Fellows of Harvard College. Distributed by the Intercollegiate Case Clearing House, Soldiers Field, Boston, Mass. 02163. All rights reserved to the contributors. Printed in the U.S.A.

[1] Loews Corporation engaged in no business transactions until February 1971, when it acquired total ownership of Loews Theatres, Inc. The operation and management of Loews Corporation was essentially a continuation of that of the acquired company. Any reference to transactions or data dated prior to the merger are actually those of Loews Theatres, Inc.

The theatres vary greatly, ranging from suburban theatres to large, deluxe "showcase" theatres. It principally exhibits motion pictures intended to appeal to all age groups of a general audience.

Through a joint venture agreement, it is involved in the planning and construction of residential developments including townhouses, condominiums, and rental apartments.

In 1968 Loews acquired 100 percent ownership of Lorillard Corporation, which it presently operates as a company division. Lorillard manufactures and sells cigarettes, including the brands of Kent, Newport, True, Old Gold, and Spring; and also markets little cigars, cigars, and chewing tobacco. The sale of manufactured tobacco products is the primary source of revenues and profits for Loews. Exhibit 1 provides a percentage breakdown of the various Loews operations.

SECURITIES PORTFOLIO OPERATIONS

Loews' management actively seeks development and expansion opportunities, and considers it necessary to maintain funds as a source of immediate financing for such opportunities. They manage a marketable security portfolio to secure a continuous return on these funds. This portfolio typically includes more than 150 different securities consisting primarily of common stocks, with the holding in each ranging from perhaps as few as 1,000 shares with a book value of $100,000 to more than 1 million shares with a book value of $43 million. For example, the portfolio included 191 common (and preferred) stocks and three bonds on August 31, 1973, and 217 stocks and four bonds on August 31, 1974.

During the past five years the entire portfolio has ranged in book value from $177 million at the beginning of fiscal year 1970 to $432.5 million at the end of fiscal 1973; and in market value from $177 million at the beginning of fiscal 1970 to $443.4 million at the end of fiscal 1972. Exhibit 2 provides a summary of the portfolio operations since 1970.

Loews' activity in the market has varied from year to year depending upon market conditions. Of the total portfolio held at August 31, 1973, about 100 different securities showed sales activity during fiscal year 1974, involving approximately $184 million in book value. This represents 43 percent of the total portfolio book value at that date.

Management of this portfolio has become increasingly important to the profitability of operations, both in terms of security gains and losses and dividend income. Together, these have represented between 20 and 30 percent of the total earnings of Loews (before interest expense, income taxes, and extraordinary items) in each of the past four years (Exhibit 2). Because of the size of the portfolio, Loews' earnings have to some degree become dependent upon the overall performance of the securities market. Exhibit 3 provides price data covering the five-year period from August 31, 1969, to August 31, 1974, for

Exhibit 1. Sources of Revenues and Earnings

	TOTAL SALES AND REVENUES					EARNINGS (LOSSES) BEFORE INTEREST EXPENSE, INCOME TAXES, AND EXTRAORDINARY ITEMS				
	YEARS ENDED AUGUST 31,					YEARS ENDED AUGUST 31,				
	(in percents)					(in percents)				
	1970	*1971*	*1972*	*1973*	*1974*	*1970*	*1971*	*1972*	*1973*	*1974*
Hotel operations	17.3	15.5	13.7	7.6	8.4	20.6	12.1	11.7	6.9	11.0
Theatre operations	6.1	5.3	5.8	4.1	4.0	9.9	3.8	3.6	4.8	5.1
Sales of manufactured products, principally cigarettes	72.3	71.3	69.3	75.8	76.3	69.0	50.9	50.5	55.2	59.5
Residential development	.5	4.4	5.8	5.7	4.5	(.1)	2.2	1.7	2.5	(6.9)
Equity income in associated companies						2.7	3.0	1.8	3.1	8.3
Other	2.6	2.1	2.9	3.8	3.8	2.0		.8		3.0
Security gains (losses)						(11.2)	19.9	15.1	11.7	.1
Dividend income	1.2	1.4	2.5	3.0	3.0	7.1	8.1	14.8	15.8	19.9

Exhibit 2. *Financial Statistics (millions of dollars, rounded)*

	8-31-69	8-31-70	8-31-71	8-31-72	8-31-73	8-31-74
Marketable Securities:						
Market value	177.0	210.2	339.5	443.4	408.5	280.8
Book value* (cost)	177.0	237.1	325.0	423.5	432.5	376.3
Pre-tax realized gains (losses) on security transactions		(11.0)	30.6	22.5	17.2	.1
Income taxes on security transactions		(5.4)	12.0	9.0	5.3	0
Net realized gains (losses) on security transactions		(5.6)	18.6	13.5	11.9	0§
Other:						
Pre-tax operating earnings†		54.9	75.9	85.0	78.6	59.4

*Represents "Investments in Securities: Other" per Loews' Consolidated Balance Sheet.

†This amount excludes all realized gains or losses on security transactions but includes all dividends received from the security portfolio.

§Actual amount $26,000; rounds to zero.

Exhibit 3. *Stock Market Data*

	NYSE INDUSTRIAL PRICE INDEX	LOEWS CORPORATION COMMON STOCK PRICE
8-31-69	55.86	31 7/8
8-31-70	46.43	25 1/8
8-31-71	58.85	52 5/8
8-31-72	67.90	51 1/8
8-31-73	61.32	23 3/8
8-31-74	41.85	13 5/8

both the New York Stock Exchange Industrial Index and Loews Corporation common stock.

ACCOUNTING METHODS

The two most common methods used to account for security investments are the *historical cost* method and the *market value* method. Both record dividends received as current period profits. They differ in the timing of recording gains or losses on security price movements. Like most accounting methods the total profit over the life of the security investment is identical under either method, but the pattern of profit recognition differs.

The *historical cost* method recognizes security price changes as profit or loss only when the security is sold. Thus price movements during the holding period are not reflected in the financial statements of that period. The only instance in which price movements are recognized prior to sale of the security is when the *lower of cost or market* rule is applied. The *LCM* rule requires that the permanent decline of a security's market value below its historical cost be accounted for as a current period loss. This is accomplished by "writing down" the balance sheet amount for securities to its lower market value.

The LCM rule is most often applied to security investments classified as current assets but not to those classified as non-current. The balance sheet classification is determined by management, subject to auditor review, based primarily on management's intention regarding the securities: "temporary" investments are classified as current; "permanent" investments as noncurrent.

The *market value* method records increases and decreases in security prices each period as a gain or a loss, regardless of whether or not the security is sold. This is accomplished by "writing up" or "writing down" the balance sheet amount for the securities each period. Hence, the balance sheet amount for securities always reflects at year end the then current market value.

Generally accepted accounting principles traditionally have required non-investment companies to use the historical cost method and investment companies (for example, mutual funds) to use the market value method. In recent years, seemingly increased general volatility of security prices has prompted both managers and auditors to rethink the conventional rules. Exhibit 4 shows Loews' method of accounting for its investment portfolio and includes excerpts from the 1974 financial statements.

QUESTIONS

1. How much pre-tax profit or loss would Loews earn on its securities portfolio in each of the fiscal years 1970 through 1974 if it used the *market value* method? If it will assist your analysis, you may assume that the cost of securities purchased (in millions) in the years 1970 through 1974 were: $120.1, 227.9, 348.5, 209.0, and 127.8, respectively.
2. How would the 1973 pre-tax profit or loss on the portfolio which you calculated in Question 1 differ if the cost of the securities purchased in 1973 were $100 million instead of $209 million?
3. As manager of Loews' security portfolio, design an evaluation system which you consider to be a fair, accurate measure of your performance. Be specific.
4. Which method of accounting more fairly presents the results of Loews' portfolio management? Which method should be used in reporting to shareholders? Why?

Exhibit 4. Loews Corporation (A)

Loews Corporation and Subsidiaries
Consolidated Balance Sheet

| | August 31, | |
	1974	1973
Assets		
Current Assets:		
Cash, including time deposits (1974, $10,640,000; 1973, $8,505,000)	**$ 23,537,000**	$ 21,314,000
Receivables—principally trade, less allowance for doubtful accounts and discounts (1974, $5,022,000; 1973, $2,919,000)	**77,944,000**	60,670,000
Inventories:		
Leaf tobacco	**223,084,000**	225,732,000
Manufactured stock	**27,707,000**	21,985,000
Materials, supplies, etc.	**9,751,000**	6,491,000
Real estate held for development and sale	**57,302,000**	47,112,000
Total current assets	**419,325,000**	383,304,000
Investments in Securities:		
Associated company	**24,259,000**	4,236,000
Other	**376,306,000**	432,472,000
Total investments in securities	**400,565,000**	436,708,000
Total current assets and investments in securities	**819,890,000**	820,012,000
Investments and Advances:		
Investments in and advances to unconsolidated companies	**4,165,000**	14,111,000
Mortgages and notes receivable (maturing through 2028 at interest rates ranging from 5% to 13%)	**47,528,000**	35,226,000
Land and other investments, at cost	**23,365,000**	19,652,000
Total investments and advances	**75,058,000**	68,989,000
Property, Plant and Equipment, at cost:		
Land	**41,834,000**	41,994,000
Buildings and building equipment	**154,880,000**	154,053,000
Machinery and equipment	**78,237,000**	71,604,000
Leaseholds and leasehold improvements	**11,322,000**	10,969,000
Total	**286,273,000**	278,620,000
Less accumulated depreciation and amortization	**92,881,000**	85,821,000
Property, plant and equipment—net	**193,392,000**	192,799,000
Other Assets:		
Cost in excess of net assets acquired	**65,519,000**	67,115,000
Trademarks	**100,033,000**	100,033,000
Patents and licenses, less accumulated amortization (1974, $5,027,000; 1973, $4,179,000)	**8,304,000**	9,152,000
Prepaid expenses, deferred charges, etc.	**11,682,000**	10,002,000
Total other assets	**185,538,000**	186,302,000
Total	**$1,273,878,000**	$1,268,102,000

Exhibit 4. (continued)

	August 31,	
	1974	1973
Liabilities and Shareholders' Equity		
Current Liabilities:		
Short-term debt	$ **80,353,000**	$ 119,515,000
Accounts payable and accrued liabilities	**57,086,000**	51,929,000
Accrued taxes:		
Federal and foreign income taxes	**10,170,000**	5,243,000
Excise and other taxes	**22,316,000**	14,754,000
Current maturities of long-term debt, less unamortized discount	**8,914,000**	11,138,000
Total current liabilities	**178,839,000**	202,579,000
Long-Term Debt, less current maturities and unamortized discount:		
Senior debt	**270,700,000**	268,235,000
Subordinated debt	**371,932,000**	372,533,000
Long-term debt—net	**642,632,000**	640,768,000
Deferred Credits and Other Liabilities:		
Deferred income taxes	**17,011,000**	17,316,000
Accrued employee benefits	**8,144,000**	6,738,000
Deferred credits and non-current liabilities	**3,617,000**	3,372,000
Total deferred credits and other liabilities	**28,772,000**	27,426,000
Shareholders' Equity:		
Common stock, authorized 30,000,000 shares of $1 par value; issued shares stated at par value	**14,791,000**	14,791,000
Additional paid-in capital	**116,522,000**	116,522,000
Earnings retained in the business	**345,003,000**	315,480,000
Total	**476,316,000**	446,793,000
Less common stock held in treasury, at cost (1974, 1,873,000 shares; 1973, 1,733,000 shares)	**52,681,000**	49,464,000
Total shareholders' equity	**423,635,000**	397,329,000
Total	**$1,273,878,000**	$1,268,102,000

Exhibit 4. *(continued)*

Loews Corporation and Subsidiaries
Statement of Consolidated Earnings and
Earnings Retained in the Business

	Year Ended August 31,	
	1974	1973
Sales and Operating Revenues:		
Sales of manufactured products and revenues of theatre and hotel operations	**$739,797,000**	$714,021,000
Other revenues, principally rent and dividends	**53,544,000**	52,415,000
Total	**793,341,000**	766,436,000
Costs and Expenses:		
Cost of sales and operating costs	**550,237,000**	505,655,000
Selling, advertising and administrative	**124,144,000**	120,266,000
Depreciation and amortization	**10,344,000**	10,124,000
Interest and amortization of debenture discount and expense	**58,579,000**	51,796,000
Income taxes	**14,158,000**	27,363,000
Total	**757,462,000**	715,204,000
Earnings Before Security Gains and Equity in Earnings of Associated Company	**35,879,000**	51,232,000
Security Gains:		
Realized gains	**70,000**	17,213,000
Less applicable income taxes	**44,000**	5,328,000
Security gains—net	**26,000**	11,885,000
Equity in Earnings of Associated Company	**9,379,000**	
Net Earnings	**45,284,000**	63,117,000
Earnings Retained in the Business, Beginning of Year	**315,480,000**	269,541,000
Cash Dividends (per share—$1.22 in 1974 and $1.21 in 1973)	**(15,761,000)**	(17,178,000)
Earnings Retained in the Business, End of Year	**$345,003,000**	$315,480,000
Earnings Per Share—Primary:		
Earnings before security gains and equity in earnings of associated company	**$2.78**	$3.61
Security gains—net		.84
Equity in earnings of associated company	**.72**	
Net Earnings	**$3.50**	$4.45
Earnings Per Share—Assuming Full Dilution:		
Earnings before security gains and equity in earnings of associated company	**$2.73**	$3.01
Security gains—net		.60
Equity in earnings of associated company	**.60**	
Net Earnings	**$3.33**	$3.61

Exhibit 4. *(continued)*

Loews Corporation and Subsidiaries
Statement of Changes in
Consolidated Financial Position

	Year Ended August 31,	
	1974	1973
Funds Provided:		
Earnings before security gains and equity in earnings of associated company	**$ 35,879,000**	$ 51,232,000
Items not currently requiring funds:		
Depreciation and amortization	**10,344,000**	10,124,000
Deferred income taxes	**54,000**	427,000
Other—net	**1,709,000**	1,094,000
Funds provided from operations exclusive of security gains and equity in earnings of associated company	**47,986,000**	62,877,000
Security gains—net	**26,000**	11,885,000
Funds provided from operations exclusive of equity in earnings of associated company	**48,012,000**	74,762,000
Dispositions of property, plant and equipment	**2,810,000**	4,773,000
Dispositions of investments and advances	**19,606,000**	16,358,000
Issuance of long-term debt	**12,871,000**	87,532,000
Reduction of cost in excess of net assets acquired attributable to income tax benefits	**2,142,000**	4,616,000
Issuance of common stock		3,517,000
Total	**85,441,000**	191,558,000
Funds Applied:		
Additions to property, plant and equipment	**12,783,000**	10,853,000
Additions to investments and advances	**25,302,000**	7,632,000
Additions to common stock held in treasury	**3,217,000**	49,394,000
Reduction of long-term debt	**12,614,000**	61,515,000
Exercise of warrants through application of 6⅞% debentures		2,834,000
Dividends paid	**15,761,000**	17,178,000
Other—net	**2,013,000**	4,121,000
Total	**71,690,000**	153,527,000
Excess of Funds Provided over Funds Applied Represented by:		
Increase (decrease) in investments in securities	**(46,010,000)***	13,178,000
Increase in working capital	**59,761,000**	24,853,000
Total	**$ 13,751,000**	$ 38,031,000
Excess of Funds Provided Over Funds Applied by Component:		
Increase (decrease) in investments in securities	**$ (46,010,000) ***	$ 13,178,000
Increase (decrease) in working capital:		
Cash, including time deposits	**2,223,000**	4,406,000
Receivables	**17,274,000**	14,210,000
Inventories	**6,334,000**	296,000
Real estate held for development and sale	**10,190,000**	(7,936,000)
Short-term debt	**39,162,000**	(17,692,000)
Accounts payable and accrued liabilities	**(5,157,000)**	14,406,000
Accrued taxes	**(12,489,000)**	10,924,000
Current maturities of long-term debt, less unamortized discount	**2,224,000**	6,239,000
Increase in working capital	**59,761,000**	24,853,000
Total	**$ 13,751,000**	$ 38,031,000

*Exclusive of equity adjustments for associated company which did not result in funds provided or applied.

NOTES TO CONSOLIDATED FINANCIAL STATEMENTS

Investments In Securities

Associated company—The Company carries its investment in Wheeling-Pittsburgh Steel Corporation (Wheeling) at cost adjusted for the Company's share of earnings and capital changes of Wheeling from dates of acquisition plus amortization of the excess of equity in net assets acquired over cost thereof. The Company reports as earnings its proportionate share of Wheeling's earnings plus amortization of the excess of equity in net assets acquired over cost thereof and provides for appropriate deferred federal income taxes on the undistributed earnings so reported.

Other—Investments in other securities are carried at cost. The cost of securities sold is determined on the identified certificate or first-in, first-out method. The Company has invested in securities in order to secure a return on funds it is holding for development and expansion opportunities. The Company regularly and actively seeks development and expansion opportunities which may require application of all or a portion of such funds. In view of the uncertainty as to when such opportunities may arise, the investment in securities has been classified as a noncurrent asset.

Other—The quoted market value of other security investments aggregated approximately $281,000,000 and $408,000,000 at August 31, 1974 and 1973, respectively. In the opinion of Management the decline in market value at August 31, 1974, does not constitute a permanent impairment of these investments.

Securities with a quoted market value of approximately $11,500,000 at August 31, 1974, are pledged as collateral in connection with the retirement plan covering hourly production employees and to secure other liabilities.

Subsequent Events

On November 11, 1974, the Company made a cash tender offer to purchase 20,000,000 shares of common and preferred stock of CNA Financial Corporation (CNA) (subject to the conditions stated in the Offer to Purchase) at a price of $5.00 per share for the common stock and $6.75 per share for the preferred stock. The Company and CNA have agreed that concurrently with the purchase of stock pursuant to the tender offer, CNA will sell, and the Company will purchase, 3,703,704 shares of a newly authorized preferred stock of CNA for $6.75 per share.

The amount required by the Company to purchase the 20,000,000 shares of stock under the offer (including commissions and other expenses) is estimated to be between $105,000,000 and $120,000,000. In addition, $25,000,000 will be required for the Company's purchase of the newly authorized preferred stock. The Company has sufficient cash, marketable securities, and other current assets to enable it to provide all such funds. Recently, market conditions have not been favorable for the sale of large amounts of securities. The Company has been informed by certain investment bankers, that they would, subject to the availability of credit to them, extend up to $85,000,000 of credit to the Company on a demand margin basis and at interest rates expected to approximate the prime brokers (call loan) rate in effect from time to time plus ½ percent, if the Company were to request such credit.

Leaseway Transportation Corp. (A)

On November 6, 1975, the Financial Accounting Standards Board issued an Exposure Draft of a proposed statement entitled, "Accounting for a Certain Marketable Securities." The Exposure Draft, if ultimately issued as proposed, would be effective for fiscal periods ending in or after late December 1975.

The relevant paragraphs of the Exposure Draft have been reproduced in full in Exhibit 3. However, a brief summary of the accounting and disclosure requirements of the proposed statement follows:

ACCOUNTING REQUIREMENTS

1. Marketable equity securities would be carried at the lower of aggregate cost or market value, as determined at each balance sheet date. Companies in industries in which the market value basis is an accepted practice may elect that practice. No distinction is to be made between amounts carried as short-term and long-term investments.
2. Except for companies in industries with specialized accounting practices, any excess of aggregate cost over market value would be charged to income. A later recovery in market price would be credited to income (up to the amount of original cost).
3. Generally, the marketable equity securities of all entities included in consolidated financial statements are to be treated as a single portfolio for purposes of comparing aggregate cost and market value.

This case was prepared by Professor William J. Bruns, Jr. and Visiting Associate Professor David A. Wilson as a basis for class discussion rather than to illustrate either effective or ineffective handling of an administrative situation.

1. For companies not following specialized industry accounting practices:
   (a) Aggregate cost and aggregate market value as of the date of each balance sheet presented.
   (b) Net realized and net unrealized gains and losses included in each income statement presented, together with the basis on which cost was determined in computing realized gains or losses.
2. For companies following specialized industry accounting practices:
   (a) Change in net unrealized gains or losses for each income statement presented.
3. For all companies:
   (a) Gross unrealized gains and losses as of the date of the latest balance sheet presented.
   (b) Significant net realized and net unrealized securities gains and losses arising after the date of the financial statements, but prior to their issuance.

By way of illustration, consider the following portfolio of equity securities held by a company at December 31, 1975 and 1976.

Securities	DECEMBER 31, 1975			DECEMBER 31, 1976		
	Cost	Market	Unrealized Gain (Loss)	Cost	Market	Unrealized Gain (Loss)
A*	$25,000	$30,000	$5,000	$25,000	$23,000	($2,000)
B*	15,000	9,000	(6,000)	15,000	17,000	2,000
C†	15,000	8,000	(7,000)	15,000	12,000	(3,000)
	$55,000	$47,000	($8,000)	$55,000	$52,000	($3,000)

*Current.
†Noncurrent.

Under the requirements of the Exposure Draft, net income in 1975 would include an unrealized loss (debit) on marketable securities of $8,000 with a corresponding valuation allowance (credit) of $8,000. In 1976, a net credit to income of $5,000 would arise from the increase in market value of the securities. A corresponding reduction of the valuation allowance to $3,000 as at December 31, 1976, would also occur. Disclosure on the balance sheet as at December 31, 1975, would be as follows:

Current assets:	
Marketable securities, carried at market (Note A)	$39,000
Noncurrent assets:	
Marketable securities, carried at market (Note A)	$ 8,000

NOTES TO THE FINANCIAL STATEMENTS

Note A. Marketable securities are carried at the lower of cost or market as at December 31, 1975, with that determination made by aggregating all marketable equity securities. Inasmuch as cost exceeded market value at December 31, 1975, marketable securities are stated at market value as of that date. The cost of marketable securities as of that date was

Current	$40,000
Noncurrent	15,000
	$55,000

At December 31, 1975, there were gross unrealized gains of $5,000 and gross unrealized losses of $13,000 pertaining to the portfolio.

The Financial Accounting Standards Board concluded that "in view of the relatively narrow scope of the project and the need for timely resolution," a period of slightly more than a month would be established for the submission of comments on the Exposure Draft by interested parties. On December 4, 1975, Mr. John L. Skipper, Vice President of Finance and Treasurer of Leaseway Transportation Corporation, sent the following letter to the FASB.

FILE REFERENCE 1034

We are opposed to the issuance of the proposed statement, "Accounting for Certain Marketable Securities" in its present form (Exposure Draft of November 6). We believe that the proposed method of accounting for investments classified as noncurrent assets at the lower of cost or market represents an unsound departure from present generally accepted accounting principles.

Specifically, we believe that:

1. a distorted earnings trend would result from applying the statement's provisions
2. an inconsistency would be established in the carrying value of noncurrent assets

3. *management's responsibility for timely reporting of losses would be usurped*
4. *"as-if" accounting is confusing*
5. *a possible shift in the placement of investment funds may result*
6. *fluctuations in earnings may be magnified by the provisions of the statement*
7. *a piecemeal approach to valuation accounting would result from adopting the statement*

Amplification of our views is contained in the following.

BACKGROUND

Leaseway Transportation Corporation was incorporated in 1960 and became a public company in 1961. Our 1974 revenues of $475 million rank us as the third largest publicly owned highway transportation company in the United States. Motor carrier transportation services account for about two-thirds of our total revenues, which includes the country's two largest contract carriers. Leasing, warehousing, and other transportation-related services account for the balance of our revenues.

Leaseway embarked upon the program of investing in marketable securities in 1971. Investments have been made primarily in preferred stocks with no heavy concentration in any one security. From the beginning, the intent of Leaseway was to make a long-range, long-term investment in these securities. These securities were classified as non-current assets in 1973, 1974 and 1975 to date.

Leaseway has a strong financial position and a highly liquid current position. The necessity to dispose of these securities to obtain working capital is remote. We presently have adequate cash to finance our operations without disposing of our long-term investment in securities. At September 30, 1975, Leaseway had over $46 million in cash and short-term investments and had an adequate supply of financing available from lenders to finance additional capital expenditures. The fact that Leaseway has both short-and long-term investments is evidence that we have no need to liquidate our non-current investments to meet our current needs for funds.

EFFECT OF PROPOSED ACCOUNTING ON FINANCIAL
STATEMENTS OF LEASEWAY TRANSPORTATION CORP.

Your attention is directed to Exhibits 1 and 2, which are attached hereto. They disclose the significant impact the proposed accounting would have on our reported net earnings and earnings per share. For 1973 and 1974, our restated net earnings and earnings per share would decrease by 11 percent and 28 percent, respectively. For the nine months ended September 30, 1975, our restated net earnings and earnings per share would increase by 21 percent. *Thus, restatement of our reported earnings to conform to the proposed accounting would result in material changes in our previously reported earnings. This may result in a serious loss of credibility of our reported earnings by investors and customers and the general public.*

Further, application of the proposed rules would result in our investment having a disproportionate effect on our reported earnings in comparison to our transportation business. At September 30, 1975, our equity securities (as defined by the proposed statement) amounted to $22 million, or, about five percent of our assets. However, the unrealized gain resulting from holding these securities for the nine months ended September 30, 1975 would amount to 18 percent of our restated earnings under the proposed rules.

ARGUMENTS AGAINST THE PROPOSED STATEMENT
Distorted Earnings Trend

We believe the trend of our earnings would be distorted, as demonstrated in the chart below, if the proposed statement is adopted. The distortion would result from fluctuations in the securities market which is unrelated to our business. Why should the whims of buyers and sellers reacting to national and international news have an effect

Leaseway Transportation Corp.
Earnings per Share by Quarters
March 31, 1973 to September 30, 1975

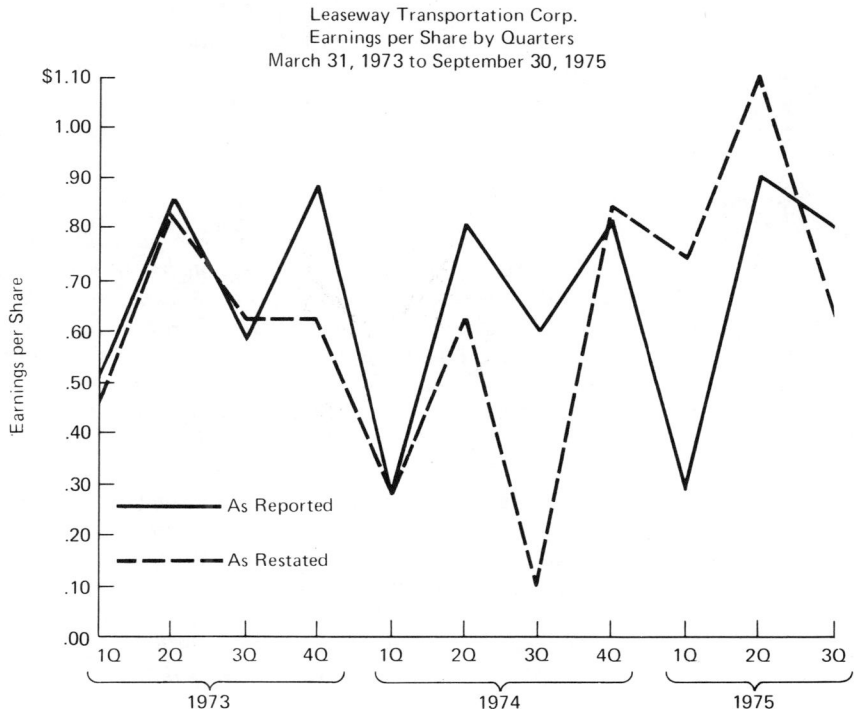

on the earnings of our company? We are not trading in securities. We are not selling securities. We have made a long-term investment. We believe the accounting for that investment should follow our investment policy.

It may be more conservative to carry long-term investments at the lower of cost or market. *But at what price conservatism and to what degree? We don't believe that the objectives can be justified by the price distortion of the earnings trends.*

Inconsistency Established

The question is, Should long-term investments be carried at market value? One answer seems to be that since a market value is available, it should be used. No other long-term investment or non-current asset is carried at market value. One reason may be that market values are not readily available for property, plant and equipment, goodwill, and similar items. Another reason may be that presumably there is no intention to dispose of the asset in the foreseeable future and it would be difficult, if not impossible, to determine what the market value might be at the date of such future disposition. This is precisely the case with marketable securities that are appropriately classified as long-term investments. The market value today is available, but what will the market value be at the date of disposal? In our view, the availability of the market value does not support the proposal to write the assets down today and up tomorrow.

Management's Responsibility

When does the loss on disposal take place for a long-term asset? For property, plant, and equipment items, it occurs when management announces its intent to dispose of such assets. Hence, the loss is recorded at the time of the management decision. So should it be with long-term investments in securities. Except for permanent impairment, the loss should be recognized when management decides to dispose of the securities. The effect of the proposed statement is to remove that decision from management and to force accounting recognition of a capital loss. In our view, it is inappropriate for the Board to usurp management's responsibility by the issuance of an accounting statement.

As responsible management we are charged with reporting timely and accurately to our shareholders and to the public the results of operations and the financial condition of the company. We believe corporate management has generally carried out this responsibility well and does not need a proliferation of rigid accounting rules to replace the exercise of sound judgment.

"As-if" Accounting

> The proposed accounting is the first step to "as-if" accounting. It says, "This is the loss I would have taken if I had sold the investment at the end of this year. There is no tax effect because if I had sold the investment, it would have resulted in a capital loss, and I don't have any if capital gain." Then, in the following year when the market value recovers, we say to our shareholders, "This is the gain I would have had if I had bought the investment this year." None of which we did or intended to do. Is the average shareholder going to understand? Will he think the accounting profession is improving communication? We don't think so.

Investment Shift

> There may be economic effects of the adoption of the proposed statement. Leaseway and other companies may not invest in preferred or common stocks in the future because of the effect such investment could have on earnings. We might invest in debt obligations to avoid the accounting problems created by the proposed statement. In the long run, this could reduce our earnings for our shareholders and could have an adverse effect on the capital market at a time when there is a shortage of investment capital, especially in equity securities.

Fluctuations in Earnings Magnified

> A doubling effect on the fluctuations in earnings could result from the adoption of the proposed statement. When interest rates on debt obligations tend to rise, market values of equity securities tend to fall. Hence, earnings are depressed by both the effect of the higher interest cost and the unrealized loss in market value of the investments. When the trend reverses, the recovery rate is likewise accelerated. The effect is to create more dramatic swings in earnings, which are unrelated to the operation of our business.

Valuation Accounting

> It is our view that the application of the proposed statement will give the wrong answer to the question at hand. We are aware of the talk of fair value, replacement value, price level adjustment, and other proposed methods of accounting valuation. We believe there may be merit in one or more of those approaches. However, we fail to see the logic of requiring that one type of long-term asset be carried at market while all other long-term assets are carried at historical cost. We believe this is not only inconsistent within the category of long-term assets, but may also be inconsistent with attempts to develop a sound approach to what the basis of accounting valuation should be.

We recognize the need for a pronouncement on this subject. Some companies have carried investments at cost in current assets. Others have carried such investments at market value. We agree that such short-term investments should be carried at the lower of cost or market.

We recognize also that some companies have classified investments as non-current assets which probably should have been classified as current assets and would therefore be subject to the lower of cost or market rule. On the other hand, there are companies which in fact do hold long-term investments for which the lower of cost or market value is inappropriate.

We believe true long-term investments should be carried at cost unless there is a permanent impairment in their value. We believe criteria should be established by the Board to define true long-term investments. The criteria could include a liquidity test, a required statement of investment policy by management in the notes to the financial statements, and such other criteria as may be required to prevent abuses. We believe this approach would result in better and more understandable accounting and reporting.

Yours truly,

John L. Skipper
Leaseway Transportation Corporation

QUESTIONS:

1. Assume that you have been assigned the task of analyzing the responses to the FASB Exposure Draft "Accounting for Certain Marketable Securities" for the members of the Board.
   (a) Comment on the issues raised in the Leaseway Transportation Corp. letter.
   (b) What would be your recommendation to the Financial Accounting Standards Board?

Exhibit 1. *Restatement of Equity Securities At Lower Of Cost Or Market*

	NET EARNINGS AS REPORTED	UNREALIZED GAIN (LOSS)	NET EARNINGS AS RESTATED	PERCENT OF CHANGE
1st Quarter, 1973	$ 3,475,098	$ (235,326)	$ 3,239,772	(6.8%)
2nd Quarter	6,158,837	(74,046)	6,084,791	(1.2)
3rd Quarter	4,001,744	139,172	4,140,916	3.5
4th Quarter	6,289,040	(2,047,201)	4,241,839	(32.6)
Total	$19,924,719	$ (2,217,401)	$17,707,318	(11.1%)
1st Quarter, 1974	$ 2,110,329	$ (148,220)	$ 1,962,109	(7.0%)
2nd Quarter	5,797,410	(1,596,141)	4,201,269	(27.5)
3rd Quarter	4,378,919	(3,743,763)	635,156	(85.5)
4th Quarter	5,802,405	325,528	6,127,933	5.6
Total	$18,089,063	$ (5,162,596)	$12,926,467	(28.5%)
1st Quarter, 1975	$ 2,222,358	$ 2,918,764	$ 5,141,122	131.3%
2nd Quarter	6,517,373	1,185,408	7,702,781	18.2
3rd Quarter	5,425,477	(1,052,962)	4,372,515	(19.4)
Total (to date)	$14,165,208	$ 3,051,210	$17,216,418	21.5

Exhibit 2. *Restatement of Equity Securities At Lower Of Cost Or Market*

	EARNINGS PER SHARE AS REPORTED	UNREALIZED GAIN (LOSS) PER SHARE	EARNINGS PER SHARE AS RESTATED	PERCENT OF CHANGE
1st Quarter, 1973	$ .47	$ (.03)	$ .44	(6.4%)
2nd Quarter	.84	(.01)	.83	(1.2)
3rd Quarter	.55	.02	.57	3.6
4th Quarter	.86	(.28)	.58	(32.6)
Total	$2.72	$ (.30)	$2.42	(11.0%)
1st Quarter, 1974	$ .29	$ (.02)	$ .27	(6.9%)
2nd Quarter	.80	(.22)	.58	(27.5)
3rd Quarter	.60	(.51)	.09	(85.0)
4th Quarter	.81	.04	.85	4.9
Total	$2.50	$ (.71)	$1.79	(28.4%)
1st Quarter, 1975	$ .31	$ .41	$ .72	132.3%
2nd Quarter	.91	.16	1.07	17.6
3rd Quarter	.76	(.15)	.61	(19.7)
Total (to date)	$1.98	$ .42	$2.40	21.2%

STANDARDS OF FINANCIAL ACCOUNTING AND REPORTING
Enterprises in Industries Not Having Specialized Accounting
Practices with Respect to Marketable Securities

7. For purposes of applying paragraphs 8–12 of this Statement, certain terms are defined as follows:

   (a) *Equity security* encompasses any instrument representing ownership shares (e.g., common, preferred, and other capital stock) or the right to acquire (e.g., warrants, rights, call options, convertible bonds) or dispose of (e.g., put options) ownership shares in an enterprise at fixed or determinable prices. The term does not encompass treasury stock or nonconvertible preferred stock that by its terms either must be redeemed by the issuing enterprise or is redeemable at the option of the investor.

   (b) *Marketable,* as applied to an equity security, means an equity security as to which sales prices or bid and ask prices are currently available on a national securities exchange or in the over-the-counter market either as reported by the National Association of Securities Dealers Automatic Quotations System or as reported by the National Quotations Bureau Inc. (provided quotations are included from at least three dealers). Restricted stock[1] does not meet this definition.

   (c) *Market price* refers to the price (see Paragraph 7(b)) of a single share or unit of a marketable equity security.

   (d) *Market value* refers to the aggregate of the market price times the number of shares or units of each marketable equity security owned by an entity. When an entity has taken positions involving short sales, sales of calls, and purchases of puts for marketable equity securities and the same securities are included in the portfolio, those contracts shall be taken into consideration in the determination of market value of the marketable equity securities.

   (e) *Cost* refers to the original cost of a marketable equity security (or, if appropriate, amortized cost for an option held or a convertible bond). When the status of an equity security changes from nonmarketable to marketable and thus comes within the definition in paragraph 7(b), its cost shall be its original cost unless a new cost basis had been assigned based on a previous recognition of an impairment of value that was other than temporary. In such a case, the new cost basis shall be its cost for the purpose of this Statement.

   (f) The *valuation allowance* for marketable equity securities represents the net unrealized loss (the amount by which aggregate cost exceeds market value) in the marketable equity securities portfolio.

   (g) The *carrying amount* of marketable equity securities is the amount at which the portfolio of marketable equity securities is reflected in the financial statements of an enterprise.

   (h) A *realized gain or loss* represents the difference between the net proceeds from the sale of a marketable equity security and its cost.

   (i) *Net unrealized gain or loss* represents the difference between the market value of marketable equity securities and their aggregate cost at any given date.

8. The carrying amount of marketable equity securities shall be the lower of their aggregate cost or market value, determined at the balance sheet date. An excess of aggregate cost over market value is accounted for as the valuation allowance.

[1] For example, stock requiring registration under the Securities Act of 1933.

Exhibit 3. (continued)

9. Realized gains and losses and changes in the valuation allowance shall be included in the determination of net income of the period in which they occur.

10. All marketable equity securities owned by an entity,[2] irrespective of balance sheet classification, shall be treated as a single portfolio for the purpose of comparing aggregate cost and market value to determine carrying amount. The portfolios of entities that are consolidated in financial statements and that do not follow specialized industry accounting practices with respect to marketable securities shall be treated as a single portfolio for the comparison of aggregate cost and market value. The portfolio of marketable equity securities owned by an entity (subsidiary or investee) that is accounted for by the equity method shall not be combined with the portfolio of marketable equity securities owned by any other entity included in the financial statements.[3] However, such an entity is, itself, subject to the requirements of this Statement.

11. The following information with respect to marketable equity securities owned shall be disclosed either in the body of the financial statements or in the accompanying notes:

    (a) As of the date of each balance sheet presented, aggregate cost and market value (each segregated between current and noncurrent assets when a classified balance sheet is presented) with identification as to which is the carrying amount.

    (b) As of the date of the latest balance sheet presented:

        (i) Gross unrealized gains representing the excess of market value over cost for all marketable equity securities in the portfolio having such an excess.

        (ii) Gross unrealized losses representing the excess of cost over market value for all marketable equity securities in the portfolio having such an excess.

    (c) For each period for which an income statement is presented:

        (i) Net realized gain or loss included in the determination of net income.

        (ii) The basis on which cost was determined in computing realized gain or loss (i.e., average cost or other method used).

        (iii) The amount included in the determination of net income representing the change in the valuation allowance.

12. An enterprise's financial statements shall not be adjusted for realized gains or losses or for changes in market prices with respect to marketable equity securities when such gains or losses or changes occur after the date of the financial statements but prior to their issuance. However, significant net realized and net unrealized gains and losses arising after the date of the financial statements, but prior to their issuance, applicable to marketable equity securities in the portfolio at the date of the most recent balance sheet shall be disclosed.

[2] For this purpose, marketable equity securities owned by an investee accounted for by the equity method shall not be considered owned by the entity (investor).

[3] This constitutes an exception to paragraph 19 of *APB Opinion No. 18* in those cases in which a subsidiary accounted for under the equity method has a net unrealized gain or loss on its portfolio of marketable equity securities that would serve to offset, in whole or in part, the net unrealized gain or loss on the portfolio of marketable equity securities of the parent or consolidated entity. If the subsidiary were consolidated and its portfolio combined with that of other entities in the consolidation in accordance with this paragraph, a different effect on consolidated net income would be produced, as compared with the equity method.

Harte-Hanks
Newspapers, Inc.
The Yakima Herald Acquisition

Newspapers have traditionally been run in a manner to keep people informed via good journalism and perhaps to persuade to a particular political or economic philosophy through editorials. Recently there has emerged a trend within the industry toward newspaper groups where management, while continuing to stress the production of high-quality newspapers, is more concerned with maximizing return on investment rather than persuading the newspaper audience to any political philosophy. Utilizing central office staffs of highly qualified and motivated managers, group newspapers, possibly best typified by Gannett or Knight, have led the way and have turned in impressive records of growth. Market recognition has followed, and the two companies currently sell at 25 to 33 times earnings. We believe Harte-Hanks is developing along comparable lines and has the potential for similar or superior earning performance. The new management team which joined the company in September of 1970 has an excellent reputation within the industry.

So begins a Wall Street report written in 1973 by White, Weld, who, it should be noted, also has underwritten Harte-Hanks' various stock offerings.

Less than three years ago, Harte-Hanks did not exist as a legal entity. There were twenty or so small corporations in Texas, each of which was controlled by the Harte and Hanks families and trusts established by them, and each of which managed a small to medium-sized newspaper. While the various companies had generally been profitable and were growing at reasonable rates, the owners

This case was prepared by Laird H. Simons, III, under the supervision of Associate Professor John K. Shank as the basis for class discussion rather than to illustrate either the effective or ineffective handling of an administrative situation.

118

recognized the need to restructure their corporate and financial affairs in order to meet the challenges and take advantage of the opportunities which the rapid changes of the early 1970s foreshadowed. Late in 1970, in events which for our purposes can be considered as simultaneous, these various corporations were brought within the rubric of one holding company, Harte-Hanks Newspapers, Inc., and a new management team was brought in.

Since that time the company has experienced rapid growth, both internally and by acquisitions. (See Exhibit 1 for 1972 financial statements.) By the time of the *Yakima Herald* acquisition, Harte-Hanks had gone public and had already expanded through acquisition into half a dozen states. (For a summary of their 1971–72 acquisitions, see Exhibit 2.)

To foster management's aim of becoming a major publicly held company to the information business, a number of rather explicit goals were established. Those directly applicable to their acquisitions policies are as follows:

1. Maintain at least 80 percent of corporate revenues from newspapers
2. Maximize the long-term value of the common shareholder equity in the company
3. Double 1971 earnings per share by July 1, 1976
4. Enjoy a price-earnings ratio that is in the upper 25 percent of the industry by July 1, 1976
5. Generate over 50 percent of total revenues from outside Texas by July 1, 1975

To this point, while non-Texas operations have accounted for 28 percent of the revenues, they have accounted for only 10 percent of the profits. This would imply that the potential earnings improvement through better productivity and market penetration are still to be realized from the recently acquired newspapers. Harte-Hanks is not buying earnings gains through acquisitions, rather it is buying the potential for earnings growth. Initially an acquisition may be slightly dilutive, but the new properties provide the basis upon which the company can effect the technological, administrative, and marketing changes that it hopes will result in significant incremental profit contribution in succeeding years.

In this regard, the company's own set of acquisition criteria are quite instructive. First, the company looks at the overall economic health of the acquiree's local market. It must be currently viable and growing in size, and must show promise of continuing improvements, both qualitatively and quantitatively. Second, the newspaper to be acquired must satisfy unique informational needs better than anyone else in the market. Every market must have its own identity regarding local news and advertising, especially, as is often the case, if the community is in the shadow of a major city. Identifying such needs requires considerable market research. Satisfying them requires intense product development. Third, the acquisition candidate must be, or have the potential for becoming in one year, the most effective means in the market for disseminating

Exhibit 1. Consolidated Balance Sheet, June 30, 1972

ASSETS		LIABILITIES AND SHAREHOLDERS' EQUITY	
Cash	$ 5,027,447	Accounts Payable	$ 2,039,158
Trade receivables	6,007,985	Accrued Expenses and	
Other current assets	2,071,960	Other Liabilities	2,001,604
Investments and		Other Current Liabilities	6,738,778
other assets	1,871,135	Long-Term Debt	11,845,276
Property, plant, and		Other Liabilities	186,558
equipment (net)	18,272,824	Common Stock	3,478,407
Intangible assets and		Additional Paid in Capital	6,955,330
deferred charges	26,143,267	Retained Earnings	26,149,507
	$59,394,618		$59,394,618

Consolidated Income Statement

	YEAR ENDING JUNE 30	
	1972	1971
Revenues		
Newspaper advertising	$39,962,983	$28,584,704
Newspaper circulation	10,655,149	7,523,219
Television revenues	3,243,794	2,903,906
Other	1,003,434	976,843
	54,865,360	39,988,672
Costs and Expenses		
Editorial, production, and distribution	30,818,868	25,109,940
Advertising, selling, general, and		
administrative	14,680,059	8,780,924
Goodwill amortization—Note L	367,490	15,694
Other	2,182,956	1,153,206
	48,049,373	35,059,864
Income before income taxes and		
extraordinary items	6,815,987	4,928,808
Income taxes	3,201,458	2,185,982
Income before extraordinary items	$ 3,614,529	$ 2,742,826
Extraordinary items, net of applicable tax—		
Note K	—	1,063,576
Net income	$ 3,614,529	$ 3,806,402
Average number of shares of common stock outstanding after giving retroactive effect to the shares issued in the reorganization and poolings of interests —Note A	3,268,989	3,119,247
Earnings per average share of common stock— Note 1:		
Income before extraordinary items	$1.11	$ .88
Extraordinary items	—	.34
Net income	$1.11	$1.22

Exhibit 2. Harte-Hanks Properties Acquired after January 1971

	MASTHEAD	DATE ACQUIRED	METHOD	PRICE (MILLIONS)	GOODWILL	PER SHARE EFFECT*
1. Journal Publishing Co. Hamilton, Ohio	*Journal News*	May 1971	cash	$ 7,634	$ 5,905	3.4¢
2. News Publishing Co. Framingham, Mass.	*South Middlesex Daily News*	June 1971	cash	4,309	3,250	1.9¢
3. Ypsilanti Press Ypsilanti, Mich.	*The Press*	September 1971	cash	1,952	1,820	1.1¢
4. Independent Publishing Co. Anderson, S.C.	*Anderson Independent and Daily Mail*	February 1972	notes	7,363	7,485	4.3¢
5. Woodbury Daily Times Woodbury, N.J.	*Daily Times*	February 1972	notes	3,039	2,638	1.5¢
6. Budde Publications San Francisco, Calif.	*San Francisco Progress*	June 1972	stock 64,908(shs)	2,220	—	N.A.
7. Republic Publishing Co. Yakima, Washington	*Yakima Herald-Republic*	September 1972	stock 482,200(shs)	12,778	—	N.A.
8. Van/De Publishing Co. California	*Pennysaver* (Orange and Santa Clara counties)	September 1972	cash and notes	6,950	6,337	3.7¢
9. San Diego Group McKinnon Newspaper Group Star News Publishing Co. Publishers Offset, Inc.	11 weekly and bi-weekly newspapers in San Diego County	October 1972	common stock 82,811 (shs) cash and notes	7,033	7,026	4.1¢
			TOTAL	$53,278	$34,461	20.0¢

*Assumes 4,320,758 shares outstanding and a 40-year amortization period.

Exhibit 3. Balance Sheet, June 30, 1972

ASSETS

Current Assets	
Cash	$ 541,839
Trade receivables, less allowance for doubtful accounts of $15,000	301,398
Current maturities of municipal bonds including accrued interest	34,635
Inventory of newsprint—at lower of cost (first-in, first-out method) or market	60,112
Prepaid expenses	9,876
Total Current Assets	947,860
Investments and Other Assets	
Long-term portion of municipal bonds	86,754
Other investments, less allowance for losses of $1,080,000	170,000
Other	44,713
	301,467
Property, Plant, and Equipment—on the basis of cost	
Land	198,337
Building and improvements	1,595,036
Equipment and furniture	1,420,114
	3,213,487
Less allowance for depreciation	1,806,433
	1,407,054
Construction and equipment installations in progress (estimated additional cost to complete of $240,000)	221,869
	1,628,923
	$2,878,250

LIABILITIES AND STOCKHOLDERS' EQUITY

Current Liabilities	
Accounts payable	$ 317,358
Accrued expenses and other liabilities	302,880
Prepaid subscriptions	68,954
Federal income taxes, including deferred	40,436
Total Current Liabilities	729,628
Stockholders' Equity	
Preferred Stock, 5% cumulative, par value $100 a share: authorized—20,000 shares; issued and outstanding—16,319 shares	1,631,900
Common Stock:	
Class A (voting): par value $10 a share; authorized—3,500 shares; issued and outstanding—2,600 shares	26,000
Class B (nonvoting): par value $10 a share; authorized—31,500 shares; issued and outstanding—23,400 shares	234,000
Additional paid-in capital	5,543
Retained earnings	251,179
	2,148,622
	$2,878,250

the information and filling the local advertising and news needs which have been identified. Finally, there must be qualified management available, either within the acquisition candidate or within Harte-Hanks, who can deal creatively with the unique characteristics, opportunities, and problems of that particular market.

Once these criteria are met, the potential acquiree must also meet several quantitative objectives before an offer will be made. The investment must be small enough in relation to the projected financial returns of the acquiree so that the discounted present value rate of return is attractive. There must be no appreciable initial dilution of earnings per share. The price paid must be less than 20 times the expected annualized earnings at the end of 12 months.

This was the framework within which the *Yakima Herald* acquisition was evaluated. It had come to the attention of Harte-Hanks that the family which owned the *Yakima Herald-Republic* was considering the sale of their entire interest. The family patriarch, W. H. Robertson, whose father had begun the paper in 1890, was 73. His sister, Helen Crum, who held most of the remaining shares, was somewhat older. Having seen what had happened to other newspapers which had passed into estates and been sold to the highest bidder, they chose to find an appropriate buyer for their life's work before retiring.

The *Yakima Herald-Republic* was attractive to a group newspaper for a variety of reasons. It serviced a natural geographic area that was partially bounded by mountains and inhabited by about 175,000 residents (46,000 households). It was the only newspaper in the area, having a circulation of about 38,000 in both its daily and Sunday editions. Papers from Spokane and Seattle with subscribers numbering several thousand, provided little competition. Yakima was a potential growth area. A fertile region of agriculture and livestock, it was not susceptible to the vagaries of the aerospace industry. It also had recently been traversed by a new superhighway. While the population had not yet grown, the growth of businesses and shopping centers was marked. These facts, when combined with the presence of the founder's grandnephew, James Tonkin, as a capable publisher who would stay on, the willingness of the patriarch to give advice as needed, and the existence of generally sound management at all levels, satisfied the qualitative criteria Harte-Hanks imposed.

The stumbling block appeared to be the price. Other groups such as Gannett and Lee had expressed interest in the paper. It would be necessary to go high, higher than the quantitative criteria would permit, to be successful in the acquisition. This would be the first exception to their rules. Harte-Hanks had stressed rapid turnaround situations where a large multiple could be paid on the assumption that substantial profit improvement was possible the first year. This was not the case with this well-run and technologically advanced paper. The asking price was in the $12 to $15 million range, or about 40 times 1971 earnings. For the 20 times earnings criterion to be met, after tax profits, now 8 percent of sales, would have to increase to 16 percent of sales (see Exhibit 3). It was clear and fully acknowledged by the company that such a large percentage improvement, while perhaps ultimately possible, would not take place in just a few years. Management's explanation for paying so much stressed the location of the newspaper. They had a strong desire to have their company geographically diversified and to this point had been unable to locate a newspaper in the dynamic growth area of the Pacific Northwest. They felt it important to have this beachhead, not to mention a satisfied publisher in an acquired company who could attend regional journalism conferences and describe the benefits of being in the Harte-Hanks group.

Having determined that the *Yakima Herald-Republic* was desirable, Harte-Hanks made an initial offer of its common stock in exchange for all the capital stock of Republic Corporation (the Herald). The Republic owners, however, had no interest in the stock of a budding newspaper group; they wanted cash. This presented a problem to Harte-Hanks, whose earnings were already suffering from the goodwill amortization of half a dozen previous acquisitions (see Exhibit 4). Republic Corporation's acquisition would result in the largest amount of goodwill yet purchased and Harte-Hanks was not willing to take on this additional earnings per share impact.

Sometime toward the end of fiscal 1972 a plan was developed which seemed to offer all parties concerned what they wanted. An agreement was worked out whereby Harte-Hanks would offer 485,200 shares of its common stock for all the outstanding capital stock of Republic. The 16,319 shares of Republic preferred stock were valued at $100 per share (par value, liquidation value, and price at which the company had redeemed shares in the past) and a price was fixed for the Harte-Hanks common (about $25) so that a ratio of approximately 4 shares for 1 was established. Class A (voting) and Class B (nonvoting) were held in exactly the same percentages by the Republic shareholders, so that those shares of Harte-Hanks common not given in exchange to the preferred stockholders were distributed according to the percentage ownership of the Republic common. Immediately upon the consummation of the deal, Harte-Hanks was to make a public offering of its own shares and to include with this offering (as a secondary offering) all of the shares given to the Republic holders and some of the shares held by Harte-Hanks insiders (see Exhibit 5 for the selling shareholders). Harte-Hanks would receive the proceeds from only 274,400 of the 800,000 shares sold and merely act as a vehicle whereby the selling shareholders could receive cash for their holdings.

This arrangement was felt by the company to be fully within the letter of Accounting Principles Board (APB) Opinion #16 (see interpretation from the *Journal of Accounting,* Exhibit 6). When they filed with the SEC, however, the Commission raised objections. It insisted that the Republic shareholders, recipients of Harte-Hanks stock, bear the risk of the market for a reasonable period before selling their Harte-Hanks shares. The period for this particular acquisition was determined by refusing to permit filing of the registration statement before the deal was signed. Thus, the length of time necessary to re-

Statement of Operations

	YEAR ENDED DECEMBER 31					YEAR ENDED June 30, 1972
	1967	1968	1969	1970	1971	
	(unaudited)	*(unaudited)*				
Revenues						
Newspaper advertising	$2,265,996	$2,419,732	$2,593,342	$2,693,969	$3,089,159	$3,339,339
Newspaper circulation	699,307	739,219	800,785	875,124	914,515	918,241
Other	62,921	48,978	64,946	81,983	54,123	62,378
	3,028,224	3,207,929	3,459,073	3,651,076	4,057,797	4,319,958
Costs and Expenses						
Editorial, production, and distribution	1,757,396	1,770,653	1,856,732	2,054,863	2,284,120	2,392,124
Advertising, selling, general, and administrative	700,146	793,239	871,034	890,496	987,008	1,067,819
Depreciation and amortization	221,933	224,913	195,601	194,537	165,434	156,386
	2,679,475	2,788,805	2,923,367	3,139,896	3,436,562	3,616,329
Income before federal income taxes and extraordinary items	348,749	419,124	535,706	511,180	621,235	703,629
Federal income taxes—Note F						
Current	151,455	191,724	281,967	267,993	291,954	361,636
Deferred (credit)	323	22,144	(11,839)	(27,154)	(13,779)	(41,084)
	151,778	213,868	270,128	240,839	278,175	320,552
Income before extraordinary items	196,971	205,256	265,578	270,341	343,060	383,077
Extraordinary items—Note B	305,122	—	—	(42,097)	(1,130,000)	—
Net income (loss)	$ 502,093	$ 205,256	$ 265,578	$ 228,244	$(786,940)	$ 383,077

Exhibit 4. *From Harte-Hanks 1972 Annual Report*

HARTE-HANKS HAS MORE AMORTIZABLE GOODWILL ON ITS BOOKS THAN ANY COMPANY IN THE INDUSTRY. ISN'T THIS A GREAT HANDICAP?

It is true that our earnings per share would have been $1.22 instead of $1.11 this past year—an increase of 30 percent instead of 26 percent— had our new affiliates joined us prior to October 1970 when the new goodwill accounting rule became effective. In our opinion, this rule should not apply to our industry. Newspapers that have secure franchises in good markets do not decline in value and, therefore, should not be subjected to an accounting rule which presupposes that a newspaper franchise is amortizable.

A case in point is our purchase of the Anderson newspapers, where we incurred $7.6 million in goodwill. Today we feel that the value of the Anderson newspapers is considerably higher than it was seven months ago when we made the purchase; yet we must write off nearly $200,000 annually in non-tax deductible goodwill for the next 40 years simply because we purchased Anderson after October 1970. I believe that most industry observers realize that the application of the goodwill to newspaper acquisitions generally produces unrealistic results, and that they will, therefore, focus their attention on earnings per share before goodwill amortization.

WHITE, WELD REPORT—FEBRUARY 12, 1973
Appendix II

The 1970 ruling of the Accounting Principles Board on purchase acquisitions presents an anomalous situation for newspapers. The ruling required the writing off of goodwill created in the "purchase" acquisition, as distinguished from a "pooling of interest" acquisition made solely for common stock, and required the writing off of such goodwill created 1971 or thereafter over a period of no more than 40 years. However, newspapers unlike most businesses, have few fixed assets relative to real worth or earning power and consequently generate considerable goodwill in a purchase acquisition. As a consequence, newspaper goodwill is essentially a capitalization of a paper "franchise" worth and reflects the difficulty of market entry. A large capital commitment is required to carry the losses incurred while a newspaper is starting up. In most cases, it is so large that it constitutes a virtual prohibition to entry. In effect most newspapers are a "legal monopoly." Thus writing off "goodwill" has less validity for the newspaper business than for other businesses. Some companies have avoided the write-off by making acquisitions with common stock on pooling of interest basis.

Exhibit 5. Selling Stockholders

The names of the Selling Stockholders, the number of shares to be sold by each of them and their respective holdings after such sales are as follows:

NAME	NUMBER OF SHARES PRESENTLY OWNED	NUMBER OF SHARES TO BE SOLD	NUMBER OF SHARES TO BE OWNED AFTER SALE
James B. Barker	100	100	—
Georgia Mayse Bassano	4,876	2,500	2,376
Walter Bassano	4,177	2,500	1,677
Anita L. Budde	18,109	9,000	9,109
Henry Budde	45,109	15,000	30,109
Conway C. Craig	70,514	1,600	68,914
Ethel M. Foster	200	100	100
Matthew Craig Gannaway	200	100	100
Houston H. Harte	673,328	4,500	668,828
Mabel Hurt	200	200	—
Robert M. Jackson	17,796	1,800	15,996
Bertie K. Mayse	12,682	1,000	11,682
Mary Jo Stone	4,876	2,000	2,876
Former Republic Stockholders			
Helen Crum	106,742	106,742	—
David R. Millen	1,540	1,540	—
Lorna R. Millen	9,122	9,122	—
Steven G. Millen	1,680	1,680	—
Ruth B. Robertson	20,353	20,353	—
W. H. Robertson	306,395	306,395	—
Iva Simmons	240	240	—
James E. Tonkin	22,499	22,499	—
Nancy Tonkin	5,022	5,022	—
Robert Wright	1,447	1,447	—
Pacific National Bank, Trustee for:			
Anne Llewelyn Millen	720	720	—
Kimberly Elaine Millen	720	720	—
Sally Tonkin	240	240	—
Susan Tonkin	240	240	—
Hiram Robertson Wright	240	240	—
Jennifer Jean Wright	80	80	—
William Carlton Wright	240	240	—
Pacific National Bank, Custodian for:			
Anne Llewelyn Millen	960	960	—
Kimberly Elaine Millen	960	960	—
Sally Tonkin	960	960	—
Stacy Tonkin	960	960	—
Susan Tonkin	960	960	—
Hiram Robertson Wright	960	960	—
Jennifer Jean Wright	960	960	—
William Carlton Wright	960	960	—

Exhibit 6. Accounting Interpretations

The Institute staff has been authorized to issue interpretations of accounting questions having general interest to the profession. The purpose of the interpretations is to provide guidance on a timely basis without the formal procedures required for an APB Opinion and to clarify points on which past practice may have varied and been considered generally accepted. These interpretations, which are reviewed with informed members of the profession, are not pronouncements of the Board. However, members should be aware that they may be called upon to justify departures from the interpretations. Unless otherwise stated, the interpretations are not intended to be retroactive.

FROM THE JOURNAL OF ACCOUNTANCY, SEPTEMBER 1971:
Pooling with "Bailout"

Question: Paragraph 48–a of APB Opinion #16 specifies that a combined corporation may not agree to directly or indirectly retire or acquire all or part of the common stock issued to effect a business combination, and paragraph 48–b specifies that a combined corporation may not enter into financial arrangements for the benefit of the former stockholders of a combining company if a business corporation is to be accounted for by the pooling of interests method. Would an arrangement whereby a third party buys all or part of the voting common stock issued to stockholders of a combining company immediately after consummation of a business combination cause the combination to not meet these conditions?

Interpretation: The fact that stockholders of a combining company may sell voting common stock received in a business combination to a third party would not indicate failure to meet the conditions of paragraphs 48–a and 48–b. "Continuity of ownership interests," a criterion for a pooling of interests under ARB #48, is not a condition to account for a business combination by the pooling of interests method under APB Opinion #16. The critical factor in meeting conditions of paragraphs 48–a and 48–b of the opinion is that the voting common stock issued to effect a business combination remains outside the combined corporation without arrangements on the part of any of the corporations involving the use of their financial resources to "bail out" former stockholders of a combining company or to induce others to do so.

Either the combined corporation or one of the combining companies may assist the former stockholders in locating an unrelated buyer for their shares (such as by introductions to underwriters) so long as compensation or other financial inducements from the corporation are not in some way involved in the arrangement. If unregistered stock is issued, the combined corporation may also agree to pay the costs of initial registration.

FROM THE JOURNAL OF ACCOUNTANCY, NOVEMBER 1972
Combination Contingent on "Bailout"

Question: An accounting interpretation of APB #16—Pooling with "Bailout"—issued in September 1971 indicates that former shareholders of a combining company may sell voting common stock received in a business combination accounted for as a pooling of interests. Would the accounting for a combination be affected by the fact that its consummation is contingent upon the purchase by a third party or parties of all or part of the voting common stock to be issued in the combination?

Interpretation: Yes. A business combination should be accounted for as a purchase if its consummation is contingent upon the purchase by a third party or parties of any *of the voting common stock to be issued. This would be the case, for example, if the parties to the combination have agreed that consummation of the combination will not occur until there is a commitment by a third party for a private purchase, a firm public offering, or some other form of a guaranteed market for all or part of the shares to be issued. Including such a contingency in the arrangements of the combination, either explicitly or by intent, would be considered a financial arrangement which is precluded in a pooling by paragraph 48–b of APB Opinion #16.*

It should be noted that this accounting interpretation does not modify the previous interpretation on Pooling with "Bailout," which states that shareholders may sell stock received in a pooling and that the corporation may assist them in locating an unrelated buyer for their shares. Although shareholders may sell stock received in a pooling, consummation of the business combination must first occur without regard to such a sale and cannot be contingent upon a firm commitment by the potential purchaser of the shares to be issued.

view the registration statement before permitting it to become effective serves to define "reasonable." While the company felt that this "interpretation" of APB #16 was in fact a change from the Opinion itself, which had no holding period requirement, it was compelled to renegotiate that portion of the deal which dealt with the timing for the secondary offering. Thus, although the agreement was signed on September 19, 1972, the secondary offering did not take place until October 25. During that period, the market price of Harte-Hanks common stock declined from $26.50 to $22.50, resulting in a significant reduction in the amount of cash received by Republic shareholders.

1. Recast the June 30, 1972, Harte-Hanks financial statements as they would have looked if the *Yakima Herald* acquisition had been made as of June 30, 1972, under:
   (a) "pooling of interest" accounting
   (b) "purchase" accounting
2. Does the acquisition qualify for "pooling of interest" treatment under generally accepted accounting principles?
3. Should the regulations regarding amortization of goodwill be suspended for newspaper companies?

Loews Corporation (B)

Loews Corporation, formed in Delaware in November 1969, operates principally as a holding company controlling more than 100 wholly owned subsidiaries.[1] Through its subsidiaries, Loews operates hotels, exhibits motion pictures through theatre ownership, develops residential real estate, and manufactures and sells tobacco products. In addition, it manages a large portfolio of securities, primarily common stock. This case focuses on the financial accounting aspects of two of Loews' major intercorporate investments: 100 percent ownership of the Lorillard Corporation in fiscal year 1969 and approximately 25 percent ownership of Wheeling-Pittsburgh Steel Corporation in fiscal year 1974.

LORILLARD ACQUISITION

The Lorillard Corporation, now operated as a division of Loews, manufactures and sells cigarettes including such brands as Kent, Newport, True, Old Gold, and Spring; it also markets other tobacco products. This division has contributed in excess of 50 percent of Loews' earnings (before interest expense, income taxes, and extraordinary items) in each of the last five years.

This case was prepared by Dennis P. Frolin and James F. Smith as a basis for class discussion rather than to illustrate either effective or ineffective handling of an administrative situation.

[1] Loews Corporation engaged in no business transactions until February 1971, when it acquired 100 percent ownership of Loews Theatres, Inc. The operation and management of Loews Corporation was essentially a continuation of that of the acquired company. Any reference to transactions or data dated prior to the merger are actually those of Loews Theatres, Inc.

Loews' primary purpose in acquiring Lorillard was to diversify into the consumer goods market. To quote Laurence A. Tisch, Chairman of the Board, in his address to shareholders on November 12, 1969:

Through the Lorillard merger, we now have a distribution apparatus channeling our products to nearly every supermarket and drugstore in the country, as well as a substantial sales capacity abroad. We are firmly launched into the consumer goods market.

At the date of acquisition, Lorillard had total assets in excess of $370 million, of which approximately 66 percent consisted of inventory and 80 percent was classified as current (Exhibit 1). Their net earnings for the 11 months ended November 30, 1968, approximated $25 million.

The merger between Loews and Lorillard was effective November 30, 1968. For each share of Lorillard stock, Loews issued $62 in principal value of $6\frac{7}{8}$ percent subordinated debentures due 1993, and one 12-year warrant to purchase one share of Loews common stock. The exercise price of the warrant was as

Exhibit 1. Lorillard Corporation and Subsidiary Companies Consolidated Balance Sheet, November 30, 1968

Assets	
Current Assets	
Cash and marketable securities	$ 15,255,760
Trade and other receivables (net)	38,007,229
Inventories	243,835,156
Total Current Assets	$297,098,145
Investment in associated companies	4,219,767
Property, plant, and equipment (net)	55,101,000
Other assets	14,858,094
Total	$371,277,006
Liabilities	
Current Liabilities	
Notes payable	$ 34,065,000
Accounts payable	9,563,708
Accrued liabilities	33,659,026
Total Current Liabilities	$ 77,287,734
Long-term debt	69,770,000
Reserves	6,719,891
Shareholders' equity	217,499,381
Total	$371,277,006

follows: $35 per share during the initial four years, $37.50 per share during the second four years, and $40 per share during the last four years.

Loews acquired all 6,478,657 common shares of Lorillard to achieve 100 percent control. It issued to Lorillard shareholders debentures with a principal value (face value) of $401,676,734 and 6,478,657 warrants in exchange for Lorillard's net assets (book value) of $217,499,381. Loews used the purchase (as contrasted to the pooling of interests) method of accounting to record the acquisition. The debentures were assigned a "fair value" of $361,509,061 and the warrants a "fair value" of $103,658,512. Exhibit 2 details price movements of both the debentures and the warrants issued by Loews. The excess of the purchase cost over the net assets acquired was recorded as an intangible asset.

In 1970, after completing an asset revaluation study, Loews reclassified the "cost in excess of net assets acquired" to reflect two major (and a few minor) adjustments: Trademarks were assigned a value of approximately $100 million and Patents approximately $13 million.

The $100 million cost assigned to Trademarks is not being amortized due to the unlimited legal life of this asset. The $13 million cost assigned to Patents is

Exhibit 2. *Loews Corporation and Lorillard Corporation, Security and Debt Prices*

LORILLARD CORPORATION

Date	Price
10–4–68	$58\frac{1}{8}$ (day prior to announcement)
10–18–68	$69\frac{3}{8}$ (record date for shareholders)
11–1–68	$68\frac{3}{4}$
11–15–68	$73\frac{7}{8}$
11–27–68	$78\frac{1}{4}$
11–29–68	80

LOEWS CORPORATION

	Debenture Offered to Lorillard Shareholders $6\frac{7}{8}$ s 1993		Warrant Offered to Lorillard Shareholders	
	Date	Price	Date	Price
First Trade	12–2–68	81	12–16–68	$31\frac{1}{2}$
One Week Later	12–9–68	$80\frac{3}{4}$	12–23–68	$32\frac{1}{8}$
Two Weeks Later	12–16–68	$78\frac{7}{8}$	12–30–68	$33\frac{7}{8}$
One Month Later	1–1–69	$81\frac{1}{4}$	1–15–69	$33\frac{1}{8}$
Two Months Later	2–1–69	$82\frac{1}{4}$	2–15–69	$36\frac{7}{8}$
Three Months Later	3–1–69	78	3–15–69	$23\frac{3}{4}$
Four Months Later	4–1–69	$76\frac{1}{2}$	4–15–69	$26\frac{1}{8}$
Five Months Later	5–1–69	$79\frac{3}{8}$	5–15–69	$24\frac{1}{2}$
Six Months Later	6–1–69	$77\frac{1}{4}$	6–15–69	17

Exhibit 3. Wheeling-Pittsburgh Steel Corporation, Five-Year Statistical Summary* (thousands of dollars)

	1974	1973	1972	1971	1970
Revenues	1,043,715	763,815	609,707	530,057	525,715
Earnings before taxes	105,418	12,781	15,048	(3,988)	(6,223)
Provision for income taxes	32,000	6,120	6,898	(3,114)	(4,039)
Net earnings	73,418	6,661	8,150	(874)	(2,184)
Earnings per share (common)	19.23	.98	1.39	(1.08)	(1.44)
Dividends declared (per common share)	.70	0	0	0	0
Stockholders' equity	313,857	245,933	242,303	237,010	240,954
Stock price:					
High	$23\frac{1}{4}$	$21\frac{5}{8}$	$24\frac{1}{4}$	$20\frac{1}{2}$	$21\frac{5}{8}$
Low	$13\frac{1}{4}$	$10\frac{1}{4}$	$15\frac{5}{8}$	$11\frac{1}{2}$	$9\frac{3}{4}$
Close	$17\frac{3}{4}$	13	$20\frac{3}{8}$	$17\frac{3}{4}$	$11\frac{1}{2}$
August 31	$19\frac{3}{4}$	$13\frac{1}{8}$			

*Calendar years.

being amortized straight line over the remaining legal lives. The approximately $135 million remaining "cost in excess of net assets" is not being amortized. This $135 million "cost in excess of net assets" has decreased, however, over the years to approximately $66 million at the end of fiscal year 1974 as a result of annual income tax benefits derived by Loews directly as a result of the Lorillard acquisition (and its liquidation as a legal entity). These tax benefits in a sense represent a reduction in the initial price paid by Loews and therefore represent a reduction in the excess of the purchase price over net assets acquired.

WHEELING-PITTSBURGH STEEL CORPORATION INVESTMENT

Wheeling-Pittsburgh Steel Corporation is an integrated steel producer engaged in the manufacture of iron, steel ingot, semi-finished, finished, and fabricated steel products. The industry is highly competitive, the giant of the industry being of course United States Steel Corporation. During 1974 Wheeling-Pittsburgh's steel production was approximately 3 percent of total industry production.

The President of Loews Corporation, Laurence Tisch, indicated in his address to the shareholders on November 19, 1974, that the

> . . . *investment in Wheeling-Pittsburgh was prompted by the favorable long-term outlook for the basic business of Wheeling-Pittsburgh and by the record of achievement of its management.*

In recent years under the leadership of Robert E. Lauterbach, Wheeling-Pittsburgh has undertaken a plan of major plant additions and modernization. In early 1974 they announced a seven-year, $250-million capital expenditure program to develop "ownership" sources of low-cost raw materials, to construct a new battery of coke ovens in its Steubenville plant, with its annual capacity of nearly 1 million tons, and to carry out an extensive rebuilding and modernization program of its blast furnaces. Steel shipments, revenues, and net earnings reached record levels in 1973; and during 1974 revenues and net earnings skyrocketed (Exhibit 3).

Loews acquired 293,000 shares of Wheeling-Pittsburgh, approximately 8 percent of the common shares outstanding, during fiscal year 1973 for $4,236,000 and carried the holding as an "Investment in Securities, at cost" on its balance sheet. During fiscal 1974 Loews acquired an additional 634,000 shares of Wheeling-Pittsburgh for $10,156,000, so that as of August 31, 1974, Loews owned approximately 25.3 percent of Wheeling-Pittsburgh outstanding common stock. Loews thus controls a substantial block of voting shares of Wheeling-Pittsburgh, though it has no direct hand in managing its operations. For example, there are no officers or directors of Loews who are also officers or directors of Wheeling-Pittsburgh. The market value of these shares at August 31, 1974, was approximately $18,308,000.

Loews recorded its investment at cost, $14,392,000. Its equity in the net assets of Wheeling-Pittsburgh exceeded the cost by $58,571,000. Having acquired in excess of 20 percent of the voting stock of Wheeling-Pittsburgh, Loews began using in 1974 the equity method to account for this investment. The excess of net assets over cost is being amortized to income over a 12-year period.

Exhibit 4 includes excerpts from the Loews Corporation 1974 Annual Report covering both the Lorillard and Wheeling-Pittsburgh investments.

ACCOUNTING METHODS

There are two methods of accounting for a business combination: the "purchase" method and the "pooling of interests" method. In terms of generally accepted accounting principles, the former can essentially be used for any combination, but the latter can be used only if certain criteria are met. The purchase method views a business combination as a purchase of one company by another, whereas the pooling method views the combination as a joining or "marriage" of the constituents. The purchase method requires that the acquired assets and liabilities be recorded at their fair value; that the excess of cost over net-asset value (occasionally referred to as goodwill), or net-asset value over cost (occasionally referred to as negative goodwill) be recorded and amortized; and that the results of operations of the acquired company be accounted for on the purchaser's financial statements only from the acquisition date.

Exhibit 4. *Loews Corporation and Subsidiaries Consolidated Balance Sheet*

Loews Corporation and Subsidiaries
Consolidated Balance Sheet

	August 31,	
	1974	1973
Assets		
Current Assets:		
Cash, including time deposits (1974, $10,640,000; 1973, $8,505,000)	**$ 23,537,000**	$ 21,314,000
Receivables—principally trade, less allowance for doubtful accounts and discounts (1974, $5,022,000; 1973, $2,919,000)	**77,944,000**	60,670,000
Inventories:		
Leaf tobacco	**223,084,000**	225,732,000
Manufactured stock	**27,707,000**	21,985,000
Materials, supplies, etc.	**9,751,000**	6,491,000
Real estate held for development and sale	**57,302,000**	47,112,000
Total current assets	**419,325,000**	383,304,000
Investments in Securities:		
Associated company	**24,259,000**	4,236,000
Other	**376,306,000**	432,472,000
Total investments in securities	**400,565,000**	436,708,000
Total current assets and investments in securities	**819,890,000**	820,012,000
Investments and Advances:		
Investments in and advances to unconsolidated companies	**4,165,000**	14,111,000
Mortgages and notes receivable (maturing through 2028 at interest rates ranging from 5% to 13%)	**47,528,000**	35,226,000
Land and other investments, at cost	**23,365,000**	19,652,000
Total investments and advances	**75,058,000**	68,989,000
Property, Plant and Equipment, at cost:		
Land	**41,834,000**	41,994,000
Buildings and building equipment	**154,880,000**	154,053,000
Machinery and equipment	**78,237,000**	71,604,000
Leaseholds and leasehold improvements	**11,322,000**	10,969,000
Total	**286,273,000**	278,620,000
Less accumulated depreciation and amortization	**92,881,000**	85,821,000
Property, plant and equipment—net	**193,392,000**	192,799,000
Other Assets:		
Cost in excess of net assets acquired	**65,519,000**	67,115,000
Trademarks	**100,033,000**	100,033,000
Patents and licenses, less accumulated amortization (1974, $5,027,000; 1973, $4,179,000)	**8,304,000**	9,152,000
Prepaid expenses, deferred charges, etc.	**11,682,000**	10,002,000
Total other assets	**185,538,000**	186,302,000
Total	**$1,273,878,000**	$1,268,102,000

Exhibit 4. *(continued)*

	August 31, 1974	1973
Liabilities and Shareholders' Equity		
Current Liabilities:		
Short-term debt	$ 80,353,000	$ 119,515,000
Accounts payable and accrued liabilities	57,086,000	51,929,000
Accrued taxes:		
Federal and foreign income taxes	10,170,000	5,243,000
Excise and other taxes	22,316,000	14,754,000
Current maturities of long-term debt, less unamortized discount	8,914,000	11,138,000
Total current liabilities	178,839,000	202,579,000
Long-Term Debt, less current maturities and unamortized discount:		
Senior debt	270,700,000	268,235,000
Subordinated debt	371,932,000	372,533,000
Long-term debt—net	642,632,000	640,768,000
Deferred Credits and Other Liabilities:		
Deferred income taxes	17,011,000	17,316,000
Accrued employee benefits	8,144,000	6,738,000
Deferred credits and non-current liabilities	3,617,000	3,372,000
Total deferred credits and other liabilities	28,772,000	27,426,000
Shareholders' Equity:		
Common stock, authorized 30,000,000 shares of $1 par value; issued shares stated at par value	14,791,000	14,791,000
Additional paid-in capital	116,522,000	116,522,000
Earnings retained in the business	345,003,000	315,480,000
Total	476,316,000	446,793,000
Less common stock held in treasury, at cost (1974, 1,873,000 shares; 1973, 1,733,000 shares)	52,681,000	49,464,000
Total shareholders' equity	423,635,000	397,329,000
Total	**$1,273,878,000**	$1,268,102,000

Exhibit 4. *(continued)*

Loews Corporation and Subsidiaries
Statement of Consolidated Earnings and
Earnings Retained in the Business

	Year Ended August 31,	
	1974	1973
Sales and Operating Revenues:		
-Sales of manufactured products and revenues of theatre and hotel operations	**$739,797,000**	$714,021,000
Other revenues, principally rent and dividends	**53,544,000**	52,415,000
Total	**793,341,000**	766,436,000
Costs and Expenses:		
Cost of sales and operating costs	**550,237,000**	505,655,000
Selling, advertising and administrative	**124,144,000**	120,266,000
Depreciation and amortization	**10,344,000**	10,124,000
Interest and amortization of debenture discount and expense	**58,579,000**	51,796,000
Income taxes	**14,158,000**	27,363,000
Total	**757,462,000**	715,204,000
Earnings Before Security Gains and Equity in Earnings of Associated Company	**35,879,000**	51,232,000
Security Gains:		
Realized gains	**70,000**	17,213,000
Less applicable income taxes	**44,000**	5,328,000
Security gains—net	**26,000**	11,885,000
Equity in Earnings of Associated Company	**9,379,000**	
Net Earnings	**45,284,000**	63,117,000
Earnings Retained in the Business, Beginning of Year	**315,480,000**	269,541,000
Cash Dividends (per share—$1.22 in 1974 and $1.21 in 1973)	**(15,761,000)**	(17,178,000)
Earnings Retained in the Business, End of Year	**$345,003,000**	$315,480,000
Earnings Per Share—Primary:		
Earnings before security gains and equity in earnings of associated company	**$2.78**	$3.61
Security gains—net		.84
Equity in earnings of associated company	**.72**	
Net Earnings	**$3.50**	$4.45
Earnings Per Share—Assuming Full Dilution:		
Earnings before security gains and equity in earnings of associated company	**$2.73**	$3.01
Security gains—net		.60
Equity in earnings of associated company	**.60**	
Net Earnings	**$3.33**	$3.61

Exhibit 4. (continued)

Loews Corporation and Subsidiaries
Statement of Changes in
Consolidated Financial Position

	Year Ended August 31,	
	1974	1973
Funds Provided:		
Earnings before security gains and equity in earnings of associated company	**$ 35,879,000**	$ 51,232,000
Items not currently requiring funds:		
Depreciation and amortization	**10,344,000**	10,124,000
Deferred income taxes	**54,000**	427,000
Other—net	**1,709,000**	1,094,000
Funds provided from operations exclusive of security gains and equity in earnings of associated company	**47,986,000**	62,877,000
Security gains—net	**26,000**	11,885,000
Funds provided from operations exclusive of equity in earnings of associated company	**48,012,000**	74,762,000
Dispositions of property, plant and equipment	**2,810,000**	4,773,000
Dispositions of investments and advances	**19,606,000**	16,358,000
Issuance of long-term debt	**12,871,000**	87,532,000
Reduction of cost in excess of net assets acquired attributable to income tax benefits	**2,142,000**	4,616,000
Issuance of common stock		3,517,000
Total	**85,441,000**	191,558,000
Funds Applied:		
Additions to property, plant and equipment	**12,783,000**	10,853,000
Additions to investments and advances	**25,302,000**	7,632,000
Additions to common stock held in treasury	**3,217,000**	49,394,000
Reduction of long-term debt	**12,614,000**	61,515,000
Exercise of warrants through application of 6⅞% debentures		2,834,000
Dividends paid	**15,761,000**	17,178,000
Other—net	**2,013,000**	4,121,000
Total	**71,690,000**	153,527,000
Excess of Funds Provided over Funds Applied Represented by:		
Increase (decrease) in investments in securities	**(46,010,000)** *	13,178,000
Increase in working capital	**59,761,000**	24,853,000
Total	**$ 13,751,000**	$ 38,031,000
Excess of Funds Provided Over Funds Applied by Component:		
Increase (decrease) in investments in securities	**$ (46,010,000)** *	$ 13,178,000
Increase (decrease) in working capital:		
Cash, including time deposits	**2,223,000**	4,406,000
Receivables	**17,274,000**	14,210,000
Inventories	**6,334,000**	296,000
Real estate held for development and sale	**10,190,000**	(7,936,000)
Short-term debt	**39,162,000**	(17,692,000)
Accounts payable and accrued liabilities	**(5,157,000)**	14,406,000
Accrued taxes	**(12,489,000)**	10,924,000
Current maturities of long-term debt, less unamortized discount	**2,224,000**	6,239,000
Increase in working capital	**59,761,000**	24,853,000
Total	**$ 13,751,000**	$ 38,031,000

*Exclusive of equity adjustments for associated company which did not result in funds provided or applied.

Exhibit 4. *(continued)*

Loews Corporation and Subsidiaries
Notes to Consolidated Financial Statements

Investments in securities:

Associated company—The Company carries its investment in Wheeling-Pittsburgh Steel Corporation (Wheeling) at cost adjusted for the Company's share of earnings and capital changes of Wheeling from dates of acquisition plus amortization of the excess of equity in net assets acquired over cost thereof. The Company reports as earnings its proportionate share of Wheeling's earnings plus amortization of the excess of equity in net assets acquired over cost thereof and provides for appropriate deferred Federal income taxes on the undistributed earnings so reported.

Other—Investments in other securities are carried at cost. The cost of securities sold is determined on the identified certificate or first-in, first-out method. The Company has invested in securities in order to secure a return on funds it is holding for development and expansion opportunities. The Company regularly and actively seeks development and expansion opportunities which may require application of all or a portion of such funds. In view of the uncertainty as to when such opportunities may arise, the investment in securities has been classified as a noncurrent asset. (Refer to Note 11 for additional information.)

Cost in excess of net assets acquired—Lorillard Corporation (Lorillard) was acquired in November 1968, liquidated and merged into Loew's Theatres, Inc. (a wholly-owned subsidiary of the Company) in July 1969 and has continued operations as a division of such subsidiary. The cost in excess of net assets acquired related to this acquisition, amounting to $128,944,000 as adjusted to date and before deduction of the estimated tax benefits referred to below, has been attributed to other intangibles which, in the opinion

of Management, have continuing value. It is the Company's policy not to amortize such excess as long as there is no diminution in value of the investment.

As a result of the aforementioned liquidation, the Company realized certain income tax benefits which have been considered to be partial recoveries of the cost in excess of net assets acquired.

The tax benefits realized to date are as follows:

Year ended August 31,	
1970	$32,477,000
1971	18,081,000
1972	6,655,000
1973	4,616,000
1974	2,142,000
Total	$63,971,000

In November 1973, the Company received an examination report from the Internal Revenue Service (IRS) advising the Company that it will seek to deny substantially all of such tax benefits for years through 1970. The IRS presumably will also seek to deny such benefits for later years. The Company does not accept the position of the IRS and filed a protest to such denial in February 1974. Should the IRS be successful in its disallowance of any portion of the above-mentioned tax benefits, such portion will accordingly be restored to cost in excess of net assets acquired.

Excise taxes—Excise taxes of $196,966,000 and $197,054,000 paid on sales of manufactured products in 1974 and 1973, respectively, are included in "sales of manufactured products and revenues of theatre and hotel operations" and "cost of sales and operating costs" in the accompanying statement of consolidated earnings and earnings retained in the business.

The pooling method requires that the acquired assets and liabilities be recorded at their "old" book values; hence there is no recorded excess of cost over net-asset value (or net-asset value over cost). The results of operations of the acquired company are recorded on the purchaser's financial statements for the entire year and for all past years. Simply stated, the total value of the entity resulting from a "pooling" is equal to the algebraic summation of the book values of the predecessor companies.

Accounting Principles Board Opinion #16 issued in August 1970 defines the criteria and rules for accounting for business combinations. Opinion #17 issued at the same time prescribes the accounting for intangible assets, including those acquired in a business combination. Simply stated, Opinion #17 requires all intangible assets to be amortized straight line over the useful life, not to exceed

Exhibit 4. *(continued)*

Loews Corporation and Subsidiaries
Notes to Consolidated Financial Statements

Investments in securities:

Associated company—The Company carries its investment in Wheeling-Pittsburgh Steel Corporation (Wheeling) at cost adjusted for the Company's share of earnings and capital changes of Wheeling from dates of acquisition plus amortization of the excess of equity in net assets acquired over cost thereof. The Company reports as earnings its proportionate share of Wheeling's earnings plus amortization of the excess of equity in net assets acquired over cost thereof and provides for appropriate deferred Federal income taxes on the undistributed earnings so reported.

Other—Investments in other securities are carried at cost. The cost of securities sold is determined on the identified certificate or first-in, first-out method. The Company has invested in securities in order to secure a return on funds it is holding for development and expansion opportunities. The Company regularly and actively seeks development and expansion opportunities which may require application of all or a portion of such funds. In view of the uncertainty as to when such opportunities may arise, the investment in securities has been classified as a noncurrent asset. (Refer to Note 11 for additional information.)

Cost in excess of net assets acquired—Lorillard Corporation (Lorillard) was acquired in November 1968, liquidated and merged into Loew's Theatres, Inc. (a wholly-owned subsidiary of the Company) in July 1969 and has continued operations as a division of such subsidiary. The cost in excess of net assets acquired related to this acquisition, amounting to $128,944,000 as adjusted to date and before deduction of the estimated tax benefits referred to below, has been attributed to other intangibles which, in the opinion

of Management, have continuing value. It is the Company's policy not to amortize such excess as long as there is no diminution in value of the investment.

As a result of the aforementioned liquidation, the Company realized certain income tax benefits which have been considered to be partial recoveries of the cost in excess of net assets acquired.

The tax benefits realized to date are as follows:

Year ended August 31,	
1970	$32,477,000
1971	18,081,000
1972	6,655,000
1973	4,616,000
1974	2,142,000
Total	$63,971,000

In November 1973, the Company received an examination report from the Internal Revenue Service (IRS) advising the Company that it will seek to deny substantially all of such tax benefits for years through 1970. The IRS presumably will also seek to deny such benefits for later years. The Company does not accept the position of the IRS and filed a protest to such denial in February 1974. Should the IRS be successful in its disallowance of any portion of the above-mentioned tax benefits, such portion will accordingly be restored to cost in excess of net assets acquired.

Excise taxes—Excise taxes of $196,966,000 and $197,054,000 paid on sales of manufactured products in 1974 and 1973, respectively, are included in "sales of manufactured products and revenues of theatre and hotel operations" and "cost of sales and operating costs" in the accompanying statement of consolidated earnings and earnings retained in the business.

40 years. Prior to Opinion #17 intangibles with unlimited life did not have to be amortized.

There are two methods used to report the results of nonconsolidated inter-corporate investments: the "cost" method and the "equity" method. The cost method views the investor and investee as separate accounting entities; the investor's investment asset reflects the initial acquisition price and remains unchanged unless the investor acquires a greater interest or disposes of a portion of its previous interest. Net income of the investee is not recorded as income by the investor; instead the investor records income only when it receives dividends from the investee. This method is the same method traditionally used for marketable securities.

The equity method views the investor and investee as a single operating entity, that is, the investor "controls" the operations of the investee. Under this method the investor records its initial acquisition at cost but the investment account subsequently reflects the investee's undistributed profit and loss activity from the acquisition date. Specifically, the investor's portion of the investee's income increases the investment account, investee losses decrease the account, and investee dividends paid to the investor are treated as a partial liquidation of the investment and therefore also decrease this account.

APB Opinion #18, effective for all fiscal periods beginning after December 31, 1971, requires that the equity method be used for investments in common stock of all unconsolidated investments large enough to create a significant influence over the operating and financial policies of the investee. It concluded that an investment of 20 percent or more of the voting stock of the investee was sufficient to evidence "significant influence." Conversely, an investment of less than 20 percent of the voting stock of the investee leads to the presumption that the investor does not have the ability to exercise "significant influence" unless such ability can be demonstrated. Prior to the issuance of APB #18, unconsolidated investments of greater than 50 percent used the equity method, less than 50 percent used the cost method.

Opinion #18 also requires the amortization on the investor's financial statement of any "cost in excess of net assets acquired" or "net assets in excess of cost" when the equity method is followed. The result of this requirement is that the equity method produces essentially the same income on the investor's income statement as would full consolidation of the investee. For this reason, use of the equity method is occasionally referred to as a "one-line consolidation."

QUESTIONS

1. Bookkeep the Lorillard acquisition: What went up or down when Loews made this purchase? In your opinion, was the determination of the "fair value" of purchase price fair? If not, how would your own determination of a "fairer value" affect the recording of the acquisition and future income statements?

2. Compare Loews' accounting for the Wheeling-Pittsburgh acquisition with its accounting for the Lorillard acquisition. How do the accounting treatments differ? In what ways are they identical?

3. Calculate Loews' 1974 return on the Wheeling-Pittsburgh investment. How important are the future operating results of Wheeling-Pittsburgh in the outcome of future ROI calculations?

4. How much profit would Wheeling-Pittsburgh have contributed to Loews' 1974 net income if the Wheeling-Pittsburgh investment had been treated as a marketable security accounted for using the "cost" method? What if the "market value" method was used?

5. What suggestions do you have for improving the accounting rules for both business combinations and significant intercorporate investments?

G. S. Holdings, Inc.

GS Holdings, Inc. began as a closely held investment company for Gerardo Schwarz, a wealthy independent oil operator. As new oil became more and more costly to locate and drill and the spectre of a comprehensive Presidential energy bill loomed on the horizon, Mr. Schwarz decided to reinvest the funds generated from his producing properties in other industries, and to raise additional capital through the sale of common shares in GS Holdings to some friends. Over the past few years, GS Holdings had grown rapidly, acquiring numerous and diverse companies at the "bargain basement" prices of the 1976–77 stock market. While GS Holdings had not yet gone public, there was considerable discussion at almost every board meeting of the appeal of a ready market for the securities of the company and of the profits to be made by Mr. Schwarz and the other directors from a public issue of the common stock. To that end, recent acquisitions had been evaluated carefully as to the effect that the acquired earning power would have on earnings per share on GS Holdings.

In late 1977, a former associate of Mr. Schwarz's approached him with an offer to buy 80% of the common stock of DN Watkins, Inc., an offshore drilling equipment manufacturer based in Corpus Christi, Texas, for $56 million in cash. The investment was found to be most attractive to GS Holdings and, accordingly, the acquisition was executed effective January 1, 1978.

During 1978, GS Holdings purchased equipment from DN Watkins for $20 million. The equipment had cost DN Watkins $12 million to manufacture and was acquired by GS Holdings solely for purposes of resale. By December 31, 1978, GS Holdings had sold half of the equipment purchased from DN Watkins, the other half still being in GS Holdings' inventory. As of December 31, 1978, GS Holdings still owed DN Watkins $15 million.

This case was prepared by Marsha M. Wilson of the University of Texas at Austin as a basis for class discussion rather than to illustrate effective or ineffective handling of an administrative situation.

143

1. Under the requirements of Opinion No. 18 of the Accounting Principles Board, it would appear that GS Holdings, Inc. should report its investment in DN Watkins, Inc. as a consolidated subsidiary. Prepare consolidated financial statements for GS Holdings, Inc. and its subsidiary, DN Watkins, Inc. (See Note.)
2. GS Holdings, Inc. would like to have a set of financial statements representing its investment in DN Watkins, Inc. as an unconsolidated subsidiary. Recast GS Holdings, Inc. financial statements so as to reflect the reporting of its investment in DN Watkins, Inc., on the equity basis. (See note.)
3. Distinguish between consolidated financial statements and the financial statements prepared using the equity method.

Note: Eighty-five percent (85%) of intercorporate dividends are excluded from taxable income. If you assume a corporate income tax rate of 48%, then the effective tax rate on intercompany dividends is (100% – 85%) X 48% = 7.2%.

Balance Sheets as of December 31, 1978 (000 omitted)

ASSETS	GS Holdings	DN Watkins
Cash	$11,000	$5,000
Accounts Receivable	65,000	95,000
Inventories	152,000	64,000
Fixed Assets, Net	200,000	40,000
Investment in DN Watkins, Inc.[1]	56,000	—
Total Assets	$484,000	$204,000
LIABILITIES AND		
OWNERS' EQUITY		
Accounts Payable	$71,000	$23,000
Income Taxes Payable	26,000	13,000
Other Current Liabilities	14,000	9,000
Long-term Debt	63,000	51,000
Capital Stock	100,000	30,000
Retained Earnings	210,000	78,000
Total Liabilities and Owners' Equity	$484,000	$204,000

[1] At cost, which equalled the fair value of the net assets of the subsidiary at the time of acquisition.

G. S. Holdings, Inc.

Income Statements for the year ended December 31, 1978 (000 omitted)

	GS Holdings	DN Watkins
Sales	$415,000	$264,000
Cost of Goods Sold	190,000	112,000
Gross Margin	$225,000	$152,000
Other Income (included dividend income)	55,000	18,000
	$280,000	$170,000
Other Expenses	75,000	63,000
Income Before Income Taxes	$205,000	$107,000
Income Tax Expense	93,000	49,000
Net Income	$112,000	$58,000
Dividends Declared and Paid	$52,000	$20,000

Xenia
Industries

As was his custom, Mr. Robert Bowen often discussed the financial statements he received on his stockholdings with an accounting friend, Mr. Andrew Franklin. Mr. Bowen had recently been appointed a director of Xenia Industries after purchasing the holdings of one of the original stockholders, and he had been making a detailed examination of the financial statements in preparation for taking an active part in the affairs of the company. Xenia's balance sheet contained among the assets an account called "Investments in Subsidiaries." Mr. Franklin suggested that Mr. Bowen seek out additional information about the nature of the items included in this account.

Further investigation revealed that Xenia had two subsidiary companies in which it owned 100 percent of the outstanding capital stock and one other company in which it had a 90 percent ownership interest. The records revealed the following investment information:

	BALANCE AT 12/31/74
1. The Oates Manufacturing Company (owned 100%), acquired January 1, 1969, at a cost of $175,000	$240,000
2. Jackson Valve Company (owned 100%), acquired January 1, 1969, at a cost of $270,000	270,000
3. Santos Mining Company (owned 90%), a Nigerian company acquired June 30, 1974, at a cost of $70,000	70,000
Total balance of "Investment in Subsidiaries" as shown on December 31, 1974, balance sheet	$580,000

This case was prepared by Dennis P. Frolin, Instructor, and Associate Professor John K. Shank as the basis for class discussion rather than to illustrate either effective or ineffective handling of an administrative situation.

Discussions with the company accountant revealed that Xenia has been recording in its investment account the undistributed earnings of the Oates Manufacturing Company. Xenia did not consolidate Oates because it was a much different business from Xenia's. The other investments were maintained at the original cost, recording revenue on Xenia's books only to the extent dividends were received. Jackson Valve was carried at cost because the management of Xenia was actively trying to divest a major part of Jackson's operations. No buyer had yet been found but negotiations were in process with several interested parties. Santos Mining was carried at cost because of management's general reluctance to count undistributed profits of a foreign subsidiary. There was, however, no particular reason to question the political or economic stability of Nigeria. Earnings of Santos were reinvested in the business as a matter of policy. It was unlikely that any of Santos' earnings would ever be repatriated.

Mr. Franklin later explained to Mr. Bowen that the above-described accounting treatments for the three subsidiaries were all within the framework of generally acceptable accounting principles, although he was uncertain as to the conditions under which each should be applied. He explained that Xenia was using the "equity" method to account for its investment in Oates, while using the "cost" method to account for its investment in both Jackson and Santos. Under the equity method, Xenia would record its share of Oates' net income (in this case 100 percent) by recording an increase in the investment account and an increase in its own (Xenia's) profits. Of course, if Oates incurred losses instead of profits, Xenia would reduce both its investment account and its own profits. Whenever Oates paid a dividend, Xenia would simply increase cash and decrease the investment account by the amount received. Thus, the company's statement that it was recording in its investment account the "undistributed earnings of the Oates Manufacturing Company" appeared accurate to Mr. Franklin. He also agreed that the "cost" method of accounting for the Jackson and Santos investments would in fact record only the *dividends* received by Xenia from these subsidiaries. Upon receipt, the Xenia cash account and its profit account would increase. Thus, the investment shown on the balance sheet would be unaffected by the profits or losses of the subsidiaries and would remain at its original cost until the investments were disposed.

Mr. Bowen had been concerned about the working capital position of Xenia Industries. He knew that the company would have to seek additional short-term borrowing from the banks and he was concerned about the effects of preparing consolidated statements upon the various parts of the Xenia financial statements, as well as the effects upon a Statement of Sources and Application of Funds. Among other things it was his impression that bankers put a great deal of emphasis upon such factors as working capital, debt-equity ratios, earnings, return on investment, and other more or less standard ratios.

Further questioning revealed that one of the important factors leading to the purchase of the Jackson Valve Company was several important patents that Jackson had developed. Jackson had charged the patent development costs to expense as they were incurred, but Xenia's management was certain these patents would contribute materially to future growth and sales for at least ten years beyond the acquisition date. The excess of purchase price over book value on this acquisition was attributable to the patents.

QUESTIONS

1. Which subsidiaries, if any, should be consolidated?
2. Prepare consolidated statements for 1974 under your assumptions from question 1. If all subsidiaries had been previously consolidated, the consolidated retained earnings on December 31, 1973, would have been $373,000.
3. Prepare a memo for Mr. Bowen analyzing the differences between the consolidated statement ratios and those of the individual firms.

Exhibit 1. *Comparative Balance Sheets*

| | DECEMBER 31 | | | |
	1973		1974	
Assets				
Current Assets:				
Cash	$129,000		$42,000	
Marketable securities	55,000		25,000	
Accounts receivable (net)	110,000		160,000	
Inventory	152,000		222,000	
		$446,000		$449,000
Long-Term Assets				
Plant and equipment	$370,000		$460,000	
Less: Accumulated depreciation	108,000	262,000	90,000	370,000
Goodwill		90,000		90,000
Patents		50,000		50,000
Other intangibles		20,000		40,000
Investment in subsidiary companies		500,000		580,000
Other assets		14,000		66,000
Total Assets		$1,382,000		$1,645,000
Liabilities and Stockholders' Equity				
Current Liabilities				
Accounts payable	$210,000		$115,000	
Accrued expenses	60,000		80,000	
Accrued taxes	62,000	$332,000	97,000	$292,000
Mortgages payable		125,000		100,000
Reserve for deferred taxes		30,000		50,000
Capital stock ($100 par)	$500,000		$540,000	
Additional paid-in capital	100,000		180,000	
Retained earnings	295,000	895,000	483,000	1,203,000
Total Liabilities and Stockholders' Equity		$1,382,000		$1,645,000

Exhibit 2. *Income Statement for Year Ended December 31, 1974*

Sales		$3,500,000
Less: Cost of sales		2,600,000
Gross Margin		$900,000
Less: Selling expenses	$400,000	
Administrative expenses	135,000	535,000
Income from operations		$365,000
Other Income and Expenses		
Deduct: Other expenses	$58,000	
Add: Equity in earnings of unconsolidated		
Oates Manufacturing subsidiary	10,000	
Dividends from unconsolidated Jackson		
Valve subsidiary	18,000	30,000
Profit before taxes		$335,000
Income taxes		102,000
Profit after taxes before extraordinary charges		$233,000
Extraordinary items (net of taxes)*		(30,000)
Net Income		$203,000

ANALYSIS OF CHANGES IN CAPITAL

Additional paid-in capital	
Balance, December 31, 1973	$100,000
Add: Premium on sale of capital stock	80,000
Balance, December 31, 1974	$180,000
Retained earnings	
Balance, December 31, 1973	$295,000
Add: Net Income	203,000
	$498,000
Deduct: Cash dividend	(15,000)
Balance, December 31, 1974	$483,000

*Because of a modernization program undertaken by the company, some excess facilities were disposed of by sale. Book value at time of sale was $110,000; originally the facilities cost $200,000. Sales price was $50,000.

Exhibit 3. Condensed Subsidiary Balance Sheets, December 31, 1974 (in thousands)

	OATES MANUFACTURING COMPANY	JACKSON VALVE COMPANY	SANTOS MINING COMPANY	TOTALS
Current Assets	$300	$130	$45	$475
Property assets (net)	50	150	35	235
Other assets	10	140	60	210
Total	$360	$420	$140	$920
Current Liabilities	$20	$70	$5	$95
Long-term debt	100	100	80	280
Owners' Equity				
Capital stock	175	200	50	425
Additional paid-in capital	—	50	—	50
Retained earnings	65	0	5	70
Total	$360	$420	$140	$920
Dividends received by Xenia Industries since acquisition through December 31, 1974	$25	$100	$ —	$125

Total owners' equity of each company at date of acquisition of stock was as follows:

	OATES MANUFACTURING COMPANY	JACKSON VALVE COMPANY	SANTOS MINING COMPANY	
Capital stock	$175	$200	$50	
Additional paid in capital	—	50	—	
Retained earnings (deficit)	—	(100)	15	
Total	$175	$150	$65	
1974 Earnings	$10	$(20)	$(10)*	

*Since acquisition, June 30, 1974.

Exhibit 4. Condensed Subsidiary Income Statements for the Year Ended December 31, 1974 (in thousands)

	OATES MANUFACTURING COMPANY*	JACKSON VALVE COMPANY	SANTOS MINING COMPANY
Sales revenue	$400	$650	$230
Cost of goods sold†	250	480	140
Administrative expenses	130	190	50
Income taxes	10	0	0
Net income (loss)	$10	$ (20)	$40
Dividends paid in 1974	0	$18	0

*Includes products purchased from Xenia and sold by Oates in 1974 (in thousands):

Production cost to Xenia	$50
Selling price from Xenia to Oates	$70
Selling price from Oates to customers	$100

Intercompany sales are offered on normal credit terms. On December 31, 1974, the balance due Xenia from Oates Manufacturing was $15,000.

†Includes depreciation of $8, $15, and $10, for Oates, Jackson, and Santos, respectively.

Greater Lafayette T.V. Cable Corporation

Communications Properties, Inc. (CPI), an Austin, Texas based company is engaged in the business of owning and operating cable television (CATV) systems. These systems distribute television signals, subscription television programming ("Pay Cable") and, in some cases, FM radio signals to subscribers served by CPI's 51 CATV systems in 109 communities. By 1976, there were 263,690 subscribers to CPI's systems. CPI estimates that based upon a measure of the number of subscribers, the company was the eighth largest in CATV operations in the United States.

In its early years, CPI achieved a growth in its subscribers through the acquisition of existing CATV systems. Many of the acquisitions were effected through an exchange of CPI common shares for the stock of the acquired company. However, in 1974, under its new President, Robert W. Hughes, the company initiated a retrenchment and consolidation process. Some of the investments in microwave and radio which were unprofitable were liquidated and emphasis at all levels was on management efficiency. In CPI's, Form 10K filed with the Securities and Exchange Commission for the year ended October 3, 1976, the company noted:

> The Federal Communications Commission (FCC) exercises compre-
> hensive regulating authority over the cable television industry. The
> FCC has broad powers to regulate cable systems in order to avoid what
> the FCC considers to be unreasonable competitive disadvantages and

---

This case was prepared by David A. Wilson, Visiting Associate Professor, from an earlier case by Associate Professor Charles Tritschler of Purdue University, as a basis for class discussion rather than to illustrate either effective or ineffective handling of an administrative situation.

prejudicial effects on existing and potential broadcasting services and to encourage cable television systems to provide services not offered by broadcast stations. . . .

The rules, regulations, and policies of the FCC affecting cable television services are in a constant state of change. A number of changes were adopted by the FCC which may have a significant impact on the cable television industry and on (CPI's) operations. . . .

The FCC has decided to leave the regulation of cable television subscriber rates to the marketplace or the local authorities, as the case may be.

The Greater Lafayette TV Cable Corporation (GLTVC) was acquired in March 1971 by Telesystems Corporations for the sum of $3,613,500. The acquisition was accounted for on a purchase basis. In April 1972, Communications Properties, Inc. exchanged 999,411 of its common shares for 100% of the outstanding common stock of Telesystems, Inc.

Immediately prior to its acquisition, GLTVC showed a net book value of $446,435. Of the acquisition price which was in excess of the net asset book value ($3,167,065), $813,039 was specifically identified as representing an increase in the value of the property, plant and equipment over its original cost. The remaining $2,354,026 represents an excess of the purchase price over the current costs of the net assets at the date of investment (see Exhibit 1). There was no adjustment on the books of account of GLTVC for the $813,039 increase in market value of its property, plant and equipment. Likewise, for income tax purposes, the original cost of the depreciable assets to GLTVC was the basis for determining depreciation expense.

In April 1976, a delegation from CPI and GLTVC appeared before a joint committee of the City Councils of Lafayette and West Lafayette to support a GLTVC request for an increase in the rates charged to subscribers in the two cities. Exhibit 2 summarizes the requested rate changes.

In support of its request, CPI noted that GLTVC had not been granted a rate increase since its inception in March 1971 to the present in spite of a period of severe inflation in most sectors of the economy. CPI went on to note that, as illustrated in Exhibit 3, the rate of return on their investment generated by GLTVC from 1972 to 1975 averaged 3.95 percent. While 1975 represented the most profitable year of the four, a state of market saturation was rapidly being approached (see Exhibit 10). CPI argued that, unlike a public utility, CATV possesses considerable risk and that a reasonable rate of return for the Lafayette subsidiary would be in the range of 15 to 18 percent per annum.

One of the expert witnesses retained by CPI for the rate request testified that in times of inflation the asset valuations and income determinations based upon original costs could often be very misleading. He noted that the left-hand column of the financial statements of GLTVC (Exhibits 5, 6, and 7) disclosed the original cost. He argued that a more appropriate basis for determining the income and rate of return generated by GLTVC would be to consider the fair market value of the assets as at the date of merger with Telesystems Corporation and an income figure adjusted for the higher depreciation and amortization dictated by the increase in asset values. He referred the joint committee to the right-hand column of Exhibits 5, 6, and 7 as those appropriate to a determination of the fairness of the rate of return earned by GLTVC.

One of the members of the joint committee, assisted by a high school civics students, concentrated his questioning on the Statement of Changes in Financial Position (Exhibit 6) and noted an apparent heavy cash flow from the subsidiary (GLTVC) to the parent. Though praising the witnesses for their technical expertise, the councilmen expressed dismay at GLTVC's producing the two different balance sheets and income statements shown in Exhibits 5 and 7. Additionally, an excerpt from the 1975 Annual Report of Communications Properties, Inc. (Exhibit 9) disclosed that, in fact, CPI paid no federal income taxes for the year ended October 31, 1975, and that any allocation to GLTVC in lieu of Federal taxes was not appropriate.

As the evening wore on, one city official remarked that he would rather watch cable TV than do its bookkeeping. The meeting was recessed for the councilmen to discuss their decision and vote on the rate increase in private deliberation.

QUESTIONS

1. If you were a member of the joint committee of the City Councils of Lafayette and West Lafayette, would you support or vote to deny GLTVC's requested rate increase?
2. If you were a consultant to CPI, what strategy would you propose for the Company to follow to maximize the likelihood of receiving the requested increase?

Exhibit 1. Allocation of Cost Purchase of Greater Lafayette TV Cable Corporation

	NET ASSETS	
	Original cost less accumulated depreciation where appropriate	$446,435
PURCHASE PRICE	Appreciation of fixed assets from book value to replacement cost	$813,039
$3,613,500	Excess of purchase price over fair market value of assets	$2,354,026

Exhibit 2. Proposed Rate Changes

GLTV herewith requests approval of the City Councils of Lafayette and West Lafayette to initiate the following changes to present service charges:

	PRESENT	PROPOSED
1. Residential, including multi-type dwelling units (i.e., duplexes, apartments and business offices)		
A. Individual Unit Billing		
Monthly Service		
First outlet	$4.90	$7.00
Each additional outlet	1.50	1.50
Other Service Charges		
Installation charge on first outlet	18.50	18.50
Relocate outlet, same premises	5.00	7.50
Installation charge each additional outlet	5.00	7.50
Transfer of service to new residence	5.00	7.50
B. Bulk Billed Accounts (apartments, trailer parks)		
Monthly Service		
First residential unit/first outlet	4.90	7.00*
Each additional residential unit/first outlet	various	5.60
Additional outlet/each additional unit	1.50	1.20*
Other Service Charges		
Installation charge for first outlet/each residential unit	18.50	18.50
Installation charge for each additional outlet in any unit	n/a	7.50
Relocate outlet/same premises	5.00	7.50
Transfer service to new residence	n/a	n/a

*80 percent of the charge for the first outlet of the same type service.

Exhibit 3. *Rate of Return Analysis*

Total Investment $3,613,500

YEAR ENDED	NET INCOME	YEARLY RETURN	AVERAGE RETURN
1972 Actual	$74,750	2.07%	2.07%
1973 Actual	$158,414	4.38%	3.23%
1974 Actual	$158,771	4.39%	3.62%
1975 Actual	$179,192	4.96%	3.95%
1976 Projected @ $4.90	$223,387	6.18%	4.40%
1976 Projected @ $7.00	$467,998	12.95%	5.75%

Exhibit 4. *Condensed Financial Statements for the Years 1972 through 1975 Inclusive*

CONDENSED STATEMENT OF INCOME*	YEARS ENDED OCTOBER 31			
	1972	1973	1974	1975
Operating revenues	$937,238	$981,154	$1,047,470	$1,191,722
Operating expenses				
Cost of service	422,379	401,592	448,675	547,854
Depreciation and amortization	246,787	165,993	178,622	197,432
Federal income taxes	173,322	255,155	261,402	267,244
Total Operating Expenses	862,488	822,740	888,699	1,012,530
Net income	$74,750	$158,414	$158,771	$179,192

*Per audited financials, adjusted for excess paid over fair value of assets at acquisition in March 1, 1971.

Exhibit 5. *Balance Sheet Adjusted for Consolidation, October 31, 1975*

Assets	SEPARATE STATEMENTS AS REPORTED	CONSOLIDATION ADJUSTMENTS DR.	(CR.)	AMOUNTS CONSOLIDATED
Current Assets				
Cash	$12,764			$12,764
Accounts receivable, net of allowance for doubtful accounts of $2,745	11,475			11,475
Prepaid expenses	11,531			11,531
Total Current Assets	35,770			35,770
Advances to parent and affiliate	1,372,529			1,372,529
Property, plant, and equipment, at cost	1,612,559	$813,039(a)		2,425,598
Less accumulated depreciation	(957,742)		(295,603)(b)	(1,253,345)
	654,817			1,172,253
Excess cost over net assets at date of acquisition, net of amortization		2,354,026(a)	(274,636)(b)	2,079,390
	$2,063,116	$2,596,826		$4,659,942
Liabilities				
Current Liabilities				
Accounts payable, trade	$15,244			$15,244
Other accrued expenses	60,396			60,396
Advance payments, subscribers	67,640			67,640
Total Current Liabilities	143,280			143,280
Stockholders' Equity				
Common stock, $100 par value; authorized 1,500 shares; issued and outstanding 750 shares	75,000			75,000
Capital in excess of par value			$(3,167,065)(a) (377,426)(c)	3,544,491
Retained earnings	1,850,836	947,665		903,171
	1,925,836			4,522,662
Less treasury stock, at cost (60 shares)	(6,000)			(6,000)
	1,919,836			4,516,662
	$2,063,116	$2,596,826		$4,659,942

Note: The accompanying consolidation entries and notes are an integral part of this statement.

Exhibit 6. *Statement of Changes in Financial Position for the Year Ended October 31, 1975*

	SEPARATE STATEMENTS AS REPORTED	AMOUNTS CONSOLIDATED
Source of funds		
Net income	$289,514	$179,192
Charges not requiring working capital in the current period:		
Depreciation	87,110	197,432
Corporate overhead charge	42,784	42,784
Amount due parent in lieu of federal income taxes, credited to advances to parent	267,244	267,244
Working capital provided by operations	686,652	686,652
Use of funds		
Additions to property, plant, and equipment	187,229	187,229
Advances to parent and affiliate	528,122	528,122
	715,351	715,351
Decrease in working capital	$28,699	$28,699
Changes in the components of working capital		
Increase (decrease) in current assets		
Cash	($1,852)	($1,852)
Accounts receivable	(7,057)	(7,057)
Prepaid expenses	8,481	8,481
	(428)	(428)
Increase (decrease) in current liabilities		
Accounts payable, trade	(7,199)	(7,199)
Other accrued expenses	2,312	2,312
Advance payments, subscribers	33,158	33,158
	28,271	28,271
Decrease in working capital	$28,699	$28,699

Exhibit 7. Statement of Income and Retained Earnings Adjusted for Consolidation for the Year Ended October 31, 1975

	SEPARATE STATEMENTS AS REPORTED	CONSOLIDATION ADJUSTMENTS DR.	(CR.)	AMOUNTS CONSOLIDATED
CATV service revenues	$1,191,722			$1,191,722
Costs and expenses				
Salaries and wages	167,953			167,953
Other operating	110,977			110,977
Selling, general, and administrative	193,640			193,640
Corporate overhead charges	42,784			42,784
Depreciation and amortization	87,110	$110,322(b)		197,432
	602,464			712,786
Income before federal and state income taxes	589,258			478,936
Federal and state income taxes				
Amount due parent in lieu of federal income taxes	267,244			267,244
State income taxes	32,500			32,500
	299,744			299,744
Net income	289,514			179,192
Retained earnings, beginning of year	1,561,322	459,917(b)		
		377,426(c)		723,979
Retained earnings, end of year	$1,850,836	$947,665		$903,171

Note: The accompanying consolidation entries and notes are an integral part of this statement.

Exhibit 8. Consolidation Entries and Notes

Consolidation Entries:

In March 1971, Telesystems Corporation purchased all of the common stock of the company for $3,613,500. The purchase price exceeded the net assets acquired by $3,167,065, of which $813,039 was specifically identifiable as plant and equipment; $2,354,026 represents excess cost over net assets at date of acquisition. The consolidation adjustments reflect the capitalization of these amounts and the recording of the related depreciation and amortization, as follows:

(a) To allocate the excess of the purchase price over recorded values at date of acquisition, aggregate credited to capital in excess of par value;
(b) To record current and prior years' depreciation and amortization of additional costs recorded in (a) above;
(c) To reclassify retained earnings at date of acquisition to capital in excess of par value.

Notes:

1. The excess cost specifically identifiable as plant is depreciated over the remaining life of the CATV system using a straight-line composite method. The excess cost over net assets at date of acquisition is amortized over 40 years.
2. These statements should be read in conjunction with the financial statements and notes thereto appearing in Exhibits 5, 6 and 7.

Exhibit 9. Excerpted from the 1975 Annual Report of Communications Properties, Inc.

Note 5—Income Taxes:
The consolidated provision for Federal and state income taxes is as follows:

	1975	1974
Current, state	$290,109	$295,161
Deferred		
Federal	497,548	619,057
State	(8,800)	(4,500)
Investment tax credit	(261,274)	(322,029)
	227,474	292,528
	$517,583	$587,689

Net deferred Federal income tax credits of $462,544 and $297,028 in 1975 and 1974 have been allocated to "equity in net loss of subsidiaries held for sale."

The provision for deferred Federal and state income taxes, arising from timing differences between financial and tax reporting, is comprised as follows:

	1975	1974
Excess of financial depreciation over tax depreciation	$13,157	($125,822)
Deferred system development costs, expensed in year incurred for tax, net of amortization	332,706	681,531
Subscriber prepayments	89,270	10,790
FCC fee refund	50,386	
Other	3,229	48,058
Investment tax credit	(261,274)	(322,029)
	$227,474	$292,528

Following is a reconciliation between the expected Federal income tax expense computed at 48 percent on income before Federal and state income taxes and equity in net loss of subsidiaries held for sale and the actual income tax expense:

	1975	1974
Expected income tax expense	$400,936	$505,671
Increase (decrease) in expected income tax resulting from:		
Depreciation and amortization not deductible for tax purposes	223,752	260,513
State income tax, net of Federal income tax effect	146,281	151,144
Investment tax credits	(261,274)	(322,029)
Other	7,888	(7,610)
	116,647	82,018
	$517,583	$587,689

The company has consolidated tax operating loss carryforwards of approximately $3,290,000 which expire in 1979 and 1980. The company also has consolidated investment tax credit carryovers of approximately $1,899,000 which expire in 1978 through 1982. As described in Note 2, the company has decided to sell its specialized common carrier microwave subsidiaries. If this is accomplished in its presently anticipated form, the consolidated net operating loss and investment tax credit carryforward would be reduced by approximately $984,000 and $502,000, respectively.

In 1975, the company's Federal income tax returns through 1974 were examined by the Internal Revenue Service (IRS). The final report has not yet been issued, but the preliminary report indicates that the IRS will attempt to permanently disallow certain deductions relating to preoperating expenses. The proposed adjustments (including the effect in 1975) would result in a reduction in the company's net operating loss carryforwards of $1,648,000 and a cash payment of $77,934. Management of the company intends to dispute the IRS if the final report is issued in its present form. The company believes it will prevail.

Exhibit 10. *Market Saturation Analysis 1972–1976*

YEAR ENDED	SUBSCRIBERS	HOMES PASSED	MARKET SATURATION	CAPITAL FUNDS TOTAL	REINVESTED PER SUBSCRIBER
1972 actual	17,497	25,100	69.7%	$90,535	$5.16
1973 "	18,502	25,700	71.9%	135,200	7.31
1974 "	19,494	26,570	73.4%	157,507	8.08
1975 "	20,883	27,405	76.2%	187,229	8.96
1976 projected	21,260	27.800	76.4%	203,000	9.55
				$773,471	

Lockheed
Aircraft Corporation

The accounting treatment of the costs of development and/or start-up of a major new program is a controversial issue. On one hand, a company may elect a conservative approach and recognize these costs as expenses of the period in which the expenditures are made—a treatment which may not produce a very satisfactory matching of costs and related revenue. On the other hand, if the costs are capitalized as assets to be matched against (potential) revenues from the project in future periods, the assets and net income of the current period may be overstated if the project is not ultimately successful. This dilemma surfaced in a major way in a recent report on the fortunes of Lockheed Aircraft Corporation (*Wall Street Journal,* June 3, 1974):

> *A huge writedown of its financially troubled L1011 "TriStar" commercial aircraft program, probably totaling at least $600 million, is the key element in a complex plan for a far-reaching financial restructuring of Lockheed Aircraft Corp., sources close to Lockheed said. . . .*
>
> *Some Lockheed critics have long contended the company was engaging in "fantasy accounting" in its handling of the books for the L1011 program and doubtless will say, in the wake of one of the biggest writeoffs in American corporate history, that the company and its auditors should have "bitten the bullet" some time ago. The auditing firm . . . has regularly qualified its opinions of the extensively footnoted Lockheed financial statements because of uncertainties over "realization of the L1011 inventories" and the maintenance of financing arrangements.*
>
> *At the end of 1973, Lockheed was carrying $1.16 billion of its total assets of $1.85 billion (and current assets of $1.56 billion) in the*

This case was prepared by Professor Thomas H. Williams, The University of Wisconsin— Madison, as a basis for class discussion rather than to illustrate either effective or ineffective handling of an administrative situation.

form of net inventories in the TriStar program. This unrecovered TriStar investment comprises the plane's development costs, initial tooling and other nonrecurring costs and production costs, less payments for planes delivered to date and customer advances on future deliveries.

Lockheed said in its latest annual report that it expected to recover this inventory through the anticipated sale of 300 TriStars, though it cautioned this could take into the early 1980s and was subject to certain variables and uncertainties. Although it had delivered 56 TriStars through 1973, Lockheed said it didn't expect to reach the point at which current production costs of each plane will be less than the sales price of planes then being delivered until mid-1974. It said the inventory at the end of 1974 would be only slightly less than a year earlier and eventual recovery of about $900 million of gross inventory depended on firm orders beyond the 129 in hand at year-end 1973.

A writedown of the L1011 inventories of about $600 million without a new cash infusion wouldn't drop Lockheed into a negative working-capital position but also wouldn't leave much room between current assets, which would drop to less than $1 billion based on the year-end $1.56 billion figure, and current liabilities, which stood at $718 million at year-end. It would, apparently, wipe out the company's retained earnings, which totaled $192.8 million at year-end.

Lockheed hasn't recorded any loss (or profit) on its L1011 deliveries to date, posting those delivered at the full sales price ($730 million in 1973 and $302 million in 1972). It has charged to income slightly over $300 million to date in general administrative expenses, however. The current sales price of an L1011 is about $20 million.

Currently, Lockheed has firm orders, including those already delivered, for 135 TriStars and second buys, or options, for 67 more, or a total of 202. Airline industry sources say, however, that prospects for substantial additional orders in the next few years are almost non-existent and, except for a few instances, airlines holding the L1011 options aren't likely to convert options to firm orders during 1974. . . .

Lockheed posted 1973 net income of $16.8 million, or $1.48 a share. This result includes an operating profit on programs other than the TriStar and new ship construction of $165.8 million and a loss of $69.7 million from general and administrative costs on the TriStar program. Sales of $2.76 billion included the $730 million from TriStars, on which zero profit or loss was recorded, as noted earlier.

REQUIRED

1. In capitalizing the development and start-up costs of its TriStar program, do you believe that Lockheed was engaging in "fantasy accounting" as alleged by some of its critics? Would your answer have been different at the outset of the program than it is now with the benefit of hindsight?

2. Assuming it is appropriate to capitalize development and start-up costs (and many companies do so):
   (a) Do you believe that the investment in the TriStar program was properly classified as a current asset—*viz.,* Inventory? Why might a corporation wish to reflect development and start-up costs as a current asset rather than some noncurrent asset such as "Other Assets"?
   (b) What justification might be offered for the policy of capitalizing the "net" production costs (the excess of current production costs over the sales proceeds from this production) of early production? (By this we mean at least the first 60 to 70 planes based on Lockheed's statement that "it didn't expect to reach the point at which current production costs of each plane will be less than the sales price of planes then being delivered until mid-1974.")
   (c) In view of the policy of capitalization adopted by Lockheed in (b) above, why do you suppose that they did not elect to capitalize the general administrative costs (presumably related to the program) rather than recognizing them as expenses of the period in which incurred?
   (d) After capitalizing the plane's development costs, initial tooling, and other nonrecurring costs, what system of matching these costs against future revenues was adopted by Lockheed? Do you believe this results in a proper matching of these costs with related revenue?
3. What do you suppose was the basis for the proposed $600 million write-down of an inventory carried at a "cost" of $1.16 billion (that is, why was the proposed write-down not some larger or smaller amount)?
4. While a major program is still in the development stage, do you believe that an auditor's qualification (or caveat) that the fairness of the financial statement presentation depends upon the "ability to realize capitalized development costs" is adequate for external investors? If not, what alternative financial data and/or auditor actions would you suggest?

PART III

Liability Recognition

Consolidation Coal Company

On September 15, 1966, the Continental Oil Company (Conoco) purchased from Consolidation Coal all its coal properties as a going concern. Continental Oil set up these coal properties as a wholly owned subsidiary and retained the name Consolidation Coal (Consol). The purchase price for this acquisition was 1,000,000 shares of Conoco common stock (valued at about $78.50 per share at the time of the acquisition). The purchase was made subject to a reserved production payment in the principal amount of $460,000,000 which Consol had sold in 1966 to the William Coal Corporation. William Coal was owned by the investment banking firm of Lehman Brothers, certain of its key employees, and certain members of their families. William Coal had borrowed the $460,000,000 from a group of institutional lenders headed by the First National City Bank of New York. The loan was secured by the production payment.

Under the terms of the production payment, William Coal was to receive each year for 16 years a portion of the gross revenues of Consol equal to 87 percent of the pre-tax profit from about 20 percent of the coal properties which Consol was actively mining. The expected life of these properties was 30 years. William Coal was also to receive 100 percent of any royalties which Consol would receive if it leased any of the specified coal properties to other mining concerns. Assuming production remained constant at 1965 levels, William Coal would receive about $44.1 million a year from 1967 through 1982 for a total of about $706 million. A schedule was set up showing the expected unpaid balance of the production payment at the end of each six-month period over the 16

This case was prepared by Assistant Professor John K. Shank with the help of Mr. Jacques Abrams as the basis for class discussion rather than to illustrate either effective or ineffective handling of an administrative situation.

years from 1967 through 1982. If production or profitability levels decreased such that the unpaid balance at the end of any six-month period was higher than the expected balance at that date, William Coal was entitled to receive the greater of 100 percent of pre-tax profits from all coal mined by Consol or $.90 per ton from coal mined in the properties subject to the production payment. This revised payment plan would then remain in effect until the unpaid balance was reduced to or below the expected level at some succeeding semi-annual check point. If production or profitability levels increased above 1965 levels, the payments to William Coal would increase proportionately and the production payment would "pay out" in fewer than 16 years.[1]

A condensed balance sheet for Consolidation Coal as of December 31, 1965, was as follows:

(in millions)			
Current assets	$100.3	Current liabilities	$ 26.4
Investments and other assets	129.1	Long-term debt	12.5
		Reserves and other liabilities	24.2
Property and equipment (net)	216.7	Shareholders' equity	383.1
Total	$446.1	Total	$446.1

An approximate balance sheet for Consol as a wholly owned subsidiary of Conoco as of September 15, 1966, was as follows:

(in millions)			
Current assets	$ 75.6	Current liabilities	$ 28.9
Investments and other assets	22.7	Reserves and other liabilities	18.3
Property and equipment (net)	27.4	Shareholders' equity	78.5
Total	$125.7		$125.7

Certain assets and liabilities of Consolidation Coal were not part of the acquisition. The significant excluded items were cash and marketable securities, investments not related to the coal properties, and long-term debt. Except for property and equipment, items were picked up by Consol at their book value. Property and equipment, as a group, was valued at the difference between the total purchase price and the book value of the other items involved.

---

[1]This is a simplified description of the agreement, focusing on its essence rather than its full complexity.

In the financial review section of the 1967 Conoco Annual Report it was noted that Consol had revenues of $279.1 million and earnings of $23.8 million for the year. Payments of $52.3 million to William Coal under the carved-out production payment plan were netted against the revenue figure for purposes of the consolidated Conoco financial statements. An approximate balance sheet for Consol at December 31, 1967, is as follows:

(in millions)			
Current assets	$ 80.0	Current liabilities	$ 30.0
Investments and other assets	20.0	Reserves and other liabilities	16.0
Property and equipment (net)	127.0	Shareholders' equity	181.0
Total	$227.0	Total	$227.0

Excerpts from the 1967 Conoco Annual Report, including complete financial statements, are reproduced as Exhibit 1.

QUESTIONS

1. Calculate the approximate gain to the shareholders of Consolidation Coal on the sale of their coal properties.
2. Do you agree with the treatment accorded the production payment by Conoco via its subsidiary, Consol?
3. If the production payment were treated as long-term debt, what would the financial statements of Consol and Conoco look like? Specifically, consider the "return on assets employed" figure for Consol, the debt-equity ratio for Conoco and the debt service coverage for Conoco.
4. What do you think of the disclosure of the production payment in the Conoco consolidated financial statements?

Exhibit 1.

Financial

Earnings In 1967 Continental's consolidated income before extraordinary gains reached a new high of $136.1 million, up 17.7% over the previous record of $115.6 million achieved in 1966. Earnings on the weighted average number of Common shares outstanding during 1967 totaled $5.51 per share, an increase of 8.5% over the $5.08 earned on a smaller number of Common shares outstanding in the prior year.

In the United States and Canada, Continental's income before extraordinary gains reached a record $121.2 million, up $8.3 million or 7.3% over earnings in 1966. The increase is attributable to the first full year of operation of the Company's coal properties and to improvements in petroleum and plant foods activities.

In the United States, Consolidation Coal Company (Consol), a wholly owned subsidiary, contributed $23.8 million to Continental's earnings in 1967. This amount is $15.7 million more than Consol's earnings in the last three and one-half months of 1966. Results from domestic petroleum refining and marketing activities also improved as sales of refined products reached new highs and product prices improved slightly. Plant foods activities increased their contribution to earnings largely because of higher operating volumes and reduced unit costs at the Company's Blytheville, Arkansas ammonia plant.

Partially offsetting these favorable factors in the U.S. were increased income taxes, higher interest and exploratory expenses, and a reduced earnings contribution from chemicals and plastics activities. Income taxes increased primarily because of higher income and suspension of the U.S. investment tax credit during the first half of the year. Exploratory expenses in the U.S. increased over the 1966 level due to an intensified search for petroleum reserves. The contribution to earnings from chemicals and plastics activities declined because of start-up costs of the Company's new ethylene and vinyl chloride monomer plants and lower sales volumes and reduced prices of polyvinyl chloride resins.

In Canada Hudson's Bay Oil and Gas Company Limited (HBOG), a 65.7%-owned affiliate, achieved record earnings as a result of major gains in the production of crude oil, natural gas, natural gas liquids, and sulfur. HBOG's earnings in 1967 totaled $22.1 million (Canadian), up 27.4% over results attained in 1966. Continental's share of HBOG's 1967 earnings, after applicable Canadian and United States income taxes on intercompany dividends, reached $10.3 million (U.S.) in 1967, an increase of $1.9 million (U.S.) or 22.5% over 1966.

In the other Western Hemisphere countries, Continental's exploration and production activities resulted in a loss in 1967 of $0.3 million, an improvement of $3.3 million over the loss of $3.6 million in 1966. Losses in both years resulted primarily from additions to the reserve for possible losses from contracts of Mexofina, S.A. de C.V., a wholly owned subsidiary operating in Mexico. The improvement in 1967 reflects increased production of crude oil in Venezuela and termination of the Venezuela-concession amortization expense.

In the Eastern Hemisphere, Continental's income before extraordinary gains reached $15.2 million in 1967, up $8.9 million over the $6.3 million earned in 1966. The gain is mainly attributable to substantially increased sales of refined products, greatly increased efficiency, improved product realizations in the United Kingdom and western Europe, and reduced expenditures for exploratory activities. Although transportation costs increased as a result of the Middle East crisis and closure of the Suez Canal in June 1967, the adverse effect on Continental's operating costs was less than for the industry as a whole. More than 95% of the Company's production of crude oil in the Eastern Hemisphere lies west of the Suez Canal.

In addition to earnings from normal operations in 1967, Continental realized an extraordinary gain of $12.9 million or $0.53 per Common share from the sale of a block of coal reserves in Washington County, Pennsylvania in June 1967. In the previous year, the Company realized an extraordinary gain of $41.3 million or $1.88 per Common share from the sale of its interest in Great Lakes Pipe Line Company in March 1966.

Dividends In December 1967, Continental paid a quarterly dividend on Common Stock of $0.70 per share, five cents per share above the previous rate. Total dividends paid on Common Stock in 1967 totaled $2.65 per share, an increase of $0.20 over payments made in 1966. Regular dividends on Preferred Stock of $2.00 per share were also paid in 1967.

Reserved Production Payment — Coal The coal reserves purchased on September 15, 1966 were subject to a reserved production payment in the primary amount of $460 million. With respect to these reserves, the holder of the production payment receives 100% of the royalty income from coal properties leased to others and such percentage of gross revenue as equals 87% of net mine revenue from coal production and sales from stipulated mines. Net mine revenue comprises revenue received from the sale of coal less related mining costs, including depreciation and administrative and selling expenses. In 1967, 87% of net mine revenue came to about 23% of gross revenue from coal production and sales from the stipulated mines. Amounts paid and accrued on the Consol production payment with respect to operations in 1967 totaled $52.3 million, including $24.2 million for interest equivalents and other costs and $28.1 million for reduction of the primary sum. After giving effect to the latter amount, the primary sum had been reduced to $429.6 million.

For financial purposes, Continental is capitalizing the costs of mining coal applicable to the reserved production payment. These costs are being amortized at a rate based on an estimate of the total costs which will be capitalized over the life of the production payment and the quantity of subject coal which will be produced for Continental's account from the stipulated mines over a period of 30 years from inception of the production payment. In 1967, $33.9 million of mining costs were capitalized and $12.6 million were amortized. Because all mining costs are being deducted for income tax purposes as incurred, provision is being made for deferred income taxes. This provision for the year 1967 came to $10.2 million.

Continental's statement of consolidated income for the year 1967 includes revenues of $279.1 million and costs and expenses of $255.3 million from Consol's

Exhibit 1. *(continued)*

coal and other activities. The revenues exclude royalty income and sales revenues applicable to the production payment. Costs and expenses reflect the capitalization and amortization of mining costs and the related deferred income taxes as previously discussed.

Revenues Continental's revenues totaled $2,255 million in 1967, up 17.8% over 1966. Sales and service revenues, which exclude excise taxes and nonoperating revenues, reached $2,083 million, an increase of 19.1% over prior-year revenues of $1,749 million. The first full year of operations of Consol and a substantial increase in the sale of refined products were the major factors accounting for the increase in revenues. Relative contributions made by the Company's principal activities to sales and service revenues in 1967 and 1966 are shown below:

| | Percent of Total | |
	1967	1966
Refined products	42%	44%
Crude oil	23	27
Natural gas	3	3
Coal and other (Consol)	13	5
Plant foods	8	9
Chemicals and plastics	8	10
Other	3	2
Total	100%	100%

Costs, Expenses, and Taxes Total costs, expenses, and taxes in 1967 came to $2,119 million, up $320 million or 17.8% over 1966. Income and other taxes of $430 million accounted for 20.3% of Continental's total costs of doing business. Costs and expenses of Consol in 1967 totaled $255 million, compared to $76 million in the last three and one-half months of 1966.

Capital Outlays Capital expenditures and investments in and advances to non-consolidated affiliates totaled a record $393.7 million in 1967, compared with $295.0 million in 1966. Capital expenditures totaled $383.5 million, an increase of $101.1 million over the previous high of $282.4 million in 1966. Major items in 1967 included $92.1 million for coal operations, $38.7 million for undeveloped offshore acreage in the United States, and $28.4 million for the 80,000-barrel-a-day refinery Continental is building in the United Kingdom.

Investments in and advances to affiliated companies in 1967 amounted to $10.2 million, compared with $12.6 million in 1966.

Source of Funds Funds derived from operations in 1967 totaled $289.2 million, an increase of 12.8% over 1966. The Company supplemented these funds with several financing arrangements.

In June 1967, the Company offered holders of its Common Stock rights to purchase one additional share of Common Stock at $59 per share for each nine shares held. Subscriptions were received for 98.8% of the 2,522,713 shares that were offered, and the remaining shares were purchased by the underwriters. Net proceeds to Continental totaled $146.1 million.

During 1967 Continental received the remaining $52.9 million proceeds of its 5⅞% Notes due 1989, which were placed in 1966 in the amount of $100 million. The Company had initially obtained $47.1 million in December 1966. In 1967 Continental also received the proceeds of the 7½%, £6.5 million sterling loan due 1993, which also had been arranged in 1966. In February 1968, Continental Oil International Finance Corporation, a wholly owned subsidiary, issued $20 million of 7% guaranteed debentures due 1980. These debentures were issued and sold outside the United States in cooperation with the U.S. Government's program to improve the nation's balance-of-payments position.

Continental has a 4½% revolving credit agreement in the amount of $100 million, all of which was available to the Company at the end of 1967. The credit, negotiated with five major banks in 1964, was utilized during the first half of 1967, but the loans were repaid in June 1967. In late 1967, the terms of the credit agreement were amended to extend its revolving feature by one year to February

1, 1969, at which time six-year term Notes may be issued at the 4½% rate.

The Company recently concluded an arrangement under which Consol has the option to lease machinery and equipment costing up to $110 million for new mines. Leases covering $24 million of facilities were executed in January 1968.

In December 1967, Continental sold carved-out (short-term) oil payments totaling $4.9 million, compared with $20.0 million sold in 1966.

In September 1967, HBOG successfully offered to the Canadian public 600,000 shares of Cumulative Redeemable Convertible Preferred Stock at a price of $51 (Canadian) per share. Net proceeds to HBOG totaled $29.5 million (Canadian). The Preferred shares have a par value of $50 and bear a 5% dividend rate. Each share is convertible into one and one-fifth shares of HBOG Common Stock until October 15, 1972 and into one Common share thereafter until October 15, 1977 unless redeemed earlier. If all of the Preferred Stock is converted into HBOG Common Stock before October 15, 1972, Continental's interest in HBOG will be reduced from 65.7% to 63.2%.

GEOGRAPHIC DISTRIBUTION OF EARNINGS AND NET ASSETS

Millions of Dollars

| | Income Before Extraordinary Gains | | Net Assets | |
	1967	1966	1967	1966
Western Hemisphere				
United States	$110.7	$104.5	$1,035.8	$ 834.1
Canada	10.5	8.4	84.1	77.6
Total U.S. and Canada	$121.2	$112.9	$1,119.9	$ 911.7
Other Western Hemisphere	(0.3)	(3.6)	39.1	44.1
Total Western Hemisphere	$120.9	$109.3	$1,159.0	$ 955.8
Eastern Hemisphere	15.2	6.3	187.0	161.4
Total	$136.1	$115.6	$1,346.0	$1,117.2

Exhibit 1. (continued)

Source and Application of Funds

Millions of Dollars

	1967	1966	1965	1964	1963
Source					
Income before extraordinary gains	$136.1	$115.6	$ 96.2	$100.1	$ 87.4
Noncash charges against income					
Depreciation, depletion, amortization, and retirements	110.3	98.3	92.8	86.8	82.7
Surrendered leases and dry hole costs	29.8	26.8	32.0	29.4	33.5
Other (including minority interest in income)	13.0	15.7	5.8	12.5	8.8
Funds derived from operations	$289.2	$256.4	$226.8	$228.8	$212.4
Common Stock issued through rights offered to Common Stockholders	146.1	—	—	—	—
Common Stock issued for assets acquired from Consolidation Coal Company	—	78.5	—	—	—
Preferred Stock issued by consolidated subsidiary	27.3	—	—	—	—
Extraordinary gains	12.9	41.3	—	—	—
Sales of fixed assets and investments	18.9	27.2	18.8	25.8	15.6
Increase in long-term debt (net)	52.3	4.3	34.8	32.0	52.4
Repayments of advances previously made to other companies	2.6	8.4	3.3	5.4	16.1
Deferred income from oil payments (net)	(9.3)	6.2	(4.4)	(1.5)	(2.8)
Other sources of funds (net)	9.0	1.6	5.4	2.3	10.3
Total funds available	$549.0	$423.9	$284.7	$292.8	$304.0
Application					
Capital expenditures—United States	$295.5	$215.7	$146.9	$156.3	$163.0
—Canada	32.1	29.8	25.0	22.4	47.0
—International (excluding Canada)	55.9	36.9	27.9	46.3	39.2
Total	$383.5	$282.4	$199.8	$225.0	$249.2
Investments in and advances to other companies	10.2	12.6	13.0	8.6	19.4
Dividends paid on Continental Common Stock	63.6	53.8	52.0	45.4	40.7
Dividends paid to Preferred stockholders, to minority interests, and to stockholders of pooled company prior to combination	8.0	7.2	7.0	6.6	4.5
Increase (decrease) in notes and accounts receivable, inventories, less current liabilities	90.4	(24.5)	3.8	26.9	24.9
Total funds applied	$555.7	$331.5	$275.6	$312.5	$338.7
Net increase (decrease) in cash and securities during the year	$ (6.7)	$ 92.4	$ 9.1	$(19.7)	$(34.7)

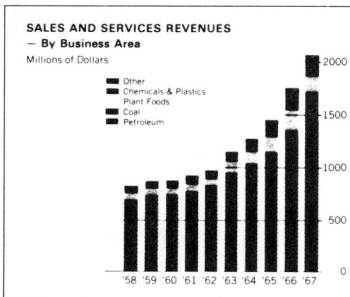

SALES AND SERVICES REVENUES
— By Business Area
Millions of Dollars

Other
Chemicals & Plastics
Plant Foods
Coal
Petroleum

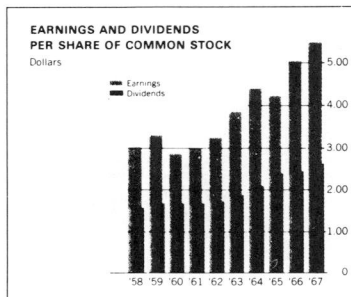

EARNINGS AND DIVIDENDS
PER SHARE OF COMMON STOCK
Dollars

Earnings
Dividends

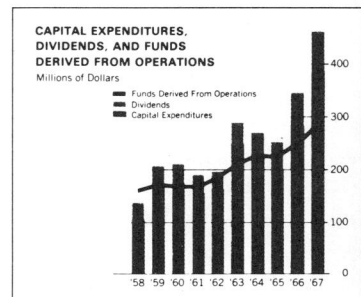

CAPITAL EXPENDITURES,
DIVIDENDS, AND FUNDS
DERIVED FROM OPERATIONS
Millions of Dollars

Funds Derived From Operations
Dividends
Capital Expenditures

Exhibit 1. *(continued)*

Accounting Policies

A summary of Continental's major accounting policies is presented below to assist the reader in evaluating the Company's financial statements and other data contained in this report.

▼ Consolidated financial statements include the accounts of Continental and majority-owned subsidiaries. Income from affiliates not consolidated is recognized only when dividends are received.

▼ Inventories of crude oil, refined products, and other merchandise are carried at cost, which is lower than market in the aggregate. Cost has been determined under the last-in, first-out method for approximately 42% of the inventories, and the cost of the remainder has been determined under the first-in, first-out and average cost methods. Materials and supplies are carried at or below average cost.

▼ Depreciation of plant and equipment is provided substantially on a straight-line method at various rates calculated to extinguish the book values of the respective items over their estimated useful lives, although accelerated depreciation rates are used for federal income tax purposes.

▼ The general policy with respect to accounting for profit and loss on disposal of property, plant, and equipment is to credit or charge such amounts to accumulated depreciation. An exception arises on the disposal of an entire property unit, in which event the profit or loss is credited or charged to income.

▼ Maintenance and repairs are charged to income. Renewals and replacements of a routine nature are charged to income, while those which improve or extend the life of existing properties are capitalized.

▼ Intangible development costs applicable to productive oil or gas wells or to the opening of new coal mines are capitalized and amortized on a unit-of-production basis. Costs of additional mine facilities required to maintain production after a mine reaches the production stage, generally referred to as "receding face costs," are charged to expense as incurred; however, costs of additional air shafts and new portals are capitalized and amortized. For federal income tax purposes, all of these costs are deducted as incurred.

▼ Costs of acquiring undeveloped acreage are capitalized. Costs of such acreage which becomes productive are amortized on a unit-of-production basis. Costs of nonproductive acreage in the United States are carried in the accounts until the properties are surrendered or otherwise disposed of, at which time the full amount is charged against income. The cost of certain foreign concessions and undeveloped leases is being amortized.

▼ Revenues from sales of carved-out production payments are deferred and are taken into income as production occurs. For federal income tax purposes, such revenues are taxable in the year received.

▼ Costs of producing oil and gas (lifting costs) applicable to production payments, which are reserved against properties which the Company has purchased, are capitalized and amortized over the Company's estimated net recoverable petroleum reserves. Costs of producing coal (mining costs) applicable to the production payment, which is reserved against properties which the Company has purchased, are capitalized and amortized using per-ton rates designed to write off the capitalized mining costs over the Company's share of the estimated tonnage to be produced in a thirty-year period. For income tax purposes, lifting and mining costs are deducted as incurred.

▼ Exploratory expenses, including geological and geophysical costs and annual delay rentals, and all dry-hole costs are charged to income as incurred.

▼ The provision for federal taxes on income is charged or credited with the estimated effect on future income taxes resulting from temporary timing differences between financial and taxable income. No such provision is made with respect to differences of a permanent nature, such as statutory depletion and the income tax deduction for intangible development costs. The provision for federal income taxes has been reduced by the amount of investment credit utilized, a procedure sometimes referred to as the "flow-through" method.

Exhibit 1. (continued)

Statement of Consolidated Income and Retained Earnings

Years ended December 31, 1967 and 1966

	1967	1966
Revenues:		
Sales and services (including excise taxes—*Note 7*)	$2,232,999,000	$1,894,563,000
Dividends, interest and other income	16,873,000	15,085,000
Gain on sale of mineral rights	4,933,000	4,951,000
	2,254,805,000	1,914,599,000
Costs, expenses and taxes:		
Costs and operating expenses	1,328,198,000	1,111,689,000
Selling, general and administrative expenses	188,306,000	159,412,000
Income and other taxes *(Note 7)*	430,160,000	376,508,000
Depreciation, depletion and amortization	110,278,000	98,298,000
Surrendered leases and dry hole costs	29,810,000	26,792,000
Interest and debt expense	23,452,000	18,597,000
Minority interest in subsidiaries' net income	8,490,000	7,671,000
	2,118,694,000	1,798,967,000
Income before extraordinary items	136,111,000	115,632,000
Extraordinary items, net of tax *(Note 10)*	12,851,000	41,284,000
Net income *(Note 10)*	148,962,000	156,916,000
Retained earnings:		
Balance at beginning of year	767,072,000	667,996,000
	916,034,000	824,912,000
Dividends paid:		
Common Stock (1967—$2.65 per share; 1966—$2.45 per share)	63,595,000	53,758,000
Preferred Stock ($2.00 per share)	4,041,000	4,082,000
	67,636,000	57,840,000
Balance at end of year	$ 848,398,000	$ 767,072,000
Per share of Common Stock:*		
Income before extraordinary items	$5.51	$5.08
Extraordinary items, net of tax	.53	1.88
Net income	$6.04	$6.96

*Based on weighted average number of Common shares outstanding and after deducting dividends paid on Preferred Stock.

See notes to consolidated financial statements.

Exhibit 1. (continued)

Consolidated Balance Sheet

December 31, 1967 and 1966

	1967	1966
Assets		
Current assets:		
Cash	$ 86,805,000	$ 118,645,000
U. S. government and other securities at cost, which approximates market	35,113,000	9,990,000
Accounts and notes receivable	405,489,000	357,263,000
Inventories *(Note 2)*	213,228,000	213,753,000
Total current assets	740,635,000	699,651,000
Investments, advances and other assets:		
Investments and advances, at or below cost	97,898,000	93,143,000
Long-term receivables from sales of property	58,449,000	46,294,000
	156,347,000	139,437,000
Property, plant and equipment, at cost		
less accumulated depreciation, depletion and amortization *(Note 3)*	1,423,182,000	1,198,649,000
Prepaid and deferred charges	34,304,000	32,018,000
	$2,354,468,000	$2,069,755,000
Liabilities and Stockholders' Equity		
Current liabilities:		
Accounts payable	$ 224,614,000	$ 253,060,000
Accrued taxes, including income taxes	94,649,000	122,263,000
Other accrued liabilities	30,173,000	28,391,000
Long-term debt due within one year	34,766,000	23,160,000
Total current liabilities	384,202,000	426,874,000
Long-term debt *(Note 4)*	415,879,000	363,557,000
Deferred credits:		
Sale of leasehold rights *(Note 5)*	40,280,000	45,446,000
Federal income taxes	59,885,000	30,553,000
Other	26,103,000	36,147,000
	126,268,000	112,146,000
Minority interest in subsidiaries	82,135,000	50,012,000
Stockholders' equity *(Note 6):*		
Preferred Stock	7,150,000	7,447,000
Common Stock	126,458,000	113,390,000
Capital surplus	363,978,000	229,257,000
Retained earnings	848,398,000	767,072,000
Total stockholders' equity	1,345,984,000	1,117,166,000
	$2,354,468,000	$2,069,755,000

See notes to consolidated financial statements.

Exhibit 1. (continued)

Notes to Consolidated Financial Statements December 31, 1967

Note 1: The inclusion of the operations of Consolidation Coal Company in the consolidated financial statements resulted in an increase in consolidated revenues and income before extraordinary items of $84,196,000 and $8,141,000, respectively, for 1966 and $279,092,000 and $23,806,000, respectively, for 1967. (See Note 3).

Note 2: Inventories at December 31, 1967 and 1966 were as follows:

	1967	1966
Crude oil and refined products	$ 93,562,000	$ 94,661,000
Plant foods	43,309,000	47,783,000
Chemicals and plastics	34,617,000	29,385,000
Coal	5,232,000	5,604,000
Other	10,420,000	10,161,000
	187,140,000	187,594,000
Materials and supplies	26,088,000	26,159,000
	$213,228,000	$213,753,000

Inventories, other than materials and supplies, are carried at cost which is lower than market in the aggregate. Cost has been determined under the last-in, first-out method for approximately 42% of the inventories and the cost of the remainder has been determined under the first-in, first-out and average cost methods. Materials and supplies are carried at or below average cost.

Note 3: Property, plant and equipment at December 31, 1967 and 1966 is summarized as follows:

	1967	1966
Petroleum production	$1,364,246,000	$1,281,495,000
Refineries and natural gas processing facilities	330,078,000	279,744,000
Petroleum marketing	201,397,000	170,819,000
Petroleum transportation	162,380,000	148,000,000
Plant foods	165,392,000	160,985,000
Chemicals and plastics	149,330,000	117,023,000
Coal and other (Consol)	145,971,000	54,733,000
Other	35,938,000	33,167,000
	2,554,732,000	2,245,966,000
Less accumulated depreciation, depletion and amortization	1,131,550,000	1,047,317,000
	$1,423,182,000	$1,198,649,000

Depreciation is provided substantially on a straight-line method at rates calculated to extinguish the book values of the assets over their estimated useful lives. In general, depletion and amortization of producing properties are provided on a unit of production basis over estimated recoverable reserves.

Effective September 15, 1966, the Company acquired the coal properties and related assets of Consolidation Coal Company, subject to a reserved production payment of $460,000,000. For financial statement purposes, certain mining costs attributable to the production payment are being capitalized annually and amortized using per ton rates designed to write off the capitalized mining costs over the Company's share of the estimated tonnage to be produced in a thirty-year period. Since these costs are deducted for income tax purposes, as incurred, a provision has been made for deferred income taxes attributable thereto. During 1966 since acquisition and during 1967, revenues of $16,145,000 and $52,294,000, respectively, have been excluded from income and applied against the production payment, including principal and interest and in 1966, closing costs. Capitalized mining costs, net of related income taxes and amortization, amounted to $3,210,000 and $11,055,000, respectively, during the same periods.

Note 4: Long-term debt at December 31, 1967 consisted of:

Continental Oil Company:

4½% debentures due 1991 (due $3,200,000 annually to 1990)	$ 90,400,000
Thirty-year sinking fund 3% debentures (due $4,000,000 annually to 1984)	64,000,000
5⅞% notes due 1989 (due $5,500,000 annually 1972 through 1988)	100,000,000

Continental Oil International Finance Corporation:*

6⅜% guaranteed notes due May 1, 1971	20,000,000

Continental Oil (U.K.) Limited:**

7½% guaranteed unsecured loan stock due 1993 (due $236,400 annually beginning 1972)	15,600,000

Hudson's Bay Oil and Gas Company Limited:†

First mortgage sinking fund bonds:

Series A, 4%, due annually to 1974 and $10,000,000 in 1975	15,858,000
Series B and C, principally 5¾%, due annually to 1977	1,580,000
Series D, 5½%, due annually 1968 through 1982 and $6,937,000 in 1983	26,182,000
Series E, 7%, $462,500 due annually in 1971 and 1972 and $555,000 due annually 1973 through 1987	9,250,000
Term loan, interest at the prime bank rate, payable in quarterly installments to April 1, 1972	12,950,000
Other notes and debentures, principally 4½% to 5%, $11,220,000 due in 1969	36,940,000
Purchase and other obligations, $6,154,000 due in 1969	23,119,000
	$415,879,000

Subsequent to December 31, 1967 Continental Oil International Finance Corporation, a wholly owned subsidiary issued its 7% guaranteed debentures due 1980 in the amount of $20,000,000.*

Continental may also borrow up to $100,000,000 from a bank under a 4½% revolving credit agreement convertible February 1, 1969 into term loans payable 1969-1975.

*These borrowings are in the form of Eurodollars borrowed outside of the U.S.

**Stated in U.S. dollars, payable in pounds sterling.

†Stated in U.S. dollars, payable in Canadian dollars.

Note 5: The sales of leasehold rights were made in 1959 and 1961 and the gain thereon was deferred and is being recorded in income, subject to income tax, as payments are received. In 1963 the Federal Power Commission asserted that these were sales of natural gas and hence were subject to the Commission's jurisdiction. During 1965 and 1966 the Courts have upheld the Federal Power Commission's jurisdiction over these sales. Further hearings on this matter are in progress before the Commission the results of which are not presently determinable; however, in the opinion of management, the final outcome will not have a materially adverse effect on the Company.

Note 6: Stockholders' equity at December 31, 1967 and 1966 consisted of:

	1967	1966
$2 cumulative convertible preferred stock, without par value: Authorized: 2,100,000 shares Outstanding: 1967—1,958,914 shares; 1966—2,040,265 shares; after deducting 59,100 shares in treasury	$ 7,150,000	$ 7,447,000
Common stock, par value $5 per share: Authorized: 28,000,000 shares Outstanding: 1967— 25,291,685 shares after deducting 142,128 shares in treasury; 1966—22,678,050 shares after deducting 149,069 shares in treasury	126,458,000	113,390,000
Capital surplus	363,978,000	229,257,000
Retained earnings	848,398,000	767,072,000
	$1,345,984,000	$1,117,166,000

Each share of preferred stock is entitled to one vote and is convertible into common stock as follows: Prior to January 1, 1969—.74 of a share; thereafter and prior to January 1, 1974—.70 of a share; and from and after January 1, 1974—.67 of a share. The preferred stock is callable on or after October 21, 1968 at $60 per share plus accrued dividends and has a liquidation value of $60 per share. The value assigned to the preferred stock is $3.65 per share which is equivalent to $5 par value

Exhibit 1. (continued)

per share on the common stock of the Company which would have been issued if the preferred stock had been converted to common stock at the initial conversion rate. In the opinion of counsel, the excess, approximately $110,500,000, of the liquidation value over the stated value does not restrict retained earnings. During 1967, 60,016 shares of common stock were issued upon conversion of 81,351 shares of preferred stock.

Under Stock Option Plans for Officers and Other Key Employees, options were outstanding at January 1, 1967 for 189,614 shares of the Company's common stock and 77,575 shares were available for the granting of options. During 1967 options for 66,000 shares were granted, options for 4,299 shares were canceled or expired and options for 30,906 shares were exercised at prices ranging from $37 to $63 per share, an aggregate of $1,685,000. At December 31, 1967, options for 220,409 shares at prices ranging from $37 to $74 per share, an aggregate of $14,011,000 were outstanding. At that same date options for 66,844 shares were exercisable and 11,575 shares were available for the granting of future options, generally not to become exercisable until at least two years after date of grant, at prices not less than market value of the Company's common stock on the date of grant.

At December 31, 1967, 1,777,648 shares of common stock were reserved for issuance including 1,449,596 shares upon conversion of preferred stock; 231,984 shares in connection with stock options; and 96,068 shares upon conversion of outstanding 5% convertible debentures.

Capital surplus was increased during 1967 by $1,531,000 resulting from the exercise of stock options and by $133,521,000 representing the excess of the net proceeds from sale over par value of 2,522,713 shares of common stock and was decreased by $324,000 resulting from the issuance of preferred stock by a majority-owned subsidiary and by $7,000 from the conversion of preferred stock.

Note 7: Income and other taxes include the following:

	1967	1966
U. S. federal and state gasoline and oil excise taxes (recovery thereof included in revenues from sales and services)	$150,232,000	$145,443,000
Income taxes:		
U. S.—federal*	30,031,000	24,670,000
U. S.—state	1,118,000	1,130,000
Foreign	61,251,000	63,200,000
	92,400,000	89,000,000

Operating taxes:		
Import duties and excise taxes— foreign	142,749,000	105,127,000
Ad valorem taxes	18,521,000	16,681,000
Production taxes	9,851,000	8,644,000
Unemployment and old age benefits taxes	9,536,000	6,231,000
Other taxes	6,871,000	5,382,000
	187,528,000	142,065,000
	$430,160,000	$376,508,000

Reduced by $818,000 in 1967 and $6,722,000 in 1966 as a result of the allowable investment tax credit and includes deferred income tax provisions of $19,596,000 in 1967 and $11,451,000 in 1966 due principally to the use of accelerated depreciation for income tax purposes but not for book purposes and the capitalization of mining costs. (See Note 3).

Note 8: The Company and certain of its subsidiaries have in effect retirement plans substantially all of which provide for contributions by the employees and the companies. Total pension expense for the year, representing the companies' contributions under the plans, was $5,843,000, of which $581,000 was with respect to prior service costs.

Note 9: The Company and certain of its subsidiaries have long-term leases on certain service stations, office buildings, ocean-going tankers, and other facilities. The aggregate rentals thereon approximated $22,600,000 in 1967 and will approximate $25,500,000 annually to 1972, then $20,600,000 annually to 1977, and in diminishing annual amounts thereafter.

The Company and one of its subsidiaries, under agreements relating to certain companies in which they have substantial stock investments, have guaranteed, directly or indirectly, payments of $32,200,000 of loans to such companies. The Company and a subsidiary are also obligated to other companies, in which they have substantial stock investments, to provide specified minimum revenues from product shipments or purchases. No significant loss is anticipated by reason of such agreements.

Note 10: Extraordinary items consist of gains from sale of coal reserves, net of $9,186,000 income taxes, in 1967 and liquidation of Great Lakes Pipe Line Company, net of $13,736,000 income taxes, in 1966 previously excluded from net income and reported as a special credit.

Report of Certified Public Accountants

ARTHUR YOUNG & COMPANY
1500 First National Building, Tulsa

The Board of Directors and Stockholders,
Continental Oil Company:

We have examined the accompanying consolidated balance sheet of Continental Oil Company and subsidiaries at December 31, 1967 and the related statement of consolidated income and retained earnings for the year then ended. Our examination was made in accordance with generally accepted auditing standards, and accordingly included such tests of the accounting records and such other auditing procedures as we considered necessary in the circumstances. We have received the reports of other public accountants with respect to their examinations of the financial statements of certain subsidiaries.

In our opinion, based upon our examination and the reports of other public accountants referred to above, the statements mentioned above present fairly the consolidated financial position of Continental Oil Company and subsidiaries at December 31, 1967 and the consolidated results of their operations for the year then ended, in conformity with generally accepted accounting principles applied on a basis consistent with that of the preceding year, after restatement to include the extraordinary item in net income for 1966, as explained in Note 10.

February 14, 1968

Arthur Young & Company

Sweet Deal Number 847

Jones owns an apartment building with a net book value of $50,000.

He will sell it for $100,000. The building grosses $17,000 per year in rentals and nets about $8,000 per year.

Smith wants to buy the building, but he has only $30,000 in cash.

Jones says that's O.K., because he will get his additional $70,000 by selling Brown an agreement entitling Brown to receive 38.8 percent of the gross rentals each year for 20 years ($6,600 per year for 20 years yields Brown 7 percent on his $70,000 investment). Then, each year Smith can just net what he pays to Brown against his gross rentals.

Smith agrees to the deal. His new balance sheet shows:

Building $30,000	Net worth $30,000

His P & L for the first year shows:

Rentals	$10,400
Expenses	9,000
Net	$ 1,400

This note was prepared by Assistant Professor John K. Shank as the basis for class discussion rather than to illustrate either effective or ineffective handling of an administrative situation.

Smith is very happy with the deal: (1) The building is not mortgaged so he can use it as collateral in other deals; (2) he can, in effect, recover the $70,000 of the purchase price which Brown provided over 20 years instead of over 40, which is the life of the building; (3) the building carries a book value of only $30,000, which should be very helpful in dealing with the tax assessors.

QUESTIONS

1. Do you concur with Smith's interpretation of the impact of the sale of his apartment building on his personal financial statement?
2. Recast all relevant financial statements as you think are appropriate to reflect fairly the effects of this transaction.

Esops
Stables

On December 16, 1976, David Lewis, President and Chief Executive Officer of Esops Stables, asked his newly hired assistant for a memo evaluating his plan to acquire Catfish Corp. via the formation of an Employee Stock Ownership Plan (ESOP). Although Ms. Robinson, a recent graduate of the Harvard Business School, knew nothing about ESOP's, she was certain her studies of corporate financial reporting and finance would serve her well.

BACKGROUND

Esops Stables is a small publicly held corporation with two lines of business: growing timber on the 100,000 acres of Alabama forest controlled by the company and raising thoroughbred race horses. Although the timber division has recently been very successful, the race horse division has proved a drag on corporate profits. In fact, the stables were currently occupied by only one horse, an Arabian of Spanish ancestry named Ali-Baba-Lu. Lu, as he is affectionately known to the Board of Directors, is not responsible for eating into the division's profits. Not only does he eat very little, but for accounting purposes Lu has long since been fully ridden off. The problem stemmed from the high overhead costs and from the fact that the division was saddled with debt.

Accordingly, Mr. Lewis thought it was time to put the division out to pasture and get into a new line of business. He had evaluated a series of proposed acquisitions, the most interesting being a proposal to market eyeglasses for

This case was prepared by Dennis P. Frolin as a basis for class discussion rather than to illustrate either effective or ineffective handling of an administrative situation.

182

chickens. Mr. Lewis viewed this as an exciting, unexploited market for two reasons. First, one of the hottest fashion trends to recently hit the United States focuses on wearing eyeglasses not for corrective but cosmetic purposes. Although this fashion trend was presently seen in only a small part of the country (namely, New York's upper East Side), Mr. Lewis was sure the idea would eventually catch on. Second, the only competition in the field, a company that marketed red contact lenses for chickens, was in the midst of a serious internal struggle (should chickens wear hard or soft lenses?). Thus it seemed like an ideal time to grab a share of the market.

In the end, however, Mr. Lewis rejected this acquisition after talking with a veterinarian who advised: "Roosters don't make passes at chicks who wear glasses."

Finally, Mr. Lewis settled on a plan to raise catfish in controlled bodies of water and to market them for consumption across the United States.

THE PLAN

The plan to acquire Catfish Corp. would consist of seven steps:

1. Esops Stables would form an ESOP for the benefit of the company's employees.
2. Esops Stables would sell, on credit, to the ESOP $1 million of Esops Stables common stock.
3. The ESOP would borrow $1 million from a local bank, pledging the common stock as collateral. This debt would also be guaranteed by Esops Stables.
4. The ESOP would use the $1 million to purchase the Catfish Corp.
5. The ESOP would sell the Catfish Corp. to Esops Stables for $1 million. This would satisfy the debt owed by the ESOP to Esops Stables for the $1 million of common stock purchased on credit.
6. Esops Stables would agree to contribute $150,000 per year for ten years to the ESOP. Esops Stables would treat the annual contribution for both accounting and tax purposes as employee compensation expense.
7. The ESOP will repay the bank $150,000 per year for 10 years to service the bank debt.[1]

Mr. Lewis was enthusiastic about this plan for four reasons. First, it expanded the equity base of the company by issuing common shares. Second, the ESOP would eliminate, perhaps totally, the pressure to create an employee pension plan, which the company currently did not have. Third, it would spare the company from adding $1 million to its already highly leveraged financial

---

[1] Repaying $150,000 per year for 10 years on a $1 million loan results in an effective interest rate of 8.14 percent.

structure. And fourth, it would provide an additional 1 percent investment tax credit as a result of recently adopted tax regulations.

GOVERNMENT SPONSORSHIP OF ESOPS

An employee stock ownership plan is a retirement plan funded with employer's stock. The stock technically goes into a trust—an ESOT—which administers accounts for each employee. ESOPs have been treated favorably in recent legislation because members of Congress have become convinced of the advantages to employers and employees of this type of benefit plan. Senator Russell B. Long, Chairman of the Senate Finance Committee and an enthusiastic supporter of ESOPs, recently said "They will act like a tonic for capitalism."

Examples of this Congressional support include ERISA (The Employee Retirement Income Security Act, also known as the Pension Reform Act) which singles out the ESOP as the only employee benefit plan that can be used for corporate borrowings. (Other employee benefit plans include, for example, profit sharing, stock bonus plans, and defined benefit pension plans.) The Trade Act of 1974 provides for guarantees by the U.S. Commerce Department of up to 25 percent of loans by banks and other lenders to leveraged ESOPs. And finally, the Tax Reduction Act of 1976 allows a 1 percent investment tax credit for investing in a qualified ESOP.

ACCOUNTING FOR ESOPS

In a letter to the FASB dated March 12, 1976, the AICPA accounting standards division has urged the FASB to deal with accounting for ESOPs as an emerging practice problem and to focus on "leveraged" ESOPs in which funds for acquiring the employer's stock are borrowed from a bank. The principal recommendations of this letter include:

1. An ESOP obligation guaranteed by an employer should be recorded (credit) as a liability (debt) on the employer's balance sheet. The offsetting debit should be a reduction of shareholders' equity. The reduction in shareholders' equity should be titled "shares held in trust for ESOP" and would be similar to the contra account called "treasury stock."
2. The employer's liability should be decreased and the shareholders' equity increased when payments are made from the employer to the ESOP. (The ESOP then remits the payment to the bank to service the debt.)
3. In addition, the employer should record the cash payment to the ESOP as employee compensation expense.

4. All shares held by the ESOP should be treated as outstanding shares in the determination of earnings per share.
5. Dividends paid on shares held by an ESOP should be deducted from retained earnings, not included as compensation expense. That is, they should be treated the same as all other dividends.

Exhibit 1 illustrates the accounting journal entries for the acquisition as proposed by Mr. Lewis and by the AICPA as they would be recorded on Esops Stables' financial statements.

Exhibit 1. Accounting Journal Entries

EVENT	MR. LEWIS		AICPA	
Create ESOP	+ Receivables	$1 Million	+ Receivables	$1 million
	+ Capital stock	$1 Million	+ Capital stock	$1 million
Acquire Catfish Corp.	− Receivables	$1 Million	− Receivables	$1 million
	+ Investment in Catfish Corp.	$1 Million	+ Investment in Catfish Corp.	$1 million
Record ESOP loan	No Entry		+ Bank loans	$1 million
			+ Shares held in trust for ESOP (contra account to shareholders' equity)	$1 million
Annual contribution to ESOP	− Cash	$150,000	(a) − Cash	$150,000
	+ Employee compensation expense	$150,000	+ Employee compensation expense	$150,000
			(b) − Bank loans	$150,000
			− Shares held in trust for ESOP	$150,000

Allen
Corporation

ACCOUNTING FOR A NEW PENSION PLAN

On January 1, 1973, the Allen Corporation discontinued its informal pension arrangement for hourly rated employees and adopted a formal plan of retirement under which the actuarially determined costs of past and current services was to be funded through a qualified pension trust. Management considered a formal plan necessary to maintain good employee relations (there was no union) and to obtain the advantages which a funded pension plan offered in comparison with the predecessor "pay-as-you-go" plan.

Previously, the company charged income with the cost of the annual pension benefits paid to retired employees. Retired employees received $235,000 in 1972 and will receive the same amount in 1973 and 1974; pension benefits are paid on December 31. The present value of the past service cost for the 435 retired employees was actuarially estimated to be $1,934,000 as of January 1, 1973, and will be funded immediately upon adoption of the formal plan. In addition, the present value of the past service cost for the 3,500 present employees was actuarially estimated at $4,614,000 as of January 1, 1973, and will be funded in 12 equal annual installments of $472,723[1] beginning January 1,

---

This case was prepared by David F. Hawkins, Professor of Business Administration, as a basis for class discussion rather than to illustrate either effective or ineffective handling of an administrative situation.

Copyright © 1976 by the President and Fellows of Harvard College. Distributed by the Intercollegiate Case Clearing House, Soldiers Field, Boston, Mass. 02163. All rights reserved to the contributors. Printed in the U.S.A.

[1] Given the fact that the implied obligation for past service cost increases periodically due to the interest factor, an amount greater than $1/_{12}$ would have to be funded each year in order to fully fund the entire $4,614,000 past service cost of present employees over a 12-year period. Assuming a 4 percent interest factor, the company would fund $4,614,000/ 9.7604767 or $472,723 each January 1 for 12 years, where 9.7604767 is the present value of an annuity in arrears for 12 periods at 4 percent.

1968. Current (normal) service cost for the 3,500 present employees was actuarially estimated at $220,000 annually as of January 1 of each year and will be funded on January 1 as incurred. A 4 percent discount rate was assumed throughout and all interest equivalents are computed as of January 1 of the appropriate year.

Selected financial data for XYZ Corporation follow:

Total assets	$47,098,000
Total liabilities	5,480,000
Capital stock	14,120,000
Retained earnings	27,498,000
Sales	57,199,000
Net income	2,009,000

Management proposed the following financial reporting for the formal pension plan:

1. Charge retained earnings with the present value of the past service cost for the 435 retired employees, net of taxes, since it related to wages of prior periods.
2. Amortize past service cost for present employees over a 25-year period, which is the estimated average remaining service life of these employees.
3. Charge income with current (normal) cost.

The $6,548,000 past service cost of retired and present employees was to be deducted for Federal income tax purposes at 10 percent per year until fully amortized. A flat 40 percent tax rate was assumed throughout.

QUESTIONS

1. Is the proposed accounting acceptable? Why?
2. Compute the defined minimum, the defined maximum, and any tax effects related to each for 1973 and 1974.
3. What information should be included in the balance sheet of Allen Corporation as of December 31, 1973; December 31, 1974?
4. Five years after the adoption of the plan, an actuary makes a new study of the assumptions on which the estimated pension costs are based. The study indicates that, due to higher than anticipated interest rates on investments and favorable mortality experience, the pension fund balance at the end of five years exceeds the balance originally expected at the end of this period. Since the company's earnings for that year are poor and its cash position is low, management decides that no contribution is to be made into the pension fund. What is the impact of this funding policy change on the company's financial statements for this year?

Measurex Corporation

Measurex Corporation designs, manufactures, and markets digital computer process control systems for producers of sheet products, primarily paper manufacturers. Measurex's equipment is designed to increase the efficiency of the production process by monitoring the physical characteristics of the material flow using a combination of radiation, infrared and optical sensors linked to a digital computer, and appropriate output devices. While Measurex's systems are most widely used in papermaking, applications exist in the tile, rubber, plastics, and metal industries.

Measurex markets its system on short- or long-term leases as well as on a sale basis. Each Measurex system sells for between $200,000 and $500,000, with an average of $275,000 to $300,000. The firm also offers short-term (12 to 42 months) and long-term (66 to 102 months) leases. Long-term leases allow the lessee to renew at the expiration of the lease term with an accompanying reduction in the monthly rental to 25 percent of the original charge; a separate charge is made for service. Lessees also retain the right to evaluate the system for the initial six months of the lease and to return the device for a refund within that period.

Incorporated in California in early 1968, Measurex has shown significant growth in revenues, profits, and assets during its corporate history (Exhibit 1). Customers have shown a clear preference for long-term leases; as of January 1972 only one user had chosen to purchase the equipment. At the same time, orders for new systems have grown from 27 in fiscal year 1971 to 46 orders in

This case was prepared by Steven E. Levy, Research Assistant, under the supervision of Associate Professor John K. Shank as the basis for class discussion rather than to illustrate either the effective or ineffective handling of an administrative situation.

Exhibit 1. *Summary of Financial Highlights*

Highlights

For the Current Year	1972	Percent Increase from 1971
Operating revenues	$16,336,000	90%
Income before extraordinary credit:		
Amount	1,727,000	67%
Per share	.71	37%
Average number of common shares	2,429,000	22%

(Dollar amounts in thousands except per-share income)	1972	1971	1970	1969	1968[1]
Operating Summary for all Years					
Operating revenues	$16,336	$ 8,613	$3,527	$ 302	
Income (loss) before taxes and extraordinary credit[2]	2,887	1,974	(25)	(781)	$ (334)
Income (loss) before extraordinary credit[2]	1,727	1,034	(25)	(781)	(334)
Extraordinary credit[2]		545			
Net income (loss)	$ 1,727	$ 1,579	$ (25)	$ (781)	$ (334)
Net income (loss) per common and common equivalent share:					
Income before extraordinary credit[2]	$ .71	$ .52	$ (.02)	$ (.72)	$ (1.16)
Extraordinary credit[2]		.27			
Net income (loss)	$ .71	$ .79	$ (.02)	$ (.72)	$ (1.16)

Financial Position at Year-End (November 30)

	1972	1971	1970	1969	1968[1]
Working capital	$ 8,021	$ 5,219	$ 764	$ 665	$ 362
Total assets	34,657	18,296	8,222	2,765	750
Capitalization:					
Long-term debt	10,386	9,033	1,649	835	62
Shareholders' equity	20,099	7,155	5,464	1,496	530

[1] From inception on January 18, 1968, to November 30, 1968.
[2] Extraordinary credit arises from reduction of provision for federal income taxes through utilization of net operating loss carry-forward.

Exhibit 1. *(continued)*

Measurex Corporation and Subsidiary Companies

Consolidated Statements of Income
for the years ended November 30, 1972 and 1971

Operating Revenues	1972	1971
Sales	$15,201,000	$8,041,000
Rental and service income	1,135,000	572,000
	16,336,000	8,613,000
Cost of sales, rentals and services	7,058,000	3,073,000
Gross profit	9,278,000	5,540,000
Selling, general and administrative expenses	6,414,000	3,458,000
	2,864,000	2,082,000
Interest income	607,000	275,000
Interest expense	(584,000)	(383,000)
	23,000	(108,000)
Income before taxes on income and extraordinary credit	2,887,000	1,974,000
Taxes on income	1,160,000	940,000
Income before extraordinary credit	1,727,000	1,034,000
Extraordinary credit—reduction of provision for federal income taxes through utilization of net operating loss carry-forward	—	545,000
Net income	$ 1,727,000	$1,579,000
Net income per common and common equivalent share:		
Income before extraordinary credit	$ .71	$ .52
Extraordinary credit	—	.27
Net income	$ .71	$ .79

See accompanying notes.

Exhibit 1. *(continued)*

Measurex Corporation and Subsidiary Companies

Consolidated Statements of Changes in Financial Position
for the years ended November 30, 1972 and 1971

Resources Provided	1972	1971
Issuances of common stock for cash	$11,210,000	$ 42,000
Issuance (cancellation) of warrants	(42,000)	70,000
Additions to long-term debt	13,160,000	10,329,000
Reduction in non-current portion of lease contracts receivable	2,417,000	4,178,000
	$26,745,000	$14,619,000

Resources Applied		
To operations:		
Net income	$(1,727,000)	$(1,579,000)
Non-working capital items entering into the determination of net income:		
Depreciation and amortization	(707,000)	(524,000)
Non-current portion of deferred taxes on income	(874,000)	(355,000)
Net book amount of systems (including installation costs) on leases converted from short-term to long-term	(741,000)	(573,000)
Additions to non-current portion of lease contracts receivable related to sales which did not create working capital	13,649,000	7,109,000
Working capital applied to operations	9,600,000	4,078,000
Payments and current portion of long-term debt	11,807,000	2,944,000
Additions to systems leased to others under short-term leases (including installation costs)	317,000	845,000
Additions to fixed assets	1,373,000	651,000
Additions to investment in new product development	915,000	631,000
Additions to residual value of systems leased to others	—	551,000
Other	(69,000)	464,000
Increase in working capital	2,802,000	4,455,000
	$26,745,000	$14,619,000

Changes in Components of Working Capital:		
Current assets—increase (decrease) in:		
Cash	$ 721,000	$ 843,000
Current portion of lease contracts receivable	1,726,000	683,000
Accounts receivable	(606,000)	1,959,000
Inventories	2,256,000	1,537,000
Prepaid expenses	(105,000)	77,000
Increase in current assets	3,992,000	5,099,000
Current liabilities—increase (decrease) in:		
Long-term debt due within one year	63,000	(66,000)
Trade accounts payable	262,000	243,000
Accrued expenses	755,000	427,000
Deferred taxes on income	110,000	40,000
Increase in current liabilities	1,190,000	644,000
Increase in working capital	$ 2,802,000	$ 4,455,000

See accompanying notes.

Exhibit 1. *(continued)*

Measurex Corporation and Subsidiary Companies

Consolidated Balance Sheet
November 30, 1972 and 1971

Assets	1972	1971
Current assets:		
Cash	$ 1,871,000	$ 1,150,000
Current portion of lease contracts receivable	2,619.000	893,000
Accounts receivable	1,457,000	2,063,000
Inventories	4,991,000	2,735,000
Prepaid expenses	26,000	131,000
Total current assets	10,964,000	6,972,000
Lease contracts receivable less current portion and valuation provision	17,222,000	5,989,000
Systems leased to others under short-term leases (including installation costs), at cost less accumulated depreciation and amortization of $261,000 (1972) and $174,000 (1971)	1,066,000	1,691,000
Residual value of systems leased to others under long-term leases	691,000	691,000
Fixed assets, at cost less allowance for depreciation	2,631,000	1,466,000
Investment in new product development less accumulated amortization of $814,000 (1972) and $451,000 (1971)	1,491,000	962,000
Other	592,000	525,000
	$34,657,000	$18,296,000

See accompanying notes.

Exhibit 1. *(continued)*

Liabilities	1972	1971
Current liabilities:		
Long-term debt due within one year	$ **210,000**	$ 147,000
Trade accounts payable	**955,000**	693,000
Accrued expenses:		
Payroll and payroll related items	**989,000**	466,000
Initial and continuing services	**421,000**	212,000
Other	**218,000**	195,000
Deferred taxes on income	**150,000**	40,000
Total current liabilities	**2,943,000**	1,753,000
Long-term debt less amount due within one year	**10,386,000**	9,033,000
Deferred taxes on income	**1,229,000**	355,000
	14,558,000	11,141,000
Contingent liabilities		
Shareholders' Equity		
Preferred stock, $1 par value: Authorized: 1,000,000 shares; issued and outstanding: none		
Common stock, without par value: Authorized: 5,000,000 shares; issued and outstanding: 2,597,284 shares (1972) and 1,927,406 (1971)	**68,000**	34,000
Additional paid-in capital	**17,865,000**	6,682,000
Retained earnings	**2,166,000**	439,000
	20,099,000	7,155,000
	$34,657,000	$18,296,000

Exhibit 1. (continued)

Measurex Corporation and Subsidiary Companies

Consolidated Statements of Shareholders' Equity
for the years ended November 30, 1972 and 1971

	Common Stock		Additional Paid-In Capital	Retained Earnings	Total
	Shares	Amount			
Balance, December 1, 1970	1,901,011	$33,000	$ 6,571,000	$(1,140,000)	$ 5,464,000
Issuance of warrants to purchase 72,000 shares of common stock			70,000		70,000
Other issuances (including 24,245 shares upon exercise of employee stock options)	26,395	1,000	41,000		42,000
Net income for the year ended November 30, 1971				1,579,000	1,579,000
Balance, November 30, 1971	1,927,406	34,000	6,682,000	439,000	7,155,000
Public offering of common stock less related expenses of $1,114,000	600,000	30,000	10,829,000		10,859,000
Cancellation of warrant to purchase 42,000 shares of common stock			(42,000)		(42,000)
Other issuances (including 65,878 shares upon exercise of employee stock options)	69,878	4,000	396,000		400,000
Net income for the year ended November 30, 1972				1,727,000	1,727,000
Balance, November 30, 1972	2,597,284	$68,000	$17,865,000	$ 2 166,000	$20,099,000

See accompanying notes.

Exhibit 1. *(continued)*

Measurex Corporation and Subsidiary Companies
Notes to Consolidated Financial Statements

1. Summary of Significant Accounting Policies

Basis of Consolidation:
The accompanying consolidated financial statements include the accounts of the Company and its subsidiaries all of which are wholly owned excepting directors' qualifying shares. All significant intercompany items have been eliminated.

Lease Accounting:
Measurex offers its customers both short-term and long-term leases. Generally, short-term leases have terms from 12 to 42 months and long-term leases have terms from 66 to 102 months.

Substantially all the amounts shown as "Sales" are represented by long-term leases accounted for on the financing method. Such method recognizes as revenue at the time of shipment of a system an amount equal to the lesser of (a) the discounted amount of future committed lease payments discounted at a rate which the Company believes approximates the customer's borrowing rate or (b) the cash purchase price of the system. The excess of the aggregate committed lease payments over the discounted amount of such payments is recognized as interest income on the sum-of-the-digits method over the term of the lease.

In years prior to 1972 it was the Company's practice to record residual value on financing leases; had this practice been continued in 1972 net income would have been increased by approximately $336,000, or $.15 per share. (In fiscal year 1972 the American Institute of Certified Public Accountants published an Accounting Interpretation recommending that in accounting for financing leases residual value not be recorded; the Company has conformed to this recommendation.)

Short-term leases are accounted for on the operating method whereby the aggregate rentals are reported as revenue on a straight-line basis over the term of the leases. Under the operating method the statement of income reflects, as expenses, depreciation of the leased property and amortization of the installation costs.

Since its inception it has been the Company's practice to grant its customers an initial period, generally six months following installation, in which to evaluate the system. During the initial period the customer may return the system and require the refund of all rentals theretofore paid. Although no systems have been returned through November 30 ,1972, provisions have been made which management believes to be sufficient to provide for losses which may result from returns.

See Note 2.

Inventory Valuation:
Purchased parts and components are stated at the lower of average cost or market. Finished sub-assemblies and systems and work in process are stated at the lower of standard cost (which approximates actual cost) or market.

See Note 3.

Properties:
The Company provides for depreciation and amortization by charges to expense which are sufficient to write off the costs of the assets over their estimated useful lives, on a straight-line basis.

The basis for computing depreciation and amortization is as follows:

Class of Property	Estimated Useful Lives
Systems leased to others under short-term leases	9 Years
Installation costs on systems leased to others under short-term leases	4 Years
Buildings	25-40 Years
Machinery and equipment	2-10 Years

Investment in New Product Development:
The Company is capitalizing new product development costs which are identifiable to significant new systems or products having a potential commercial value; those costs not meeting these criteria are charged to selling, general and administrative expense currently. The capitalized costs are being amortized to expense over the anticipated useful life of the system or product, or three years from the beginning of routine production, whichever is shorter. Costs applicable to projects abandoned are written off in the year of abandonment.

See Note 5.

Taxes on Income:
Deferred taxes are provided on all significant differences between taxable income and pre-tax income as shown in the accompanying consolidated statements of income except taxes are not provided on the income of the Company's Domestic International Sales Corporation subsidiary inasmuch as management believes that the payment of taxes on such income can be deferred indefinitely by investing and distributing such income as the DISC regulations allow.

Investment tax credit on fixed assets is recognized on the flow-through method. Generally, it is the Company's policy to allow the end-user of the leased Measurex system to claim the related investment tax credit; unclaimed investment tax credit is recognized by the Company either as additional sales or as financing income over the term of the lease.

Exhibit 1. *(continued)*

Notes to Consolidated Financial Statements, continued

Deferred taxes arise principally as a result of the following differences between taxable income and pre-tax income as shown in the accompanying consolidated statements of income:

(a) new product development costs which have been deferred in the accompanying financial statements are expensed for tax purposes,

(b) long-term leases, which are reported under the financing method for financial statement purposes, are reported under either the installment method or the operating method for tax purposes, and

(c) losses upon non-collection and system return are deducted for tax purposes as the losses are incurred.

See Note 8.

Net Income per Common and Common Equivalent Share:
Net income per common and common equivalent share has been computed based upon the average number of common shares outstanding during the year assuming the exercise of employee stock options and stock warrants to the extent that such options and warrants were dilutive. In this computation, the proceeds from the assumed exercise of the options and warrants are assumed to have been used to purchase shares of common stock at the average market price for the period such options and warrants were outstanding. The number of shares used in the computation was 2,429,000 in 1972 and 1,994,000 in 1971.

2. Lease Contracts Receivable

Lease contracts receivable are summarized below:

	1972	1971
Aggregate lease payments to be received under long-term leases accounted for under the financing method	$25,939,000	$9,079,000
Less unearned financing income	4,449,000	1,774,000
	21,490,000	7,305,000
Less amount due within one year	2,619,000	893,000
	18,871,000	6,412,000
Less reserve for non-collection and system returns	1,649,000	423,000
	$17,222,000	$5,989,000

For a more complete description of lease transactions, see Note 1—"Lease Accounting."

The aggregate amount of principal payments due in years subsequent to 1972 are set forth below:

1973	$ 2,619,000
1974	3,048,000
1975	3,201,000
1976	3,343,000
1977	3,277,000
Thereafter	6,002,000
	$21,490,000

With respect to certain leases which have been or will be accounted for under the financing method, the Company has arranged financing with Manufacturers Hanover Trust Company ("Manufacturers") in amounts not to exceed $7,456,000 through November 30, 1973. Pursuant to such arrangement, the Company sells to Manufacturers such lease contracts receivable and related equipment on a full recourse basis and participates with Manufacturers in revenues received from the customers pursuant to purchase or lease renewal options. The effective interst rate of this arrangement varies between 8¾% and 10%. As of November 30, 1972 the Company had received $3,456,000 from Manufacturers pursuant to this agreement and was contingently liable to Manufacturers for approximately $2,990,000 of such amount.

3. Inventories

Inventories are as follows:

	1972	1971
Purchased parts and components	$3,077,000	$1,232,000
Finished sub-assemblies and systems	1,064,000	1,085,000
Work in process	850,000	418,000
	$4,991,000	$2,735,000

See Note 1—"Inventory Valuation."

4. Fixed Assets

Details of fixed assets less allowance for depreciation are set forth below:

	1972	1971
Buildings (under construction in 1971)	$1,127,000	$ 350,000
Machinery and equipment	1,025,000	537,000
Leasehold improvements	—	9,000
	2,152,000	896,000
Less allowance for depreciation (see Note 1—"Properties")	293,000	164,000
	1,859,000	732,000
Land	772,000	734,000
	$2,631,000	$1,466,000

Exhibit 1. *(continued)*

5. New Product Development

Total new product development expenditures:

	1972	1971
Capitalized (before amortization)	$ 915,000	$ 631,000
Charged to operating expenses currently	953,000	634,000
	$1,868,000	$1,265,000
Amortization of capitalized costs	$ 363,000	$ 273,000

See Note 1—"Investment in New Product Development."

6. Long-Term Debt

Details of long-term debt are presented below:

	1972	1971
Credit agreement with banks	$ 8,935,000	$7,110,000
4% mortgage payable in annual installments of $83,000	249,000	332,000
8¾% mortgage payable in monthly installments from 1973 to 1998	1,050,000	380,000
Capitalized lease obligations on equipment used by Measurex (8¾% interest rate)	362,000	158,000
2% above prime subordinated note	—	1,200,000
	10,596,000	9,180,000
Less amount due within one year	210,000	147,000
	$10,386,000	$9,033,000

The credit agreement with Bank of America and Manufacturers Hanover Trust Company allows the Company to borrow up to $20,000,000 through November 30, 1973. The funds borrowed as of November 30, 1973 are repayable in 66 monthly installments beginning in December 1973. The monthly installments are determined by a formula related to the Company's rental receipts, but in no case will the installments be less than 1/66th of the November 30, 1973 borrowed funds.

Borrowings under the credit agreement bear interest at ½% above the prime interest rate to November 30, 1973 and thereafter at 1% above prime. In addition, the Company is required to maintain compensating balances with the bank equal to the greater of 20% of the borrowed funds or $1,000,000; such compensating balance requirements at November 30, 1972 raise the Company's cost of borrowed funds under this agreement to approximately 7½% per annum.

The credit agreement prohibits payment of cash dividends and requires the Company to keep working capital and indebtedness within specified levels. As collateral for the credit agreement, the banks may require the Company to assign its rights to future rentals on certain systems leased to end users. As of January 23, 1973, the banks had not requested any collateral.

As of January 23, 1973, borrowings under the credit agreement have increased to $11,565,000.

The aggregate amount of principal payments of long-term debt required to be paid for each of the five years following fiscal year 1972 is set forth below:

1973	$ 210,000
1974	1,817,000
1975	1,802,000
1976	1,693,000
1977	1,661,000
Thereafter	3,413,000
	$10,596,000

Subsequent to November 30, 1972, the Company arranged for a $7 million Eurocurrency borrowing.

7. Profit-Sharing Plans

The Company presently has an employee cash profit-sharing plan whereby up to 10% of the consolidated pre-tax income may be contributed to the plan. The plan is subject to annual renewal and has been renewed for 1973. The Company's contributions under the plan are set forth below:

	Percent of Pre-Tax Income	Amount
Year ended November 30, 1972	7.9%	$248,000
Year ended November 30, 1971	8.2%	178,000

The Company also has an annually renewable bonus plan whereby the Company's president is paid 1% of pre-tax (and pre-profit-sharing) income.

8. Taxes on Income

The components of taxes on income are as follows:

	1972	1971
Provision for federal income taxes which would be required in the absence of the availability of the net operating loss carry-forward		$545,000
Deferred taxes	$1,283,000	475,000
Investment tax credit (recognized under the flow-through method)	(123,000)	(80,000)
	$1,160,000	$940,000

As of November 30, 1972 the Company had a net operating loss carry-forward for federal income tax purposes of approximately $9,000,000 of which amount approximately $500,000 will expire in 1973, $700,000 in 1974, $1,500,000 in 1975, $400,000 in 1976 and $5,900,000 in 1977, if not theretofore used to reduce taxable income. If the net operating loss carry-forward is utilized, it will not affect financial statement income in the year of utilization but will reduce federal income taxes otherwise payable.

Exhibit 1. *(continued)*

Notes to Consolidated Financial Statements, continued

In 1972 the Company formed a Domestic International Sales Corporation ("DISC"). Through the proper utilization of a DISC, federal income taxes on transactions with foreign customers may be indefinitely deferred. The 1972 statement of income includes $430,000 of DISC-related income for which no federal income tax provision has been made inasmuch as management believes they will be able to defer the payment of such tax indefinitely.

See Note 1—"Taxes on Income."

9. Qualified Stock Option Plans

Under the Company's qualified stock option plans, 405,000 shares of common stock have been reserved for granting of options to officers and key employees of which 150,000 shares are subject to shareholder approval. Options may be granted at prices not less than 100% of the fair market value of the stock at the date of grant and become exercisable either ⅓ each year commencing two years from the date of grant or ¼ each year commencing one year from the date of grant. Options expire if not exercised within five years from the date of grant. Information concerning options granted under the plans is set forth below:

	Shares Available for Grant	Options Outstanding		
		Shares	Price per Share	Total
Balance, December 1, 1971	30,802	179,124	$.33-$15	$1,670,000
Additional shares reserved for grant	150,000			
Options granted	(58,750)	58,750	$17-$32	1,424,000
Options terminated	9,852	(9,852)	$10-$32	(147,000)
Options exercised		(65,878)	$.33-$15	(331,000)
Balance, November 30, 1972	131,904	162,144	$.33-$32	$2,616,000
Options exercisable at November 30, 1972		30,286	$.33-$15	$ 280,000

10. Warrants

At November 30, 1972, the Company has the following warrants to purchase common stock outstanding:

Shares	Price per Share	Expiration Date
12,000	$15.00	December 29, 1975
18,000	$13.33	May 30, 1977

Auditors' Report

To the Board of Directors
Measurex Corporation

We have examined the consolidated balance sheet of Measurex Corporation and Subsidiary Companies as of November 30, 1972, and the related consolidated statements of income, shareholders' equity and changes in financial position for the year then ended. Our examination was made in accordance with generally accepted auditing standards and accordingly included such tests of the accounting records and such other auditing procedures as we considered necessary in the circumstances. We previously examined and reported upon the consolidated financial statements of Measurex Corporation and Subsidiary Companies for the year ended November 30, 1971.

In our opinion, the above-mentioned financial statements present fairly the consolidated financial position of Measurex Corporation and Subsidiary Companies at November 30, 1972 and 1971, and the consolidated results of their operations and changes in financial position for the years then ended, in conformity with generally accepted accounting principles applied on a consistent basis, except for the change, with which we concur, in accounting for residual value on finance leases as described in Note 1 of Notes to Consolidated Financial Statements.

Lybrand, Ross Bros. + Montgomery

Lybrand, Ross Bros. & Montgomery
Palo Alto, California

January 23, 1973

1972 and 50 in the first half of 1973. A significant number of users have been repeat customers. Measurex has financed the growth in outstanding leases by maintaining lines of credit with domestic banks and through Eurocurrency borrowings. In addition, the firm has spent large sums on research and development throughout its history; in January 1972 it held four domestic patents and had applied for nine domestic and 34 foreign patents.

Measurex made a public offering of common stock in March 1972. Issued at $20, the shares quickly rose to $40 and were quoted, in November 1973, in the mid-$20's. Measurex's stock attracted a substantial following among institutional investors and brokerage houses, having been selected "No. 1 Baby Blue Chip" in a poll of Western security analysts. Analysts predicted earnings per share of $.85 to $.90 in fiscal year 1973 and $1.20 in 1974. At the same time, a number of individuals and publications called attention to alleged flaws in several aspects of Measurex's accounting practices. Yet, as 1973 drew to a close, corporate officials strongly defended the firm's policies and institutional analysts continued to recommend the purchase of Measurex shares.

QUESTIONS

1. What rate of discount is Measurex using to compute the present value of its "lease contracts receivable"? (Hint: What is the present value of the payment streams discounted at 4 percent? at 6 percent?)[1]
2. What number would Measurex report for "sales" revenue in 1972 if the lease payments were discounted for 10 percent?
3. What is the impact of the discount rate on the reported earnings of Measurex? How do you think that discount rate should be determined?
4. Evaluate Measurex's inventory, tax, depreciation, and R & D accounting policies in terms of the firm's general reporting strategy.
5. What is the relationship between Measurex's accounting practices and its overall corporate strategy?

---

[1] In considering Question 1, you may assume that the timing of receipt of the aggregate cash flows from the long-term lease contracts receivable is as follows:

	1972	1971
1972	$ —	$1,109,000
1973	3,162,000	1,300,000
1974	3,680,000	1,324,000
1975	3,864,000	1,301,000
1976	4,037,000	1,314,000
1977	3,953,000	914,000
1978	2,415,000	908,000
1979	2,415,000	909,000
1980	2,413,000	—
Total	$25,939,000	$9,079,000

Huff
Manufacturing, Inc.

Jennifer Sims, the Controller of Huff Manufacturing, Inc., and her assistant, Thomas Lind, had just returned from an all morning session with representatives of Lease, Inc. concerning the possibility of Huff's leasing a major addition of new equipment that was due to be brought on line during the next several months. Elizabeth Zemelka, Huff's President, had requested that they evaluate the lease versus buy option for this major addition so that she could finalize her capital expenditure budget which would be submitted to the corporate headquarters finance committee.

BACKGROUND INFORMATION

Huff Manufacturing, Inc. was a small privately held company which sold a limited line of rubber products. Historically, revenues and profits had been generated almost exclusively from its line of solid rubber balls, marketed as playthings for children and pets. The recent successful introduction of handballs and squash balls in the sporting goods market and a line of rubber household products has provided the company with a more diversified revenue base.

Huff was founded in 1952 by Tsezar Hufflovich, a 48-year-old mechanical engineer who 15 years earlier had immigrated to this country with his family. Unable to locate employment suitable to his background, but responsible for the

This case was prepared by Dennis P. Frolin and James F. Smith as a basis for class discussion rather than to illustrate either effective or ineffective handling of an administrative situation.

feeding of several mouths, he spent his first four years working as a machine operator for a small rubber products manufacturer in New York City. His next nine years were spent as a mechanical engineer for an engineering firm in Brooklyn. It was during these years that Mr. Hufflovich became convinced that his talents would never be fully utilized by his employer, a fact that was a source of constant frustration to him. He took considerable pride in his ability to innovate, but this was a quality that his employer seemed to stifle rather than promote. Consequently, he often spent time privately contemplating a new idea, dreaming that he might one day use one of these innovations to start his own business.

Finally, in November 1951, wrought with frustration and confident that he could successfully implement an idea which he had been pondering for some time, he bade his employer a final farewell. After doing considerable research he had concluded that by making certain fundamental changes in the configuration of the machinery which he had operated during his initial four years in the country (machinery which had remained essentially unchanged over the years) he could produce a line of premium quality solid rubber balls—the product which not coincidentally had been the "bellwether" of his first employer—at costs significantly lower than those prevailing in the industry.

In June 1952, financed by his life savings and those of a trusting comrade, he purchased the business of a small struggling rubber products manufacturer in New York. He happily renamed the company Huff Manufacturing, abbreviating Hufflovich because he felt that it would be more appealing to the American consumer. His engineering innovation proved to be quite successful, and by marketing his product at a significantly reduced price he was able to operate the business at a sufficient profit.

Huff Manufacturing prospered over the years as a private company. In 1967, during the height of the corporate acquisition years, Huff was acquired in a stock-for-stock swap by an aspiring conglomerate holding company. Mr. Huff continued as president until 1972 at which time he wisely liquidated his stock holding, resigned his position, and bought a McDonald's franchise, which he now operates in southern Florida.

Huff Manufacturing continues to exist as a legal entity 100 percent owned by the parent-holding company and is currently managed by Ms. Zemelka, Mr. Hufflovich's replacement. Ms. Zemelka along with six other top Huff executives is a salaried employee who participates in the parent's Performance Achievement Reward System (PARS). PARS determines an executive's annual bonus payment by weighting the division or subsidiary's level of and growth in market share, profits, return on sales, and return on assets. The actual PARS distribution received in any year by an executive is left to the discretion of a parent-level compensation committee.

Each of the four measures of performance weighted by PARS is explicitly defined in the Manual for Executive Compensation (MEC). Profits are defined

Exhibit 1. *Pro Forma Financial Statements**

Balance Sheet		1976 (IN THOUSANDS)
Cash†		$1,500
Accounts receivable		4,000
Inventory		3,000
Property, plant, and equipment	$43,000	
Accumulated depreciation	13,000	
		30,000
Other Assets		9,300
Total assets		$47,800
Current liabilities		$5,100
Long-term debt†		24,100
Owners' equity		18,600
Total liabilities and equity		$47,800

Profit and Loss Statement:	1976 (IN THOUSANDS)
Sales	$50,000
Cost of sales	26,000
Gross profit	$24,000
Expenses	
Selling	7,000
General and administrative	1,620
Profit before tax	$15,380
Tax expense	7,380
NOPAT§	$8,000

*Excludes Balance Sheet and Profit and Loss Statement effect of investment in machinery.
†Allocated by corporate headquarters to each division or subsidiary.
§As defined in the case.

as annual net operating profits after tax (NOPAT) and the asset base for return on assets (ROA) calculations is defined as the book value of accounts receivable, inventory and gross property, plant, and equipment.

The NOPAT calculation excludes interest charges, and the asset base in the ROA calculation excludes cash balances because external debt and cash balances are managed centrally in corporate headquarters. The balance sheet amounts for both cash and debt indicate corporate allocations rather than actual funds employed or owed by a division or subsidiary.

Exhibit 1 details the budgeted income statement and balance sheet for 1976 *excluding* the impact of the proposed acquisition of new equipment. The actual results for 1975 showed a NOPAT of $7.6 million on an asset base of $48.1 million.

CAPITAL EXPENDITURE PROCEDURES

Each division or subsidiary is responsible for selecting its own priority ranking of capital investment projects, which is then reviewed by the corporate head-quarters finance staff. The minimum corporate-wide hurdle rate applied to all capital expenditure requests is 11 percent. Projects that do not meet this criterion are routinely rejected at the division level. For projects meeting the minimum return criterion, the following factors are then subjectively weighted to assist in the priority ranking:

1. Projects to improve safety, work convenience, or regulatory compliance
2. Projects to improve product design and quality
3. Projects designed to increase profit, justified primarily by
    (a) cost reduction
    (b) an increase in production capacity for existing products
    (c) new capacity for the manufacture and distribution of a new product

In the absence of an extreme imbalance between funds requested and funds available, corporate headquarters is reluctant to reorder or severely deny the capital expenditure budget submitted by a division. Instead the headquarters prefers to rely on the PARS plan to motivate and regulate capital expenditure requests.

Lease agreements proposed by a division to acquire capital assets are included in a separate informational section of the capital expenditure budget and are subject to final approval by headquarters. PARS requirements account for lease payments as an annual operating rental expense.

LEASE VERSUS BUY DECISION

The proposed acquisition could be arranged either as a straight purchase, to be financed by long-term secured installment financing through a commercial bank, or as a long-term lease. In either case the investment is expected to generate a minimum annual NOPAT of $1,920,000 *excluding* the annual depreciation or rent expense, depending on the method of acquiring the asset. Exhibit 2 details the terms of both the purchase and lease options. Exhibit 3 details the cash flow analysis of the purchase/borrow option prepared by the corporate headquarters finance staff.

1. Analyse the alternative modes of acquisition of the new equipment:
   (a) purchase to be financed through a long term note secured by the equipment;
   (b) a long term lease
2. Assume that a third alternative is to acquire the equipment with cash presently in the bank. How would this option revise your answer to (1) above?
3. What non-quantitative considerations would enter the ultimate decision process?

Exhibit 2. Investment Data

MACHINERY

Cost	$10 million
Useful life	10 years*
Qualifies for 10% investment tax credit §	
Depreciation method	Straight line*

LOAN TERMS

Principal amount	$10 million
Lending rate	8%
Term	10 years
Repayment schedule	$1,490,300 annually†
Secured by equipment	
Compensating balance requirement	10% of original amount borrowed

LEASE TERMS

Lease life	10 years
Annual rental	$1,295,050†

*For tax purposes useful life is eight years, and the depreciation method is sum-of-the-years digits. Tax rate is 48 percent.

†Assume lump sum payment at each year end.

§For financial reporting purposes the company defers recognition of I.T.C. and amortizes it over the asset life on a straight line basis.

Exhibit 3. Cash Analysis–Purchase of Machinery

YEAR	ANNUAL DEBT SERVICE	INTEREST EXPENSE	TAX DEPRECIATION*	INVESTMENT TAX CREDIT	TAX SHIELD†	NET CASH FLOW§	PRESENT VALUE OF NET CASH FLOW**
1	$1,490,300	$800,000	$2,222,222	$1,000,000	$2,450,667	$960,367	$865,195
2	1,490,300	744,776	1,944,444	0	1,290,825	(199,474)	(161,898)
3	1,490,300	685,134	1,666,666	0	1,128,864	(361,436)	(264,279)
4	1,490,300	620,721	1,388,888	0	964,612	(525,688)	(346,287)
5	1,490,300	551,154	1,111,111	0	797,887	(692,413)	(410,913)
6	1,490,300	476,023	833,333	0	628,491	(861,809)	(460,758)
7	1,490,300	394,881	555,555	0	456,209	(1,034,091)	(498,079)
8	1,490,300	307,247	277,781	0	280,812	(1,209,488)	(524,829)
9	1,490,300	212,677	0	0	102,049	(1,388,251)	(542,702)
10	1,490,300	110,387	0	0	52,986	(1,437,314)	(506,200)
	$14,903,000	$4,903,000	$10,000,000	$1,000,000			$2,850,750

*As reported on the income tax return.
†48% of Interest Expense plus Tax Depreciation. Year 1 includes the $1,000,000 I.T.C.
§Represents the net of Annual Debt Service and Tax Shield.
**At 11% minimum corporate hurdle rate.

Greyhound Leasing

and

Financial Corporation (A)

For a number of years, the Accounting Principles Board (APB) and its successor, the Financial Accounting Standards Board (FASB) have grappled with the resolution of problems associated with the accounting for leases by both lessors and lessees. The first pronouncement, APB Opinion # 5, issued in September 1964 considered the reporting of lease transactions in the financial statements of lessees. Its companion pronouncement, APB Opinion # 7, issued in May 1966 and effective for fiscal periods beginning after December 31, 1966, considered the reporting issues from the perspective of the lessor. In 1972 and 1973 two further Opinions were issued (# 27 and # 31, respectively) clarifying some aspects of the lease-reporting process and requiring a fuller disclosure in the footnotes to lessee's financial statements of the commitments under lease contracts.

The requirements of the Opinions of the APB notwithstanding, there was still considerable debate within the accounting profession as to the adequacy of the prescribed disclosure. Accordingly, one of the initial research questions addressed by the Financial Accounting Standards Board was that of accounting for leases. The first Exposure Draft issued in the fall of 1975 was withdrawn in the wake of a deluge of letters of comment from interested parties who felt that the accounting procedures prescribed in the Draft did not result in full or fair disclosure of the economic substance of the lease transaction.

After almost a full year of deliberation, on July 22, 1976, the FASB issued a revised Exposure Draft. The complex Exposure Draft ran to 111 pages and, if adopted, would have established standards of financial accounting and reporting for both lessees and lessors. The general requirements of the Draft may be summarized as follows:

Leases which meet any of the following four criteria would be capitalized and accounted for as assets and liabilities ("capital" leases including direct financing and sales-type leases).

1. Ownership is transferred to the lessee at the end of the lease.
2. The lease contains a bargain purchase option.
3. The lease term is 75 percent or more of the leased property's estimated economic life.
4. The present value of the minimum lease payments is 90 percent or more of the fair value of the leased property, less any investment credit retained by the lessor.

Leases which do not meet any of the above criteria would be classified as "operating" leases for which rentals generally should be charged to operations as they become payable.

If adopted, the Exposure Draft would have been applicable to leases entered into or revised on or after January 1, 1977. Retroactive application of the provisions would be encouraged but would not be required until annual or interim periods beginning after late December 1980.

The Exposure Draft did propose special accounting rules for the lessor for a subset of capital leases called leveraged leases. The FASB argued that such leases possessed a unique combination of characteristics such that they result in "an overall economic effect that is distinct from that of other transactions."

The leveraged lease was defined in the Draft as one possessing the following characteristics:

1. It meets the criterion of a direct financing lease (that is, a capital lease in which the lessor is providing only a financing function and is not also reaping a profit margin as a dealer in the item leased) except for the 90 percent of fair value criterion noted above.
2. At least three parties are involved in the transaction: a lessee, a lessor (the "equity participant"), and a long-term creditor.
3. The financing provided by the long-term creditor is nonrecourse as to the general credit of the lessor. The amount of the financing is sufficient to provide the lessor with substantial leverage in the transaction.
4. The lessor's net investment as defined below declines during the early years once the investment has been completed and rises during the later years of the lease before its final elimination.

The Exposure Draft states:

A lease meeting the preceding definition shall be accounted for by the lessor using the method described in paragraphs 42–46; other leases shall be accounted for [accordingly]. . . .

> 42. *The lessor shall record his investment in a leveraged lease net of the nonrecourse debt. The net of the balances of the following accounts shall represent the initial and continuing investment in leveraged leases:*
>
> a. *Rentals receivable, net of that portion of the rental applicable to principal and interest on the nonrecourse debt*
>
> b. *A receivable for the amount of the investment tax credit to be realized on the transaction*
>
> c. *The estimated residual value of the leased asset*
>
> d. *Unearned and deferred income consisting of (i) the estimated pre-tax lease income (or loss), after deducting initial direct costs, remaining to be allocated to income over the lease term and (ii) the investment tax credit remaining to be allocated to income over the lease term*[14]
>
> *The investment in leveraged leases less deferred taxes arising from differences between pre-tax accounting income and taxable income shall represent the lessor's net investment in leveraged leases for purposes of computing periodic net income from the lease, as described in paragraph 43.*
>
> 43. *Given the original investment and using the projected cash receipts and disbursements over the term of the lease, the rate of return on the net investment in the years*[15] *in which it is positive shall be computed. The rate is that rate which when applied to the net investment in the years in which the net investment is positive will distribute the net income to those years (see Appendix E, Schedule 3) and is distinct from the interest rate implicit in the lease. . . . In each year, whether positive or not, the difference between the net cash flow and the amount of income recognized, if any, shall serve to increase or reduce the net investment balance. The net income recognized shall be composed of three elements, two of which, pre-tax lease income (or loss) and investment tax credit, shall be allocated in proportionate amounts from the unearned and deferred income included in net investment, as described in paragraph 42; the third element is the tax effect of the pre-tax lease income (or loss) recognized, which shall be reflected in tax expense for the year. The tax effect of the difference between pre-tax accounting income (or loss) and taxable income (or loss) for the year shall be charged or credited to deferred taxes. The accounting prescribed in paragraph 42 and in this paragraph is illustrated in Appendix E.*

The example in Appendix E provides data for a hypothetical leveraged lease and illustrates the flow of income under the proposed method.

Schedules 1, 2, and 3 beginning on page 211 set out the example provided in the FASB Exposure Draft.

---

[14]It is recognized that the investment tax credit may be accounted for other than as prescribed in this Statement, as provided by Congress in the Revenue Act of 1971.

[15]The use of the term "years" is not intended to preclude application of the accounting prescribed in this paragraph to shorter accounting periods.

APPENDIX E
ILLUSTRATIONS OF ACCOUNTING AND FINANCIAL STATEMENT
PRESENTATION FOR LEVERAGED LEASES

110. This Appendix contains illustrations of the accounting and disclosure requirements of this Statement as applied to a leveraged lease. The illustrations do not attempt to encompass all circumstances that may arise in connection with leveraged leases; rather, the illustrations are based on a single example of a leveraged lease, the terms and assumptions for which are stated in Schedule 1. The elements of accounting and reporting illustrated for this example of a leveraged lease are as follows:

1. Leveraged lease example—terms and assumptions, Schedule 1.
2. Cash flow analysis by years, Schedule 2.
3. Allocation of annual cash flow to investment and income, Schedule 3.
4. Journal entries for lessor's initial investment and first year of operation, Schedule 4.
5. Financial statements including footnotes at end of second year.
6. Accounting for a revision in the estimated residual value of the leased asset assumed to occur in the eleventh year of the lease (from $200,000 to $120,000):
   (a) Revised allocation of annual cash flow to investment and income, Schedule 5.
   (b) Balances in investment accounts at beginning of the eleventh year before revised estimate, Schedule 6.
   (c) Journal entries, Schedule 7.
   (d) Adjustment of investment accounts, Schedule 8.

Exposure Draft

SCHEDULE 1
Leveraged Lease Example—Terms and Assumptions

Cost of leased asset (equipment)	$1,000,000
Lease term	15 years, dating from January 1, 1975
Lease rental payments	$90,000 per year (payable last day of each year)
Residual value	$200,000 estimated to be realized one year after lease termination. In the 11th year of the lease the estimate is reduced to $120,000
Financing:	
Equity investment by lessor	$400,000
Long-term nonrecourse debt	$600,000, bearing interest at 9% and re-payable in annual installments (on last day of each year) of $74,435.30
Depreciation allowable to lessor for income tax purposes	Seven-year ADR life using double-declining balance method for the first two years (with the half-year convention election applied in the first year), sum-of-years digits method for remaining life, depreciated to $100,000 salvage value
Lessor's income tax rate (federal and state)	50.4% (assumed to continue in existence throughout the term of the lease)
Investment tax credit	10% of equipment cost or $100,000 (realized by the lessor on last day of first year of lease)
Initial direct costs	For simplicity, initial direct costs have not been included in the illustration.

SCHEDULE 2
Cash Flow Analysis by Years

YEAR	1 GROSS LEASE RENTALS AND RESIDUAL VALUE	2 DEPRECIATION (FOR INCOME TAX PURPOSES)	3 LOAN INTEREST PAYMENTS	4 TAXABLE INCOME (LOSS) (COL. 1-2-3)	5 INCOME TAX CREDITS (CHARGES) (COL. 4 × 50.4%)	6 LOAN PRINCIPAL PAYMENTS	7 INVESTMENT TAX CREDIT REALIZED	8 ANNUAL CASH FLOW (COL. 1-3+5-6+7)	9 CUMULATIVE CASH FLOW
Initial investment	—				—		$100,000	$(400,000)	$(400,000)
1	$90,000	$142,857	$54,000	$(106,857)	$53,856	$20,435	—	169,421	(230,579)
2	90,000	244,898	52,161	(207,059)	104,358	22,274	—	119,923	(110,656)
3	90,000	187,075	50,156	(147,231)	74,204	24,279	—	89,769	(20,887)
4	90,000	153,061	47,971	(111,032)	55,960	26,464	—	71,525	50,638
5	90,000	119,048	45,589	(74,637)	37,617	28,846	—	53,182	103,820
6	90,000	53,061	42,993	(6,054)	3,051	31,442	—	18,616	122,436
7	90,000	—	40,163	49,837	(25,118)	34,272	—	(9,553)	112,883
8	90,000	—	37,079	52,921	(26,672)	37,357	—	(11,108)	101,775
9	90,000	—	33,717	56,283	(28,367)	40,719	—	(12,803)	88,972
10	90,000	—	30,052	59,948	(30,214)	44,383	—	(14,649)	74,323
11	90,000	—	26,058	63,942	(32,227)	48,378	—	(16,663)	57,660
12	90,000	—	21,704	68,296	(34,421)	52,732	—	(18,857)	38,803
13	90,000	—	16,957	73,043	(36,813)	57,478	—	(21,248)	17,555
14	90,000	—	11,785	78,215	(39,420)	62,651	—	(23,856)	(6,301)
15	90,000	—	6,145	83,855	(42,263)	68,290	—	(26,698)	(32,999)
16	200,000	100,000	—	100,000	(50,400)	—	—	149,600	116,601
Totals	$1,550,000	$1,000,000	$516,530	$33,470	$(16,869)	$600,000	$100,000	$116,601	

SCHEDULE 3
Allocation of Annual Cash Flow to Investment and Income

	1	2	3	4	5	6	7
			ANNUAL CASH FLOW		COMPONENTS OF INCOME†		
YEAR	LESSOR'S NET INVESTMENT AT BEGINNING OF YEAR	Total (from Schedule 2, col. 8)	Allocated to investment	Allocated to income*	Pretax income	Tax effect of pretax income	Investment tax credit
1	$400,000	$169,421	$134,833	$34,588	$9,929	$(5,004)	$29,663
2	265,167	119,923	96,994	22,929	6,582	(3,317)	19,664
3	168,173	89,769	75,227	14,542	4,174	(2,104)	12,472
4	92,946	71,525	63,488	8,037	2,307	(1,163)	6,893
5	29,458	53,182	50,635	2,547	731	(368)	2,184
6	(21,177)	18,616	18,616	—	—	—	—
7	(39,793)	(9,553)	(9,553)	—	—	—	—
8	(30,240)	(11,108)	(11,108)	—	—	—	—
9	(19,132)	(12,803)	(12,803)	—	—	—	—
10	(6,329)	(14,649)	(14,649)	—	—	—	—
11	8,320	(16,663)	(17,382)	719	206	(104)	617
12	25,702	(18,857)	(21,079)	2,222	637	(321)	1,906
13	46,781	(21,248)	(25,293)	4,045	1,161	(585)	3,469
14	72,074	(23,856)	(30,088)	6,232	1,789	(902)	5,345
15	102,162	(26,698)	(35,532)	8,834	2,536	(1,278)	7,576
16	137,694	149,600	137,694	11,906	3,418	(1,723)	10,211
Totals		$516,601	$400,000	$116,601	$33,470	$(16,869)	$100,000

*Lease income is recognized as 8.647 percent of the unrecovered investment at the beginning of each year in which the net investment is positive. The rate is that rate which, when applied to the net investment in the years in which the net investment is positive, will distribute the net income (net cash flow) to those years. The rate for allocation used in this Schedule is calculated by a trial-and-error process. The allocation is calculated based upon an initial estimate of the rate as a starting point. If the total thus allocated to income (column 4) differs under the estimated rate from the net cash flow (Schedule 2, column 8) the estimated rate is increased or decreased, as appropriate, to derive a revised allocation. This process is repeated until a rate is selected which develops a total amount allocated to income that is precisely equal to the net cash flow. As a practical matter, a computer program is used to calculate Schedule 3 under successive iterations until the correct rate is determined.

†Each component is allocated among the years of positive net investment in proportion to the allocation of net income in column 4.

213

As expected, the Exposure Draft drew many letters of comment, particularly from equity participants in leveraged lease situations. The comment by Mr. B. A. Roth, Executive Vice President Finance of Greyhound Leasing and Financial Corporation together with an example based upon an actual lease entered into by Greyhound are included in Exhibit 1.

QUESTIONS

1. How does a leveraged lease differ from other "capital" leases?
2. Do you concur with the position with respect to leveraged leases advocated by the FASB?
3. How would you respond to the arguments raised in Mr. Roth's letter to the FASB?

Exhibit 1. GLFC Leveraged Lease Terms and Assumptions

Cost of leased asset	$42,500,000
Lease term	15 years, dating from January 31, 1975
Lease rental payments	$4,710,606 per year (payable last day of each year)
Residual value	$6,375,000 estimated to be realized the same day as lease termination
Financing	
Equity investment by lessor	$8,500,000
Long-Term nonrecourse debt	$34,000,000, bearing interest at 9-7/8% and repayable in annual installments (on last day of each year) of $4,353,194
Depreciation allowable to lessor for income tax purposes	12-year ADR life using double-declining balance method for the first two years—sum-of-years digits method for remaining life, depreciated to $2,125,000 salvage value
Lessor's assumed income tax rate (Federal)	48% (assumed to continue to exist throughout the term of the lease)
Investment tax credit	10% of equipment cost or $4,250,000 (assumed to be realized by lessor on last day of the 6th month of lease)
	Allocated to income using a sum-of-the-months digits basis

Leveraged Lease Income Analysis

MONTH	INTEREST METHOD (LESSOR PRE-TAX ACCOUNTING METHOD)	FASB PROPOSED METHOD
6	318,659	1,923,975
18	595,711	1,398,084
30	557,834	914,053
42	520,967	353,325
54	485,271	
66	450,976	
78	418,328	
90	387,603	
102	359,134	
114	333,279	
126	310,458	
138	291,137	
150	275,849	
162	265,197	
174	259,860	541,242
180	101,839	801,423
Total	5,932,102	5,932,102

Exhibit 2. Letter of Comment by Mr. B. A. Roth

GREYHOUND LEASING &
FINANCIAL CORPORATION

Greyhound Tower
Phoenix, Arizona 85077
602 248-4900

September 27, 1976

Director of Administration
File Reference 1002 - 019
Financial Accounting Standards Board
High Ridge Park
Stamford, CT 06905

Dear Sir:

In response to your request, we are setting forth herein the comments of Greyhound Leasing & Financial Corporation ("GLFC) with respect to certain matters covered in the current study of the Financial Accounting Standards Board ("FASB") of proposed changes in accounting for lessees and lessors.

GLFC is an independent lessor engaged principally in the business of equipment financing. The Company, a pioneer in the leasing business, has twenty-two (22) years of experience and is one of the largest leasing companies in the industry. The following comments are, therefore, the views of an independent lessor as to the prospective changes to lease accounting.

Lessor Accounting

Although the guidelines in the Exposure Draft on balance reflect the economic substance of lease transactions, we note conceptual inconsistencies in the criteria set forth therein as it relates to leveraged lessor accounting. The Exposure Draft assumes there is a significant difference between direct financing leases and leveraged leases and therefore sets forth different accounting treatment for the types of leases. We do not believe that the substance of a leveraged lease is dramatically different from that of a financing lease for the reasons set forth hereafter. In addition, we believe that the prescribed accounting method for leveraged leases results in extreme front-loading of income in a non-conservative manner and an illogical income stream over the life of the lease which does not relate to the true economic yield of the transaction. Therefore, we strongly recommend that the FASB allow lessors to account for leveraged leases under one of two alternatives, (a) either the same accounting guidelines as direct finance leases or (b) the method prescribed in the Exposure Draft. It is not proposed that the method prescribed for leveraged leases in the recent Exposure Draft be prohibited; rather only that a lessor be permitted to use for his leveraged leases either the accounting prescribed for leveraged leases or the accounting method prescribed for direct finance leases.

The reasons for our conclusions and recommendations are as follows:

1. The existence of non-recourse debt of a leveraged lease does not sufficiently change the economic substance of the lease or sufficiently differentiate the lease from a direct financing lease to justify the recognition of income in such a radically and dramatically different fashion. This is because borrowed capital is the essence of the leasing business and all transactions are constructed with borrowed capital. The difference in the capital utilized in a leveraged lease and a direct financing lease is that in a leveraged lease the borrowed capital is secured by the leased property and is non-recourse to the lessor. This distinction has an effect only in case of liquidation of the asset because of default where the liquidation value of the asset is less than the amount of the non-recourse debt. Since liquidation value of the asset generally exceeds the amount of the non-recourse debt (thus making the non-recourse feature of debt irrelevant), the distinction between non-leveraged and leveraged leases is more a theoretical rather than practical or significant one. Accordingly, we do not believe this minor distinction should result in the requirement of radically different accounting treatment for leveraged lease transactions if a lessor should wish to elect a method of recognizing income identical to that for direct finance leases.

2. The proposed accounting method for leveraged leases allows the lessor to front-load a significant amount of income in a manner which is difficult to relate to the true financial yield, where the return is related to the total investment in the asset, rather than the "equity" in a lease. It also causes the lessor to have a large gap in its stream of recorded income during the term of the lease. The effect of the accounting for leveraged leases is that the income stream is amortized in neither a logical nor a rational manner even after the lessor makes a reasonable assumption for reinvestment income derived from cash flow timing differences. In addition, the front-loading of the income stream causes the lessor greater asset risk because in the early years the carrying values of the leased assets would usually be significantly in excess of the market value. As an example, we have attached an income analysis (Exhibit A) comparing methods of accounting for a leveraged lease recently consummated by Greyhound Leasing & Financial Corporation. The income differential if the leveraged lease accounting is used rather than direct finance lease accounting is that the lessor records as income an additional amount of $2,407,689 (after-tax) in the first eighteen (18) months of the lease. This amount increases through the 42nd month to $2,596,266 (after-tax). Then, there is no direct income recognized on the lease until the 174th month, resulting in a gap of 132 months without recording income on a lease with a 180-month

term. Furthermore, while this calculation uses a conservative fifteen (15) percent valuation for its residual, an adjustment of the residual valuation to twenty (20) percent results in additional income recorded in the early term of the lease. The effect of this accounting treatment is obviously material and hardly conservative.

3. The accounting for leveraged leases results in the flow of cash and tax benefits entering into the determination of the income stream. Since these items enter into the economics of constructing all lease transactions, it is possibly logical to include these items in the determination of the income stream. However, the logic should also apply to two-party leases. The Board has elected a more conservative method for amortizing income on two-party leases. We see no reason for differentiating the income stream for tax benefits and cash flow simply because of third-party non-recourse debt. Accordingly, we believe that direct finance lease accounting should be available for all leases.

4. There are many methods of calculating yields on leases. In our opinion the one of greatest relevance is the method that measures the flow of income through the financial statements. The FASB method for leveraged leases results in an after-tax yield of 45.3 percent on the lease described in the example in paragraph 2 above. In our opinion this is not the most accurate method of calculating the yield and additionally, this yield is significantly in excess of the yield calculated and assumed for prudent management purposes.

In summation, if left to our decision, Greyhound Leasing would choose not to use the FASB's proposed method of accounting for leveraged leases. Because of the front-loading of income, the effect of non-replacement of leases during a business downturn when utilizing the prescribed leveraged lease accounting method will be significantly more dramatic than would result from non-replacement of leases on the direct finance method. This dramatic effect could cause pressure on leasing companies to replace expired leases with leases to marginal credit companies. In essence, the accounting could result in the lack of prudent business judgment.

Therefore, we recommend that, instead of the FASB requiring implementation of the designated leveraged lease method of accounting as the only one, the designated method be prescribed as one of two alternatives for a leveraged lease, the other alternative being the method prescribed for direct financing leases.

Very truly yours,

GREYHOUND LEASING &
   FINANCIAL CORPORATION

By _____
      B. A. Roth
      Executive Vice President-Finance

Golden Stores, Inc.

Golden Stores, Inc. operated a chain of department and mail-order stores in the western United States. The chain had experienced a large expansion in recent years, both as a result of opening new stores and the continuing increase in the region's retail sales. Golden Stores' financial condition was sound (see Exhibits 1 and 2). The past few years, however, had seen the growing use of liberal credit terms as a sales tool. By 1974, the company's credit sales had reached 50 percent of its total sales. This trend, although not new, had important implications from the point of view of the company's finances and accounting.

As indicated in Exhibit 2, Golden Stores' credit sales increased from 41 percent of $165 million in 1970 to 50 percent of $202 million in 1974, or from $68 million to $101 million. Thus, substantially all of the sales increase in the past five years had been additional credit sales. The company was very much aware of this trend; in fact, Golden Stores had been stressing its credit facilities in order to gain new sales, and planned to continue this emphasis in the future.

Mr. James Voss, Treasurer of Golden Stores, was cognizant of the effect that the company's expanding credit volume had on its financial needs. He pointed out that the company's receivables averaged about eight months' credit sales, and that the period was increasing annually. Obviously, this growth in receivables created a major financing need for the company.

Two "long-term" credit plans were offered by Golden Stores to its customers. Almost all credit customers used one of these two plans. The volume of monthly

---

Exhibit 1. Consolidated Balance Sheet at December 31, 1974 (all amounts in thousands)

CURRENT ASSETS

Cash and U.S. Treasury bills		$10,755
Accounts receivable (less $5,900 reserve*)		68,540
Inventories, at lower of cost or market		35,278
Prepayments		1,434
Total Current Assets		$116,007
Investments, at or below cost		10,671
Property, plant, and equipment cost	$28,278	
Less: depreciation	12,474	
Net		15,804
Debenture discount		169
Total Assets		$142,651

CURRENT LIABILITIES

Accounts payable		$5,118
Accrued expenses		4,638
Federal income taxes		7,355
Other taxes payable		3,694
Short-term notes payable		30,217
Total Current Liabilities		$51,022
5% debentures, due 1996		17,500
Stockholders' equity		
Capital stock—$1.00 par value	$11,250	
Paid in surplus	3,420	
Retained earnings	59,459	
Total Stockholders' Equity		74,129
		$142,651

*Comprising deferred finance charges on installment accounts and a provision for bad and doubtful debts (see bottom of Exhibit 3).

Exhibit 2. Comparative Income Statement Data, 1970 to 1974

	(in millions of dollars)				
	1974	1973	1972	1971	1970
Net sales	$202	$186	$180	$178	$165
Net income before taxes	20.2	16.9	16.7	17.2	16.7
Year-end receivables (net) (see Exhibit 3)	68.5	58.7	54.0	50.4	44.4

Exhibit 2. *(continued)*

	(in percentages)				
Realized gross margin*	36.0%	35.3%	35.4%	35.8%	36.0%
Credit sales/total sales	50	47	46	44	41
Installment plan	37	38	39	38	37
Revolving credit	13	9	7	6	4

*Gross margin (sales less cost of goods sold), expressed as a percentage of net sales.

account sales was very small, as customers usually preferred either to pay cash at the time of the sale or to finance their purchases over a period of several months.

The more popular plan was based on a regular installment agreement on some specific purchases. Customers would make a down payment on the articles they selected, and pay off the balance plus a finance charge over an agreed period of time.[1] Most of the sales under this plan were so-called "big ticket" items, such as household appliances and furniture, where a single purchase represented a large dollar amount.

In recent years, however, Golden Stores had also offered customers with proven credit worthiness the opportunity to finance their purchases of less expensive items, particularly clothing, under a revolving credit plan. Under this plan, approved customers were permitted a monthly maximum purchase on credit. At the same time, they made a monthly payment in reduction of the unpaid balance of their account, the payment being calculated as one-twelfth of the total balance. In this way, one year's credit was allowed, and customers could re-utilize the credit granted to them as they paid off their account. Under this plan, a monthly finance charge of 1 percent of the month's average credit balance was assessed.

ACCOUNTING IMPLICATIONS

The accounting policies that Golden Stores applied to credit sales had been determined when these sales were only a small proportion of the company's total volume. Normal accrual accounting was used; that is, the sale was shown as revenue at the time of purchase, and the profit on the sale was recognized in full at that time. Finance charges on the credit sales were taken into income on a time basis, according to the monthly balances on accounts receivable. The

[1] The "add-on" for finance charges was 12½ percent on a year's contract; that is, 8⅓ percent of the face value of the average account, on the basis of the eight-month average for accounts receivable. Thus, the finance charges represented about 7.7 percent (.083/1.083) of the amount of outstanding installment receivables.

"prepaid" finance charge on installment plan sales was deferred and shown on the balance sheet as a reserve deducted from accounts receivable. Because revolving credit charges were assessed monthly, there was no need for deferral of these finance charges.

During 1975, as the trend of rising credit sales volume continued, it became apparent to the company's management that their present policies, in effect, produced two possibly unfortunate results. First, immediate recognition of the profit on credit sales meant that the income taxes also had to be provided for and paid, often before a major part of the sales price had been collected in cash. Second, this immediate profit recognition meant that the company's financial statements indicated a source of funds from profits that was, in part, counterbalanced by an application of funds to increased investment in accounts receivable. Both of these phenomena tended to make management's task more difficult: the first because of the cash drain, and the second because of the misleading source of funds that was being indicated.

CHANGE FOR TAX PURPOSES

During 1974 Golden Stores' tax advisor pointed out to the company's management that it could defer paying income taxes on the profit from its installment sales until the actual cash was received. The Internal Revenue Service permitted retailers such as Goldern Stores to prorate the gross profit on such sales over the period in which payment was received (Regulation #1.453-1). This had the effect of deferring the gross profit on those sales represented by outstanding accounts receivable. This accounting method was known as the "installment method," and was regarded by the IRS as a remedy to the inequity that arises if income tax is assessed on income not yet actually received in cash.

To illustrate the installment method, suppose Golden Stores had used the method in calculating its 1974 income tax. From the $59.2 million installment accounts receivable (Exhibit 3) would first be deducted the amount representing the finance charge add-ons, 7.7 percent or $4.6 million. To this net receivables amount, $54.6 million, would be applied the 1974 gross margin percentage, 36.0 percent (Exhibit 2), giving $19.7 million deferred gross margin. Because the average installment account receivable is paid within about eight months, for simplicity it can be assumed that this $54.6 million in receivables will be collected in 1975. Thus, in 1975 Golden Stores would have to pay taxes on the $19.7 million gross margin deferred from 1974. However, the company would have a new deferral in 1975 arising from the new receivables accumulated during that year.

One complication of the installment method of accounting for tax purposes was the possibility of double taxation in the year following the changeover to the new method. This double taxation arose because, prior to the changeover, income taxes had already been paid on total profits as determined by accrual

Exhibit 3. *Accounts Receivable Data, 1970 to 1974 (December 31)*

| | (in millions of dollars) | | | | |
	1974	1973	1972	1971	1970
Installment accounts	$59.2	$54.7	$51.2	$48.0	$42.6
Revolving charge accounts	12.8	6.6	4.8	4.0	2.5
Miscellaneous accounts	2.4	2.9	3.0	3.1	3.6
	$74.4	$64.2	$59.0	$55.1	$48.7
Less: Reserve*	5.9	5.5	5.0	4.7	4.3
Net Total	$68.5	$58.7	$54.0	$50.4	$44.4

*See note to balance sheet. The Reserve is comprised of:
  1. Deferred finance charges on installment accounts, and
  2. Provision for bad and doubtful accounts. Thus

| | (in millions of dollars) | | | | |
	1974	1973	1972	1971	1970
Deferred finance charges on installment accounts* (7.7% as per text footnote 1)	4.56	4.21	3.94	3.70	3.28
Provision for bad and doubtful accounts	1.34	1.29	1.06	1.00	1.02
Total reserve	5.90	5.50	5.00	4.70	4.30

accounting, regardless of whether the total sales providing these profits had been collected in cash. In the changeover year, the gross profit from the uncollected sales of the previous year, already taxed in that year, would be taxed a second time when the cash was received. The only way this double taxation could be avoided was for the retailer to convert all of his receivables to cash at the end of the year before the change to the installment method. Golden Stores' tax advisor explained that this could be accomplished by selling the year-end installment sales receivables to a "factor," who would give the company cash (less the factor's service charge) for the receivables and would then collect the receivables himself.

The installment method of tax calculation appeared attractive to Golden Stores' management because the tax deferral would improve the company's cash flow. They inquired of their tax advisor whether the same method could be used on their revolving credit sales, but were told that the IRS was awaiting a judgment from a Superior Court before agreeing to extend the method to revolving credit plans. Nevertheless, management decided to apply the method to their installment receivables beginning January 1, 1976.

1. If Golden Stores had adopted the installment method on January 1, 1970, by what amount would their cash flow have been improved in the years 1970-1974. (Assume a 50 percent tax rate, ignore the provision for doubtful accounts, and disregard the service charge paid to the factor for converting January 1, 1970, installment receivables into cash.)

2. Should Mr. Voss also adopt the installment basis of accounting for reporting to Golden Stores' stockholders? What factors should he consider in his analysis? Should all retail businesses use the installment method of recognizing gross profit?

Trans Union
Corporation

The following excerpt is taken from the President's Letter in the 1972
Trans Union Corporation Annual Report:

> . . . *your management has become quite concerned about the serious
> understatement of our reported earnings that is caused by the way in
> which we are required to handle our "deferred taxes." The deferred
> tax account arises primarily because, in order to encourage the con-
> struction of all types of rail cars, we are permitted to depreciate our
> tank cars much more rapidly for tax purposes than they actually wear
> out. While the accounting for deferred taxes is somewhat complicated,
> the understatement of earnings can be readily grasped by referring
> to page 10 where we compute out net income for the year 1972.*
>
> *On page 10 we have set out the gross revenues for 1972 and have
> then deducted the related expenses. All of the expenses which we
> have deducted on this page have already been paid or will be paid in
> early 1973. The one exception to this statement is deferred taxes,
> which we have deducted in the amount of approximately $13.4 million.
> Unlike the other expenses,* this $13.4 million will not be paid for an
> average of approximately 18 years! *During the 18-year period we are
> not required to pay any interest on this amount, but we are still re-
> quired to deduct it today just as though it had already been paid.*
>
> *It is common knowledge that a dollar due in 18 years is not worth
> a dollar today. Who would pay one dollar today for just the right to
> receive one dollar 18 years from now? The same principle applies to*

This case was prepared by Guillermo J. Fernandez, Research Assistant, under the supervision of Associate Professor John K. Shank as the basis for class discussion rather than to
illustrate either the effective or ineffective handling of an administrative situation.
Copyright © 1974 by the President and Fellows of Harvard College. Distributed by the
Intercollegiate Case Clearing House, Soldiers Field, Boston, Mass. 02163. All rights reserved
to the contributors. Printed in the U.S.A.

expenses. An obligation to pay $13.4 million in 1990 does not require us to set aside $13.4 million today. If we were to set aside only half that amount today and were to earn 4% interest on it, it would total $13.4 million in 1990.

In other words, when a liability is due at some time in the future, simple logic says we should discount the amount to determine what the real liability is today. If that were done in our case, we would deduct substantially less than $13.4 million in determining our 1972 income, and our earnings per share would be materially higher.

Our statement that we will pay the deferred taxes 18 years from now is quite conservative. There are well known authorities who argue cogently that the $13.4 million will really never be paid unless the Company were to liquidate its tank car fleet and go out of business, and very likely not even then. These authorities include one of the very top auditing firms and the head of one of the most prestigious graduate schools of business in the country.

We have been forced to account for our deferred taxes by ignoring the 18-year delay in payment, because the Accounting Principles Board (APB) has so ruled. It is interesting to note that at one time the APB created a subcommittee of its own members to study the problem of deferred taxes. In 1966 that committee expressed a preference for discounting, but the APB overruled them. The APB prohibited discounting until a further research study could be made, but they have actually done nothing on the subject in the six years since that time.

It is also pertinent to point out that the handling of deferred taxes required by the APB is directly contrary to the handling they require for pension liabilities. If an employee works for us in 1972 and thereby acquires the right to receive a pension of $1,000 in the year 1990, the APB will not permit us to deduct $1,000 in 1972 but will permit a deduction of only the discounted amount of such future payment. This is directly opposite to the treatment they require for deferred taxes, and the reason for this inconsistency has never been explained by the APB.

The APB is being replaced by a new body known as the Financial Accounting Standards Board. It is only now being formed, but when it is functioning we would hope that it would address itself to this problem. In the meantime we wanted you to understand the situation in order to properly appraise the quality of our earnings.

Excerpts from the financial statements and footnotes for 1972, along with the auditors' opinion, are reproduced as Exhibit 1.

The casewriter discussed the deferred tax issue with Mr. Donald B. Romans, a graduate of a well-known Eastern business school who is Vice President Finance for Trans Union.

WALL STREET REACTION TO TRANS UNION'S ACTIONS

Mr. Romans stated that the "market" seemed to be totally insensitive to the qualitative issues raised by the President in the Annual Report. Trans Union is listed on both the New York and London Stock Exchanges.

Mr. Romans further stated that security analysts in their research reports regarding Trans Union agree with the company's viewpoint and philosophy but that this agreement, in his opinion, has not been reflected in the company's price earnings ratio or its stock price. Some research reports have mentioned that the deferred income tax charges in the income statement appear "excessive," but in no instance have the analysts actually adjusted the reported earnings per share accordingly.

DEFERRED TAXES: DEBT? EQUITY? NEITHER?

Mr. Romans expressed the view that analysts for the bond rating agencies, such as Moody's, routinely treat deferred income taxes as equity capital in computing debt-equity ratios and coverage of fixed charges in their evaluation procedures. He went on to recount the following incident. While having lunch with three bankers, he requested that each independently compute the company's debt-equity ratio. Three different numbers were produced! Deferred income taxes were considered by one of the bankers to be equivalent to debt, by one of the bankers to be equivalent to equity, and by one of the bankers to be properly disregarded altogether in making the computation. The latter approach, Mr. Romans added, is most common among debtors and analysts. He feels that most of them seem either to disregard the balance sheet's deferred income taxes account entirely or to adopt the more conservative approach and consider it as debt, despite the fact that the Company and its auditors are very careful not to label the item as a liability.

MANAGEMENT VERSUS THE ACCOUNTING PROFESSION

Mr. Romans expressed the opinion that the "market" will never adopt an earnings measurement scheme different from that required in the Annual Report by the accountants, no matter how strongly management objects. He went on, "It appears that security analysts and investors give more credence to earnings per share as computed by the certified public accountants than to the economic realities of discounted cash flows. Stockholders, bankers, and analysts acknowledge the facts as we presented them, but they hesitate in applying this to the valuation process for our common stock.

"In essence," Mr. Romans concluded, "management is at the mercy of the accountants in terms of the quality of the earnings as perceived by the investment community."

QUESTIONS

1. Estimate the impact on the 1972 and 1971 financial statements if deferred taxes were discounted as proposed by Mr. Van Gorkom.
2. In your opinion, should deferred taxes be discounted?
3. Consider carefully the strategy adopted by Trans Union in this matter. What options are open to them? Why did they select the approach they did? What can they gain? What can they lose? What would you do as Mr. Van Gorkom in the 1973 Annual Report?

Auditors' Report

To the Stockholders of Trans Union Corporation:

We have examined the consolidated balance sheet of Trans Union Corporation (a Delaware corporation) and subsidiaries as of December 31, 1972, and December 31, 1971, and the related consolidated statements of income, retained earnings, additional capital, and source and use of funds for the five years ended December 31, 1972. Our examination was made in accordance with generally accepted auditing standards, and accordingly included such tests of the accounting records and such other auditing procedures as we considered necessary in the circumstances.

In our opinion, the accompanying consolidated balance sheet and consolidated statements of income, retained earnings, additional capital, and source and use of funds present fairly the financial position of Trans Union Corporation and subsidiaries as of December 31, 1972, and December 31, 1971, and the results of their operations and the source and use of funds for the five years ended December 31, 1972, in conformity with generally accepted accounting principles consistently applied during the periods.

Arthur Andersen & Co.

Chicago, Illinois,
January 22, 1973.

Exhibit 1. *Consolidated Balance Sheet*

Trans Union Corporation and Subsidiaries

Consolidated Statement of Income

	1972	1971
Revenues:		
Net Sales	$135,387	$110,324
Services	153,931	145,936
Net Income from Finance Lease Business	1,223	570
Net Income from 50% Owned Companies	1,202	1,483
Interest Income	1,642	1,992
Royalties and Other	1,573	1,585
Amortization of Investment Tax Credit	462	432
	$295,420	$262,322
Costs and Expenses:		
Cost of Sales	$102,123	$ 83,433
Cost of Services	81,492	79,282
Selling, General and Administrative Expenses	46,747	40,965
Interest Expense	19,693	18,026
Minority Interest in Ecodyne Corporation	335	—
	$250,390	$221,706
Net Income Before Income Taxes	$ 45,030	$ 40,616
Provision for Income Taxes:		
Current	$ 4,750	$ 2,418
Deferred	13,440	13,980
Investment Tax Credit (Deferred)	890	1,172
	$ 19,080	$ 17,570
Net Income Before Extraordinary Items	$ 25,950	$ 23,046
Extraordinary Items, Net of Income Taxes	—	6,060
Net Income (Including Extraordinary Items)	$ 25,950	$ 29,106
Per Share of Common Stock—		
Net Income Before Extraordinary Items	$2.61	$2.32
Extraordinary Items	—	.61
Net Income (Including Extraordinary Items)	$2.61	$2.93

Exhibit 1. *(continued)*

Trans Union Corporation and Subsidiaries

Consolidated Balance Sheet

			December 31	
Assets			**1972**	1971
			(Dollars in thousands)	
Cash			**$ 23,181**	$ 18,381
Accounts Receivable, including $56,675,000 and $51,812,000, respectively, due within one year			**63,393**	59,716
Inventories (lower of cost or market):	**1972**	1971		
Materials and Supplies	**$ 20,638**	$ 20,728		
Finished and In Process	**23,593**	16,912	**44,231**	37,640
Prepaid Expenses and Deferred Charges			**12,809**	11,833
Investments:				
Land Held for Resale, at cost	**$ 34,276**	$ 31,225		
Finance Lease Subsidiaries	**13,307**	8,942		
Goodwill of Acquired Businesses	**14,650**	12,565		
7% Debentures due in 1974	**8,500**	8,500		
Other	**12,647**	6,592	**83,380**	67,824
Tank Car Lease Fleet (minimum future rentals under existing leases at December 31, 1972 total $287,981,000, of which $68,414,000, is due within one year):				
Cost	**$578,846**	$567,435		
Accumulated Depreciation	**(175,514)**	(173,156)	**403,332**	394,279
Ocean Vessel Fleet (minimum future receipts under existing contracts at December 31, 1972 total $106,185,000, of which $28,121,000, is due within one year):				
Cost	**$104,370**	$ 78,351		
Accumulated Depreciation	**(28,084)**	(25,447)	**76,286**	52,904
Fixed Assets, at cost:				
Land	**$ 3,686**	$ 2,755		
Building and Leasehold Improvements	**37,608**	35,555		
Equipment	**53,796**	47,570		
Accumulated Depreciation	**(33,619)**	(30,026)	**61,471**	55,854
			$768,083	$698,431

231

Exhibit 1. *(continued)*

Liabilities, Deferred Items and Stockholders' Equity			December 31	
			1972	1971
			(Dollars in thousands)	
Accounts Payable			**$ 26,842**	$ 18,071
Accrued Expenses			**29,830**	28,095
Federal Income Taxes Payable			**4,720**	5,820
Borrowed Debt:	**1972**	1971		
Due within one year	**$ 79,191**	$ 53,776		
Due from one to five years	**119,068**	115,586		
Due after five years	**157,349**	167,901	**355,608**	337,263
Total Liabilities			**$417,000**	$389,249
Minority Interest In Ecodyne Corporation			**6,073**	—
Deferred Items:				
Federal Income Taxes	**$132,530**	$119,090		
Investment Tax Credit	**10,550**	10,100	**143,080**	129,190
Stockholders' Equity:				
Preferred Stock	**$ —**	$ —		
Common Stock	**10,577**	10,526		
Additional Capital	**68,788**	59,194		
Retained Earnings	**129,006**	115,983		
Less Reacquired Common Stock, at Cost	**(6,441)**	(5,711)	**201,930**	179,992
			$768,083	$698,431

The accompanying notes and summary of accounting principles and
practices are an integral part of this statement.

Exhibit 1. *(continued)*

Trans Union Corporation and Subsidiaries

Consolidated Statement of Source and Use of Funds

	1972	1971
Source of Funds		
Net Income before Extraordinary Items	$ 25,950	$ 23,046
Depreciation	24,097	24,625
Deferred Income Taxes and Investment Tax Credit	13,890	14,670
Tank Car, Vessel and Other Fixed Asset Disposals (book value)—		
Cost	20,638	24,243
Less Accumulated Depreciation	(16,763)	(19,411)
Total from Operations	$ 67,812	$ 67,173
Funds Provided from Extraordinary Items	—	7,705
New Borrowings	57,166	51,117
Proceeds from Public Sale of Stock of Ecodyne Corporation	13,897	—
Other Sources of Funds	9,343	664
	$148,218	$126,659
Use of Funds		
Fixed Asset Additions—		
Tank Car Lease Fleet	$ 27,868	$ 40,318
Ocean Vessel Fleet	26,019	494
Other Fixed Assets	11,690	9,115
Investment In—		
Land Held for Resale	3,051	1,242
Nonconsolidated Subsidiaries	4,365	(1,376)
Purchase of Companies	4,454	1,814
Increase in Cash, Accounts Receivable and Inventories, etc.	18,754	28,490
Repayment of Borrowed Debt	39,090	35,039
Cash Distributions of Partnerships Prior to Pooling	—	—
Cash Dividends	12,927	11,523
	$148,218	$126,659
Cash Dividends Per Share	$1.31	$1.24

Note: Disposals are larger than normal in 1970, 1971
and 1972 due to the accelerated retirement of
older tank cars.

Exhibit 1. *(continued)*

Trans Union Corporation and Subsidiaries

Consolidated Statements of Retained Earnings and Additional Capital

	1972	1971
Retained Earnings:		
Balance at Beginning of Year as Previously Reported		
Restatement for Company Added through Pooling of Interests		
Balance at Beginning of Year as Restated	$115,983	$ 98,912
Net Income (including extraordinary items)	25,950	29,106
Income of Partnerships Prior to Pooling Transferred to Additional Capital	—	—
Cash Dividends	(12,927)	(11,523)
Adjustment Due to Difference in Fiscal Year of Pooled Company	—	(512)
Balance at End of Year	$129,006	$115,983
Additional Capital:		
Balance at Beginning of Year as Previously Reported		
Restatement for Company Added through Pooling of Interests		
Balance at Beginning of Year as Restated	$ 59,194	$ 57,819
Increase Due to Public Sale of Stock of Ecodyne Corporation	8,156	—
Option Price of Stock Issued over Amount Added to Common Stock	1,438	1,175
Transfer from Common Stock for Change to $1 Par Value....	—	—
Transfer to Common Stock for 2½ for 1 Stock Split	—	—
Net Changes in Partner's Equity in Pooled Businesses Previously Operated As Partnerships	—	—
Other	—	200
Balance at End of Year	$ 68,788	$ 59,194

Exhibit 1. *(continued)*

Notes to Consolidated Financial Statements

Income Per Share

Net Income per share amounts have been computed on the basis of the average number of shares outstanding after adjustment for poolings of interests. Distribution of 400,000 shares held in escrow in connection with a 1970 acquisition is contingent upon future earnings increases of the acquired business; these shares are not included in earnings per share computations and are not dilutive.

Extraordinary Items

The extraordinary items include the following:

	1971	1970	1969
	(Dollars in thousands)		
Gain on sale of 50% stock interest in Phoenix Manufacturing Company, less applicable income taxes of $2,410,000	$4,570	$ —	$ —
Net recovery from claims in connection with losses in 1962 on a missile site contract, less applicable income taxes of $3,270,000 in 1970 and $1,800,000, in 1969	—	3,400	1,625
Gain arising from insurance recovery on damaged vessel, less applicable income taxes of $1,410,000	1,490	—	—
Loss on sale of Graver Tank & Mfg. Co., less applicable income tax credit of $1,340,000	—	(1,510)	—
Net	$6,060	$1,890	$1,625

Sale of Stock of Subsidiary

During 1972, a wholly-owned subsidiary of Trans Union, Ecodyne Corporation, sold newly issued shares of its common stock in a public offering. This sale resulted in a 15% minority interest in the ownership of Ecodyne. The proceeds of this sale, amounting to $13,897,000, net of commissions and expenses, were credited to minority interest ($5,738,000) and to additional capital ($8,156,000).

Retirement Plans

The Company and its subsidiaries provide retirement benefits for most employees through pension and other retirement plans. The total retirement expense provision was $2,390,000 in 1972 and $2,230,000 in 1971 for all plans, including amortization of prior service pension costs over a twenty year period. The Company's policy is to fund pension costs as they are accrued. At December 31, 1972, the total of the pension funds were in excess of the actuarially computed value of vested benefits. Unfunded prior service costs under the pension plans were approximately $5,500,000 as of the most recent valuation date.

Borrowed Debt

Details of borrowed debt at December 31, 1972 are as follows:

	(Dollars in thousands)
Equipment Trust Certificates, 5.85%-9.875% (7.91% average rate) payable in annual installments through 1991 (secured by tank cars with original cost of approximately $251,000,000)	$168,232
Notes payable, 5½%-8½% payable in installments through 1983 (secured by first and second mortgages on vessels with original cost of approximately $78,000,000 and assignment of future revenues under vessel charters of approximately $35,000,000 and accounts receivable of approximately $1,000,000)	54,813
Sinking Fund Debentures, 3¾%-5% payable in annual installments through 1986	34,432
Equipment Trust Notes at prime rate (6% at December 31, 1972), due August 30, 1974 (secured by tank cars with original cost of approximately $27,000,000)	20,401
Commercial paper, 5.50% average rate	35,110
Bank Notes, at prime rate due January, 1974 . . .	15,000
Other Debt	27,620
	$355,608

Exhibit 1. *(continued)*

Sinking fund debentures and equipment trust certificates have been reacquired for sinking fund purposes in the principal amounts of $5,361,000 at December 31, 1972, and $7,116,000 at December 31, 1971, and have been deducted from the appropriate debt captions in the accompanying consolidated balance sheet.

The aggregate amounts due on debt obligations for each of the five years following December 31, 1972, are as follows:

		(Dollars in thousands)	
1973:	Commercial paper	$35,110	
	Other	44,081	$79,191
1974:	Equipment Trust Debt	$33,382	
	Other	24,552	57,934
1975			26,892
1976			20,219
1977			14,023

Capital Stock

The capital stock of the company at December 31, 1972 and 1971 was as follows:

	Shares	Par Value
		(Dollars in thousands)
Preferred stock, $1 par		
5,000,000 shares authorized in 1972 and 1971		
None issued	—	—
Common stock, $1 par		
20,000,000 shares authorized in 1972 and 1971		
Issued—		
December 31, 1972	10,576,748	$10,577
December 31, 1971	10,526,371	$10,526

The changes in common shares issued in 1972 and 1971 are due entirely to the exercise of stock options which are described elsewhere in these footnotes.

Reacquired Common Stock

Changes in reacquired common stock during 1971 and 1972 were as follows:

	Shares	Cost
		(Dollars in thousands)
Balance at January 1, 1971 as previously reported	265,753	$6,894
Restatement for pooling of interests	(98,750)	(1,970)
Balance at January 1, 1971 as restated	167,003	$4,924
Purchases	24,627	985
Reissued in purchase acquisition	(7,118)	(198)
Balance at December 31, 1971	184,512	$5,711
Purchases	19,000	730
Balance at December 31, 1972	203,512	$6,441

Commitments

The Company has various contractual commitments entered into in the normal course of business including approximately $156,000,000 related to construction of nine new ocean vessels which are scheduled for delivery in 1973, 1974, and 1975. Long-term charters have already been obtained for certain of these vessels.

Future commitments for rentals under leases for space, vessels and equipment aggregate $13,279,000 payable, $1,992,000 in 1973, $1,684,000 in 1974, $1,530,000 in 1975, $1,471,000 in 1976, $1,274,000 in 1977 and the remainder in varying annual amounts through 1995.

Poolings of Interests

During the period 1968-1972 the Company acquired the following businesses in pooling of interests transactions:

Year	Business	Principal Activity	Number of Trans Union Shares Issued
1972	Vennard & Ellithorpe Ltd.	Sulphur handling and conversion	98,750
1971	Trans Union Ocean Shipping Group	Ocean shipping	600,000
1971	McKenzie-Ris Mfg. Co.	Manufacture heat exchangers	112,000
1970	Environmental Developers, Inc.	Multiple family housing developer	300,000*

*Plus up to 400,000 additional shares contingent upon future earnings increases of Environmental Developers.

Exhibit 1. *(continued)*

Trans Union Corporation and Subsidiaries

Notes to Consolidated Financial Statements

The accompanying financial statements have been restated in the year of acquisition to include the accounts of these companies for the periods prior to their respective acquisitions. The restatement in 1972 to reflect the acquisition of Vennard & Ellithorpe Ltd. had an insignificant effect (less than 1% of revenues and net income in any year) on previously reported operations as well as on 1972 operations.

The holding company reorganization effective June 1, 1969, pursuant to which Trans Union became the parent of Union Tank Car Company, was accounted for in the same manner as a pooling of interests, and consequently, at the time the transaction became effective, the consolidated financial statements of Trans Union for 1968 and prior years were identical to the previously reported statements of Union Tank Car Company.

Stock Options

The stock option plan for officers and key employees provides that options granted become exercisable over four years from date of grant at a price per share which is not less than 100% of market value on the date the options are granted.

Options outstanding at December 31, 1972 were as follows:

Year of Grant	Number of Shares	Option Price and Market Value at Date of Grant Per Share	Total
1968	9,000	$35.56	$ 320,040
1969	28,975	26.62-31.50	785,955
1970	20,375	24.56	500,410
1971	23,000	42.00	966,000
1972	22,750	44.12	1,003,730
Total	104,100		$3,576,135

Options became exercisable as follows:

	1972	1971
Number of Shares	27,163	39,729
Option Price—		
Per Share	$24.56-42.00	$24.56-35.56
Total	$837,261	$1,127,431
Market Value at Date Exercisable—		
Per Share	$40.00-47.12	$39.62-45.50
Total	$1,117,903	$1,686,522

Options were exercised as follows:

Number of Shares	50,377	40,687
Option Price—		
Per Share	$24.56-35.37	$24.56-30.15
Total	$1,481,423	$1,146,828
Market Value at Date Exercised—		
Per Share	$40.00-47.75	$35.62-45.75
Total	$2,179,275	$1,667,366

On options exercised, $1 per share has been credited to common stock and the balance of the option price has been credited to additional capital. No charges or credits have been made to income for stock options. There were 100,634 and 80,762 additional shares of common stock reserved for the granting of options at December 31, 1971 and 1972, respectively.

Cancellations due to employee terminations or option expirations totaled 3,883 shares in 1972 and 2,563 shares in 1971.

Finance-Lease Subsidiaries

The investment in nonconsolidated finance-lease subsidiaries is carried at cost, plus equity in undistributed earnings since date of acquisition. The excess of this investment over the underlying book value of these subsidiaries represents purchased goodwill and amounts to $942,000.

The combined condensed financial statements of these finance-lease subsidiaries follow on the next page.

Worldwide Trade Corporation

On February 18, 1974, Mr. William Girod, Chairman of the Board of the Worldwide Trade Corporation was examining the Annual Report in preparation for the forthcoming annual stockholders' meeting.

Mr. Girod knew that each year an increasing number of shareholders were examining the annual statements with increased expertise. In particular, he was aware that at the prior year's shareholders' meeting there had been some questions regarding the corporate income taxes paid by Worldwide which he had not been able to answer satisfactorily. Furthermore, the Securities and Exchange Commission had recently adopted revised disclosure requirements for income tax expense. Therefore, despite the fact that the company's fiscal year reporting did not require it to comply with the new ruling this period, Mr. Girod suspected that there would be extensive inquiries made on this subject at the coming meeting. He proceeded to contact Mr. William Fifer, Worldwide's Treasurer and Vice President of Finance, in order to have the necessary information prepared.

THE COMPANY

Worldwide could be classified as a mini-conglomerate, with consolidated sales of $35 million and net income before income taxes of $4.2 million for the 1973 fiscal year.

This case was prepared by Guillermo J. Fernandez, Research Assistant, under the supervision of Associate Professor John K. Shank as the basis for class discussion rather than to illustrate effective or ineffective handling of an administrative situation.

The company's main subsidiary, Worldwide Oil Corporation, had originated with the Girod family's ownership of oil wells in Texas in the late 1930s. Worldwide Oil Corporation emerged from World War II in a very strong financial position as a fully integrated producer and refiner. Expansion into Latin America and Europe was actively pursued and by the end of the 1950s crude production, refining, and marketing had been established in several countries. In addition, a shipping company, Panamanian Worldwide Tankers Corporation, had been acquired in 1966. It was chartered in Panama and operated from Panama City.

In 1958 a diversification move was made with the purchase of Worldwide Home Appliance Corporation, which was a full-line producer of home appliances with subsidiaries in the United States and in Europe. The present crude oil shortages had delayed further expansion in the petrochemicals field.

INCOME TAXES

Mr. Fifer proceeded to analyze the 1973 consolidated income tax expense in order to arrive at its composition and determine the variance with the current corporate tax rate of 48 percent. In addition, he had to reconcile the difference between the tax provision and the actual tax payable, which gave rise to deferred income taxes.

His examination of the consolidated income statements and related supporting schedules disclosed the following:

1. Permanent income differences
   (a) Income included on the book which was excluded for tax purposes.
       (1) $500,000 insurance proceeds received on the policy held by Worldwide on the life of the late Mr. Crow, former President of International Operations, deceased in August 1973.
       (2) $55,000 interest income on Westchester County Sewage Authority Bonds.
       (3) $24,000 which represents 85 percent of the dividend income received from domestic corporations. These investments represent less than 20 percent of the equity of such corporations and, therefore, are recorded using the cost method of accounting for investments.
       (4) $488,000 which represents 50 percent of the earnings of Worldwide's Domestic International Sales Corporation, a wholly owned corporation. Earnings of international sales subsidiaries of domestic corporations are taxed only when distributed. However, 50 percent of the earnings are considered as taxable dividends to the shareholders even if actual payment does not occur. The remainder is taxed upon actual distribution. Worldwide, however,

does not expect ever to make such distribution and, therefore, no deferred tax is provided.

(5) $216,000 net income of Panamanian Worldwide Tankers Corporation. This income is tax exempt since it is derived from and permanently reinvested in a country with very liberal tax provisions for foreign corporations.

(b) Taxable income which is not considered to be income for financial reporting purposes.

(1) $330,000 proceeds of stock purchase warrants which expired in August 1973 and were not exercised. This amount was originally credited to Additional Paid-in Capital for accounting purposes, but it is considered as current income for tax purposes.

2. Timing income differences

(a) Income recognized earlier for accounting purposes than for tax purposes.

(1) $236,000 excess of accrued sales revenue on installment sales over the amounts collected by Worldwide Home Appliance Corporation. Accrual accounting is used for stockholders' statements, while installment accounting is used for tax purposes. This amount represents the excess of recognized accrual income over the taxable installment income.

(2) $122,000 net income of Worldwide Oil Corporation's Chilean branch which cannot be repatriated due to that country's present currency restrictions. U.S. taxes on blocked foreign income are deferred until restrictions disappear or actual repatriation is made.

(b) Income recognized earlier for tax purposes than for financial reporting purposes.

(1) $250,000 service contract fees of the home appliance subsidiary collected in 1973, which are recognized as collected for tax purposes but are amortized over the warranty period for book purposes. This amount represents the excess of collections in 1973 over the amount amortized for financial reporting purposes.

3. Permanent expense differences

(a) Expenses included in the books which are not deductible for tax purposes.

(1) $87,000 of life insurance premiums paid on policies for key

executives for which Worldwide is the beneficiary. Premiums and ultimate proceeds of life insurance policies for which the company is the beneficiary are both excluded in income tax calculations.

(2) $98,000 amortization of goodwill not allowed for tax purposes.

(b) Expenses deductible for tax purposes which are not shown in the financial statements.

(1) $30,000 excess statutory depletion over the cost-based depletion recorded as expense on the books.

(2) $5,000 capital appreciation on 100 shares of stock donated to Harvard University. The original cost of the stock was $10,000 and the fair market value at the time of the donation was $15,000. The tax laws allow a deduction for the full market value, limited to a maximum of 5 percent of taxable income. The donation was expensed at cost for book purposes.

4. Timing differences for expenses

(a) Expenses recognized earlier for tax purposes than for book purposes.

(1) $233,000 excess of accelerated depreciation over straight-line.

(2) $157,000 excess of capitalized research and development expenses over the amount amortized for reporting purposes. Worldwide capitalizes research and development expenses on the books but expenses such items as incurred for tax purposes.

(b) Expenses recognized later for tax purposes than for book purposes.
(1) $43,000 excess book deduction for warranty expense. The reserve method of accounting for an expected warranty liability is not allowed for tax purposes. Worldwide's home appliance subsidiary has provided $69,000 of warranty expense on its books, while $26,000 was the actual cash outlay for the period.

5. Investment tax credit and tax on capital gains

(a) The tax law provides a 7 percent credit for new qualified property against the taxes payable, subject to a maximum limitation. Worldwide had qualified investments totaling $570,000 for a $40,000 tax credit (well under the limitation). Worldwide uses the "flow-thru" method to account for this credit.

(b) $96,000 capital gains tax on a $319,000 net long-term capital gain arising from the sale of 15 percent interest in Safeguard Warehouse

Corp. The tax was the lowest under the two alternatives allowed by the law. The capital gain was included in the net income before taxes.

With this information Mr. Fifer proceeded to prepare the necessary reconciliations.

QUESTION:

1. Prepare the necessary tax reconciliations.

NVF
Company

In late 1968, NVF Company, a manufacturing firm, made an exchange offer to the shareholders of Sharon Steel Corporation. For each share of Sharon common, the holder was to receive $70. of 5 percent subordinated debentures and 1.5 common stock purchase warrants. By March 1, 1969, approximately 86 percent of the Sharon common shares had been tendered and, as a result, the 1969 NVF Annual Report recorded the effects of the transaction. Because of the sizable difference between the coupon rate on these debentures and the rate required by the market, a significant bond discount asset (deferred debt expense) appeared among NVF's assets. It is interesting to note that the New York Stock Exchange originally refused to list these debentures because of the uncertainty that the interest payments would be covered.

QUESTIONS

1. What was the cash equivalent value of the Sharon stock acquired? What was the book value of the stock acquired?
2. What disclosures should be included, either on the balance sheet or in the footnotes, to fairly represent this financial situation to the shareholder?
3. NVF is amortizing this discount on the "straight-line" method. What advantages does this method have? What disadvantages?

This case was prepared by Laird H. Simons, III, Research Assistant, under the supervision of Associate Professor John K. Shank as the basis for class discussion rather than to illustrate either effective or ineffective handling of an administrative situation.

4. The Accounting Principles Board has recommended, but not required, showing the discount as a "contra-liability" (that is, netted against the principal amount of the liability). How does this improve the situation?

5. A growing minority (of purists?) feels that this netting process should be combined with discount amortization using the "compound interest" method. Why does this come closer to representing the economic realities of the situation? Why might a company desire to avoid this method as long as it is optional?

6. What was the yield rate at date of issue on the 5 percent debentures? Compute interest expense on the debentures for 1969 as NVF would calculate it and under a market yield calculation approach.

NVF COMPANY AND SUBSIDIARIES
Consolidated Balance Sheet

	December 31	
	1969	**1968** pro forma— unaudited (note 2)
Assets		
Current assets:		
Cash and short-term securities	$ 4,635,000	$ 3,910,000
Receivables, less allowance for doubtful accounts of $274,000 and $245,000	34,019,000	26,484,000
Inventories (note 3)	47,258,000	46,393,000
Other current assets	112,000	358,000
Total current assets	86,024,000	77,145,000
Properties at cost, less accumulated depreciation, depletion and amortization (note 4)	130,088,000	136,437,000
Deferred debt expense (note 1)	51,881,000	56,609,000
Prepaid expenses and other assets	4,831,000	1,530,000
	$272,824,000	$271,721,000
Liabilities and Stockholders' Equity		
Current liabilities:		
Notes payable	$ —	$ 2,000,000
Long-term debt payable within one year	10,811,000	6,321,000
Accounts payable	15,500,000	10,999,000
Wages, salaries and other employee costs	10,944,000	12,618,000
Federal and state taxes on income (note 6)	1,751,000	315,000
Other current liabilities	3,079,000	4,820,000
Total current liabilities	42,085,000	37,073,000
Long-term debt (note 7)	39,209,000	49,089,000
Accrued employee benefits	2,802,000	2,652,000
Noncurrent and deferred income taxes (note 6)	12,560,000	9,954,000
Minority interest	15,490,000	14,720,000
	112,146,000	113,488,000
5% subordinated debentures, due 1994 (note 8)	93,886,000	99,066,000
Excess of equity over cost of investment (note 2)	18,182,000	19,685,000
Stockholders' equity (note 9):		
Preferred stock, $1 par value; 5,000,000 shares authorized in 1969, none issued	—	—
Common stock, $1 par value; authorized, 10,000,000 shares (1,000,000 in 1968); issued 967,408 shares (731,787 in 1968)	967,000	732,000
Capital in excess of par value	29,981,000	27,966,000
Retained earnings	17,662,000	10,784,000
Total stockholders' equity	48,610,000	39,482,000
	$272,824,000	$271,721,000

(1) Acquisition of Sharon Steel Corporation:

Under an exchange offer, the company acquired, as of March 1, 1969, 1,415,235 common shares of Sharon Steel Corporation (approximately 86%) in exchange for $99,066,000 principal amount of 5% subordinated debentures due 1994 and 2,122,852 common stock purchase warrants. Deferred debt expense of $56,609,000 attributable to the 5% subordinated debentures was recorded and is being amortized on the "bonds outstanding" method. The value of $22,129,000 assigned to the warrants issued with respect to the exchange has been reflected as part of the cost of investment in Sharon.

(2) Principles of Consolidation:

The consolidated statements include the accounts of NVF Company and all of its subsidiaries. Sharon Steel Corporation and subsidiaries have been included for the year, with appropriate adjustment made for pre-acquisition income. At the date of acquisition, Sharon's net worth exceeded the cost of investment by $19,835,000. This amount is being amortized into income over a ten-year period.

For the purpose of providing a comparison, 1968 financial statements have been presented on a pro forma basis, consolidating the financial statements of NVF and Sharon for that year on the assumption that the acquisition of Sharon by NVF had been effected as of January 1, 1968.

(3) Subordinated Debentures:

The 5% subordinated debentures due 1994 are redeemable in whole or in part at any time at the option of the company at prices reducing 1/4 of 1% each year from 105% on December 31, 1969. Additionally the company is required to make cash sinking fund payments on January 1 of each year for five years commencing 1989 to retire by redemption 10% of the outstanding debentures on the November 15 immediately preceding each such January 1 less any debentures previously retired.

The warrants issued in connection with the acquisition of Sharon Steel Corporation entitle the holders thereof to purchase one share of common stock of NVF at $22 per share. The principal amount of any of the 5% subordinated debentures due 1994 held by a warrant holder may be applied by him toward payment of the purchase price upon exercise of the warrant. The warrants expire on January 31, 1979. The purchase price is subject to adjustment in certain events.

Accounting for Liabilities: Three Questions

1. What is a liability? Najeeb E. Halaby was employed as Chairman and Chief Executive Officer of Pan American World Airways, Inc. until March 22, 1972, when he was forced to resign by the Board of Directors. Prior to his resignation, Pan American reported losses as follows:

1969	$30 million
1970	48 million
1971	46 million

In accordance with his employment contract, Mr. Halaby continued to receive his base salary of $100,000 per year after his forced resignation. If we assume that his contract expired on December 31, 1975, Mr. Halaby is entitled to and will receive subsequent to his resignation the following amounts:

1972	$ 75,000 (9 months)
1973	100,000
1974	100,000
1975	100,000

Consider now the accounting question of recording Mr. Halaby's compensation.

This case was prepared by Dennis P. Frolin as a basis for class discussion rather than to illustrate either effective or ineffective handling of an administrative situation.

Copyright © 1975 by the President and Fellows of Harvard College. Distributed by the Intercollegiate Case Clearing House, Soldiers Field, Boston, Mass. 02163. All rights reserved to the contributors. Printed in the U.S.A.

Three possibilities come to mind:

1. Pan American has incurred a liability and an expense as of March 22, 1972, for Mr. Halaby's future compensation of $375,000.
2. Pan American has incurred a liability and created an asset as of March 22, 1972, for Mr. Halaby's future compensation of $375,000.
3. Pan American has neither incurred a liability nor an expense, nor created an asset as of March 22, 1972. Instead the corporation will have an expense in each of the future periods for the amount paid to Mr. Halaby.

Define for financial accounting purposes the term *liability*. Operationally this should mean that only those items meeting your definition appear on the right-hand side of your balance sheets. Does Pan American have a liability on March 22, 1972? Why or why not?

2. For a liability with a *known cost,* how is interest accounted for?

On January 1, 1975, a company places through an investment counselor a three-year $1-million term note with a private investor. The note has an annual interest rate of 8 percent of the face value, pays interest semi-annually on July 1 and January 1 and matures January 1, 1978. The investor paid $1 million to the counselor, who paid the company $950,000 in cash after deducting the agreed upon $50,000 "finder's fee."

Calculate the interest expense for each of the three years and the amount of the liability on the balance sheet at the end of each of the three years.

3. For a liability with an *unknown cost,* how is interest accounted for?

On January 1, 1975, a company issues a $1,000 five-year 20 percent bond at par, receiving cash of $1,000. Each December 31 the outcome of a coin flip determines whether any interest is paid. If the outcome is heads, $200 is paid; if tails, no interest is paid. The face amount of $1,000 is payable on January 1, 1980.

Calculate the interest expense for 1975 assuming the flip shows heads. What if it shows tails?

United Brands—The Case of the Disappearing Hung Convertible

Late in 1968, United Fruit Company issued over $250 million of $5\frac{1}{2}$ percent convertible subordinated debentures, due 1994, in connection with the acquisition of AMK Corporation. The debentures were convertible into United Brands' (the merged entity) common at one share for each $55 face value of debentures. The stock of United Brands did not do well subsequently and the debentures were selling at 64 in early 1973, having dipped earlier into the 50's.

In January 1973, the company, pursuant to a plan of recapitalization and a pledge to offer debenture holders a package with a more attractive market value than the convertible issue, announced that it would offer new debentures and cash for the old debentures. Details of the exchange were forthcoming the following month. If more than $20 million face value of the old debentures were tendered, the company obligated itself to acquire any amount offered up to $80 million. The exchange offer of $10 cash and $60 principal amount of a new $9\frac{1}{8}$ percent subordinated debenture, due 1998, in exchange for each $100 principal amount of the $5\frac{1}{2}$ percent issue was to remain open for approximately three weeks.

In March 1973, at the termination of the exchange offer, $125,000,000 principal amount of the $5\frac{1}{2}$ percent debentures had been exchanged, reducing outstanding debt by approximately $50,000,000 and reducing potential dilution of common stock from debt conversion by approximately 50 percent.

This case was prepared by Professor John K. Shank as a basis for class discussion rather than to illustrate either effective or ineffective handling of an administrative situation.

Copyright © 1972 by the President and Fellows of Harvard College. Distributed by the Intercollegiate Case Clearing House, Soldiers Field, Boston, Mass. 02163. All rights reserved to the contributors. Printed in the U.S.A.

1. Summarize what someone who accepted the exchange offer gave up and what he or she got.
2. How large is the gain or loss that United Brands will realize on the exchange?
3. How will United Brands account for the transaction?
4. What was the effective dollar cost to United Brands over the period 1968–72 for the use of the $125,000,000 in tendered debentures? Do the financial statements fairly reflect this cost?

Exhibit 1. Consolidated Balance Sheet (in thousands)

Assets

	DECEMBER 31 1972	DECEMBER 31 1971
Current Assets		
Cash	$ 18,894	$ 21,514
Marketable securities, at cost which approximates market	64,225	49,082
Receivables, less allowance for doubtful accounts of $3,561 (1971—$2,723)	119,847	92,289
Inventories	94,412	83,696
Growing crops	29,678	31,885
Materials and supplies	25,331	28,441
Prepaid expenses	10,997	11,593
Total Current Assets	363,384	318,500
Investments at long-term receivables (Note 3)	67,417	44,324
Deferred charges	11,197	12,736
Property, plant, and equipment, net (Note 4)	331,018	334,530
Trademarks and leaseholds (Note 5)	50,249	49,882
Excess of cost over fair value of net assets acquired (Note 5)	279,069	285,255
Assets held for disposal, at estimated realizable value (Note 11)	15,505	24,000
	$1,117,839	$1,069,227

Liabilities and Shareholders' Equity

	DECEMBER 31 1972	DECEMBER 31 1971
Current Liabilities		
Notes and loans payable to banks	$ 43,419	$ 28,933
Accounts payable and accrued liabilities	87,692	92,806
Long-term debt due within one year	14,719	7,656
U.S. and foreign income taxes (Note 10)	22,820	19,874
Deferred U.S. and foreign income taxes (Note 10)	10,882	11,436
Total Current Liabilities	179,532	160,705
Long-term Debt (Note 6)	402,487	380,280
Accrued severance and other social benefits (Note 7)	34,596	37,095
Other liabilities and deferred credits	7,689	13,158
Total Liabilities	624,304	591,238
Shareholders' Equity (Notes 6, 8, and 9)		
$3.00 cumulative convertible preferred stock	2,738	2,769
$1.20 cumulative convertible preference stock	29,610	29,610
$3.20 cumulative convertible preference stock	7,452	7,452
Capital stock, $1 par value	10,773	10,781
Warrants and options to purchase capital stock (Notes 8 and 9)		
Capital surplus	366,322	366,303
Income retained in the business (Note 6)	76,640	61,074
Total Shareholders' Equity	493,535	477,989
	$1,117,839	$1,069,227

251

Exhibit 1. *(continued)*

NOTE 6—LONG TERM DEBT.

Long-term debt comprises the following:

	1972	1971
	(in thousands)	
$5\frac{1}{2}$ percent subordinated debentures, due 1994, redeemable at approximately 5 percent above par in 1973 and at slightly lesser amounts thereafter, convertible into capital stock at $55.00 a share, with sinking fund redemptions commencing in 1980 at annual rates of 4 percent (1980–1984), 7 percent (1985–1989) and 9 percent (1990–1993) of the principal amount outstanding on January 31, 1980, less unamortized debt discount of $7,032,000 in 1972, $7,560,000 in 1971	$ 251,548	$ 242,020
$6\frac{1}{2}$ percent subordinated debentures, due 1988, redeemable at approximately 5 percent above par in 1973 and slightly lesser amounts thereafter with required sinking fund redemptions of $1,200,000 in each of the years 1975–1978, $1,800,000 in each of the years 1979–1983, and $2,400,000 in each of the years 1984–1987, less unamortized debt discount of $4,570,000 in 1972, $5,009,000 in 1971	25,395	24,956
Eurodollar loans payable to banks at interest rates generally $\frac{3}{4}$ of 1 percent over the London interbank rate, $30,000,000 matures in 1975 and the balance matures 1973–1980	80,134	62,500
$6\frac{7}{8}$ percent subordinated notes due in annual installments of approximately $1,761,000 from 1973–1979	12,324	14,085
Other loans, notes, and debentures and other liabilities payable to banks and others with interest rates from $4\frac{1}{2}$ percent to 9 percent including $10,000,000 with interest to $\frac{1}{2}$ percent over prime rate, maturing from 1973 to 1997	47,805	39,375
Less current maturities	(14,719)	(7,656)
	$ 402,487	$ 380,280

Southland—The Case of the Dubious Debt Expense

In March 1972, The Southland Corporation decided to force the conversion of its $5\frac{1}{2}$ percent convertible subordinated debentures which were carried in the 1971 financials at $39.4 million. Conversion was induced by announcing that the company would be redeeming all outstanding convertible debentures one month hence by paying the necessary call premium of 5 percent above par value. During that month all debenture holders would have the option of converting their holdings at a rate of 4.202 shares of common stock per $100 face value of debentures. The OTC bid price for the common stock stood at $36.80 at that time.

QUESTIONS

1. Why had the debenture holders not converted earlier?
2. Make sure you fully understand how the company has accounted for this conversion.
3. Assuming the debentures were issued in January 1969, what was the total dollar cost paid by Southland for the use of these funds from 1969 to 1972? *Be careful because this is a loaded question.*
4. To what extent does "GAAP" reflect "fair" accounting for the cost of convertible debt?

This case was prepared by Professor John K. Shank as a basis for class discussion rather than to illustrate either effective or ineffective handling of an administration situation.

Copyright © 1972 by the President and Fellows of Harvard College. Distributed by the Intercollegiate Case Clearing House, Soldiers Field, Boston, Mass. 02163. All rights reserved to the contributors. Printed in the U.S.A.

Exhibit 1. *Southland Corporation Consolidated Balance Sheet*

Assets

	December 31 1972	December 31 1971
Current Assets:		
Cash.	$ 33,120,375	$ 38,563,851
Cash investments	26,193,151	—
Accounts and notes receivable (Note 3).	46,024,739	39,366,520
Inventories, at the lower of cost or market	53,747,359	49,076,601
Deposits and prepaid expense.	8,099,136	8,649,379
Investment in property (Note 4)	35,598,687	25,561,540
Total Current Assets	202,783,447	161,217,891
Investments in Affiliates (Note 2)	19,568,903	8,371,942
Other Assets	1,729,878	1,200,133
Property, Plant and Equipment (Note 5)	165,270,306	155,688,095
	$389,352,534	$326,478,061

Liabilities and Shareholders' Equity

	1972	1971
Current Liabilities:		
Long-term debt due within one year.	$ 6,757,630	$ 6,718,133
Accounts payable and accrued expense.	86,313,975	67,302,432
Income taxes.	1,800,241	3,508,187
Total Current Liabilities	94,871,846	77,528,752
Deferred Credits (Note 7)	15,620,385	14,437,289
Reserves for Self Insurance	2,615,183	2,187,878
Long-Term Debt, due after one year (Note 6)	82,042,893	95,191,759
Contingencies and Commitments (Note 9)		
Shareholders' Equity (Notes 6 and 8):		
Common stock, $.01 par value, authorized 40,000,000 shares, issued and outstanding 15,917,385 and 13,685,704 shares.	159,174	136,857
Additional paid-in capital.	153,464,415	99,149,745
Earnings retained in the business	40,578,638	37,845,781
	194,202,227	137,132,383
	$389,352,534	$326,478,061

See notes to financial statements.

Exhibit 1. *(continued)*

	Year ended December 31	
	1972	1971
Common Stock:		
The Southland Corporation.	$ **136,857**	$ 81,162
Shares issued in poolings	**—**	5,325
Balance January 1, restated for poolings.	**136,857**	86,487
Exercise of stock options.	**671**	750
3% Stock dividend.	**4,592**	3,939
Conversion of notes and debentures.	**17,054**	4,769
Purchase acquisition.	**—**	142
Stock split—3-for-2	**—**	40,770
Balance December 31.	**159,174**	136,857
Additional Paid-in Capital:		
The Southland Corporation.	**99,149,745**	78,381,952
Pooled companies.	**—**	289,266
Balance January 1, restated for poolings.	**99,149,745**	78,671,218
Exercise of stock options.	**786,363**	1,077,480
3% Stock dividend.	**14,001,161**	11,840,486
Conversion of notes and debentures.	**39,527,146**	7,183,224
Purchase acquisition.	**—**	418,107
Stock split—3-for-2	**—**	(40,770)
Balance December 31.	**153,464,415**	99,149,745
Earnings Retained in the Business:		
The Southland Corporation.	**37,845,781**	30,576,349
Pooled companies.	**—**	3,950,978
Balance January 1, restated for poolings.	**37,845,781**	34,527,327
Net earnings for the year	**20,365,987**	17,796,595
	58,211,768	52,323,922
Less:		
Cash dividends.	**3,491,311**	2,423,341
Cash paid in lieu of fractional shares	**136,066**	210,374
3% Stock dividend	**14,005,753**	11,844,426
	17,633,130	14,478,141
Balance December 31.	**40,578,638**	37,845,781
Total Shareholders' Equity (Notes 6 and 8).	**$194,202,227**	$137,132,383

See notes to financial statements.

	Year ended December 31	
	1972	1971
Source of Funds:		
From operations:		
Net earnings before extraordinary item.	**$ 20,365,987**	$ 17,299,759
Depreciation	**17,862,325**	16,246,787
Deferred income taxes and other credits	**1,183,096**	1,214,478
Funds provided by operations.	**39,411,408**	34,761,024
Extraordinary item.	**—**	496,836
5% Convertible subordinated debentures	**30,000,000**	—
Long-term debt.	**7,782,559**	11,398,085
Conversion of notes and debentures.	**39,544,200**	7,187,993
Exercise of stock options.	**787,034**	1,078,230
Value of shares issued in purchase acquisition	**—**	418,249
Increase in accounts payable, accruals and income tax.	**17,303,597**	2,576,062
Property retirements and sales	**4,619,882**	3,676,514
Decrease in cash and cash investments.	**—**	7,144,275
Other	**977,548**	—
	$140,426,228	$ 68,737,268
Application of Funds:		
Payment of long-term debt	**$ 11,347,728**	$ 6,954,314
Conversion of notes and debentures.	**39,544,200**	7,187,993
Cash dividends.	**3,491,311**	2,423,341
Cash paid in lieu of fractional shares	**136,066**	210,374
Investments in affiliates	**11,196,961**	8,273,942
Property, plant and equipment.	**32,064,418**	31,494,017
Increase in cash and cash investments	**20,749,675**	—
Increase in accounts and notes receivable	**6,658,219**	2,900,307
Increase in inventories	**4,670,758**	3,729,842
Increase in investment in property.	**10,037,147**	4,605,838
Net assets of business purchased	**—**	418,249
Other	**529,745**	539,051
	$140,426,228	$ 68,737,268

See notes to financial statements.

NOTE 6—LONG-TERM DEBT:

At December 31, 1972, long-term debt and amounts due within one year were as follows:

	Amount outstanding	Current portion	Balance included in long-term debt
5¾% Promissory notes due 1976	$10,312,500	$ 3,437,500	$ 6,875,000
4%–9% Real estate and equipment notes (mature 1973 to 1995)	37,938,023	3,320,130	34,617,893
5% Convertible subordinated notes due 1984	6,000,000	—	6,000,000
5¾% Convertible subordinated notes due 1987	4,550,000	—	4,550,000
5% Convertible subordinated debentures due 1987	30,000,000	—	30,000,000
	$88,800,523	$ 6,757,630	$82,042,893

The 5% and 5¾% convertible notes and the 5% convertible debentures may, at the option of the holders, be converted at any time into common stock of the Company at the ratios, respectively, 85.55, 69.78, and 23.94 shares of stock for each $1,000 of principal. As to the notes, these ratios decrease to 75.29 and 66.33 shares on January 1, 1975 and December 1, 1977, respectively. At December 31, 1972, there were 1,548,999 shares of common stock reserved for the conversion of the notes and debentures. Principal payments on the notes are due annually beginning in 1975 and 1978 respectively, in amounts equal to 10% of the aggregate principal amount outstanding one year prior to the date of the first required payment.

Under a revolving credit facility with certain banks the Company may borrow, repay and reborrow up to $32,000,000 at an interest rate equal to ¼% above the prime rate. On or before July 2, 1973, the banks have agreed to make a term loan to Southland in an amount up to $32,000,000. No amounts were borrowed under this facility at December 31, 1972, nor does the Company anticipate any borrowings thereunder to the date it terminates on July 2, 1973.

At December 31, 1972, the aggregate amount of long-term debt maturities is as follows for the years ended December 31: 1973—$6,757,630; 1974—$6,513,087; 1975—$6,809,419; 1976—$3,260,273; 1977—$3,278,497.

The agreements under which the promissory notes and the convertible notes were issued place certain restrictions on the payment of cash dividends. Under the most restrictive of these provisions, retained earnings totaling $38,400,000 at December 31, 1972, were not so restricted.

Other provisions of the agreements include requirements as to maintenance of working capital and net worth. The Company has complied with these requirements.

Reliance
Group, Incorporated

Reliance Group, Incorporated operates two businesses: insurance and leasing. The following information about the company includes:

1. 1974 comparative balance sheets (as reported in the 1974 Annual Report)
2. 1975 comparative balance sheets (as reported in the 1975 Annual Report) 1975 income statement, and relevant footnotes
3. June 14, 1976, press release

Examine the 1974 and 1975 balance sheet treatment of the company's outstanding preferred stock issues. Footnote 3 describes the preferred stock issued by a subsidiary in 1975 to acquire Commonwealth Land Title Insurance Company. Footnote 13 describes the preferred stock issued by Reliance Group, Incorporated. The "Series B" preferred stock was issued in 1968 to acquire Reliance Insurance Company. The "Series C" preferred stock was issued subsequently in a (partial) exchange offer for the "Series B" preferred stock.

QUESTIONS

1. In what ways are Reliance's preferred stock issues similar to long-term debt? In what ways are they dissimilar?
2. Are the preferred stocks enough similar that they should be accounted for as long-term debt and recorded in the liability section of the balance sheet?

3. Calculate the impact on Reliance's debt-equity ratio and fixed charges coverage ratio if the preferreds are accounted for as liabilities.
4. How does the 1974 accounting treatment differ from the 1975 accounting treatment for the preferred stocks? Is the 1975 treatment adequate? Is it an improvement? How would you account for the preferred stocks?

Exhibit 1. *Reliance Group, Incorporated and Subsidiaries Consolidated Balance Sheet*

Reliance Group, Incorporated and Subsidiaries
Consolidated Balance Sheet

Assets December 31	1974	1973 (Restated)
Marketable securities—principally of insurance subsidiaries:		
Common and preferred stocks, at quoted market (cost $239,553,000 and $340,990,000) (note 3)	**$160,427,000**	$ 339,144,000
Bonds—at amortized cost (quoted market $466,112,000 and $386,844,000)	**539,741,000**	403,220,000
Cash (note 6)	**60,122,000**	79,162,000
Accounts and notes receivable, less allowances of $4,938,000 and $4,345,000 (note 4)	**122,290,000**	118,775,000
Finance lease receivables (note 4)	**92,179,000**	100,002,000
Computer rental equipment—at cost, less accumulated depreciation and unamortized investment grants of $178,368,000 and $133,990,000 (note 2)	**167,699,000**	191,026,000
Container rental equipment—at cost, less accumulated depreciation of $31,753,000 and $25,450,000	**76,252,000**	50,302,000
Prepaid acquisition costs and other prepaid expenses	**76,698,000**	74,673,000
Policy and first mortgage loans	**41,402,000**	42,285,000
Real estate—at cost, less accumulated depreciation of $5,076,000 and $4,618,000	**28,296,000**	27,455,000
Furniture, fixtures, computers and other equipment—at cost, less accumulated depreciation of $11,271,000 and $9,307,000	**17,222,000**	15,804,000
Costs of businesses acquired in excess of amounts allocated to tangible net assets	**11,711,000**	14,895,000
Other assets	**45,724,000**	40,104,000
	$1,439,763,000	$1,496,847,000
Liabilities and Shareholders' Equity		
Unearned insurance premiums	**$ 243,370,000**	$ 226,020,000
Unpaid insurance losses and loss expenses, and policy claims pending	**388,031,000**	343,693,000
Future life policy benefits	**114,827,000**	110,584,000
Notes payable (note 6)	**293,636,000**	274,905,000
Accounts payable and accrued expenses	**99,830,000**	97,383,000
Federal and foreign income taxes (note 5)	**34,361,000**	51,849,000
	1,174,055,000	1,104,434,000
Debentures and subordinated notes (note 6)	**182,631,000**	166,595,000
Minority interests	**6,380,000**	8,873,000
Shareholders' equity (note 12):		
Preferred stock—redemption value $116,352,000 after treasury securities	**4,380,000**	4,380,000
Common stock	**3,075,000**	3,059,000
Additional paid-in capital	**127,197,000**	126,846,000
Retained earnings (note 13)	**134,399,000**	187,834,000
Unrealized losses on common and preferred stocks (note 3)	**(54,052,000)**	(2,180,000)
Treasury securities—at cost	**(138,302,000)**	(102,994,000)
	76,697,000	216,945,000
Commitments and contingencies (notes 14 and 15)		
	$1,439,763,000	$1,496,847,000

Exhibit 1. *(continued)*

Reliance Group, Incorporated and Subsidiaries
Consolidated Balance Sheet

Assets December 31	1975	1974 (Restated)
Marketable securities of insurance subsidiaries:		
Common and preferred stocks—at quoted market (cost $261,224,000 and $239,553,000) (note 4)	$ 250,592,000	$ 160,427,000
Bonds—at amortized cost (quoted market $480,416,000 and $348,828,000)	553,323,000	422,457,000
Invested cash	41,675,000	117,284,000
Cash (note 7)	37,087,000	60,122,000
Accounts and notes receivable, less allowances of $5,487,000 and $4,938,000 (note 5)	121,758,000	122,290,000
Finance lease receivables (notes 5 and 7)	24,898,000	92,179,000
Computer rental equipment—at cost, less accumulated depreciation and unamortized investment grants of $208,156,000 and $178,368,000 (note 2)	133,259,000	167,699,000
Container rental equipment—at cost, less accumulated depreciation of $41,335,000 and $31,753,000	85,199,000	76,252,000
Deferred policy acquisition costs and prepaid expenses	79,576,000	76,698,000
First mortgage and policy loans	41,396,000	41,402,000
Real estate—at cost, less accumulated depreciation of $7,113,000 and $5,076,000	39,400,000	28,296,000
Furniture, fixtures and other equipment—at cost, less accumulated depreciation of $15,429,000 and $11,271,000	20,120,000	17,222,000
Costs of businesses acquired in excess of amounts allocated to tangible net assets	9,495,000	11,711,000
Other assets (note 11)	59,806,000	40,876,000
	$1,497,584,000	$1,434,915,000

Exhibit 1. (continued)

Liabilities and Shareholders' Equity	December 31	1975	1974 (Restated)
Unearned insurance premiums		$ 248,864,000	$ 243,370,000
Unpaid insurance claims, related expenses and policy claims pending		448,221,000	388,031,000
Future policy benefits		141,079,000	114,827,000
Notes payable (note 7)		190,957,000	293,636,000
Limited recourse financing (note 7)		28,939,000	–
Accounts payable and accrued expenses		107,956,000	99,830,000
Federal and foreign income taxes, principally deferred (note 6)		27,223,000	34,361,000
		1,193,239,000	1,174,055,000
Debentures and subordinated notes (note 7)		180,560,000	182,631,000
Minority interests:			
Preferred stock of a subsidiary (note 3)		30,000,000	–
Other		7,825,000	6,380,000
		37,825,000	6,380,000
Shareholders' equity (notes 1, 13 and 14):			
Preferred stocks—par value		4,380,000	4,380,000
—difference between par value and redemption value		111,970,000	111,972,000
Redemption value of preferred stocks		116,350,000	116,352,000
Common Stock—par value		3,078,000	3,075,000
Additional paid-in capital		127,240,000	127,197,000
Retained earnings		99,866,000	129,551,000
Difference between par value and redemption value of preferred stocks		(111,970,000)	(111,972,000)
Unrealized loss on common and preferred stocks (note 4)		(10,302,000)	(54,052,000)
Treasury securities—at cost		(138,302,000)	(138,302,000)
		85,960,000	71,849,000
Commitments, contingencies, dividends and transfers of funds (notes 14, 15 and 16)			
		$1,497,584,000	$1,434,915,000

262

Exhibit 2. *Consolidated Statement of Operations*

Reliance Group, Incorporated and Subsidiaries
Consolidated Statement of Operations

Year Ended December 31	1975	1974 (Restated)
Revenues:		
Insurance premiums earned	$685,791,000	$585,129,000
Investment income of insurance companies	57,134,000	51,004,000
Equipment rentals and earned income on lease contracts (note 2)	97,997,000	105,041,000
Consulting and software	32,896,000	33,573,000
Other (note 7)	1,877,000	4,228,000
	875,695,000	778,975,000
Expenses:		
Policy claims and adjustment expenses	438,521,000	366,304,000
Policy acquisition costs and other insurance expenses	239,424,000	194,304,000
Policyholders' benefits and dividends	66,627,000	55,748,000
Depreciation-rental equipment (note 2)	49,401,000	55,882,000
Cost of sales-services	28,478,000	28,096,000
Interest	41,135,000	48,474,000
Selling, general and administrative (note 8)	37,721,000	50,397,000
	901,307,000	799,205,000
Operating loss from continuing operations before taxes and minority interests	(25,612,000)	(20,230,000)
Federal and foreign income tax benefits (note 6)	8,783,000	10,903,000
Minority interests (note 3)	(3,011,000)	(768,000)
Operating loss from continuing operations	(19,840,000)	(10,095,000)
Net realized gain (loss) on insurance investments (note 6)	3,786,000	(36,870,000)
Loss from continuing operations	(16,054,000)	(46,965,000)
Discontinued operations (note 9)	(8,082,000)	(4,206,000)
Loss before extraordinary items	(24,136,000)	(51,171,000)
Extraordinary items (note 10)	(2,715,000)	6,500,000
Net loss	$(26,851,000)	$(44,671,000)
Per-share information:		
Loss from continuing operations	$(4.27)	$(7.30)
Discontinued operations	(1.38)	(.55)
Loss before extraordinary items	(5.65)	(7.85)
Extraordinary items	(.46)	.85
Net loss	$(6.11)	$(7.00)
Average number of common shares outstanding	5,865,000	7,665,000

Appreciation of $43,750,000 in 1975 and depreciation of $51,872,000 in 1974, in the market value of investments in common and preferred stocks, have not been included in the Consolidated Statement of Operations but have been recorded in Shareholders' Equity (note 4).

Exhibit 3. *Consolidated Statement of Changes in Shareholders' Equity*

Reliance Group, Incorporated and Subsidiaries
Consolidated Statement of Changes in Shareholders' Equity

Year Ended December 31	1975	1974 (Restated)
Additional Paid-In Capital:		
Balance, beginning of year	$ 127,197,000	$ 126,846,000
Change arising from stock option and purchase plans, and contingent obligations	43,000	351,000
Balance, end of year	$ 127,240,000	$ 127,197,000
Retained Earnings:		
Balance, beginning of year as previously reported	$ 134,399,000	$ 187,834,000
Restatement for foreign currency translation (note 1)	(4,848,000)	(1,767,000)
Balance, beginning of year as restated	129,551,000	186,067,000
Net loss	(26,851,000)	(44,671,000)
	102,700,000	141,396,000
Less dividends (note 14):		
Common Stock ($.10 and $.40 per share)	587,000	2,857,000
Series B Preferred Stock ($.55 and $2.20 per share)	441,000	1,763,000
Series C Preferred Stock ($.65 and $2.60 per share)	1,806,000	7,225,000
Balance, end of year	$ 99,866,000	$ 129,551,000
Unrealized Loss on Common and Preferred Stocks:		
Balance, beginning of year	$ (54,052,000)	$ (2,180,000)
Appreciation (depreciation), after applicable taxes and minority interests of $1,502,000 and $2,166,000	43,750,000	(51,872,000)
Balance, end of year	$ (10,302,000)	$ (54,052,000)
Treasury Securities—at Cost:		
Balance, beginning of year	$ (138,302,000)	$ (102,994,000)
Acquisition of 1,968,147 common shares in exchange for the issuance of 9⅞ % Debentures due in 1999	—	(21,598,000)
Purchase of 1,500,000 common shares	—	(13,154,000)
Purchase of 185,377 stock purchase warrants expiring in 1987	—	(556,000)
Balance, end of year	$ (138,302,000)	$ (138,302,000)

Exhibit 2. *(continued)*

3. Acquisition	On January 31, 1975, a financing subsidiary of the Company, Reliance Financial Services Corporation ("RFSC"), acquired complete ownership of Commonwealth Land Title Insurance Company ("Commonwealth") from Provident National Corporation ("Provident") in exchange for the issuance of 300,000 shares of Series A Preferred Stock of RFSC, which shares have a redemption value of $100 per share and an annual cumulative dividend of $10 per share. Commencing October 31, 1980, RFSC is required to redeem 20,000 shares per year of the Series A Preferred Stock at $100 per share for a total redemption value of $30,000,000. At December 31, 1975 the $30,000,000 redemption value is included in minority interests in the Company's consolidated balance sheet. In addition, based on 7½ times the average annual after-tax earnings of Commonwealth in excess of $3,000,000 over a period of five years, Provident may receive up to an additional 100,000 shares of Series A Preferred Stock of RFSC. Under the agreement the average annual after-tax earnings of Commonwealth was $2,362,000 through December 31, 1975.

The acquisition of Commonwealth at a cost of $30,600,000, has been recorded based on the purchase method of accounting, with the accounts of Commonwealth adjusted accordingly. Commonwealth's revenues of $36,219,000 and net income of $2,665,000 since February 1, 1975 are included in the consolidated statement of operations. Preferred dividend requirements of $2,750,000 on the RFSC Series A Preferred Stock, since the date of acquisition of Commonwealth, are included in minority interests in the consolidated statement of operations.

13. Capital Stock, Stock Options and Warrants	Authorized Common Stock consists of 50,000,000 shares, $.25 par value. At December 31, 1975, there were 5,866,027 common shares outstanding, excluding 6,446,077 shares held in the treasury. The changes consisted of:

Year Ended December 31	1975	1974
Outstanding, beginning of year	5,852,426	9,256,106
Issued under contingent obligation incurred in connection with an acquisition	—	23,187
Issued under stock option and purchase plans	13,525	41,280
Issued upon conversion of preferred stock	76	—
Received in exchange for issuance of 9⅞% Debentures due in 1999	—	(1,968,147)
Received under cash offer to purchase	—	(1,500,000)
Outstanding, end of year	5,866,027	5,852,426

During 1974, the Company reacquired 3,468,147 shares of Common Stock—1,968,147 in exchange for the issuance of 9⅞% Debentures due in 1999 in the ratio of $14 principal amount of debentures for each common share, and 1,500,000 under a cash offer to purchase stock at $8.50 per share. These common shares, reacquired at a net cost of $34,752,000 including expenses, are being held in the treasury.

Authorized Preferred Stock consists of 25,000,000 shares, $1.00 par value. At December 31, 1975, the outstanding Preferred Stock consisted of 801,756 shares of $2.20 convertible Series B Preferred Stock (excluding 799,050 shares held in the treasury) and 2,778,951 shares of $2.60 nonconvertible Series C Preferred Stock.

The Series B Preferred Stock has one vote for each six shares, cumulative dividend rights of $2.20 a share (see note 14) and is redeemable at the Company's option at various prices declining to $55 a share. Each share is convertible into approximately 1.53 shares of Common Stock, for a total of 1,224,905 common shares as of December 31, 1975. The Company is required to redeem the 801,756 outstanding shares of Series B Preferred Stock at $55 a share for a total redemption value of $44,097,000. Assuming all previously converted and reacquired shares of Series B Preferred Stock are used toward satisfying required redemptions, the outstanding shares would not have to be redeemed prior to July 1, 1993.

The Series C Preferred Stock has cumulative dividend rights of $2.60 a share (see note 14) and is redeemable at the Company's option any time after June 30, 1983 at

Exhibit 3. (continued)

various prices decreasing to $26 a share. The Company is required to redeem the Series C Preferred Stock at $26 a share commencing July 1, 1988 for a total redemption value of $72,253,000. During the years 1988 through 1997, the Company is required to redeem 138,948 shares a year, and from 1998 through 2002 is required to redeem 277,895 shares a year.

The balance sheet at December 31, 1975 reflects preferred stocks at redemption value and the balance sheet at December 31, 1974 has been reclassified accordingly.

14. Dividends and Transfers of Funds

During 1975, the Board of Directors of the Company determined to omit the quarterly dividends on Common Stock and the quarterly dividends of $.55 per share on the Series B Preferred Stock and $.65 per share on the Series C Preferred Stock. The dividends on the preferred stocks are cumulative. At December 31, 1975, the accumulated and unpaid preferred dividends amounted to $6,741,000 ($1,323,000 or $1.65 per share, on the Series B Preferred Stock and $5,418,000 or $1.95 per share, on the Series C Preferred Stock). If dividends on a Series (either "B" or "C") of Preferred Stock shall be in arrears in an amount equal to 1½ times the annual dividend, then the holders (as a class) of that Series in arrears shall be entitled to elect two members of the Board of Directors of the Company.

Dividends on Common Stock cannot be resumed until all accumulated and unpaid dividends on preferred stocks have been paid in full. In addition, under the terms of a loan agreement, Common Stock dividends may not exceed 75% of the aggregate of consolidated net income after December 31, 1971 over the aggregate of Preferred Stock dividends paid after December 31, 1971. Under this formula, at December 31, 1975, an additional $39,000,000 of net income would have been required before the Company could pay dividends on its Common Stock.

17. Subsequent Event

On January 29, 1976, the Company announced that its principal subsidiary, Reliance Insurance Company plans to sell through a prospectus $50,000,000 of nonconvertible, sinking-fund preferred stock through a public underwritten offering. The offer will take place upon the effective date of a registration statement to be filed with the Securities and Exchange Commission as soon as possible after obtaining regulatory and other approvals.

RELIANCE INSURANCE COMPANY REGISTERS

$50 MILLION PREFERRED STOCK OFFERING WITH SEC

PHILADELPHIA, PA., June 14, 1976---Reliance Insurance Company
announced today that it had filed a registration statement with the
Securities and Exchange Commission relating to a proposed public
offering of 2,000,000 shares of non-convertible, sinking fund, Series A
Cumulative Preferred Stock. The shares will be offered at a proposed
price of $25 per share, and a required sinking fund will commence
June 1, 1987 to retire the entire issue by June 1, 2001. White, Weld
& Co., Incorporated will be manager of the underwriting group to offer
the shares publicly.

Proceeds to the company from the sale of the shares will be added
to its general funds and will be used primarily to increase its investment
portfolio.

- more -

NEWS

**RELIANCE
INSURANCE
COMPANIES**

FOR RELEASE: IMMEDIATE

NEWS ITEM NO:

FOR ADDITIONAL INFORMATION: John T. Leatham
Executive Vice President
Reliance Group, Incorporated
(212) 573-8300

National Headquarters ☐ 4 Penn Center Plaza, Philadelphia, Pennsylvania 19103 ☐ Telephone 215 · 864-4000

267

PART IV

Issues in Corporate Financial Reporting

Total
Electronics
Corporation (A)

Total Electronics Corporation (TEC) is a vertically integrated manufacturer and distributor of complex electronics equipment for both military and civilian markets. Founded and incorporated in California in 1964, the firm has grown primarily through a combination of intensive new product development and the acquisition of other high technology firms. Such mergers have often been accomplished with cash payments, but several larger acquisitions involved instead the use of convertible securities.

TEC made its first public offering in early 1966 and its stock was subsequently afforded a price-earnings ratio high enough to facilitate the use of equity-based instruments for acquisitions. Yet, by the end of 1970, TEC's stock had fallen substantially in price and an antitrust consent decree in that year prevented the firm from making any further major acquisitions. Thus, in the period 1970–73, TEC's management concentrated on internal growth within the constraints of the firm's complex capital structure.

Exhibit 1 presents data on outstanding issues of TEC securities.

Exhibit 2 provides information on TEC's performance in fiscal year 1973.

QUESTION

1. Based on the information in the case, calculate TEC's primary and fully diluted earnings per share for the 1973 fiscal year. Assume that APB Opinion #15 applies to all outstanding securities. You may also assume a 50 percent tax rate.

This case was prepared by Steven E. Levy, Research Assistant, under the supervision of Associate Professor John K. Shank as the basis for class discussion rather than to illustrate either the effective or ineffective handling of an administrative situation.

271

Exhibit 1. Outstanding Securities Issues, December 31, 1973

ISSUE	ISSUE DATE	AMOUNT	ISSUE PRICE	COUPON RATE/ STATED DIVIDEND RATE	CONVERSION RATE	PRIME RATE AT TIME OF ISSUE	MATURITY/ EXPIRATION
I. Convertible Debentures	12/67	$15,000,000	$1000/bond	3.75%	Each bond convertible into 12 shares of common	6.00%	1987
II. Convertible Preferred Stock Series A	3/68	$12,000,000	$ 100/share	$5.00	Each share convertible into 2.75 shares of common	6.00%	–
III. Convertible Preferred Stock Series B	10/68	$25,000,000	$ 100/share	$6.50	Each share convertible into .3 shares of common	6.25%	–
IV. Convertible Debentures	1/70	$20,000,000	$ 987.50/bond	6%	Each bond convertible into 50 shares of common	8.50%	1985
V. Convertible Preferred Stock Series C	4/70	$10,000,000	$ 100/share	$5.25	Each share convertible into 4 shares of common	8.00%	–
VI. Common Stock Purchase Warrants	9/68	5 million warrants	–	–	Each warrant convertible into 1 share of common at exercise price of $60	6.50%	1988
VII. Common Stock Purchase Warrants	2/66	200,000 warrants	–	–	Each warrant convertible into 1 share of common at exercise price of $10	5.00%	1982

Exhibit 2. TEC Data, Fiscal Year 1973

A. Profit before tax $20,400,000
   Tax   10,200,000

   Net income after tax   10,200,000
   Preferred dividends   2,750,000

   Net income to common stock $ 7,450,000

B. Common shares outstanding (12/31/72)   3,200,000 shares
   Common stock offering (3/31/73)   120,000 shares
   Common shares outstanding (12/31/73)   3,320,000 shares

C. Price per share (1/1/73) $32.75
   Average price per share for fiscal year 1973 $28.00
   Price per share (12/31/73) $26.25

Gulf & Western
Industries, Inc. (B)

Jack Abel was in doubt. What were the earnings of Gulf & Western Industries, Inc.? Recently, when questions of this type had occurred, he had frequently given them to Bob Dennis to obtain clearer understanding and analysis. Calling Bob Dennis in, Jack Abel handed him a thick file saying:

> *Bob, I really don't know how to approach this. Earnings per share seems to be one of the most frequently utilized indicators of a firm's performance. However, we need to know more than just the EPS for this year. The effect on future earnings of conversions of convertible securities or exercise of warrants or options is important. We need some indication of the effects of these already contracted future changes of capital structure on EPS. Some years ago, the accountants came to our rescue and began to compute "fully diluted" earnings per share. But in Gulf & Western's case, . . .*

As the sentence trailed off, Bob Dennis picked up his file and returned to his desk.

GULF & WESTERN INDUSTRIES

Gulf & Western Industries, Inc. is a large conglomerate with revenues in excess of $2.5 billion. Gulf & Western Industries had pursued an active acquisition strategy throughout its corporate history. As a result, the firm had outstanding a

This case was written by Ray G. Stephens under the supervision of Dennis P. Frolin as the basis for class discussion rather than to illustrate either effective or ineffective handling of an administrative situation.

number of hybrid securities including convertible debentures, convertible preferreds, and stock purchase warrants (Exhibit 1).

Gulf & Western's holdings were widely diversified. Their 1975 Annual Report divided the company into nine groups: (1) Manufacturing, (2) Food and Agricultural Products, (3) Natural Resources, (4) Paper and Building Products, (5) Leisure Time, (6) Automotive Replacement Parts, (7) Consumer Products, (8) Financial Services, and (9) Apparel Products.

Page 66 of the 1975 financial statement (year ending July 31, 1975) showed:

Net earnings	primary	$4.49
	fully diluted	$3.67

Exhibit 1. Note E—Long-term and Convertible Subordinated Debt

Note E — Long-term and Convertible Subordinated Debt

	July 31 1975	1974
Long-term debt includes:		
Notes payable to institutional investors, interest 4¾% to 9⅞%, averaging approximately 6½%, due 1976 to 2004	$220,695,000	$172,764,000
6% subordinated debentures due 1978 to 1988	50,019,000	50,885,000
7% subordinated debentures due 2003, net of unamortized discount of $47,719,000 at July 31, 1975 and $40,478,000 at July 31, 1974 (effective interest rate of 11%)	83,303,000	75,264,000
5% debentures due 1979 to 1988, convertible into common stock of the Company at $26.76 a share	49,898,000	49,898,000
Notes payable to banks due 1976 to 1986:		
Interest at or above (primarily ½%) the prevailing prime rates	76,263,000	61,149,000
Interest ½% above the prevailing prime rates, with effective interest limited to a maximum of 7½% to 8¾% from date of note to date of interest payment	110,000,000	60,000,000
Interest at 115% to 120% of the prevailing prime rates	47,500,000	47,500,000
Interest 6% to 11%, averaging approximately 8%	190,900,000	190,521,000
Other notes and debentures, interest 4½% to 10½%, averaging approximately 7¼%, due 1976 to 1999, net of unamortized discount of $1,341,000 at July 31, 1975 and $1,550,000 at July 31, 1974	159,567,000	87,044,000
	$988,145,000	$795,025,000
Less current maturities	45,894,000	36,697,000
	$942,251,000	$758,328,000
Convertible subordinated debt includes:		
5½% debentures, due 1992 and 1993, convertible into common stock of the Company at $28.17 a share, may be redeemed at 104¼% of face	$336,137,000	$336,137,000
5¾% debentures and notes, due 1976 to 1990, convertible into common stock of the Company from $21.66 to $23.58 a share, may be redeemed at 103.3% of face	76,882,000	82,708,000
5½% notes, due 1979 to 1987, convertible at July 31, 1975 into common stock of a subsidiary, Kayser-Roth Corporation, at $35.00 a share (to be convertible into 228,572 shares of the Company's $2.50 Series D convertible preferred stock subsequent to the merger referred to in Note B), may be redeemed at 105.05% of face	20,000,000	
	$433,019,000	$418,845,000
Less current maturities	1,115,000	2,194,000
	$431,904,000	$416,651,000

Maturities of long-term and convertible subordinated debt during the five years ending July 31, 1980, are:

1976	$ 47,009,000
1977	80,932,000
1978	71,450,000
1979	47,531,000
1980	102,289,000

The Company has complied with restrictions and limitations required under terms of various loan agreements. Consolidated retained earnings unrestricted as to the payment of cash dividends at July 31, 1975 was $189,500,000.

The conversion prices of convertible debt are subject to anti-dilution provisions.

Exhibit 1. *(continued) Note F—Capital Stock*

277

Note F—Capital Stock

	Shares			
	Authorized July 31		Outstanding July 31	
	1975	1974	1975	1974
Cumulative, convertible preferred stock, recorded at $2.50 par value:				
$3.875 Series C—convertible into 3.508 shares of common, may be redeemed at $104.00 a share, $100.00 liquidation value, (outstanding excludes 191,169 shares held in treasury)	1,200,000	1,200,000	749,559	751,924
$2.50 Series D—currently convertible into 1.488 shares of common, is redeemable beginning in 1981 at $42.50 a share (but cannot be redeemed unless the market value of common reaches a specified amount, initially $36.52 a share),$40.00 liquidation value . . .	2,500,000		774,984	
Undesignated	1,300,000	3,800,000		
Cumulative, non-convertible preferred stock:				
$5.75 series, 5% sinking fund requirement, may be redeemed at $103.00 a share, recorded at $100.00 liquidation value, (outstanding excludes shares held in treasury—11,917 at July 31, 1975 and 29,134 at July 31, 1974)	635,578	654,066	354,482	355,753
Common stock recorded at $1.00 par value:				
(outstanding excludes shares held in treasury—1,490,000 at July 31, 1975 and 1,500,000 at July 31, 1974)	150,000,000	150,000,000	30,615,666	31,105,572

Each share of the preferred and common stock is entitled to one vote.

Preferred stock outstanding at July 31, 1975 does not include 225,000 shares of $3.875 Series C reserved under the stock purchase plan (see below), and up to 50,000 shares of $2.50 Series D reserved for issuance under terms of an agreement with former shareholders of an acquired business as set forth in Note B.

Common stock outstanding at July 31, 1975 does not include 1,519,154 shares reserved under the stock option incentive plans (see below); 897,366 shares reserved under the stock purchase plan (see below); 15,457,729 shares reserved for exercise of warrants expiring 1978 and 1986 at a total exercise price of $402,830,000; 17,284,554 shares reserved for issuance upon conversion of an aggregate of $462,917,000 principal amount of convertible debt; and 3,857,030 shares reserved for conversion of convertible preferred stock outstanding and the shares of $2.50 Series D convertible preferred stock reserved for issuance.

The conversion prices of the cumulative convertible preferred stock and the exercise prices of warrants and options are subject to anti-dilution provisions.

The Company's 1964 Stock Option Incentive Plan provides for the issuance of qualified options to key employees to purchase common stock of the Company at a price not less than fair market value on the date of grant.

The Company's 1973 Key Employees Stock Purchase Plan provides for the issuance of non-qualified options to key employees to purchase shares of the Company's $3.875 Series C convertible preferred stock or common stock at a price not less than fair market value on the date of grant. When an employee exercises an option for shares of either class of stock, his option for shares of the other class is automatically rescinded.

In reviewing the credit file, Bob Dennis ascertained that uncertainty in determining Gulf & Western's EPS had occurred previously. During 1973, Gulf & Western came under attack by a number of financial analysts and columnists (Exhibits 2 and 3). Of particular concern to the financial analysts and columnists was the calculation of Gulf & Western's fully diluted EPS for the 1972 fiscal year, an issue of unusual importance given the firm's rather complex capitalization. Exhibit 8 contains some relevant portions of APB Opinion #15 used in these calculations.

The file also contained the 1973 and 1974 calculations of EPS by a previous analyst (Exhibit 4). His analysis raised the following questions about the practices utilized by Gulf & Western Industries in determining their EPS for financial statements:

1. Gulf & Western's practice of applying the proceeds of the exercise of warrants and options, under the "treasury stock" method, to the repurchase of outstanding convertible debt
2. The "purchase" of convertible debt at beginning of the fiscal year market prices, rather than at an average price for the fiscal year
3. The inclusion in income, utilizing the amortization method, of bond discount profit generated by convertible "repurchase"
4. Application of a below normal corporate tax rate to interest savings from debt "repurchase"

Just at that moment, Jack Abel came in. "What would be the effect on EPS if the company's stock price was equal to its book value?" Jack said, "Once stock price falls below book, I can't help but worry." Gulf & Western's 1975 year-end book value was $28.25 per share.

1. Analyze the alternative methods for calculating fully diluted earnings per share presented in Exhibits 3 and 4. Given your knowledge of APB Opinion #15 and the excerpts from *Unofficial Interpretations of APB No. 15* in Exhibit 7, do you feel that Gulf & Western's method of accounting for dilution is proper and fairly represents the realities of the firm's position?
2. Examine the excerpts from Note A from Gulf & Western's 1974 and 1975 Annual Reports (Exhibit 5). Given that the firm utilized the same method in calculating diluted earnings in both fiscal years, how would you evaluate the disclosure to investors contained in these notes? How could the Notes be improved to provide better disclosure?

3. Using Exhibit 6 and 7, calculate a 1975 EPS on a fully diluted basis which you feel is proper and fairly represents the realities of the firm's position.

4. How would Gulf & Western's calculation of fully diluted earnings be affected by an increase in the price of the firm's common stock? How would your calculation be affected by a similar price increase? Calculate approximate 1975 earnings on a fully diluted basis utilizing both methods, assuming a stock price of $28.25.

Exhibit 2.

The following story appeared in Alan Abelson's column, "Up and Down Wall Street," in *Barron's* of February 12, 1973:

We were reminded again of the creative side of bookkeeping by the current controversy surrounding Gulf & Western. No, we don't mean the brawl with A&P. Or, whether or not the prospective acquisition of Talcott National will violate antitrust laws. Rather, we're referring to the dispute over how G&W calculates its fully diluted earnings per share.

In one corner are G&W and its auditors, Ernst & Ernst.

In the opposite one is a trio of analysts: Sidney J. Heller, director of the Conglomerate Service of Sterling, Grace & Co.; and Ted O'Glove and Robert Olstein, who run the "Quality of Earnings Report" for Coenen & Co. By G&W's lights, in fiscal '72, on a fully diluted basis, it earned $3.30 a share. Working independently and in separate reports, Heller and the two Os come up with the same total—$2.61 a share—as the true fully diluted figure.

The analysts (who, lest we be accused of impartiality, deserve high marks for a very professional job) base their argument on APB No. 15 and its subsequent "Accounting Interpretation." No. 15 laid down certain guidelines for determining fully diluted per share earnings and the interpretation elaborated on these. We blanch at even attempting to translate accountantese into English. Essentially, though, the issue turns on whether in doing its calculations, G&W properly accounted for the proceeds from the hypothetical exercise of outstanding warrants and options.

G&W chose to use those mythical proceeds to buy in convertible debentures; in doing so, moreover, it used prices at the beginning of the year rather than a yearly average price (which, as it turned out, was higher). The benefits for G&W were twofold: (a) since its converts were selling considerably below par, it was able to enrich earnings by the amount of the discount; (b) by reducing the amount of convertible debentures outstanding, it also softened the dilutive impact of those securities on the per share figure.

What G&W should have done, the analysts say, was to use those hypothetical funds raised from warrants and options to retire straight, rather than convertible, debt and invest the rest in government securities or commercial paper (all of this, after theoretically buying in 20 percent of the common). Heller, in his report, points out that except for National General, all other conglomerates he is familiar with calculate their fully diluted net in this fashion. Hence, he concludes, "what G&W is doing in this instance makes their earnings non-comparable to those of most other companies." In like vein, O'Glove and Olstein charge that in purchasing the convertible debt rather than the straight debt, in utilizing debt discount and beginning-of-year bond

Exhibit 2. *(continued)*

purchases in making fully diluted per share earnings calculations, G&W "violated" the accounting interpretation of APB No. 15.

What's helpful to reported earnings today, paradoxically, could prove a drag in future. O'Glove and Olstein put it this way: "The unrealistic assumptions on the part of GW and its auditors regarding fully diluted earnings per share can best be exemplified by the following example. Assume GW's earnings from operations jump 15 percent per year for the next two fiscal years and the prices of the company's convertible bonds move substantially over par. At the end of two years, GW's earnings would be approximately $93 million, up from fiscal 1972's reported $70 million. Also further assume that the warrants are exercised, the company utilizes the money to retire the 5½ percent convertible debentures, and the 5¼ debentures are converted by its holders.

"We believe that these assumptions, if anything, are fair to GW and do not represent unrealistic events. Under the aforementioned assumptions, the primary earnings per share would be $3.31, or the same as fiscal 1972, despite a more than 30 percent increment in after-tax dollar earnings. In essence, what we are saying, if GW's stock price moves upward, it would probably have a highly opposite negative effect on earnings per share computations. Thus, investors should be aware of the fact that an increasing stock price could have a negative impact on earnings per share, and hence work against the stock price moving up to the same degree as after tax earnings."

G&W and its auditors counter that the "interpretation" of APB is unofficial and that their practice is both consistent (they calculated the same way last year) and fully compatible with No. 15. Our colleague, Steve Anreder, checked in with Chief Accountant Burton of the SEC to see if he had any feelings, pro or con, and discovered that the agency is actively studying the matter (as they say in official argot). "It would appear," comments Burton, "that Gulf & Western followed the letter of the opinion. But the question is whether they followed the spirit as well."

Exhibit 3. Calculation of EPS of Gulf & Western Industries, Inc., Fiscal Year Ended July 31, 1972*

	EARNINGS OR CREDIT (MILLIONS OF DOLLARS)		SHARES (MILLIONS)		EPS
Primary earnings	63.9		19.4	(1)	$3.30
Conversion of Series C Preferred	3.2	(2)	1.4	(3)	
	67.1		20.8		3.22
Conversion of convertible debt	14.4	(4)	9.9†		
	81.5		30.7		2.66
Exercise of warrants	10.9	(5)	4.7	(6)	
Fully diluted EPS	92.4		35.4		2.61

Notes

1. Assumes conversion of Series A and B Preferred Stocks as common stock equivalents.
2. Represents elimination of dividend requirements on Series C Preferred.
3. Shares issued in conversion of Series C Preferred.
4. Assumes 50 percent tax rate on investment income.
5. Repurchase of public debt with average rate of 7.5 percent; assumed tax rate of 50 percent.
6. Assumes repurchase of 20 percent of outstanding common stock at average price of $35 per share. Given outstanding warrants and options for 8 million shares at aggregate exercise price of $406 million, 3.3 million shares would be repurchased with $292 million remaining for debt repurchase.

Sources: Thornton O'Glove and Robert A. Olstein, "Quality of Earnings Report" Coenen & Co., Inc.), January 24, 1973.
Sidney J. Heller, " Conglomerate Service" (Sterling, Grace & Co., Inc.), January 1973.
*Calculation based on APB Opinion #15 (analysts' calculation).
†Convertible debt.

RATE	AMOUNT	CONVERSION PRICE	EQUIVALENT SHARES	MARKET PRICE 7/31/72
5½%	$385 million	$56.70	6.8 million	83
5¼%	98 million	43.60–49.02	2.2 million	95
5%	50 million	53.87	0.9 million	NA
	$533 million		9.9 million	

Exhibit 3. (continued)

Calculation of Fully Diluted Earnings per Share (in thousands)

	EPS.	Earnings	Shares
	YEAR ENDED JULY 31, 1972		
Net earnings and average common and common equivalent shares per financial statements		$69,411	19,372
Less dividends on preferred stock other than common equivalents		5,519	
Primary Earnings Per Share	$3.30	$63,892	19,372
Calculation of fully diluted earnings per share			
(1) Assume exercise of warrants and options			7,993
(2) Assume purchase of treasury stock			(3,277)
(3) Assume retirement of convertible debt and interest saving net of tax		18,948	4,716
(4) Convert the balance of convertible debt and interest savings net of tax		4,128	2,029
(5) Convert $3.875 Series C convertible preferred and savings on preferred dividends		3,191	1,435
Fully Diluted Earnings Per Share	$3.27	$90,159	27,552
Conclusion	Less than 3% Dilution		

Source: Gulf & Western Industries, Inc., 1973 10K Report.

Notes

1. Includes interest savings and bond discount. Interest savings calculated at average rather than marginal tax rate. "Repurchase" at price prevailing at beginning of fiscal year rather than average price.
2. The 1972 Gulf & Western Industries, Inc. Annual Report shows (p. 22) both primary and fully diluted as $3.30 per share.

Exhibit 4-A. *Calculations of Earnings Per Share of Gulf & Western Industries, Inc. Fiscal Year Ended July 31, 1973*

PRIOR ANALYST'S ALTERNATIVE CALCULATIONS

	EARNINGS OR CREDIT	SHARES	EPS
	(THOUSANDS)	(THOUSANDS)	
Primary earnings	83,791	18,217	$4.60
Exercise of warrants and options		8,042	
Treasury stock purchase (20% of 13,945)		(2,789)	
Repurchase of convertible (1) (2) debt (at 48% tax rate)	10,840		
Convert balance of debt (at 48% tax rate)	2,348		
Convert Series C Preferred	2,917		
	99,896	26,356	$3.79
As reported by Gulf & Western	106,892	26,356	$4.06

Notes

1. Prices used for purchase were beginning of year prices, higher than average prices. If actually repurchased, this would have resulted in pre-tax book profit of $58,030,000.
2. If debt were retired instead of convertibles, then shares would increase by approximately 6,198,623 and additional income at average of 7.5 percent would result in an after-tax (48 percent tax rate) increase of $12,720,000. Fully diluted EPS would then be $3.46.

Exhibit 4-B. Calculations of Earnings Per Share of Gulf & Western Industries, Inc. Fiscal Year Ended July 31, 1974

PRIOR ANALYST'S ALTERNATIVE CALCULATIONS

	EARNINGS OR CREDIT	SHARES	EPS
	(THOUSANDS)	(THOUSANDS)	
Primary earnings	$ 95,575	16,139 (1)	$5.92
Exercise of warrants and options		8,313	
Repurchase of treasury stock (20% of 15,553)		(3,111)	
Repurchase convertible debt (48% tax rate) (2) (3)	13,169		
Retire subordinated debt	1,735		
Convert Class C Preferred	2,636	1,319	
	$113,115	22,660	$4.99
As reported by Gulf & Western	$121,132	22,660	$5.35

Notes

1. Note that Series A and B preferred were called during 1974.
2. Prices used for purchase were beginning of the year prices, higher than average prices. If actually repurchased, this would have resulted in pre-tax book profit of $157,935,000.
3. If debt were retired instead of convertibles, then shares would increase by approximately 6,198,623 and additional income at an average of 7.5 percent would result in an after-tax (48 percent) increase of $12,121,512. Fully diluted EPS would then be $4.34.

Exhibit 5. Gulf & Western Industries, Inc., Earnings Per Share

1974

Primary earnings per share amounts are based on the weighted average common and dilutive common equivalent (the Company's $1.75 Series A and $3.50 Series B convertible preferred stock) shares outstanding during the respective periods.

In computing fully diluted earnings per share the following additional assumptions are made:

1. exercise of all options and all warrants
2. use of the proceeds of such assumed exercises to purchase, at market prices, 20 percent of the outstanding common shares for the treasury and part of the Company's convertible debt
3. conversion of the remaining convertible preferred stock and debt.

1975

Primary earnings per share amounts are based on the weighted average common and dilutive common equivalent (primarily the Company's $1.75 Series A and $3.50 Series B convertible preferred stock, all of which were converted to common shares or redeemed as of April 1, 1974) shares outstanding during the respective periods.

In computing fully diluted earnings per share the following additional assumptions are made:

1. exercise of all options and all warrants
2. use of the proceeds of such assumed exercises to purchase, at market prices, 20 percent of the outstanding common shares for the treasury and Company debt (including convertible debt)
3. conversion of the remaining convertible preferred stock and debt, if any

Exhibit 6-A. Calculation of Fully Diluted Earnings Per Share, Year Ended July 31, 1975

	EPS	EARNINGS	SHARES
		(IN THOUSANDS)	
Net earnings and average common shares outstanding		$140,055	30,040
Assumed exercise of dilutive options and purchases of treasury stock (net)			18
Less dividends on preferred stock (none of which are common equivalents)		(5,138)	
Primary earnings per share	$4.49	$134,917	30,058
Reverse dilutive effect of options included in primary calculation			(18)
			30,040
Calculation of fully diluted earnings per share:			
(1) Assume exercise of all warrants and options—Schedule A			16,592
(2) Assume purchase of treasury stock—Schedule A			(6,123)
(3) Assume retirement of convertible debt and interest savings net of tax—Schedule A		$ 19,415	
(4) Assume purchase of other debt and interest savings net of tax—Schedule A		1,682	
		$ 21,097	10,469
(5) Convert $3.875 Series C convertible preferred—749,559 shares × 3.508 and savings on preferred dividends Convert $2.50 Series D convertible preferred—774,984 shares × 1.488 × 36/360 (issued June 26, 1975) and savings on preferred dividends		2,905	2,629
(6) Effect of dilution in affiliates earnings per share		188	115
		(600)	
	$1.79	$ 23,590	13,213
Fully diluted earnings per share	$3.67	$158,507	43,253

	POTENTIAL	
	Additional Shares	Cash Proceeds
I. Warrants and Options		
Warrants to purchase common at $26.621 a share	14,857	$395,508
Warrants to purchase common at $12.18 a share	601	7,322
Options under the stock option incentive plan with average price of $14.47 a share	518	7,498
Options under the stock purchase plan with average price of $13.04 a share	616	8,032
	16,592	$418,360
II. Treasury Stock Purchase		
Common shares o/s at 7/31/75	30,616	
Percent limitation	20%	
Total shares to be purchased	6,123	(6,123)
Year-end price (higher than average)	$ 21.25	
Cash needed	$130,114	(130,114)
Balance of cash to purchase debt		$288,246

Exhibit 6-A. *(continued)*

	Price of Debt on 8/1/74	Principal Amount	Interest Saved, Gross
III. *Convertible Debt to be Retired*			
5¼% convertible at $21.66–$23.58	$64	$ 76,882	$ 4,036
5½% convertible at $28.17	54¾	336,137	18,488
5% convertible at $26.76	77	49,898	2,495
		$462,917	$25,019
IV. *Other Debt to be Retired*			
7% subordinated	55	30,156	2,168
		$493,073	$27,187

Effect on Shares:

	Shares
5¼% convertible	(49,204)
5½% convertible	(184,035)
5% convertible	(38,421)
	$ 16,586
7% subordinated	(16,586)
	$ 0
	10,469

Summary

	Earnings	*Shares*
Steps I, II and III as per above	$25,019	
Apply tax at effective rate of 22.4% based on three-year average	(5,604)	
	$19,415	
Step IV as per above	$ 2,168	
Apply tax at effective rate of 22.4% as above	(486)	
	$ 1,682	
	$21,097	10,469

Source: Gulf & Western Industries, Inc., 1975 10-K Report.

288

Exhibit 6-B. *Calculation of Fully Diluted Earnings Per Share, Year Ended July 31, 1974*

	EPS	EARNINGS	SHARES
		(IN THOUSANDS)	
Net earnings and average common and common equivalent shares per financial statements		$100,646	32,278
Less dividends on preferred stock other than common equivalents		(5,071)	
Primary earnings per share	$2.96	$ 95,575	32,278
Calculation of fully diluted earnings per share:			
(1) Assume exercise of warrants and options—Schedule A			16,626
(2) Assume purchase of treasury stock—Schedule A			(6,222)
(3) Assume retirement of convertible debt and interest savings net of tax—Schedule A		$ 20,007	
(4) Assume purchase of other debt and interest savings net of tax—Schedule A		2,636	
		$ 22,643	10,404
(5) Convert $3.875 Series C convertible preferred—751,924 shares × 3.508 and savings on preferred dividends		2,914	2,638
	$1.96	$ 25,557	13,042
Fully diluted earnings per share	$2.68	$121,132	45,320

Exhibit 6-B. (continued)

	POTENTIAL		Price of Debt on 8/1/73	Principal Amount	Interest Saved, Gross
	Additional Shares	Cash Proceeds			
I. Warrants and Options					
Warrants to purchase common at $26.621 a share	14,770	$395,508			
Warrants to purchase common at $12.18 a share	600	7,323			
Options under the stock option incentive plan with average price of $13.78 a share	626	8,627			
Options under the stock purchase plan with average price of $12.78 a share	630	8,048			
	16,626	$419,506			
II. Treasury Stock Purchase					
Common shares o/s at 7/31/74	31,106				
% limitation	20%				
Total shares to be purchased	6,222 (6,222)				
Average price (higher than year-end price)	$ 12.54				
Cash needed	$78,024 (78,024)				
Balance of cash to purchase debt		$341,482			
III. Convertible Debt to be Retired					
5¼% convertible at $21.66–$23.58		(61,617)	$74½	$ 82,708	$ 4,342
5½% convertible at $28.17		(211,767)	63	336,137	18,488
5% convertible at $26.76		(37,424)	75	49,898	2,495
		$ 30,674		$468,743	$25,325
IV. Other Debt to be Retired					
7% subordinated		(30,674)	65	47,191	3,337
	10,404	$ 0		$515,934	$28,662

290

	Effect on	
Summary	Earnings	Shares
Steps I, II and III as per above	$25,325	
Apply tax at effective rate of 21% based on three-year average	(5,318)	
	$20,007	
Step IV as per above	$ 3,337	
Apply tax at effective rate of 21% as above	(701)	
	$ 2,636	
	$22,643	10,404

Source: Gulf & Western Industries, Inc., 1975 10–K Report.

Exhibit 6-C. Calculation of Fully Diluted Earnings Per Share, Year Ended July 31, 1973

	EPS	EARNINGS	SHARES
		(IN THOUSANDS)	
Net earnings and average common and common equivalent shares per financial statements		$ 89,216	36,434
Less dividends on preferred stock other than common equivalents		(5,425)	
Primary earnings per share	$2.30	$ 83,791	36,434
Calculation of fully diluted earnings per share:			
(1) Assume exercise of warrants and options—Schedule A			16,084
(2) Assume purchase of treasury stock—Schedule A			(5,578)
(3) Assume retirement of convertible debt and interest savings net of tax—Schedule A		$ 16,594	10,506
(4) Convert the balance of convertible debt and interest savings net of tax—Schedule A		3,590	3,148
(5) Convert $3.875 Series C convertible preferred—752,724 shares × 3.486 and savings on preferred dividends		2,917	2,624
	$1.42	$ 23,101	16,278
Fully diluted per share	$2.03	$106,892	52,712

292

POTENTIAL

	Additional Shares	Cash Proceeds
I. Warrants and Options		
Warrants to purchase common at $26.62\tfrac{1}{} a share	14,216	$380,655
Warrants to purchase common at $26.62\tfrac{1}{} issued during year	232	6,192
Warrants to purchase common at $12.18 a share	600	7,323
Other warrants	22	600
Options with average price of $15.05 a share	1,014	15,256
	16,084	$410,026

II. Treasury Stock Purchase		
Common shares o/s at 7/31/73	27,890	
% limitation	20%	
Total shares to be purchased	5,578	
Average price (higher than year-end price)	$ 15.04	
	(5,578)	
Cash needed	$83,865	
		(83,865)
Balance of cash to purchase debt		$326,161

III. Convertible Debt to be Retired			Price of Debt on 8/1/72	Principal Amount	Interest Saved, Gross
5\tfrac{1}{4}% debentures convertible at $21.80–$24.51		(81,406)	$96	$ 84,798	$ 4,452
5\tfrac{1}{2}% convertible at $28.35		(244,755)	81\tfrac{3}{4}	299,393	16,467
	10,506	$ 0		$384,191	$20,919

293

Exhibit 6-C. (continued)

IV. Convert Balance of Debt				
5½% convertible at $28.35	1,296		$ 36,745	$ 2,021
5% convertible at $26.94	1,852		49,898	2,495
			86,643	
	3,148		$470,834	$ 4,516

	Effect on	
	Earnings	*Shares*
Summary		
Steps I, II and III as per above	$20,919	10,506
Apply tax on above at effective rate of 20.5% based on three-year average	(4,288)	
	$16,631	
Other warrants	(37)	10,506
	$16,594	10,506
Step IV as per above	$ 4,516	3,148
Apply tax at effective rate of 20.5% as above	(926)	
	$ 3,590	3,148

Exhibit 7. Selected Prices of Gulf & Western Convertible Securities

	1.75 A PFD	3.50 B PFD	3.875 C PFD	$5\frac{1}{4}$ S 87	$5\frac{1}{4}$ S 7A	$5\frac{1}{2}$ S 92–93
7/31/71	94.25	114.00	57.38	80.00	—	68.25
Avg., fiscal 72	111.53	137.81	65.98	88.57	—	77.48
7/31/72	120.00	143.63	69.00	93.50	—	83.00
Avg., fiscal 73	99.94	116.57	56.65	86.44	—	74.54
7/31/73	85.25	106.00	50.38	71.50	§	64.50
Avg., fiscal 74	85.68	107.19	51.29	71.63	70.96	63.65
7/31/74	*	†	43.75	61.25	64.75	56.00
Avg., fiscal 75	—	—	52.61	74.66	77.38	63.06
7/31/75	—	—	76.00	100.00	99.13	80.13

Source: *Value Line Convertible Survey.* Year ends are last July quote and averages are of monthly ending quotes in this survey.

*Called March 28, 1974, at $92.00. Average is for preceding seven months. Quoted February 25, 1974, at 81.13.

†Called March 29, 1974, at $112.50. Average is for preceding seven months. Quoted February 25, 1974, at 100.50.

§Second smaller issue with same interest rate and maturity, January 1974. Average in 1974 is for seven months.

40. ORIGINAL ISSUE PREMIUM OR DISCOUNT ON CONVERTIBLE SECURITIES

Question: What happens to original issue premium or discount when convertible securities are assumed to be converted and common stock is assumed to be issued for earnings per share computations?

Answer: Any original issue premium or discount amortized during the period (to compute the effective interest deducted from net income for a debt security) is eliminated from net income in arriving at earnings applicable to common stock. The unamortized original issue premium or discount balance at the date of assumed conversion (the ending balance plus the amount amortized during the period) is then ignored for earnings per share computations. The if converted method only assumes conversion of the securities; it does not assume retirement. The converted securities are assumed to be held by the issuer as treasury securities during the period being reported upon and balance sheet accounts related to those securities are not affected by the assumed conversion. Note that these assumptions are made only for earnings per share computations; the issuer's balance sheet and net income for the period are not affected in any way by the assumptions made for earnings per share computations.

77. DEBT PURCHASED UNDER PARAGRAPH 38

Question: What debt may the issuer assume is purchased when the provisions of Opinion paragraph 38 apply?

Answer: The issuer may select any debt which is eligible to be retired for assumed purchase when the provisions of Opinion paragraph 38 apply. This includes convertible debt (both common stock equivalents and other potentially dilutive securities) except that convertible debt may not be assumed purchased if the purchase would be antidilutive (that is, result in less dilution). Debt is eligible to be retired when it either may be "called" or is trading and could be purchased in the market.

The same debt is assumed purchased for both primary and fully diluted earnings per share computations. Different amounts of debt may be assumed purchased, however, since different market prices may have to be used for the primary and fully diluted computations for the treasury stock method. The average market price of the debt during each quarter for which the computations are made is used for both the primary and fully diluted computations under Opinion paragraph 38.

Munchies, Inc.

On April 10, 1975, the Executive Committee of Munchies, Inc. convened its quarterly meeting to review and finalize its interim financial results for the first three months of the year. Normally, by this time the committee had a preliminary but generally accurate impression of what the numbers would look like. Thus the meeting sometimes revolved around relatively minor accounting questions and more often around polishing the statement presentation and any accompanying remarks management wished to include.

Today's meeting was expected to be less than typical for three reasons. First, Munchies had switched from FIFO to LIFO to account for its refined sugar inventories for the year ended December 31, 1974. As a result, this would be the first interim report prepared on a LIFO basis. Second, Munchies, like all its competitors, was still enduring the economic shock waves of a tumultuous sugar market—shock waves which were clearly felt in recent income statements. Third, Munchies had asked its independent certified public accountants to "certify" its quarterly report. Although such certification was not required, Munchies was aware of the rumors that the SEC would soon require increased auditor involvement with the interims. Thus management hoped to gain a large amount of low-cost publicity in the financial press by being a pacesetter in this matter.

BACKGROUND

Munchies was conceived one evening in 1968 by two graduates of a well known Eastern business school while sharing a large batch of special "homemade"

This case was written by Dennis P. Frolin and James F. Smith as a basis for class discussion rather than to illustrate either effective or ineffective handling of an administrative situation.

brownies with some of their friends. Envisioning a world full of millions of young people who also loved brownies, they decided to offer their product to the local market. Thus, it all began.

From its modest beginning, Munchies grew from a private firm to a small publicly held company in 1972. A common stock issue floated in that year provided the necessary financing for a significant investment in highly automated candy production machinery and placed 38 percent of the company in the hands of investors unrelated to either the original owners or the management. By the end of 1974 Munchies, Inc. had assets of approximately $27 million and annual revenues of about $45 million. Exhibit 1 presents the Munchies, Inc. balance sheets and income statement for the years ended December 31, 1973 and 1974. The majority of Munchies' assets are current, with inventories (principally sugar) comprising about 20 percent of the total. They operate three plants located in the Far West and Southwest, with a headquarters in their native state of California. They produce numerous chocolate and chocolate covered candies but their two primary products are "Munch-ets"—small bits of multi-colored, candy-coated chocolates in various animal shapes—and "Munch-eternal"—a large chocolate-covered caramel, nougat, nut and fruit bar.

The operation consists essentially of purchasing raw materials, mixing and processing the materials to make candy items, and selling the candy to both distributors and retail outlets. Their principal raw material is sugar; other ingredients, though insignificant in terms of inventory value, are numerous. They include corn syrup, honey, molasses, milk solids, emulsifiers, fruits, nuts, and artificial flavors and colors.

The production process is relatively simple, and is fully mechanized. "Fondant," a soft creamy-smooth mixture used in all the products, is produced using a continuous fondant-making machine (Exhibit 2). A syrup consisting primarily of sugar is prepared in a cooker, delivered to a cooled rotating drum, and automatically scraped from the drum into a rectangular box fitted with spindles and baffles called the "beater." Here the syrup is mechanically agitated giving it a property which allows it to be stored and later reheated for molding without repeating the cooking and drum-cooling cycle. The "fondant" is poured from the "beater" into shallow trays where it is stored for later molding. The molding process is done automatically by a machine called a "mogul." The cooled and set fondant pieces are then ejected from the molds onto a conveyor which carries them forward for chocolate or candy covering. The finished candy is automatically packaged, and is shipped normally within a week. This process allows Munchies to maintain minimal finished goods inventory, the value of which is immaterial relative to total inventory.

THE ACCOUNTING SYSTEM

Munchies uses a very simple cost accounting system. Planning and budgeting for the coming year is carried out in November and December when monthly sales

Exhibit 1. *Balance Sheet, December 31, 1973, 1974*

ASSETS

Current Assets	1974	1973
	(in thousands)	
Cash	$ 1,310	$ 5,380
Accounts receivable	6,090	3,560
Refundable Federal income taxes	5,000	
Marketable securities	0	210
Inventories	6,200	6,800
Total Current Assets	$18,600	$15,950
Property, plant, and equipment (net)	8,100	7,580
Other assets	400	370
Total Assets	$27,100	$23,900

LIABILITIES AND EQUITY

Current Liabilities		
Accounts payable	$ 9,750	$ 5,140
Bank notes payable	3,400	400
Accrued expenses	2,600	1,220
Total Current Liabilities	$15,750	$ 6,760
Long-term debt	5,440	5,840
Stockholders' equity	5,910	11,300
Total Liabilities and Equity	$27,100	$23,900

Profit and Loss Statement, Year ended December 31

Net sales	$44,770	$29,190
Cost of sales	49,120*	19,450†
Gross profit (loss)	$ (4,350)	$ 9,740
Selling, general, and administrative	6,010	6,340
Other expenses	420	420
Profit before tax	$(10,780)	$ 2,980
Federal income tax	(5,390)	1,490
Net income (loss)	$ (5,390)	$ 1,490
Earnings per share §	$ (2.03)	$ .56

*LIFO.
†FIFO.
§2,650,000 common shares outstanding.

Exhibit 2. *Continuous Fondant-making Machine*

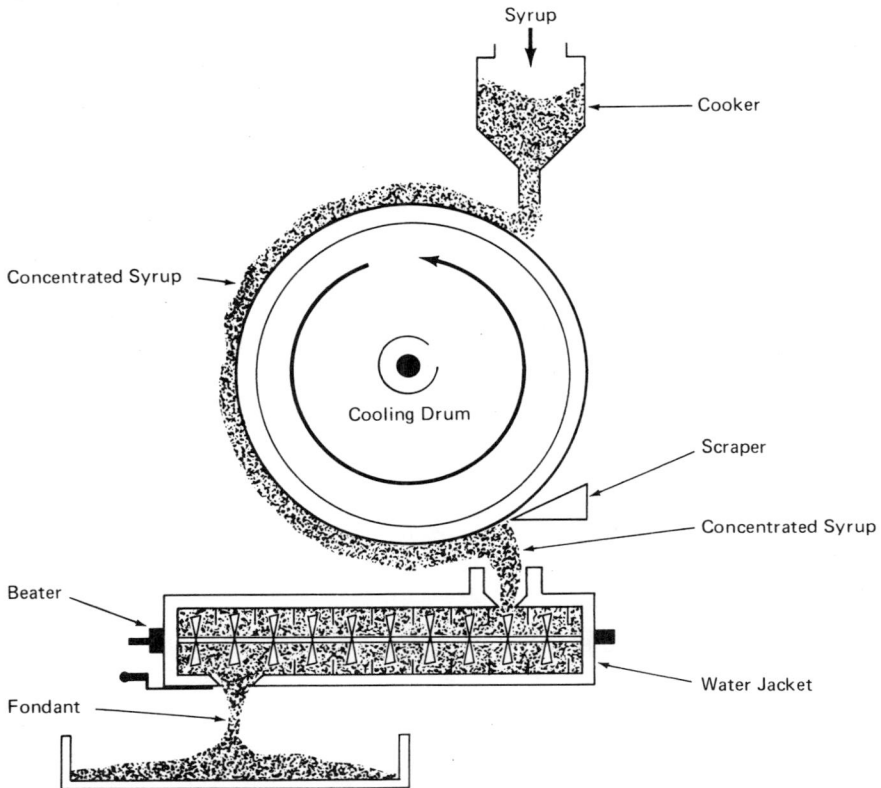

targets and production schedules are formalized. The planning committee devotes considerable time to designing an explicit but tentative sugar purchasing strategy. It also forecasts the coming year's average wholesale refined cane sugar cost. This forecasted average cost serves as the standard cost for recording *both* the *purchase* and *use* of refined sugar. In the past, sugar prices were stable enough during the year that using an annual average as the standard was adequate for both internal and external reporting needs. Recent volatility in prices however may cause this policy to be changed.

Exhibit 3 illustrates the mechanics of the cost accounting system. By using a standard cost for refined sugar, both positive and negative purchase price variances are identified immediately. The net price variance at the end of the year is treated as an increase or decrease in the cost of goods sold on the income statement. During 1974, the price variance recorded on each quarter's purchases was reported in the quarter's interim results. Thus, in the Profit and Loss Statement, the cost of goods sold for the first quarter of 1974 was decreased by $1.2 million as a result of *favorable* price variance experienced in first quarter purchases.

Exhibit 3. *Standard Cost System: Illustrative Transactions*

TRANSACTIONS	Refined Cane Sugar Inventory		Cost of Sales	
(A)	B.I 650*			
Purchased 4 million pounds of	(A) 1,280	(B) 1,920	(B) 1,920	
refined sugar	(D) 380		(C) 320	(D) 380
at market price .40 = 1,600				(E) 1,860 §
at standard .32 = 1,280	EI 390†			
Unfavorable				
variance 320				

	Price Variance		Accounts Payable	
(B)**				
Requisitions from inventory:	(A) 320	(C) 320		(A) 1,600
Increase cost of sales and				
decrease inventory at standard				
6 million pounds at .32 = 1,920				

(C)
Close price variance account
to cost of sales

	Profit/Loss	
(D)		
Adjust inventory and cost of	(E) 1,860	
sales to reflect year-end		
physical inventory		

Actual quantity .   3 M lbs.
X LIFO standard   .13/lb

LIFO standard value   390
Inventory balance   10

Required adjust-
ment   380

(E)
Close cost of sales to profit/
loss account

*5 million pounds at 1973 standard of $.13.
†3 million pounds at 1973 standard of $.13.
§Consumed 6 million pounds:
     4 million at .32   = 1,280
     2 million at .13   =   260
     Unfavorable var.   =   320
                    1,860

**Note that in reality this transfer increases first work-in-process inventory then finished goods inventory, and eventually cost of sales. For the sake of illustration the intermediate steps have been eliminated.

The 1974 results in total (Exhibit 1) include $16 million of *unfavorable* price variance on the purchase of refined sugar. If an actual instead of a standard cost system were used, the net effect for the year would be essentially unchanged as long as physical inventory levels remain fairly constant.

A physical inventory is taken at the end of each year, and the inventory and cost of sales accounts are adjusted to reflect the actual quantities of inventory on hand. Assuming the annual standard cost of refined sugar differs from one year to the next, the year-end adjustment also makes any necessary LIFO correction (FIFO in 1973). Since the entire year's charge outs (credits) from the refined sugar account are at the *current year's standard cost,* a LIFO adjustment to cost of sales and raw materials is necessary if more sugar is used than purchased. Alternatively, a FIFO adjustment is necessary regardless of the purchase/use relationship since the "old" inventory (first in) must be the first out, that is, it must go to cost of sales. For example, in 1974 the cost of sales account (including the $16 million unfavorable purchase price variance) before adjustment was $49,470,000. However, all the refined sugar used had been charged through the inventory accounts and into cost of sales at the $.20 per pound 1974 standard cost. Since the ending inventory of refined sugar for the year had decreased by 5 million pounds and since the beginning inventory for 1974 was at the 1973 standard of $.13 per pound, the correction for the LIFO liquidation consisted of decreasing (credit) the cost of sales by $350,000 (5 million pounds X $.07) to $49,120,000 and increasing (debit) the refined sugar inventory account by the same amount.

CURRENT OPERATIONS

Inventory costs spiraled during 1974 reflecting very tight supply conditions; the price of sugar rose to unprecedented heights throughout 1974, peaking in December (Exhibit 4).

In June of 1974, Munchies' management decided that to minimize inventory carrying costs and cash flow burdens, they would attempt to cut the sugar inventory to approximately two-thirds of the physical level maintained at the end of 1973. They had succeeded in cutting it by 10 percent at the end of 1974, and by nearly 30 percent at the end of March 1975.

At the end of 1974 Munchies switched from FIFO to LIFO for refined cane sugar inventory to better reflect rising sugar prices in cost of sales and to minimize income tax payments. Exhibit 5 details the quantity and cost of refined sugar inventory.

Munchies' management expects the cost of sugar to decline during 1975— from $.52 per pound in January to approximately $.20 by year end. Based upon these expectations, and their purchasing strategy, they established a $.32 per pound standard cost for 1975. As expected during the first quarter of

Exhibit 4. *Average Wholesale Refined Cane Sugar Prices at New York (excludes excise tax)*
(in cents per pound)

YEAR	JAN-UARY	FEB-RUARY	MARCH	APRIL	MAY	JUNE	JULY	AU-GUST	SEPTEM-BER	OCTO-BER	NOVEM-BER	DECEM-BER	AVER-AGE
1970	11.1	10.9	10.9	10.9	10.9	11.3	11.3	11.3	11.4	11.4	11.4	11.4	11.2
1971	11.4	11.4	11.7	11.6	11.6	11.6	11.8	11.8	11.8	11.8	11.8	11.8	11.7
1972	11.8	12.2	12.2	12.4	12.4	12.4	12.4	12.4	12.4	12.4	12.2	12.2	12.3
1973	12.2	13.2	13.2	13.3	12.7	12.7	13.2	13.7	13.7	14.1	15.0	12.8	13.3
1974	14.3	16.1	20.0	20.0	24.8	28.5	31.9	33.8	39.5	40.8	54.9	59.2	32.0
1975	51.8	49.2	42.0										

Exhibit 5. Refined Cane Sugar Inventory

	QUANTITY	STANDARD COST	AMOUNT (IN THOUSANDS)
December 31, 1973	49.2	.13	$6,400†
March 31, 1974	49.4§	.20	9,900†
December 31, 1974	44.3	.13	5,800*
March 31, 1975	34.4	.13	4,500*

STANDARD COSTS ESTABLISHED BY MUNCHIES:

1973 = $.13 per pound
1974 = .20 per pound
1975 = .32 per pound

*LIFO basis.
†FIFO basis.
§Purchased approximately 50 million pounds of sugar during this quarter; about 49 million pounds were consumed in operations. This was considered to be about "normal," given Munchies previous policy of maintaining a three months' sugar inventory.

1975, they recorded unfavorable price variances on sugar purchases totaling $3.4 million (see Exhibit 6).

Sugar shortages also forced Munchies to purchase substantial quantities of sugar from some suppliers with whom they had conducted no previous business. In February 1975, it was discovered that about $300,000 of the December 31, 1974, refined sugar inventory was contaminated and therefore not usable. This sugar remains in inventory at March 31, 1975, and management expects that they will "dump" it by year end.

With regard to new product development, by the end of 1974 Munchies' management believed that it was on the threshold of a major breakthrough in the industry. They were developing "Munch-tyne," a new candy bar that cleans teeth; it consists of fondant, nougat, crispies, and pumice. During the first quarter of 1975, the research and development costs for this project totaled $900,000. Management expects that this amount represents approximately 75 percent of the total R & D costs to be incurred during 1975, and that the candy bar will be on the market (for at least a test) in the last quarter of this year.

EXECUTIVE COMMITTEE MEETING

On April 10, 1975, the Executive Committee met to discuss the issuance of the interim report to shareholders and the Securities and Exchange Commission 10Q filing for the first quarter of 1975. The following are excerpts from that meeting:

Exhibit 6. Summary of Refined Cane Sugar Purchases, First Quarter 1975

MONTH	MILLIONS OF POUNDS	ACTUAL PURCHASE PRICE PER POUND	AMOUNT (IN THOUSANDS)
January	4.2	.52	$2,190
February	6.6	.49	3,240
March	14.2	.42	5,970
	25.0		$11,400
	25.0 at 1975 standard of $.32		$ 8,000
	Unfavorable price variance		$ 3,400

W. Brock   (President) You each have had a chance to review the preliminary report from Bill's people for the first quarter of the year (Exhibits 7 and 8). I think Bill should give a brief explanation of the report, and then we'll open it for discussion.

Bill Boyer   (Controller) The comparative first quarter balance sheets (Exhibit 7) and income statements (Exhibit 8) include the 1975 results on a LIFO basis and the first quarter 1974 results on both a FIFO and LIFO basis. We published the FIFO results last year but we may want to restate for the accounting switch. There are several important items to note. First, as expected the inventory value is down significantly from last year; this was caused by the switch from FIFO to LIFO and the reduction in sugar inventories on hand from three months' operating needs to nearly two months'. It looks like we should reach our goal of reducing inventory to two months' operating requirements by mid-year. Second, we experienced a near quadrupling of cost of sales because of the outrageous sugar prices of recent months. Sugar last January was $.14. This January it was over $.50. Third, the "SG&A" account includes $900,000 of R & D expenses for the "Munch-tyne" project. Finally, despite the unfavorable results of this quarter, I feel certain that we can turn it around by year end, and that the 1975 numbers will look good. Sales are at an all-time high and should be maintained or possibly bettered during the rest of the year. Our costs are temporarily high but it's just a matter of taking our lumps now because of extraordinarily high sugar and R & D costs. It will turn around in the second half of the year. So let's discuss!

George Whitman   (Treasurer) Bill, one thing that is bothering me is that these preliminaries seem to be comparing apples and oranges. How can we place

Exhibit 7. *Balance Sheet, March 31, 1974, 1975*

	(A)	(B)	(C)
		(IN THOUSANDS)	
		FIFO	*LIFO*
ASSETS	*1975*	*1974*	*1974*
Current Assets			
Cash and marketable securities	$ 1,160	$ 3,800	$ 3,800
Accounts receivable	7,910	3,400	3,400
Refundable Federal income taxes	5,880	0	0
Inventories*	4,800	10,200	6,700
Total Current Assets	$19,750	$17,400	$13,900
Property, plant, and equipment (net)	8,320	7,880	7,880
Other assets	210	320	320
Total Assets	$28,280	$25,600	$22,100
LIABILITIES AND EQUITY			
Current Liabilities			
Accounts payable	$11,010	$ 5,850	$ 5,850
Other	8,200	2,345	595
Total Current Liabilities	$19,210	$ 8,195	$ 6,445
Long-term debt	5,440	5,840	5,840
Stockholders' equity	3,630	11,565	9,815
Total Liabilities and Equity	$28,280	$25,600	$22,100

*See Exhibit 5 for value of refined cane sugar included in total inventory.

Exhibit 8. *Profit and Loss Statement, Quarter ended March 31, 1974, 1975*

	(A)	(B)*	(C)
		(IN THOUSANDS)	
		FIFO	*LIFO*
	1975	*1974*	*1974*
Net sales	$14,640	$ 8,640	$ 8,640
Cost of sales†	16,700	6,600	10,100
Gross profit	$ (2,060)	$ 2,040	$ (1,460)
S.G. & A. and other	2,500§	1,510	1,510
Pre-tax income	$ (4,560)	$ 530	$ (2,970)
Taxes	(2,280)	265	(1,485)
Net income	$ (2,280)	$ 265	$ (1,485)
Earnings per share	$ (.86)	$ .10	$ (.56)

Exhibit 8. *(continued)*

*Column (B) are the numbers from the first quarter interims published in 1974. Column (C) represents the controller's restatement to a LIFO basis.

	1975	FIFO 1974	LIFO 1974
†Consists of:			
Refined sugar consumed			
at standard	$11,200	$ 6,400	$ 9,900
Purchase price variance	3,400	(1,200)	(1,200)
Other	2,100	1,400	1,400
	$16,700	$ 6,600	$10,100

§Includes R & D cost of $900,000.

LIFO and FIFO statements side by side? We don't have any choice but to restate the first quarter of 1974 on a LIFO basis, do we?

Bill Boyer Our '74 records were maintained on the FIFO basis, and more importantly our '74 interims were issued on that basis. It seems to me that it would only serve to confuse the shareholder if we were to make these '74 numbers different from those he received last year.

George Whitman Bill, what could be more confusing for the shareholder than to look at these statements (Columns A and B, Exhibit 8) and conclude that last year's first quarter was $2.5 million more profitable than this year's. He'll think we're going down the tube—and it will all be due to a mere accounting change. If your calculations are correct on the income statement for the first quarter of '74 using LIFO (Column C, Exhibit 8), we actually lost nearly $1.5 million in that quarter. Quite different from a $265,000 profit and certainly more realistic.

Bill Boyer I see your point, George, but I'm not sure that I agree we should make a restatement. Perhaps Ernie (Ernest J. Young, a CPA with a "Big Eight" accounting firm and audit partner in charge of the Munchies audit) will know what to do.

Tom Reed (Vice President Finance) Bill, I don't know about LIFO apples and FIFO oranges, but it seems to me that our '75 cost of sales number is far too high. This number was computed by simply multiplying the volume of sugar consumed during the quarter by the *current* standard cost of $.32 per pound of sugar. But we consumed nearly ten million pounds more sugar than we purchased during the quarter, and that ten million pounds came from *last year's* inventory, which we valued at $.13 per pound. That difference of $.19 per pound on the

LIFO inventory liquidation represents a $1.9 million decrease in cost of sales—which makes the quarter look much better. I know we would have to make a LIFO liquidation adjustment if this were year end. Don't we have to make one each quarter?

Larry Luden   (Vice President Operations) Tom, the biggest part of that LIFO liquidation, as you call it, is only temporary. True, we don't need the high inventory level that we had at the end of '73, but the inventory goal (two-thirds of the 1973 volume) you people set is unreasonable. Business is on the upswing, and there is no way we can operate with that low inventory level. I think that by year end it will be back to about 80 percent of what it was in '73. So how much LIFO inventory are we really liquidating? I suspect that by year end we will have liquidated about 5 million pounds—not ten. So at most the adjustment should be about $1 million for the year.

Bill Boyer   And maybe that should be spread equally over the four quarters.

Tom Reed   The fact is that the sugar inventory in this first quarter is down substantially. I think cost of sales should reflect that liquidation.

Bill Boyer   Looks like another question for Ernie.

Sam Schrafft   (Vice President Purchasing) What bothers me about that $16.7 million cost of sales figure is that we've dumped $3.4 million of the *unfavorable* purchase price variance into the account, even though we think that by the end of the year the variance in that account will net to zero. To me that doesn't make sense. Your numbers make my purchasing department look like the culprit, but we all knew the cost would exceed the $.32 standard for at least the first six months this year. I think cost of sales should be calculated each quarter based on the expected average annual cost—and that's our standard. Without that variance we'd be in the black for '75—where we should be. The way the statement is now, it looks like we're having another bad year. I thought '75 was going to be a good year.

Tom Reed   What you say is true, Sam, but you can't deny that we had to pay top dollar for sugar last quarter, and I think this statement has to reflect that.

George Whitman   I agree with Sam—the first quarter of '74 is a prime example. We all agree that the year '74 was a disaster, but with the $1.2 million *favorable* price variance included in cost of sales as it is in these preliminaries, we looked like sure winners in that first quarter. Without that variance we were in the red, where we belonged. If we know the year is going to be rough, we should reflect that in our quarterly report. The same reasoning should apply for a good year.

Tom Reed   The fact still remains that the first quarter of '74 was good, even though the year turned out to be poor. And the first quarter of '75 has been a bad one. I think the quarterlies should report what actually happened during that quarter.

Bill Boyer   May I suggest a compromise. I think we would all agree on one thing—that by year end this variance will be at worst no more than it is now. So why can't we simply spread the $3.4 million equally over four quarters. And, before one of you asks, it seems that we have to raise the same question about the R & D expenses. They are unusually high in the first quarter, but will probably be only about $300,000 for the rest of the year. So, do we spread the total $1.2 million evenly over four quarters or do we show the $900,000 in the first quarter and only $100,000 in each of the next three?

Tom Reed   You know where I stand.

Sam Schrafft   Tom, when we make policy decisions regarding inventory, pricing, R & D or whatever, we are generally doing so in a time horizon of at least one year and often longer, but almost never one quarter. So, if we have a strong idea of where those decisions are leading us in a year, I think the quarterlies should reflect that direction.

Tom Reed   Just because we expect a good year doesn't mean we should report four good quarters. If we have a bad quarter, we should report a bad quarter. I hate to be the bearer of all bad news, but I think there is one more thing we have to table. We all know that we have some sugar sitting in inventory that cost us about $300,000 which turned "sour" this quarter. We know it's bad and I think we should write it off—now.

Bill Boyer   Tom, we've filed suit to recover those losses so maybe we shouldn't write it off. Our legal counsel is of the opinion that we can expect full recovery; but then lawyers are eternal optimists until the verdict is in. Perhaps it's simply another question of whether we should take it all now or spread it over four quarters. You know it just occurred to me that, depending on which of these adjustments Ernie makes, we could report a "super" first quarter—and the remaining three may look bad in comparison. We could argue about these things indefinitely. Hopefully Ernie will have the answers.

W. Brock   I would like to make a couple of points here. First, remember we want an "opinion" attached to this report, but it sounds like Ernie won't opine unless he can do a "full blown" audit. I don't think we can afford that. We also have time pressure to get the quarterly out and the 10Q in. We can't wait until mid-year to report our first quarter. It seems to me that he knows our business well enough to issue an opinion without the "full" audit, but he thinks there are too many risks involved. Second, most of what we have discussed here today are decisions to be made by us, not Ernie: We'll discuss our decisions with Ernie later. Third, it does seem that our accounting should somehow be consistent with how we make policy decisions. At the same time, maybe the real question is how Wall Street uses these quarterlies. After all, this is our most concise form of communicating with the investment community. When I was at business school in the mid-Sixties, I was sure I knew the answer to that question. You took four times the quarterly earnings per share, applied a price earnings ratio, and were off to the races. I'm not so sure that's how it works today. Finally, Bill, you're wrong—we can't argue about these things forever, at least not on company time. Let's vote on each of the issues.

QUESTIONS

1. How should Munchies, Inc. account for its sugar inventory for the first quarter of 1975?
2. How should the possible effects of the suit to recover the $300,000 loss be reflected on the financial statements of the first quarter of 1975?
3. How does Wall Street use quarterly reports?

Lambert International, Inc.

Lambert International, Inc. was a conglomerate operating a number of diverse business operations on a worldwide basis. Its stock was traded in New York. Over the last 12 months it had become known as a "growth" stock. As a result, a number of the major mutual funds had acquired large holdings of the stock during the previous six months. This active buying had been in large part responsible for a rapid rise in the company's stock price.

Typically, the company's interim statements presented on a comparative basis the current quarter and year to date: the company's sales; income before taxes, provision for taxes; income before extraordinary items; extraordinary items (including related tax effects); and net income. No balance sheet was provided. Also, unless a change had been made in accounting principles, no footnotes were included. The company's auditor did not express an opinion on the interim statements. In addition to the financial presentation, the interim reports included a brief letter from the President to the shareholders highlighting the important activities of the period covered, and anticipated key events in the near future.

The following Board of Directors' discussion of the first quarter interim statements for Lambert International took place in early April. The statements were due to be released later in the month:

Lawrence   (Vice President) The figures for the first quarter don't look good. However, I believe we have it in our power to push them over the same period results for last year, if we want to so do.

This case was prepared by Professor David F. Hawkins as a basis for class discussion rather than to illustrate either effective or ineffective handling of an administrative situation.

Copyright © 1973 by the President and Fellows of Harvard College. Revised February 1973.

Franklin   (outside director) What do you mean by that?

Lawrence   Let me explain. Last year we earned $.52 per share for the first quarter, which was the best we had ever done to date for that period. This year we have only $.47 per share, before any adjustments to my accounting decisions that you may wish to make.

Morris   (President) Frankly, I think it is imperative that we report a good first quarter. Last year our earnings were a record high and our fourth quarter was extremely strong. In fact, it was our best quarter ever. . . .

Powers   (outside director) Yes, I know. But didn't we pull a lot of income into the last quarter from this year to get those results? For example, we cut advertising, accelerated foreign dividend receipts, picked up DISC tax savings for the first time, deferred maintenance, accelerated equipment purchases to get the investment tax credit, recognized income on advanced shipments. . . . It seems to me that what we did was to "rob Peter to pay Paul." Now we have to pay the price.

Morris   I admit we pushed a bit, but the fact is the stock market reacted favorably to our strong finish to last year and our stock price has really started to climb. In fact since mid-January our price-earnings ratio has gone from 21 times to 24 times this year's estimated earnings, which the market estimates will be higher than last year. I don't think we can afford to lose this stock price momentum.

Lawrence   I am convinced that if we report earnings for this quarter that are not substantially above last year's first quarter results we will see our price-earnings ratio decline. This is a very "nervous" stock market we are in. The Dow is high, but it is subject to wide fluctuations on a daily basis.

Braun   (Vice President Marketing) Why are the first quarter earnings less than last year? What are the causes and dollar value? What options do we have? I for one want to keep the stock's price-earnings ratio up.

Lawrence   Here is an analysis of the differences between this year and last year: First, because we deferred maintenance on a worldwide basis from last year to this year, our first quarter maintenance costs are up by 2 cents a share over last year. Also, since the first quarter is normally the heaviest maintenance period of the year, we have an extra 2 cents per share charge above what the average will be for the next three quarters, which have fairly equal maintenance expenditures.

I have charged the extra 4 cents maintenance to the first quarter.

Second, our DISC tax deferrals in this quarter ran at the rate of 3 cents per share. This is our peak export period. It is over one-third of the year's projected DISC tax saving of 8 cents, which we can flow through to income.

Last year's fourth quarter was the first time we had material DISC tax savings. In that case we credited all of the savings to that quarter's income.

Now, I believe we should spread our DISC tax savings equally over the full year on a quarter-by-quarter basis. So, I picked up 2 cents for this quarter and deferred 1 cent. Actually the DISC tax impact on earnings is a "plus" from last year at this time.

Braun   Do we have to spread the benefit?

Lawrence   No. We can pick up the DISC earnings as earned. However, I felt "spreading" was the preferred approach.

Powers   It all depends on how you define "preferred."

Lawrence   Next, we have the costs of relocating the Southern Paper Sioux Springs plant and offices. These came to 3 cents a share. Actually, we had planned to do that last year, but put it off because we didn't want to hurt last year's earnings. I included all of that cost in the first quarter.

Morris   I talked to Bill [Lawrence] about these charges which are depressing earnings and he tells me that it is good accounting to recognize costs and defer revenues. I suspect he is correct, but do we necessarily have to do this for interim reports?

Bill, you have some more items don't you?

Lawrence   Yes. This first quarter includes a dividend of 4 cents per share, we got from our Brazilian subsidiary in March. Since we account for this subsidiary on the cost basis, we only pick up income from it as it is received in dividends in the U.S.A.

Morris   Last February I felt we were having earnings problems, so I put extra pressure on Brazil to repatriate some dividends. As you know, they were held up by legal problems from getting these funds to us last year.

Cohen   (Vice President Personnel) What do the dividends from overseas cost-basis investments look like this year?

Morris   Well, I think we can get about 10 cents per share's worth in the last quarter, but between now and then I am not very hopeful. Incidentally, 10 cents is all we budgeted for from foreign dividends this year.

Frankly, while domestic and exports sales and profits are on track from regular operations, our overseas operations are down. In fact, that is the principal reason for our problems. In particular the new Italian company, Grazini, which we picked up late last year and included in the consolidated results on a pooling of interest basis is a real "lemon."

I have to admit we were in a big hurry to acquire it. We wanted its full year profits to be included in the full year's results. As you know its profits were up some 200 percent over the previous year.

Peter [Pike], why don't you explain the situation to us?

Pike   (Vice President International) Well, the company is still delivering operating profits, but its inventories and receivables turned out to be overstated. Once our internal auditors got in last January and examined what we had bought, they found a lot of obsolete and damaged inventories. Also, the receivables bad debt reserves were too low. In addition, some equipment was still carried on the books, but it couldn't be found. Then, some more equipment should be written off. It is junk.

All this amounts to a 6 cents per share write-off. . . .

Lawrence   I charged it to operating income. That's what Opinion #9 requires.

Morris   Of course, we have a lawsuit in the Italian courts against the Grazini brothers to recover these amounts.

Braun   What do you think our chances are of collecting?

Morris   Very slim. However, I thought it was worth the effort. Perhaps to protect their name they'll settle out of court. They are not dishonest. They're just poor bookkeepers.

Outside of the Grazini problem, I expect our foreign operations will deliver their budgeted share of this year's earnings per share by December 31.

Braun   Bill [Lawrence], how do you charge the major advertising program we had in March?

Lawrence   I figure we spent about 2 cents a share above our average monthly budget. The principal cost was the "unusual" TV show and related radio and newspaper advertising. All of this was charged to March.

Braun   The benefits will come in April, May, and June, won't they? In fact so far this month, our sales are up just as we planned. It seems to me that—to quote you from an earlier meeting—"proper matching of costs and revenues" should require us to defer this "extra" 2 cents per share to the second quarter.

Morris   What about investment tax credit benefits?

Lawrence   Well, you'll recall we pushed the buying of qualified property from the first quarter of this year into the fourth quarter of last year. As a result, we only have a 1 cent per share benefit in the first quarter of this year, which we flow through to earnings.

Our projected credits for the year are worth 12 cents per share. This is fairly certain, as most of the orders for the property have been placed.

Morris   Can we pull some of these into the first quarter? After all, if we don't, our effective tax rate will be different from that for the year as a whole.

Lawrence   I'm not sure. If we did that we would have to take a second look at our DISC tax benefits accounting also.

Morris   Are our projected DISC benefits as sure as our projected ITC benefits?

Lawrence   They're fairly sure, but not as certain as the ITC benefits.

There are two more items I wanted to mention. First, I have picked up in the first quarter one-third of the third quarter advertising costs related to this year's special fall campaign. I'll pick up another third in the next two quarters.

This special program, which is in addition to our normal advertising costs, is going to cost about 6 cents per share above our regular advertising costs, which are run fairly evenly throughout the year.

Second, due to the change in the dollar relative to many overseas currencies we had an exchange gain of 4 cents per share. I did not include this in the first quarter results. In my opinion, by year end we could end up with currency losses. So, I feel it is wise to defer this gain as a possible offset against future losses.

Morris   Thank you, Bill [Lawrence].

Well, here's our problem. The security analysts are predicting we will make nearly 60 cents for the first quarter. We don't have that kind of performance now. However, I feel that if we don't report 60 cents our price-earnings ratio will drop.

If this happens, I am fearful that our merger negotiations with Apex in Cleveland and Contrelli in Italy will collapse—or not produce the earnings per share impact we expected. We need the earnings of both of these companies and at least one more merger to meet our forecasted profits for this year.

As I reported to the finance committee last month, these two mergers under negotiation will be for our stock and will be accounted for as a pooling of interest. . . . The Apex price-earnings ratio based on our offering price is 20 times this year's projected earnings. . . . The Contrelli family is interested in us because they feel we are a growth stock. . . .

Well, gentlemen, what do you think we should do?

QUESTION

1. What are Lambert International's first quarter earnings per share?

Ramada
Inns, Inc.

In December 1974, the Financial Accounting Standards Board exposed for comment a proposed statement dealing with the translation of foreign currency transactions and foreign currency financial statements. The Exposure Draft proposed the use of the temporal method for translation, which uses exchange rates approximating those in effect at the time transactions occur. The temporal method is similar in application and effect to the monetary–nonmonetary method which was already being used by a number of United States corporations. The FASB also proposed that translation gains and losses be included in reported net income in the accounting period when they arise.

In response to the Exposure Draft, Carl D. Long, Group Vice President and Chief Financial Officer, wrote to the Financial Accounting Standards Board on April 25, 1975. His letter is reproduced below.

MR. LONG'S LETTER

April 26, 1975

Financial Accounting Standards
 Board
High Ridge Park
Stamford, Connecticut 06905

Dear Sirs:

Following is our response to the Exposure Draft "Accounting for the Trans-

---

lation of Foreign Currency Transactions and Foreign Currency Financial Statements." Specifically our response discusses and illustrates what we consider to be a mismatching of revenue and expenses which can occur through the application of current rates to long-term debt, in conjunction with the use of historical rates for fixed assets.

I. Effect of Exposure Draft Policies on Ramada's Reported Profits

The effect is shown in the following paragraphs using Ramada's European operations (Ramada Europe) as an example. Ramada translates its foreign currency financial statements into U.S. dollars using the current–noncurrent method and any resulting translation gains or losses are included in current net income. As of February 28, 1975, Ramada Europe's consolidated balance sheet and its balance sheet exposure (stated in equivalent U.S. dollars and based on the current–noncurrent translation method) was as follows:

	BALANCE SHEET (AT FEBRUARY 28, 1975)	EXPOSURE Unexposed	Exposed
Cash, receivables	$ 2,777	$	$ 2,777
Inventory, prepaids	317		317
Net fixed assets	35,434	35,434	
Deferred and other	1,490	1,490	
	$40,018	$36,924	$ 3,094
Short-term payables	$ 3,091		$ 3,091
Long-term debt			
Swedish kronor	5,465		
German DM	16,090		
French francs	2,751		
Belgian francs	5,026		
	$29,332	$29,332	
Equity and dollar debt	$ 7,595	$ 7,595	
	$40,018	$36,927	$ 3,091
Net exposure (long)			$ 3

Several points are apparent from the above balance sheet and exposure report:

1. Ramada Europe is very capital intensive (essentially all fixed assets represent the cost of hotels which are 100 percent owned by Ramada Europe).
2. Ramada Europe has financed its hotels largely with foreign currency debt (most debt is 15- to 25-year mortgage debt).
3. Ramada's exposure to translation gains and losses under the current-noncurrent method is negligible.

Ramada's European exposure changes drastically under the translation methods proposed in the FASB draft, as shown below. (Hereafter in this response, we will refer to the translation method proposed in the FASB draft as the monetary–nonmonetary method.)

	BALANCE SHEET (AT FEBRUARY 28, 1975)	EXPOSURE Unexposed	EXPOSURE Exposed
Cash receivables	$ 2,777	$	$ 2,777
Inventory, prepaids	301	301	
Net fixed assets	35,434	35,434	
Deferred and other	1,490	1,490	
	$40,002	$37,225	$ 2,777
Short-term payables	$ 3,091		$ 3,091
Long-term debt			
Swedish kronor	5,875		
German DM	17,606		
French francs	3,121		
Belgian francs	5,375		
	$31,977		$31,977
Equity and dollar debt	$ 4,934	$ 4,934	
	$40,002	$ 4,934	$35,068
Net exposure (short)			($32,291)

To determine the effect which the monetary–nonmonetary translation method would have on Ramada's earnings, we have prepared balance sheets for Ramada Europe for each quarter beginning with the first quarter of 1973, and have computed translation gains or losses for each quarter using the monetary-nonmonetary method. The balance sheets and the basis for their preparation are shown and described in Attachment A. To summarize this attachment we present below the translation gains or losses which would have been reported for each quarter. Also, to illustrate the magnitude of these gains and losses, we have presented Ramada's reported consolidated net income (for all domestic and foreign operations) for the same quarters.

QUARTER	REPORTED CONSOLIDATED NET INCOME	TRANSLATION GAIN (LOSS)
1973: Second quarter	$4,047,000	$(1,647,000)
Third quarter	5,485,000	(1,284,000)
Fourth quarter	2,025,000	1,611,000
1974: First quarter	1,955,000	836,000
Second quarter	3,220,000	(1,631,000)
Third quarter	3,455,000	1,118,000
Fourth quarter	23,000	(1,800,000)
1975: First quarter	1,042,000	(2,714,000)
Second quarter		1,173,000*
Total		$(4,338,000)†

*Through April 21, 1975.

†Gross losses are $9,076,000 and gross gains, $4,738,000, for a net of $4,338,000.

The large gains and losses shown above illustrate the magnitude of profit fluctuations which Ramada can expect in the future if it must apply the monetary–nonmonetary translation method to its European operations.

In connection with the above comparison we would like to point out the following additional facts.

1. Ramada's primary business activity is the operation of its company-owned hotels. In 1975 this activity will account for about 75 percent of consolidated sales and almost 100 percent of foreign sales. The cost of Ramada Europe's hotels represents slightly more than 10 percent of consolidated fixed assets, and its foreign currency long-term debt also represents slightly more than 10 percent of consolidated long-term debt.

2. In addition to the European exposure of approximately $32,000,000 (under the monetary–nonmonetary method), Ramada has a further exposure of about $13,000,000 in Canadian dollars. The Canadian currency has not been nearly as volatile as European currencies, but quarterly U.S./Canadian dollar fluctuations of 2 to 3 percent are not uncommon and fluctuations of this magnitude would produce additional gains or losses of $260,000 to $390,000 per quarter.

3. The translation gains and losses might be reduced somewhat through the recording of deferred taxes. However, we presently believe that deferred taxes would apply to only about 50 percent of the gross translation gains or losses. (Hence, net translation gains and losses would be about 75 percent of the amounts shown above.)

*Exhibit 1. Attachment A, Ramada Europe Balance Sheets**

	AS REPORTED USING RAMADA'S CURRENT-NONCURRENT METHOD	AS REPORTED BUT USING TRANSLATION METHOD PROPOSED IN FASB DRAFT AND EXCHANGE RATES ON DATES SHOWN									
		4-21-75	2-28-75	11-30-74	8-31-74	5-31-74	2-28-74	11-30-73	8-31-73	5-31-73	2-28-73
Cash receivables	$ 2,777	$ 2,666	$ 2,777	$ 2,555	$ 2,388	$ 2,472	$ 2,333	$ 2,416	$ 2,555	$ 2,444	$ 2,305
Inventories, prepaids	317	301	301	301	301	301	301	301	301	301	301
Net fixed assets	35,434	35,434	35,434	35,434	35,434	35,434	35,434	35,434	35,434	35,434	35,434
Deferred and other	1,490	1,490	1,490	1,490	1,490	1,490	1,490	1,490	1,490	1,490	1,490
Total	$40,018	$39,891	$40,002	$39,780	$39,613	$39,697	$39,558	$39,641	$39,780	$39,669	$39,530
Short-term payables	$ 3,091	$ 2,967	$ 3,091	$ 2,844	$ 2,658	$ 2,751	$ 2,596	$ 2,689	$ 2,844	$ 2,702	$ 2,566
Long-term debt in local currency	29,332	30,817	31,977	29,238	27,507	28,616	27,001	27,827	29,422	28,169	26,519
Equity and debt in U.S. dollars	7,595	7,595	7,595	7,595	7,595	7,595	7,595	7,595	7,595	7,595	7,595
Translation gain (loss)		(1,488)	(2,661)	53	1,853	735	2,366	1,530	(81)	1,203	2,850
Total	$40,018	$39,891	$40,002	$39,780	$39,613	$39,697	$39,558	$39,641	$39,780	$39,669	$39,530
Translation gain (loss) for quarter		$ 1,173	$ (2,714)	$ (1,800)	$ 1,118	$ (1,631)	$ 836	$ 1,611	$ (1,284)	$ (1,647)	

*Ramada Inns, Inc. reports earnings on a calendar quarter basis; however, foreign earnings are cut off one month early. That is, Ramada earnings for the quarter ended March 31, 1975, include foreign earnings for the quarter ended February 28, 1975.

NOTES TO ATTACHMENT A

Foreign exchange markets have been very volatile since 1971 and all indications point to continued volatility for the foreseeable future. In this response we are attempting to demonstrate the effects of this volatility on Ramada, assuming use of the monetary-nonmonetary translation method.

We have done this by starting with actual Ramada Europe figures as of February 28, 1975, and then restating these figures as though the assets which existed at that time were in existence each quarter for the past two years. Actual foreign exchange rates were used for each quarter to restate local currency debt, current assets, and current liabilities.

Attachment I does not consider depreciation or repayment of long-term debt. However, this is not significant because (a) depreciation has no effect on translation gains or losses; and (b) repayment of long-term debt for the two-year period would be under $1,000,000 or 3 percent of total debt.

Figures used in the extreme left-hand column are actual reported figures as of February 28, 1975, with one exception. On April 15, 1975, our Swedish subsidiary received SK 8 million (about U.S. $2 million), which represented the proceeds of a long-term mortgage. We attempted to draw down this commitment before February 28, but certain technical matters prevented this.

The February 28 balance sheet has been restated as though this commitment had been drawn down by February 28.

II. Ramada's View of Its Exposure From European Operations

We feel that the monetary–nonmonetary translation method is not appropriate for Ramada and that this translation method violates the accounting principle of matching revenue and expenses when applied to Ramada.

In our opinion the proper translation method for a company such as Ramada is the "current rate" method. Our reasoning for this opinion can first be illustrated by reference to the following flow chart, which describes our approach in building, financing, and operating a foreign hotel.

From the flow chart it is apparent to us that only our equity and U.S. dollar loans are exposed. These are exposed because foreign currency earnings and cash flow are used to pay dividends and repay U.S. dollar loans. Following this reasoning, the current rate method is the appropriate method for Ramada, since under this method our translation gains and losses would be equal to our total dollar loans and equity, times the percentage by which the U.S. dollar changes in value relative to the local currency in each country of operation.

Under the current rate method our net balance sheet exposure would be "long" by about $7,600,000. It should be noted that exposure under the current rate method is the opposite of monetary–nonmonetary exposure. For

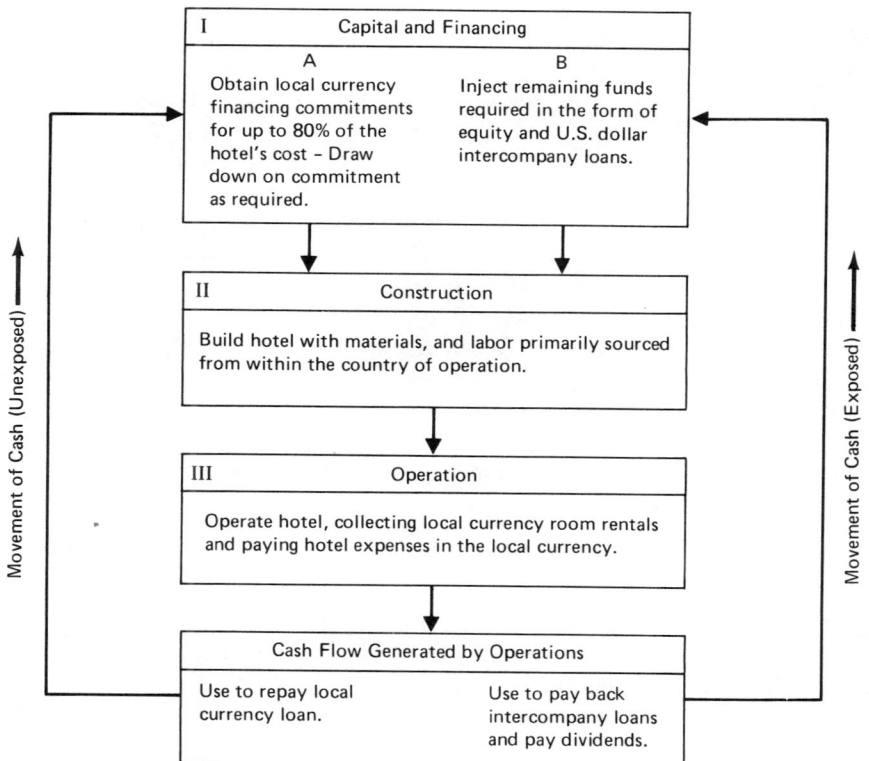

example, under the current rate method we would realize a translation gain when the dollar devalued, whereas a loss would result under the monetary-nonmonetary method.

We have not adopted the current rate method because it is not permissible under present accounting rules. We therefore have adopted the current-noncurrent method, which is permitted and which provides much more realistic results for Ramada than the monetary-nonmonetary method.

III. General Discussion

Our argument against the monetary-nonmonetary method is made on the basis of "compatibility," or Objective E of the Exposure Draft. That is, we feel that the monetary-nonmonetary method, when applied to Ramada, produces results which are not compatible with expected economic effects.

Objective E was rejected by the FASB. One reason given was that "The proposed objective is impractical because foresight would be required to identify the future economic effects of a rate change at the time it occurs." We disagree that the objective is impractical because it is clear to us that a decline in the value of the dollar will increase Ramada's earnings and cash flow in terms of U.S. dollars, while an increase in the value of the U.S. dollar will decrease our earnings and cash flow in terms of U.S. dollars.

Other arguments against compatibility contained in the draft opinion related to areas such as imports and exports, commitments for purchases or sales in another foreign currency, and so forth. These arguments do not apply to a company such as Ramada which is almost entirely dependent on the local economy.

The Exposure Draft also mentioned the opposing views that (a) historical costs should be measured in terms of dollars versus (b) historical costs should be measured in terms of the foreign currency. The Board adopted view (a) and rejected view (b). However, the Board's main reason for adoption of view (a) seemed to be that it is mathematically possible to determine the dollar equivalent of the cost of an asset on the date of acquisition. We agree that the use of dollar historical costs for fixed assets is mathematically possible, but we feel that it should not be the only acceptable method and in fact feel that it is not the proper method for us to use.

IV. Conclusions, Recommendation

The monetary-nonmonetary method as proposed in the draft would essentially force us to finance all future foreign hotels with U.S. dollars in order to minimize translation losses. This would be unfortunate because (1) it would be against the U.S. public interest, as it would cause an outflow of U.S. dollars; (2) it would hamper our expansion if the U.S. government should again impose controls such as the former OFDI regulations; (3) financing in U.S. dollars runs counter to what we should do from an economic standpoint.

We could reduce or eliminate our present exposure under the monetary–nonmonetary method by entering into forward foreign exchange transactions. However, this is not an argument for the monetary–nonmonetary method because such transactions can be costly; and like U.S. dollar financing, they don't make sense from an economic standpoint.

In our opinion the monetary–nonmonetary translation method is not appropriate for Ramada or other capital intensive companies which have similar operations. We believe that the current rate method is clearly the most appropriate for Ramada, and that the Board should permit the use of this method— at least for certain types of companies such as Ramada.

However, if the Board does not wish to permit the use of the current rate method at this time we recommend the following alternatives.

1. Use of the current–noncurrent method

or

2. Use of the monetary–nonmonetary method along with deferral of gains and losses that relate to long-term debt used to finance fixed assets.

We are anxious to meet with members of the Financial Accounting Standards Board to further discuss the figures, arguments, and comments in this response at any time, and in this connection ask that you contact the undersigned or Donald W. Hair, our Director of International Accounting.

QUESTIONS

1. Does the method of financing foreign operations which Ramada has adopted make good economic sense?
2. Ramada says it has not adopted the current rate method because it was not permissible (yet it is the most widely used method in many countries). Can you, however, verify that the balance sheet exposure would be "long" by $7,600,000 under that method?
3. If the average of all foreign currencies in which Ramada Europe has borrowed devalued 10 percent versus the dollar in 1976, approximate the translations gain or loss which Ramada Europe would report in 1975 under the monetary–nonmonetary method? The current rate method? The current–noncurrent method?
4. Consider the gains and losses shown on the tables on page 320. If you were part of Ramada's management, how would you explain these gains and losses in your reports to shareholders and lenders?
5. With the adoption of FASB Statement #8, what actions *should* Ramada take? What actions do you think they *will* take?

Drago
Chemical

In October 1974, Mr. Ralph Reeves, Managing Director of Drago Chemical, was reviewing his Financial Director's proposal for changes in the company's management control system. The proposed changes, prepared at Mr. Reeves' request, made explicit provision for inflation accounting.

Drago Chemical's manufacturing was centered in Southern England. The company's major products included PVC, plasticizers, polyethylenes, surfactants, and herbicides. The heads of the five manufacturing divisions and the several staff departments reported to the Managing Director. Over 30 percent of the company's sales were outside the United Kingdom (although mostly within the EEC).

The capital investments of each division were carefully reviewed at the corporate level; in most respects, however, each division manager was free to pursue his business objectives. For control purposes, a division was organized as an investment center. Each was expected steadily to improve current performance while pursuing long-term viability. In August 1974, all divisions had a positive ROI. Nevertheless, there were wide variances in their returns; the two least profitable divisions had ROIs of 2 and 4 percent.

Although pleased with Drago's current financial performance (Exhibits 1 and 2), Ralph Reeves had by mid-1974 become concerned about the impact of inflation on the firm's profitability (Exhibit 3). Accordingly, he had asked his financial director to study the internal impact of inflation. He knew the subject of external reporting was under active study in the U.K. (Exhibit 4). However, he felt that Drago's approach to this issue for management control and for performance appraisal should be independent of statutory requirements for external reporting and for the Inland Revenue Service.

Mr. Reeves was impressed by the simplicity and comprehensive approach of the Financial Director's report (Appendix A). Nonetheless, he wondered if the proposed procedures would adequately reflect what happened to his stocks of raw materials, works in process, and finished goods. During the last 18 months, this stock had dropped about 2 percent in tonnage, although the mix of products had remained almost the same. In the same period, however, the rapid rise in the prices of raw materials had inflated the value of his stock from slightly over £6.6 million to £11.6 million (£8.5 million on February 28, 1974). (As was common in the U.K., stock was valued on a first-in, first-out basis.) This stock represented about 60 days of purchases.

Mr. Reeves was also mindful of a recent chance conversation with the head of Drago's most important union. The union head had been complimentary of the company's recent profits (Exhibit 1), which he had just seen. Then he had expressed the hope that all who had helped to achieve those results could share amicably in the obviously ample rewards.

Of equal concern to Mr. Reeves was a recent letter that Drago's Chairman had sent to the stockholders. The Chairman had hailed the firm's record performance in sales and earnings; he added that he intended to pay an increased dividend for the year, "up to the maximum" then permitted. Mr. Reeves was partly reassured, since Drago's pre-tax profit of £2,960,000 came only after deduction of a special one-time contribution of £900,000 to the corporate pension fund. (This was to recognize the fund's increased liabilities, "an inevitable consequence of inflationary pressures upon remuneration.") For that reason, Mr. Reeves felt that the company's real earnings were somewhat higher than the announced figure.

Mr. Reeves had a further bit of relevant information: in the last six months, Drago had incurred a tax liability of £1,598,000 as a result of operations. However, the company had acquired considerable new equipment during the same period. Since the associated tax credits were large enough to balance the liability, no tax would have to be paid.

QUESTIONS

1. How much inflation-adjusted profit do you believe Drago earned during the last 18 months?
2. Should this inflation-adjusted profit figure be the basis for calculating the firm's return on investment?

Exhibit 1. Profit and Loss Summary

	FULL YEAR ENDING FEBRUARY 28, 1974	HALF YEAR ENDING AUGUST 31, 1974
	(THOUSANDS OF POUNDS)	
Turnover	48,002	40,080
Trading profit before following deductions	4,604	3,806
Depreciation	980	492
Interest charges	802	354
Profit before tax	2,822	2,960
Tax	1,524	1,599
Profit after tax	1,298	1,361

Exhibit 2. Balance Sheet

	MARCH 1, 1973	FEBRUARY 28, 1974
Assets		
Cash	103	158
Debtors (accounts receivable)	9,614	11,413
Stock (inventory)	6,614	8,512
Fixed assets	8,684	9,103
	25,015	29,186
Liabilities and Net Worth		
Accounts payable	8,276	12,109
Short-term debt	2,010	1,400
Long-term debt	5,040	5,040
Net worth	9,689	10,637
	25,015	29,186

Exhibit 3. *Inflation in the United Kingdom, 1963-1973*

YEAR	RETAIL PRICE INDEX	ANNUAL INFLATION	CUMULATIVE INFLATION
1963	100	—	—
1964	103	3%	3%
1965	108	5%	8%
1966	112	4%	12%
1967	115	3%	15%
1968	121	5%	21%
1969	127	5%	27%
1970	135	6%	35%
1971	148	10%	48%
1972	158	7%	58%
1973	173	10%	73%

Exhibit 4. *The State of Inflation Accounting in the United Kingdom, October 1974**

In London, the Sandilands Committee on Inflation Accounting is hard at work in an attempt to produce its recommendations by early 1975. Last May, the Institute of Chartered Accountants published its provisional statement of standard accounting practice No. 7 (SSAP 7). This contains proposals for adapting conventional historic cost accounts to conditions of inflation. The statement supports the current purchasing power or general price level method of adjustment. *The accountants point out that management must be able to appreciate the effects of inflation on costs, profits, distribution policies, dividend cover, borrowing power, return on investment, and cash requirements.*

Although the Institute opinion supports the current purchasing power method, the Sandilands Committee is still analyzing the advantages and disadvantages of the replacement cost method. The replacement cost method has many supporters in industry who argue that it is better to use a more complex system in an effort to approach the truth than to use a rigid, easy to apply formula which will always be inaccurate.

The ease of applying the current purchasing power system for the company and the ease of auditing it for the accountant make the system an attractive one. Although the Sandilands Committee has made no disclosures on which way it is leaning, many feel that it will attempt a synthesis of the two methods. There is currently a loophole in SSAP 7 allowing companies to revalue assets as well as to apply a rigid index to their original purchase cost. If the Sandilands Committee decides to support this decision, the controversy over the two systems may become irrelevant.

*From the *Financial Times,* October 3, 1974.

Appendix A.

To: Mr. Ralph Reeves, Managing Director
From: Mr. John Thompson
Date: October 7, 1974

Pursuant to our discussion of last month, I have investigated the feasibility of incorporating an inflation accounting approach into our ongoing Management Control System. It is my opinion that while many aspects of an inflation accounting approach are counterbalancing insofar as their ultimate impact on the firm's profit, the overall impact on profits could be sufficiently significant that we should move to an inflation accounting approach for internal purposes, effective January 1. The rest of this memorandum details the approach I believe we should follow, with Exhibit A showing how these procedures would have impacted our stated earnings for the year ending February 28, 1974, and the half year ending August 31, 1974, and Exhibit B showing the critical calculations in depth.

Debtors, Creditors, Stock, and Fixed Assets are all subject to inflation adjustments, which will affect the company's real profitability. Accordingly I plan to process these items each quarter to take into account the impact of inflation during the quarter. *The Economist* Intelligence Unit's index (E.I.U.)* will be used on an annual basis to revalue our Fixed Assets. The Retail Price Index (R.P.I.) will be used on other assets and liabilities.

Quarterly, all Assets and Liabilities will be adjusted for inflation using only the Retail Price Index (the base value of Fixed Assets being the calculated E.I.U. values as of March 1 each year). If anything, we are understating the specific effect of inflation on the company since chemical industry raw material prices have soared in the past 12 months. The table below gives a brief feel for the magnitude of the changes in our plant values as a result of using the E.I.U. index.

*E.I.U. Index is an industry replacement value index created by *The Economist* Intelligence Unit of *The Economist* magazine. The E.I.U. produces 16 indices for various industries. An industry index is established by selecting a number of different types of standard equipment representative of the industry. The number of deliveries of a piece of equipment determines its relative importance. The change in the manufacturer's sale price over a certain period of time is then considered and weighted according to the relative importance of each piece of equipment to determine the E.I.U. The weighting of the various pieces of equipment is revised as the items become obsolete.

| | | NET BOOK VALUE | |
	Historical	Current Purchasing Power as of August 31, 1974
		(in thousands of pounds)
Plant A	1,538	2,392
Plant B	452	820
Plant C	360	604

The specific procedure for calculating the effect of inflation is as follows, and the impact worked out in detail for the year ending February 28, 1974, is shown in Exhibit B.

A. Net Monetary Assets (Debtors less Creditors)

> The closing Retail Price Index is divided by the opening Retail Price Index. The percentage uplift multiplied by the value of the opening net monetary assets is the loss (profit if net monetary liability) to be offset against the historically recorded profits.

B. Stock

> The index to be used for the opening stock must be backdated to allow for the period over which that stock was purchased (if two months' stock in hand, then the opening index is the average index of those two months). This index is divided into the closing index, etc., as above.
>
> The closing stock, on a similar basis, would yield a constant purchasing power profit in the period. Thus,

$$\frac{\text{RPI at closing date}}{\text{RPI at average of last two months}} \times \text{Value of closing stock}$$

$$\text{Value of closing stock} - \text{Profit in period}$$

C. Fixed Assets

> The depreciation charge is to be uplifted by the proportion of historical costs to current value.

EXHIBIT A

IMPACT OF INFLATION ON COMPANY ACCOUNTS

	YEAR ENDING FEBRUARY 28, 1974	HALF YEAR ENDING AUGUST 31, 1974
	(IN THOUSANDS OF POUNDS)	
Profits before tax per conventional accounts	2,822	2,960
Taxes	1,524	1,599
Profit after tax conventional accounts	1,298	1,361
Adjustments		
(1) Stocks (restatement of stocks at beginning and end of year)	(638)	(668)
(2) Depreciation (additional depreciation due to adjusting fixed asset values)	(457)	(304)
(3) Monetary items (gain due to excess of monetary liabilities over monetary assets)	573	278
Net adjustments	(522)	(694)

EXHIBIT A (continued)

Profit before tax expressed in £'s of current purchasing power at the end of the period	2,300	2,266
Taxes	1,524	1,599
Profit after tax in £'s of current purchasing power	776	667

EXHIBIT B

CALCULATION OF CHANGE IN CORPORATE PROFITS MOVING FROM HISTORICAL COST ACCOUNTING TO INFLATION ADJUSTED ACCOUNTING (MARCH 1, 1973–FEBRUARY 28, 1974)

1. Summary Balance Sheet Data from Exhibit 2

	MARCH 1, 1973	FEBRUARY 28, 1974
Net monetary assets (cash plus debtors, creditors, short-term debt, long-term debt)	(5,609)	(6,978)
Stock	6,614	8,512
Net book value (fixed assets)	8,684	9,103

2. Retail Price Index

December 31, 1972	158
January 31, 1973	160
February 28, 1973	160.6
December 31, 1973	173
January 31, 1974	175
February 28, 1974	177

3. Fixed Assets adjusted by E.I.U. Index

March 1, 1973	11,550
February 28, 1974	12,106

4. Calculation of Impact of Inflation on Profits

GAIN/(LOSS)

$$\text{Net Monetary Assets} \quad 5,609 \times \frac{177}{160.6} \qquad -5,609 = \quad 573$$

$$\text{Opening Stock} \quad 6,614 \times \frac{177}{(158 + 160.6) \times .5} \qquad -6,614 = (735)$$

$$\text{Closing Stock} \quad 8,512 \times \frac{177}{(173 + 177) \times .5} \qquad -8,512 = \quad 97$$

$$\text{Depreciation} \quad \frac{11,550}{8,684} \times 980 \times \frac{177}{160.6} \qquad - \quad 980 = \quad 457$$

Forever
Stores, Inc.

Karl Stone, President and principal stockholder of Forever Stores, Inc., sat at his desk reflecting on the condition of his business in general, and on the 1973 results (see Exhibits 1 and 2) in particular. It hadn't been a great year, he mused, but it hadn't been a disaster either. At least he didn't have to worry about the energy crisis; his 94 jewelry stores were all located in high pedestrian-traffic areas of major metropolitan areas, and he had recently been assured by his regional managers that there had been no noticeable slump in sales. Still, Stone felt mildly uncomfortable about another problem in the U.S. economy that didn't seem to want to go away: inflation. He felt that if he could only get some feel for the parameters of the situation as it affected Forever, he would be better able to deal with it. With this in mind he called his assistant, a recent graduate of a well-known Eastern business school, into his office.

"Carole," he began, "I have the feeling that we're getting clobbered by rising prices, but these statements look as healthy as ever. Since it looks as though inflation is here to stay, at least for a while, I think that this might be a good time to review some of our financial policies: capital structure, dividend policy, credit policies, things of that sort. But I have to be able to *see* what I'm fighting first; I need *information*. Do you see what I'm driving at?"

Carole Schultz shifted in her chair. "Yes, I believe I do," she replied. "What you're referring to are price-level adjusted financial statements; the techniques involved here have been part of GAAP for years, but have been largely ignored in practice. They relate a company's reported results to general price-level changes in the economy."

This case was prepared by David Clark, MBA student, under the supervision of Associate Professor John K. Shank as the basis for class discussion rather than to illustrate either effective or ineffective handling of an administrative situation.

Stone leaned back, looking slightly relieved. "Excellent. What do you need to construct these statements?"

"First, I'll need a table of the Gross National Product Implicit Price Deflator (GNPI) going back to 1963, the year the company was formed," she responded, "but I can get that at the library (see Exhibit 3). Then, in addition to the basic financial statements, I'll need schedules that show the age of individual items in our 'nonmonetary', accounts: Plant and Equipment, Other Current Assets, Other Assets, Other Liabilities, and Common Stock and Surplus (Exhibit 4). I'll get on it right away."

"Fine," replied Stone. "While you're at it, I'd like you to think about the implications of the figures you come up with. I'd like to know what kinds of decisions the price-level adjusted data will help us make, and I'd also like to get your ideas on some of the weaknesses or pitfalls that we should watch out for. I have a meeting with another director later today, so I'd like to go over your results with you before then. I'll see you at three."

Carole got up and turned to leave. Before she reached the door Stone called out, "Oh, and don't worry about lunch; I'll send one of the boys out for sandwiches."

Exhibit 1. Comparative Balance Sheets

	DECEMBER 31	
	1973	1972
	(IN MILLIONS OF DOLLARS)	
Current Assets		
Cash	$ 2.3	$ 2.3
Accounts receivable	56.3	53.7
Inventories (FIFO)	34.3	32.7
Deposits	0.6	0.6
	93.5	89.3
Plant and equipment	10.6	10.6
Less accumulated depreciation	3.9	3.4
	6.7	7.2
Investments (at cost)	3.5	3.5
	$103.7	$100.0
Current Liabilities		
Accounts payable	$ 31.5	$ 29.9
Accruals	4.4	4.2
Other current liabilities	1.4	1.3
	37.3	35.4

Exhibit 1. *(continued)*

Long-term debt	15.3	14.9
Deferred taxes	10.5	10.1
Capital stock	33.6	33.6
Retained earnings	7.0	6.0
	40.6	39.6
	$103.7	$100.0

Exhibit 2. *Statement of Income and Retained Earnings for year ended December 31, 1973 (in millions of dollars)*

Sales		$100.0
Cost of goods sold (FIFO)		
Opening inventory	$32.7	
Purchases	81.6	
Closing inventory	34.3	80.0
Gross Margin		20.0
Depreciation		0.5
Other Expenses		13.8
Operating Profit		5.7
Interest (at 7.5%)		1.7
Profit before tax		4.0
Profit after tax		$ 2.0
Retained earnings, December 31, 1972		$ 6.0
		8.0
Less: Dividends paid, 1973		1.0
Retained earnings, December 31, 1973		$ 7.0

Exhibit 3. *Implicit Price Deflators for Gross National Product for years 1963–1973* (1958 = 100)*

YEAR	GNPI	RELATIVE TO INDEX AT 12/31/73	RELATIVE TO INDEX AT 12/31/72
1963	107.2	1.478	1.377
1964	108.8	1.456	1.357
1965	110.9	1.428	1.331
1966	113.94	1.390	1.296
1967	117.59	1.347	1.255
1968	122.30	1.294	1.207
1969	128.20	1.235	1.152
1970	135.24	1.171	1.092
1971	141.60	1.118	1.043
1972	146.10	1.084	1.010
1973	153.94	1.029	—

QUARTERLY AVERAGES

1972		RELATIVE TO 12/31/73	RELATIVE TO 12/31/72
I	144.85	1.093	1.019
II	145.42	1.089	1.015
III	146.42	1.082	1.008
IV	147.63	1.073	1.000

1973			
I	149.81	1.057	—
II	152.46	1.039	—
III	155.06	1.021	—
IV	158.36	1.000	—

*Source: U.S. Department of Commerce, Bureau of Economic Analysis: *Survey of Current Business,* February 1974, for 1973 data; 1972 *Business Statistics* for all other data.

Exhibit 4. *Chronological Analysis of Selected Accounts (all amounts in millions of dollars)*

PLANT AND EQUIPMENT

Year Acquired	Gross Investment	Accumulated Depreciation* 12/31/72	Net Amount	
			12/31/72	12/31/73
1963	$ 3.6	$1.8	$1.8	$1.6
1965	1.5	0.6	0.9	0.8
1968	2.4	0.6	1.8	1.7
1970	2.1	0.3	1.8	1.7
1971	1.0	0.1	0.9	0.8
	$10.6	$3.4	$7.2	$6.7

COMMON STOCK AND SURPLUS

Year Acquired	Amount
1963	$16.8
1966	8.4
1970	8.4
	$33.6

DEPOSITS, INVESTMENTS, AND DEFERRED TAXES

For simplicity, assume that entire amounts appearing on the 1972 statements were acquired in 1968.

*All Plant and Equipment depreciated straight-line over 20 years.

QUESTIONS

1. Prepare the 1973 financial statements for Forever Stores, Inc. on a general price level adjusted basis.
2. What kinds of decisions do the price level adjusted financial statements facilitate
   (a) for management?
   (b) for investors or potential investors?

The Investment
Tax Credit

Exposure Draft October 22, 1971, Proposed APB Opinion Accounting for Investment Tax Credits

This proposed Opinion was drafted on the basis of the bill (HR 10947) passed by the House October 6 and will require that benefits arising from investment tax credits be accounted for as reductions of income tax expense over the periods in which the cost of the related property is charged to income. In taking final action, the Board will, of course, take into consideration any changes in relevant provisions of the law as finally enacted that differ substantially from those provisions in the House bill.

Issued by the Accounting Principles Board of the
American Institute of Certified Public Accountants
for Comment from Persons Interested in Financial Reporting.

Comments should be received by November 30, 1971, and addressed to Richard C. Lytle, Administrative Director, APB at the Institute's Offices, 666 Fifth Avenue, N.Y., N.Y. 10019

INTRODUCTION

1. The United States Internal Revenue Code from time to time has provided for selective tax benefits as incentives to accomplish desired objectives, such as stimulating investment in certain types of property. This Opinion states the views of the Accounting Principles Board on the appropriate accounting for investment tax credits (job development credits).

2. This Opinion supersedes APB Opinion No. 2, *Accounting for the "Investment Credit,"* except the Addendum thereto, and APB Opinion No. 4 (Amending No. 2), *Accounting for the "Investment Credit,"* and paragraph 4 of APB Opinion No. 11 *Accounting for Income Taxes.* This Opinion should be applied to regulated companies in accordance with the provisions of the Addendum to APB Opinion No. 2.

DISCUSSION

3. Under the United States Internal Revenue Code the investment tax credit resulting from expenditures for qualifying property is claimed as a credit against income taxes otherwise payable. This, for income tax purposes, benefits from investment tax credits depend on two conditions: (1) an investment in qualifying property and (2) the existence of taxable income. Two principal methods have been followed in accounting for benefits arising from investment tax credits:

    a. The "flow through" method reduces income tax expense for the periods in which expenditures create tax benefits. This method is premised on the view that realization of the benefit of the investment tax credit is effected by the generation of taxable income and that realization does not depend on, or relate to, future productive use of the related property (so long as the property is held for the qualifying period for income tax purposes) or to revenues earned during subsequent periods. Under this method the investment tax credit is viewed as a selective tax reduction in the periods taxes otherwise payable are reduced by the credit. Thus, the tax credit is not considered to be a reduction of the cost of the property acquired.

    b. The "deferral" method defers the benefit arising from the investment tax credit and amortizes that benefit as a reduction of income tax expense over the periods in which the cost of the related property is charged to income. Under this method the investment tax credit is viewed in substance as a reduction of, or offset to, the cost of the property that results in the credit. The tax credit is not viewed as resulting in a reduction of income tax expense prior to the time the cost of the related asset is charged to income. Thus, the tax benefit follows the accounting for the related asset and is reflected in income proportionately as the cost of the asset is charged to income.

OPINION

4. The Board concludes that benefits arising from investment tax credits should be accounted for as reductions of income tax expense over the periods

in which the cost of the related property is charged to income, as discussed in paragraph 3b.[1] The Board believes that this conclusion will result in a more meaningful presentation of the economic facts to investors and other users of financial statements. Amortization of the tax benefits deferred should be proportional to the amortization of the related expenditures.

5. Investment tax credits should be recognized as deferred investment tax credits only to the extent that the benefits (a) have been utilized as offsets against income taxes payable, (b) would have been utilized as offsets against income taxes otherwise payable except for the effect of timing differences, (see paragraph 36 of APB Opinion No. 11) or (c) having not been so utilized or applied, are subject to unusual circumstances so that utilization is assured beyond any reasonable doubt at the time the credits arise. The benefits recognized under (a), (b), or (c) should be amortized to income tax expense in accordance with the provisions of paragraph 4.

6. If legislation were to be enacted providing that the depreciable tax basis of any property qualifying for investment tax credit be reduced to the extent of the credit, the amount of such reduction would have an effect similar to a timing difference (APB Opinion No. 11) and should be so treated. The balance of the tax reduction arising from the investment tax credit should be amortized in accordance with the provisions of paragraphs 4 and 7.

7. Investment tax credits may be unused because of the absence of taxable income or because of limitations provided in the Internal Revenue Code. Benefits of investment tax credit carryforwards should not be recognized as deferred credits except as set forth in paragraph 5. When unused investment tax credit carryforwards are recognized in a period subsequent to the period in which the related expenditure was made, the benefits should be recorded as deferred credits and amortized to the current and future periods as the remaining cost of the related property is depreciated.

8. The amount of benefits of investment tax credits that enter into the provision for income taxes and into the amounts of taxes payable in a period should be disclosed. Amounts of benefits of investment tax credits not utilized in the reduction of taxes payable (together with expiration dates) and that portion of those amounts recognized because of the effect of timing differences or because utilization is assured beyond any reasonable doubt should be disclosed (paragraph 5b and c).

9. The conclusions of this Opinion should be applied in all situations unless the results of application would be clearly immaterial in relation to the income tax provision, net income, and the trend of earnings.

---

[1] In certain circumstances the benefit related to an investment tax credit may be realized in a financing transaction (usually by a lending institution) as an element of the "yield" on the financing. The benefits of such tax credits may be recognized over the appropriate term of the financing transaction.

If the investment tax credit serves to reduce income taxes otherwise payable by a lessee of property, the benefits should reduce income tax expense over the periods in which the related charge is made to income.

10. This Opinion shall be effective for all benefits of investment tax credits arising under legislation enacted subsequent to December 31, 1970 as a part of the United States Internal Revenue Code. Similar benefits arising under taxation laws of other countries should be accounted for in a manner consistent with the concepts of this Opinion.

NOTES

Opinions of the Accounting Principles Board present the conclusions of at least two-thirds of the members of the Board, which is the senior technical body of the Institute authorized to issue pronouncements on accounting principles.

Board Opinions are considered appropriate in all circumstances covered but need not be applied to immaterial items.

Covering all possible conditions and circumstances in an Opinion of the Accounting Principles Board is usually impracticable. The substance of transactions and the principles, guides, rules, and criteria described in Opinions should control the accounting for transactions not expressly covered.

Unless otherwise stated, Opinions of the Board are not intended to be retroactive.

Council of the Institute has resolved that Institute members should disclose departures from Board Opinions in their reports as independent auditors when the effect of the departures on the financial statements is material or see to it that such departures are disclosed in notes to the financial statements and, where practicable, should disclose their effects on the financial statements. (Special Bulletin, *Disclosure of Departures from Opinions of the Accounting Principles Board,* October 1964). Members of the Institute must assume the burden of justifying any such departures.

SENATE BARS RULE CHANGE
ACCOUNTING UNIT FAVORED

By H. Erich Heinemann

The United States Senate, in a little noticed action, has vetoed an attempt by the accounting profession to tighten the rules governing the financial reporting of the proposed 7 per cent "job development" tax credit.

While the Senate action will have an immediate impact on company financial reporting practices, accounting leaders said yesterday that its ultimate consequences would be far broader.

Philip L. Deflies, chairman of the Accounting Principles Board, the senior rule-making body of the profession, charged yesterday that "the involvement of Congress in the setting of accounting principles could represent a dangerous precedent and a decided step backwards for the long, hard effort to achieve uniformity in financial reporting."

Other Systems Cited

Mr. Deflies, who is also managing partner of Lybrand Ross Bros. & Montgomery, said that as many as three or more accounting methods would be possible under the Senate's rule.

"If accounting principles must be established by the Legislative process," he stated, "they should provide for one method."

Leonard M. Savoie, executive vice president of the American Institute of Certified Public Accountants, said that the Senate--which acted with the formal support of the Administration--had "cut the ground out from under" both the Accounting Principles Board and the Securities and Exchange Commission, which had backed the original A.P.B. action.

Mr. Savoie said that he was hopeful that the Conference Committee, which must iron out the differences between the House and Senate versions of the Revenue Act of 1971, would knock out the accounting amendment, which was introduced by Senator Wallace E. Bennett, Republican of Utah.

If the provision stayed in, he said, "the door would be open" for any industry that didn't like a ruling of the A.P.B.--he mentioned insurance and petroleum in particular--to run to Washington for relief.

Last month, after carefully lining up support from the S.E.C. (and it was thought at the time, the Administration) the A.P.B. ruled that if the tax credit became law, then companies would be required to report the tax savings that would result over the useful life of the equipment involved.

The Board specifically disallowed the so-called "flow-through" accounting method that was widely used when the previous investment tax credit was in force, which in some companies had had the effect of producing marked increases in reported profits, as all the tax savings were taken the first year.

The deferral and amortization method that it had approved, the Board said, "will result in a more meaningful presentation of the economic facts to investors and other users of financial statements."

But according to Charls E. Walker, Under Secretary of the Treasury, the relatively lower profits that would be reported under the deferral method "might operate to diminish the job-creating effect of the credit" since businessmen would "have less motivation to purchase new equipment."

The Senate, in accepting this argument, voted that "no taxpayer shall be required, without his consent, to use, for purposes of his financial reports, any particular method of accounting for the credit allowed by section 38, and (2) a taxpayer shall disclose, in any financial report made by him, the method of accounting for the credit allowed by section 38 used for purposes of such report."

Illustrations on Effect on Reported Earnings of Alternate Accounting Treatments for the Investment Credit

	FINANCIAL ACCOUNTING TREATMENT			*Cumulative Balance Sheet Deferral*
	Flow-thru	*Defer-ral*	*Differ-ence*	
CONSTANT AFTER-TAX PROFIT BEFORE APPLICATION OF INVESTMENT CREDIT	$140 M	$140 M	0	0

PROFIT AFTER APPLICATION OF INVESTMENT CREDIT

(a) Individual Investment*

YEAR				
1	$210 M	$147 M	$ 63 M	$ 63 M
2	140 M	147 M	(7 M)	56 M
3	140 M	147 M	(7 M)	49 M
4	140 M	147 M	(7 M)	42 M
5	140 M	147 M	(7 M)	35 M
6	140 M	147 M	(7 M)	28 M
7	140 M	147 M	(7 M)	21 M
8	140 M	147 M	(7 M)	14 M
9	140 M	147 M	(7 M)	7 M
10	140 M	147 M	(7 M)	0
11	140 M	140 M	0	0
12	140 M	140 M	0	0

(b) Level Flow Investment†

1	$210 M	$147 M	$ 63 M	$ 63 M
2	210 M	154 M	56 M	119 M
3	210 M	161 M	49 M	168 M
4	210 M	168 M	42 M	210 M
5	210 M	175 M	35 M	245 M
6	210 M	182 M	28 M	273 M
7	210 M	189 M	21 M	294 M
8	210 M	196 M	14 M	308 M
9	210 M	203 M	7 M	315 M
10	210 M	210 M	0	315 M
11	210 M	210 M	0	315 M
12	210 M	210 M	0	315 M

(c) Intermittent Investment§

1	$210 M	$147 M	$ 63 M	$ 63 M
2	140 M	147 M	(7 M)	56 M
3	140 M	147 M	(7 M)	49 M
4	210 M	154 M	56 M	105 M
5	140 M	154 M	(14 M)	91 M
6	140 M	154 M	(14 M)	77 M

	FINANCIAL ACCOUNTING TREATMENT			Cumulative Balance Sheet Deferral
	Flow-thru	Defer-ral	Differ-ence	
CONSTANT AFTER-TAX PROFIT BEFORE APPLICATION OF INVESTMENT CREDIT	$140 M	$140 M	0	0
PROFIT AFTER APPLICATION OF INVESTMENT CREDIT				
7	210 M	161 M	49 M	126 M
8	140 M	161 M	(21 M)	105 M
9	140 M	161 M	(21 M)	84 M
10	210 M	168 M	42 M	126 M
11	140 M	161 M	(21 M)	105 M
12	140 M	161 M	(21 M)	84 M

Assumptions

1. Constant after-tax profit before application of investment credit of $140,000 in years 1 through 12.
2. Federal taxes payable before application of investment credit is $140,000 in years 1 through 12.
3. Productive life of each investment is 10 years and, for simplicity, assume straight-line depreciation.

*Assumes an individual investment in qualifying property of $1,000,000 in year 1 and for illustrative purposes, a $0 investment in years 2 through 12.

†Assumes a level flow of investment in qualifying property of $1,000,000 for each of years 1 through 12.

§Assumes an intermittent investment in qualifying property of $1,000,000 in years 1, 4, 7, and 10 and for illustrative purposes, a $0 investment in years 2, 3, 5, 6, 8, 9, 11, and 12.

A VOTE FOR GIMMICKRY

Over the years, the accounting profession has had to cope with two forces that sometimes are in conflict.

On the one hand, it has professional and certain legal obligations to set and maintain acceptable and consistent standards for certifying the fairness and accuracy of corporate financial reports. On the other, it is faced with pressures from clients seeking to present their reports in ways most convenient to their own purposes.

Now, it would appear, yet another force, the United States government, is involving itself more heavily in the delicate balance of interests. From all appearances, moreover, the government is entering the lists not on the side of consistent standards but on the side of short-term convenience.

The argument is over how companies and their accountants should handle the proposed 7% tax credit on capital investment which President Nixon is pushing as an economic stimulant. The accounting profession, through its rule-making Accounting Principles Board, wants the tax-saving effect of the credit spread over the life of the capital equipment purchased, on the ground that this single method would make earnings reports consistent with each other and reduce year-to-year distortions.

The administration, on the other hand, fears that the APB approach would weaken the stimulative effect of the tax credit by preventing a quick recovery of the full 7% by companies that wanted to apply it to their earnings immediately.

Last week, the Senate sided with the administration, voting a provision into its version of the tax bill that would prohibit application of the APB rule. The APB says this could leave companies with a choice of three or more different ways of accounting for the tax credit and represents a decided step backwards "for the long, hard effort to achieve uniformity in financial reporting."

Indeed it does. And the reason all this comes about is the government's effort to make the economy, and its own record, look good through employment of a tax gimmick. In other words, the government is trying to do much the same thing responsible accountants have been trying to get corporations not to do for so many years.

The tax law still hasn't passed both houses of Congress. The APB may still win its point, but the chances don't look particularly bright. It is one thing to persuade a corporation to abide by "generally accepted accounting procedures." But it is something else again to persuade a government.

The Wall Street Journal, November 23, 1971. Reprinted by permission.

October 27, 1967

Mr. Clifford V. Heimbucher, Chairman
Accounting Principles Board
The American Institute of Certified
   Public Accountants
666 Fifth Avenue
New York, New York

Dear Mr. Heimbucher:

   I am sure that you have been deluged with comments about the airline industry and the flow through of investment credit. From an
accounting and a security analyst standpoint I can well understand
your position, but I think you are taking on a lot of responsibility
in which, by the farthest stretch of the imagination, you have no
authority. By this I mean you are forcing changes in market share for
various companies.

   I am sure you are well aware of the $1.487 billion difference in
retained earnings that the major trunks told Mr. Ackley that they
would not have if they were forced to amortize the investment credit.
Metropolitan Life and Chase Manhattan, which have been two of the
leading lenders, have in times of severe problems been willing to give
the carriers straight debt equal to 1.5 times the sum of convertibles
plus net worth. Make it just one-to-one and you will see you are preventing carriers from buying $3 billion worth of equipment over the
next decade. The gross plant of the entire industry is only $5 billion.

   In the interests of conversatism, or perhaps fear of the SEC, do
you really want to have that much control over companies' fortunes?
Also, are you sure you have considered the disservice you are doing to
the American travelling public by withholding the benefits of improved
service and possible lower fares from them?

   Enough is enough!

                              Sincerely,

                              Charles H. Brunie,
                              Partner
                              Oppenheimer & Company

CHB/g

THE FINANCIAL ANALYSTS FEDERATION

Tower Suite, 219 East 42nd Street, New York, N.Y. 10017
(212) 687-3882

THE HONORABLE RUSSELL B. LONG
THE UNITED STATES SENATE
WASHINGTON, D. C.

THE HONORABLE WILBUR B. MILLS
CHAIRMAN, HOUSE WAYS AND MEANS
   COMMITTEE
THE HOUSE OF REPRESENTATIVES
WASHINGTON, D. C.

THE HONORABLE WALLACE F. BENNETT
THE SENATE FINANCE COMMITTEE
THE UNITED STATES SENATE
WASHINGTON, D. C.

THE HONORABLE HAROLD R. COLLIER
MEMBER, HOUSE WAYS AND MEANS
   COMMITTEE
HOUSE OF REPRESENTATIVES
WASHINGTON, D. C.

THE HONORABLE AL ULLMAN
THE HOUSE OF REPRESENTATIVES
WASHINGTON, D. C.

THE HONORABLE CLINTON P. ANDERSON
THE UNITED STATES SENATE
WASHINGTON, D. C.

THE HONORABLE CARL T. CURTIS
THE UNITED STATES SENATE
WASHINGTON, D. C.

THE HONORABLE HERMAN E. TALMADGE
THE UNITED STATES SENATE
WASHINGTON, D. C.

THE HONORABLE JOHN W. BYRNES
THE HOUSE OF REPRESENTATIVES
WASHINGTON, D. C.

THE HONORABLE JACKSON E. BETTS
THE HOUSE OF REPRESENTATIVES
WASHINGTON, D. C.

IDENTICAL TELEGRAMS

November 19, 1971

"THE FINANCIAL ANALYSTS FEDERATION WISHES TO FILE AN OBJECTION TO
THE AMENDMENT TO THE TAX BILL H.R. 10947, PARAGRAPH C, PAGE 5, BY THE
SENATE, GIVING COMPLETE FREEDOM TO CORPORATIONS IN THE METHOD OF
ACCOUNTING FOR THE INVESTMENT TAX CREDIT IN THEIR FINANCIAL REPORTING.
WE URGE THAT THIS PROVISION BE STRICKEN FROM THE BILL IN THE CONFERENCE
COMMITTEE.

THE FINANCIAL ANALYSTS FEDERATION IS THE PROFESSIONAL ORGANI-
ZATION OF 13,000 SECURITY ANALYSTS AND INVESTMENT MANAGERS WHO REPRE-
SENT, DIRECTLY OR INDIRECTLY, A LARGE SEGMENT OF ALL INSTITUTIONAL AND
INDIVIDUAL INVESTORS IN THE UNITED STATES.

OUR OBJECTIONS TO THIS PROVISION ARE TWOFOLD. FIRST, WE DO NOT
BELIEVE ACCOUNTING AND REPORTING STANDARDS SHOULD BE ESTABLISHED BY
LEGISLATION, ESPECIALLY WITHOUT OPPORTUNITY FOR HEARING FROM INVESTORS
WHO ARE AFFECTED BY SUCH STANDARDS. THIS PROVISION UNDERCUTS THE
ESTABLISHED AUTHORITY OF THE SECURITIES AND EXCHANGE COMMISSION AND
THE ACCOUNTING PRINCIPLES BOARD FOR THE DETERMINATION OF ACCOUNTING

STANDARDS. WE FEAR THAT THIS ACTION, IF FINALLY ADOPTED BY THE CONGRESS, WILL ENCOURAGE SPECIAL INTEREST GROUPS TO ATTEMPT TO BRING ABOUT OTHER CHANGES IN ACCOUNTING STANDARDS FOR THEIR BENEFIT THROUGH THE LEGISLATIVE PROCESS. WE BELIEVE THIS WILL RESULT IN A GROWING LOSS OF CONFIDENCE IN CORPORATE FINANCIAL REPORTING TO THE DETRIMENT OF INVESTORS.

SECOND, THE PROVISION PERMITS A VARIETY OF ACCOUNTING TREATMENTS OF THE TAX CREDIT. OUR FEDERATION HAS FOR MANY YEARS WORKED TO NARROW OR REDUCE THE NUMBER OF ALTERNATIVE ACCOUNTING METHODS. ANY MOVE TOWARD INCREASING THE NUMBER OF ALTERNATIVE METHODS IS A BACKWARD STEP IN REPORTING TO INVESTORS, RESULTING IN MISLEADING COMPARISONS OF THE FINANCIAL RESULTS OF PUBLIC CORPORATIONS.

THE CONGRESS HAS ALWAYS SHOWN GREAT CONCERN FOR THE PROTECTION OF THE INVESTOR. WE URGE THAT THIS PROVISION IN H. R. 10947 IN REGARD TO FINANCIAL REPORTING OF THE TAX CREDIT BE RECONSIDERED FOR ITS AFFECT ON INVESTORS. WE BELIEVE THAT THE CONTINUOUS LONGTERM IMPROVEMENT IN CORPORATE REPORTING TO INVESTORS IS BEING SACRIFICED FOR THE SHORTRUN BENEFIT OF A LIMITED NUMBER OF CORPORATIONS AND THAT A DANGEROUS PRECE-DENT IS BEING ESTABLISHED."

(SIGNED) WALTER P. STERN, PRESIDENT
THE FINANCIAL ANALYSTS
FEDERATION
219 EAST 42ND STREET
NEW YORK, NEW YORK 10017

THE SECRETARY OF THE TREASURY
Washington

Dec. 2, 1971

Dear Mr. Stern:

This is in response to your telegram dated November 19, 1971, to Senator Long and Representative Mills, a copy of which was sent to me, relating to the Senate amendment to H.R. 10947 concerning the financial accounting treatment of the Job Development Investment Credit.

The Treasury Department supports the actions of the Senate in providing that a corporation shall retain the option of accounting for the credit in its financial statements on either the "flow-through" or the "deferral" method.

The Department's primary concern in seeking the credit is to stimulate the economy and create jobs by encouraging the purchase of new machinery and equipment. We believe that a requirement that corporations may only amortize the benefits of the credit over the service life of the asset in their financial statements may have an adverse impact on the intended effects of the credit.

When the Administration decided to press for the enactment of the Job Development Investment Credit, one of the factors that was considered was the manner in which such a credit would affect corporate reported earnings. The decision to request a restoration of the credit was based, in part, on the assumption that the present optional treatment of the credit for financial accounting purposes would be continued.

The Treasury Department has often stated that it believes that the establishment of accounting principles is solely within the province of the accounting profession and the Securities and Exchange Commission. However, because of the exceptional circumstances surrounding the accounting treatment of the credit and because of its critical relationship to the stimulation of the economy through the Job Development Investment Credit, we are compelled to support the actions of the Senate in dealing with the financial accounting treatment of the credit.

The Treasury Department strongly supports the efforts of the accounting profession to narrow the range of permissible accounting practices. Furthermore, we hope that our support for the Senate's action is in no way interpreted as a precedent for any future efforts to legislate financial accounting principles. Nevertheless, the strategic importance of the credit in the overall economic program--to create jobs through the stimulation of capital investment--requires that the Treasury Department support the efforts of the Senate to retain the present optional accounting treatment of the Job Development Investment Credit.

If you have any further questions, please feel free to contact us.

Sincerely yours,

Charles E. Walker
Acting Secretary

Mr. Walter P. Stern
President
The Financial Analysists Federation
219 East 42nd Street
New York, New York 10017

November 17, 1967

Mr. Stanley S. Surrey
Assistant Secretary
Treasury Department
Washington, D.C.

Dear Stanley:

This letter is to take issue with the Treasury Department position expressed in your letter of November 8 to the Accounting Principles Board, on accounting for income taxes.

It seems to me that the Treasury Department letter misses the point as to what the accountants' problem is. Economists tend to think in macroeconomic terms about aggregate cash flows, and from that point of view, perhaps, the investment credit is something like a rate reduction. But the accountants' problem is to give a meaningful report of the results of operation of a particular firm during a particular period on a basis that can be intelligently compared with similar reports for other firms or for other periods. From that viewpoint there is all the difference in the world between a reduction in the rate of tax imposed on income, and a credit against tax measured by something wholly unrelated to income in the current period. Neither the purpose nor the effect of the credit can be altered by referring to its association with the capital asset to which it relates as "artificial," or as a mere "mechanical method by which [a rate] reduction is measured or implemented in the statute." What the credit is and was intended to be is a form of subsidy for capital investment; what is artificial, and a mere mechanical method by which the subsidy is implemented, and a source of seemingly interminable semantic confusion, is the fact that the credit was incorporated into the income tax law instead of being separately enacted as a subsidy measure.

Allocation of taxes between current expense and capital account is a recurring and commonplace accounting procedure. Real estate taxes are charged to current expense or to plant accounts according to whether the plant is in service or under construction. Sales taxes on goods used for plant construction are charged to plant account.

If the federal government were to impose an excise tax on the purchase of airplanes, for example, that would be treated as part of the cost of the airplane and charged off over its useful life, not all at once. The investment credit is in purpose and effect much more nearly a negative exercise tax on capital investment than a reduction of rate of tax on income, and as such, it should be reflected, like a positive excise, over the useful life of the asset in question.

November 17, 1967

I am, perhaps, most troubled by the following sentence in the Treasury letter:

> "Furthermore, a mandate to defer the benefit arising from the investment credit could well blunt its effectiveness as an incentive to modernization and expansion."

I can find nothing in any part of the description of the intended incentive affect of the credit that depends in any way upon the credit being immediately reflected in income. The whole analysis was in terms of a rather sophisticated consideration of discounted cash flows, in which the credit was regarded essentially as reducing the cost of a capital investment without affecting the projected yield. The only way I can imagine that the accounting treatment would affect the incentive to invest is that under a flow-through method of accounting a management would see the investment credit as presenting an opportunity to show higher immediate earnings -- or to cover up a drop in earnings -- by making an otherwise undesirable capital investment and having the credit reflected immediately as a decrease in current income tax expense. This form of added inducement seems to me to involve a higher cost in terms of honesty and integrity of corporate financial reporting that we should be willing to pay.

The last sentence of the Treasury letter says that it would be unfortunate for the accounting profession to be bound by "ad hoc characterizations" of tax benefits. I agree whole-heartedly with that sentiment, but it seems to me that what is ad hoc about the investment credit is its incorporation into the income tax law, not its association with capital investment.

Sincerely,

William D. Andrews
Professor of Law
Harvard Law School

AMERICAN INSTITUTE OF CERTIFIED PUBLIC ACCOUNTANTS

666 FIFTH AVENUE
NEW YORK, N.Y.   10019

STATEMENT OF THE ACCOUNTING PRINCIPLES BOARD
ON ACCOUNTING FOR THE INVESTMENT CREDIT

DECEMBER 9, 1971

The Accounting Principles Board has had to defer its efforts to develop a single uniform method of accounting for the investment credit in view of congressional action permitting taxpayer choice of accounting method of recognizing the benefit of the credit.

The APB had circulated a proposal for public comment with the intent of establishing uniform accounting by year end. This proposal would have required that, for reporting income to shareholders, benefits from the investment credit be spread over the lives of the related assets. This would have ruled out the use of any other method, such as the "flow through" method under which the entire amount of the credit is taken into income in the year in which income taxes are reduced by the credit.

The APB did not discuss further the merits of the accounting methods or the comments received on its proposal, since Congress has stated that no taxpayer shall be required to use any particular method of accounting for the credit in reports subject to the jurisdiction of any federal agency.

The congressional action requires consistency in the use of the accounting method selected, unless the Treasury Department consents to a change. The designation of another agency, the Treasury Department, to approve changes in accounting methods may hamper the APB's efforts to further improve reporting to investors since the APB has recently issues a pronouncement permitting changes in accounting methods only when the new methods are preferable.

The APB unanimously deplores congressional involvement in establishing accounting principles for financial reports to investors, which largely have been the responsibility of the Securities & Exchange Commission and the accounting profession. The APB further deplores congressional endorsement of alternative accounting methods, especially since there has been strong demand by congressmen and others for the elimination of alternative methods which confuse investors.

Stirling Homex

During the late 1960s a number of companies, spurred by the Department of Housing and Urban Development's (HUD) $67-million "Operation Breakthrough," attempted to revolutionize the technology of the housing industry. One of these companies, Stirling Homex, pioneered the concept of "modular" housing, which used many of the techniques of automobile assembly to mass produce, transport, and install large numbers of completed housing units in clusters. The substantial savings in labor costs due to mass production and the ability to construct entire housing projects on site in a matter of days were especially attractive to federal, state, and local housing authorities searching for ways to improve housing, particularly for lower income groups.

Stirling Homex was started in 1967 by William and David Stirling, Jr., brothers who ran a small home-building company in Avon, New York. The company obtained risk capital from Harper Sibley, Jr., a Western Union heir who was an experienced construction investor, in order to begin mass production. Homex estimated it could build a modular home, exclusive of land, for between $16,000 and $25,000. From the beginning, the company attracted considerable national publicity through its technological innovations and its close identification with HUD. Several HUD bureaucrats joined the Homex management and HUD Secretary George W. Romney was flown by Homex to Avon to see the company's facilities. Homex used some of its first modular units for a suburban Rochester housing project with 275 dwelling units; on-site construction was completed in 36 hours. In 1969, the company developed a system of jacks to

This case was prepared by Assistant Professor M. Edgar Barrett with the assistance of Jonathan Brown, Research Assistant, as a basis for class discussion rather than to illustrate either effective or ineffective handling of an administrative situation.

raise modules so other units could be slipped under them without the use of a crane. The next year Homex sent a 2,000-ft.-long train of modules to Corinth, Mississippi, to supply emergency housing after a hurricane destroyed hundreds of homes. Homex was the first to transport modular units by train.

Between 1969 and 1970 when Homex went public, the company sold most of its units in the Rochester area, more than half, according to some sources, to companies in which the Homex management had investments. The offering prospectus showed earnings of $1 million on sales of $10 million for fiscal 1969. The public issue of stock came out in February 1970 at $16.50 a share and doubled within 24 hours. By the middle of March Homex stock was selling for $51.75.

In 1970 Homex won a HUD contract to construct a 13-story apartment house in Memphis. The company also said it had a "tentative understanding" with the Greater Gulfport (Miss.) Housing Development Corporation to build $100 million worth of modular housing. To produce for what the company saw as a lucrative market in the South, Homex planned to lease a 350,000-sq. ft. plant in Gulfport. The plant would be financed by county industrial revenue bonds to be approved by local voters.

The 1971 Annual Report revealed Homex's intention to market its products to a broader consumer spectrum. In addition to public housing projects and high-rise apartments, the company was offering modular units for townhouses, private residences, college housing, efficiency apartments, hotels, and motels. During the year the company doubled its manufacturing facilities at Avon and created the U.S. Shelter Corporation, a wholly owned subsidiary, to provide construction and permanent financing for its customers. Earnings per share were $.24 in fiscal 1970 and $.37 in 1971. Management anticipated increased sales and revenues for fiscal 1972.

REVENUE RECOGNITION

Stirling Homex recognized the sale of a modular unit when it was produced if the unit was assigned to a specific contract and if there was an identified site plan and a financially capable purchaser. Homex did not require progress payments from its buyers nor did the company demand that the housing site itself be approved by the purchaser. Some of the contracts were in the form of letters of intention to buy from reputable institutions such as public housing authorities whose final decisions were often delayed by red tape, changing budgets, or the necessity of seeking voter approval through public referenda.

According to people familiar with the company, Homex's profit margin came essentially from the production of modular units; revenues from installation operations, recognized on a percentage of completion basis, were allocated on an estimated break-even point. Neither the February 1970 offering prospectus nor the July 1970 Annual Report broke down revenues and costs between production and installation. The 1970 Annual Report stated that "contracts generally provided for payment upon completion and receipt of all approvals necessary for occupancy, or for payment upon completion of each respective phase." Because of the quality of its receivables, due in the most part from public housing authorities, no provision for doubtful accounts was considered necessary.

Exhibit 1 contains a complete set of Homex's audited financial statements for the fiscal year ended July 31, 1971.

Exhibit 1. *Stirling Homex Corporation and Consolidated Subsidiaries Consolidated Balance Sheets July 31, 1971 with comparative figures for 1970*

Stirling Homex Corporation and Consolidated Subsidiaries

Consolidated Balance Sheets July 31, 1971 with comparative figures for 1970

Assets

	1971	1970
Current assets:		
Cash (Note 11)	$ 3,196,457	2,778,077
Preferred stock proceeds receivable (Note 2)	19,000,000	—
Receivables (Notes 1 and 3)	37,845,572	15,486,119
Inventories (Note 5):		
Raw materials, work in process and salable merchandise at lower of cost (first-in, first-out) or replacement market	2,614,200	2,167,603
Land held for development or sale, at cost	1,878,343	1,583,621
Prepaid expenses and other current assets	226,530	124,765
Total current assets	64,761,102	22,140,185
Investment in unconsolidated subsidiary (Note 1)	1,134,579	—
Long-term receivables (Note 4)	4,225,349	541,124
Property, plant and equipment at cost, less accumulated depreciation and amortization: 1971—$733,705; 1970—$230,921 (Notes 6 and 8)	9,426,941	5,245,745
Deferred charges, less accumulated amortization: 1971—$586,011; 1970—$153,894 (Note 7)	2,558,792	944,109
	$82,106,763	28,871,163

See accompanying Notes to Consolidated Financial Statements.

Exhibit 1. *(continued)*

Liabilities and Stockholders' Equity

	1971	1970
Current liabilities:		
Current portion of long-term debt (Note 8)	$ 295,630	333,036
Notes payable to banks—unsecured (1971—6 to 6½%; 1970—8 to 8½%) (Note 11)	37,700,000	11,700,000
Accounts payable	4,025,254	2,480,834
Due to unconsolidated subsidiary (Note 1)	76,894	—
Accrued expenses and other liabilities	577,377	232,819
Current and deferred income taxes (Note 9)	3,528,125	1,387,338
Total current liabilities	46,203,280	16,134,027
Long-term debt (Note 8)	236,588	496,489
Deferred income taxes (Note 9)	2,098,767	587,265
Option deposit on land contract (Note 5)	235,000	—
Stockholders' equity:		
$2.40 cumulative convertible preferred stock (Note 2): Authorized 500,000 shares, $1.00 par value; shares subscribed: 1971—500,000 (aggregate involuntary liquidation value— $20,000,000); 1970—none	500,000	—
Common stock (Notes 2 and 10): Authorized 15,000,000 shares, $.01 par value; shares issued: 1971—8,909,200; 1970—8,897,400	89,092	88,974
Additional paid-in capital (Note 2)	26,554,453	8,446,738
Retained earnings	6,370,333	3,117,670
	33,513,878	11,653,382
Less treasury stock at cost (60,000 shares)	180,750	—
Total stockholders' equity	33,333,128	11,653,382
Commitments and contingencies (Note 11)		
	$82,106,763	28,871,163

Exhibit 1. (continued)

Financial Summary

Stirling Homex Corporation and Consolidated Subsidiaries

Consolidated Statement of Income Year ended July 31, 1971 with comparative figures for 1970

	1971	1970
Revenues:		
Manufacturing division—trade (Note 3)	$29,482,271	16,492,770
Installation division (Note 3):		
Trade	7,230,878	5,601,357
Affiliate	—	459,941
Equity in undistributed net income of subsidiary (Note 1)	134,579	—
Total revenues	36,847,728	22,554,068
Costs and expenses:		
Cost of sales:		
Manufacturing division	17,729,078	9,919,327
Installation division	6,601,413	5,240,388
Administrative and selling expenses	4,048,113	2,390,604
Interest expense	1,838,461	648,181
Total costs and expenses	30,217,065	18,198,500
Income before Federal and state income taxes	6,630,663	4,355,568
Federal and state income taxes (Note 9):		
Current	368,000	1,965,982
Deferred	3,010,000	354,397
	3,378,000	2,320,379
Net income	$ 3,252,663	2,035,189
Average common shares outstanding (Note 12)	8,881,938	8,649,483
Earnings per common share (Note 12)	$ .37	.24

See accompanying Notes to Consolidated Financial Statements.

Exhibit 1. (continued)

Stirling Homex Corporation and Consolidated Subsidiaries

Consolidated Statement of Changes in Financial Position
Year ended July 31, 1971 with comparative figures for 1970

	1971	1970
Source of working capital:		
Net income	$ 3,252,663	2,035,189
Expenses not requiring outlay of working capital:		
Depreciation and amortization	529,116	220,227
Amortization of deferred charges	432,117	133,288
Deferred income taxes (noncurrent)	1,511,502	184,776
Undistributed net income of finance subsidiary	(134,579)	—
Working capital provided from operations	5,590,819	2,573,480
Net proceeds from sales of stock:		
Public offering of common stock	—	5,985,715
Private sale of common stock	—	516,500
Common stock issued under qualified stock option plan	37,200	—
Public offering of preferred stock	18,570,633	—
Long-term borrowings	51,402	124,677
Decrease in long-term receivables	10,000	43,421
Option deposit received on land contract	235,000	—
Total source of working capital	24,495,054	9,243,793
Application of working capital:		
Purchase of treasury stock	180,750	—
Additions to property, plant and equipment	4,710,312	4,422,506
Additions to deferred charges	2,046,800	735,093
Reduction in long-term debt	311,303	3,052,140
Increase in noncurrent portion of long-term receivables	3,694,225	—
Investment in unconsolidated subsidiary	1,000,000	—
Total application of working capital	11,943,390	8,209,739
Increase in working capital	$12,551,664	1,034,054

See accompanying Notes to Consolidated Financial Statements.

Exhibit 1. (continued)

	1971	1970
Changes in working capital:		
Increase in current assets:		
Cash	$ 418,380	1,357,917
Preferred stock proceeds receivable	19,000,000	—
Receivables	22,359,453	12,286,631
Inventories	741,319	1,236,215
Prepaid expenses and other current assets	101,765	34,973
	42,620,917	14,915,736
Increase in current liabilities:		
Current portion of long-term debt and notes payable		
to banks :	25,962,594	10,721,700
Accounts payable and accrued expenses	1,888,978	2,155,635
Due to unconsolidated subsidiary	76,894	—
Current and deferred income taxes	2,140,787	1,004,347
	30,069,253	13,881,682
Increase in working capital	$12,551,664	1,034,054

During the year ended July 31, 1971, the Company assigned $4,650,000 of its accounts receivable, without recourse, to an unconsolidated subsidiary for which that subsidiary paid $4,650,000 to the Company. See Note 1.

Exhibit 1. (continued)

Stirling Homex Corporation and Consolidated Subsidiaries

Consolidated Statements of Additional Paid-in Capital and Retained Earnings
Year ended July 31, 1971 with comparative figures for 1970

Additional Paid-In Capital

	1971	1970
Balance at beginning of period	$ 8,446,738	1,949,813
Excess of proceeds over par value of 400,000 shares of common stock issued in public offering (less expenses of $118,285)	—	5,981,715
Excess of proceeds over par value of 129,000 shares of common stock issued in private sales (less applicable expenses)	—	515,210
Excess of proceeds over par value of 500,000 shares of preferred stock issued in public offering (less expenses of $429,367) (Note 2)	18,070,633	—
Excess of proceeds over par value of 11,800 common shares issued under stock options (Note 10)	37,082	—
Balance at end of period	$26,554,453	8,446,738

Retained Earnings

	1971	1970
Balance at beginning of period	$ 3,117,670	1,082,481
Net income	3,252,663	2,035,189
Balance at end of period	$ 6,370,333	3,117,670

See accompanying Notes to Consolidated Financial Statements.

Exhibit 1. (continued) Notes to Consolidated Financial Statements July 31, 1971

Notes to Consolidated Financial Statements July 31, 1971

(1) Principles of Consolidation

The consolidated financial statements include the accounts of the Company and its subsidiaries except for U. S. Shelter Corporation, its financing subsidiary (all of which are wholly-owned). The Company carries its investment in all subsidiaries at equity in the underlying net assets. On consolidation, all significant accounts and transactions with consolidated subsidiaries have been eliminated.

The following are condensed financial statements of the unconsolidated financing subsidiary:

Balance Sheet
July 31, 1971

Assets

Cash	$ 5,171
Accounts receivable—unbilled (Note a)	4,950,000
Other assets	24,593
Due from parent company	76,894
	$5,056,658

Liabilities and Stockholder's Equity

Notes payable—bank (7%) (Note b)	$3,750,000
Payables, accruals and other liabilities	172,079
Stockholder's equity	1,134,579
	$5,056,658

Statement of Income
From date of Incorporation
(September 25, 1970) to July 31, 1971

Finance income	$544,946
General and administrative expenses (including interest expense of $54,917)	263,367
	281,579
Federal and state income taxes—current	147,000
Net income	$134,579

Notes:

(a) Accounts receivable includes $4,650,000 relating to accounts assigned to U. S. Shelter by the Company for which U. S. Shelter remitted cash.

(b) The subsidiary has obtained an unsecured $15,000,000 line of credit from a bank. These funds are being used in financing transactions involving customers of the Company. The Company has not guaranteed this line of credit.

(2) Preferred Stock Offering

On July 29, 1971, the Company, through its underwriters, offered 500,000 shares of $2.40 cumulative convertible preferred stock to the public at $40 per share. Net proceeds of $19,000,000, after deducting an underwriting discount, were received by the Company on August 5, 1971. Additional paid-in capital has been credited with the net proceeds received less the par value of the stock issued ($500,000) and expenses related to the offering ($429,367).

The preferred stock is nonvoting except for certain defined events which would significantly affect the preferred stockholders' equity interests. The preferred shares are convertible into 1,379,310 common shares subject to adjustment in certain events, including stock split-ups and stock dividends. At its option, the Company may redeem the preferred stock at an initial price of $50 per share, as of August 1, 1971, ranging downward annually to $40 per share as of August 1, 1981 and thereafter.

(3) Receivables

The Company enters into various modular housing sales contracts which contain an allocation of the sales price between modules (based upon published price lists) and installation work. Sales of modules (Manufacturing Division) are recognized when units are manufactured and assigned to specific contracts. Installation work (Installation Division) is recorded on the percentage of completion method. The contracts generally provide for payment upon completion and receipt of all approvals necessary for occupancy, or for payment upon completion of each respective phase. "Unbilled" receivables represent recorded sales on contracts in process for which billings will be rendered in the future in accordance with the contracts.

Receivables consist of:

	July 31, 1971	July 31, 1970
Contract receivables:		
Billed	$10,382,626	10,559,145
Unbilled	24,633,799	4,626,370
Total	35,016,425	15,185,515
Income tax refund receivable (Note 9)	2,498,672	—
Current portion of long-term receivables (Note 4)	12,500	17,500
Other receivables	317,975	283,104
	$37,845,572	15,486,119

361

Exhibit 1. (continued)

Stirling Homex Corporation and Consolidated Subsidiaries

Notes to Consolidated Financial Statements (continued) July 31, 1971

(3) Receivables (continued)

Substantially all sales are to local housing authorities and sponsors who qualify for financial assistance from Federal agencies of the U. S. Government or who have made arrangements for long-term financing. In light of this, no provision for doubtful accounts is considered necessary.

See the condensed financial statements of U. S. Shelter Corporation in Note 1 for information with respect to receivables assigned by the Company to U. S. Shelter Corporation.

(4) Long-Term Receivables

Long-term receivables consist of:

	July 31, 1971	July 31, 1970
Mortgages receivable:		
Mortgage due June 1, 1974—payments of $2,500 due quarterly with interest at the prime commercial rate in effect on the interest payment date	$ 241,624	256,624
Mortgage due June 30, 1975—payments of $25,000 due June 30, 1973 and June 30, 1974 and the balance due June 30, 1975. Interest payable annually at the prime commercial rate in effect on the interest payment date	302,000	302,000
	543,624	558,624
Less installments due within one year (Note 3)	12,500	17,500
	531,124	541,124
Long-term portion of contract receivables—unbilled	3,694,225	—
	$4,225,349	541,124

The mortgage notes are secured by mortgages on the property sold.

(5) Inventories

Inventories of the Company consist of the following:

	July 31, 1971	July 31, 1970
Raw materials	$1,439,960	963,664
Work in process	1,001,632	139,531
Salable merchandise	172,608	1,064,408
	$2,614,200	2,167,603

Land held for development or sale is recorded at cost plus real estate taxes, mortgage interest and other related carrying costs. The Company has entered into a contract to sell a parcel of the land with costs of $673,017 for a sale price of $2,100,000. The Company has received non-refundable payments of $235,000 which have been accounted for as an option deposit.

(6) Property, Plant and Equipment

Property, plant and equipment consist of the following:

	Useful Life	July 31, 1971	July 31, 1970
Land and land improvements	20	$ 1,136,499	1,002,067
Buildings	10 & 45	4,822,055	1,702,924
Machinery, equipment and tools	2—10	1,735,396	1,071,515
Furniture, fixtures and office equipment	5—10	942,131	500,951
Other	1—15	135,952	27,998
Construction in progress		1,388,613	1,171,211
		10,160,646	5,476,666
Less accumulated depreciation and amortization		733,705	230,921
		$ 9,426,941	5,245,745

The straight-line method of depreciation is used for all depreciable assets. Depreciation expense for the years ended July 31, 1971 and 1970 is $529,116 and $220,227; respectively.

Exhibit 1. *(continued)*

(7) Deferred Charges

The unamortized balance of deferred charges consist of:

	Amortization Period	Unamortized Balance July 31, 1971	July 31, 1970
Patents pending and trademarks	Legal Life	$ 171,680	88,660
Training and professional development . .	3 years	491,641	148,636
Research and development . .	5 years	671,897	84,496
Project and production start-up costs	2 to 5 years	844,028	503,539
Property acquisition costs	(a)	379,546	118,778
		$2,558,792	944,109

(a) Expenditures in connection with property acquisition will be added to the cost of property subsequently acquired.

In the event of project abandonment or other circumstances causing a loss of value to deferred items, the related unamortized costs are charged to current operations.

(8) Long-Term Debt

Long-term debt consists of the following:

	July 31, 1971	July 31, 1970
Mortgages maturing at various dates through December 31, 1976 and bearing interest at rates ranging from 4¾% to 6%	$443,176	704,615
Installment contracts and lease purchase agreements maturing at various dates through August, 1974	89,042	124,910
	532,218	829,525
Less payments due within one year	295,630	333,036
	$236,588	496,489

Land, buildings and equipment with a net book value of $2,223,803 and $2,232,091 as of July 31, 1971 and July 31, 1970, respectively, are encumbered under the above agreements.

(9) Income Taxes

Deferred taxes relate principally to manufacturing division and installation division sales, depreciation, deferred costs and capitalized costs. None of the Company's tax returns have been examined by the Internal Revenue Service. The tax refund included in Note 3 relates to refundable advance tax payments and the planned amendment of the prior year's tax returns.

(10) Stock Options

The Company has a qualified stock option plan in effect whereby options to purchase shares of common stock may be granted to officers and key employees at not less than the fair market value on the date of grant. During February, 1971, authorized shares under the plan were increased from 400,000 to 900,000 shares. Options expire five years after the date of grant and are exercisable in cumulative installments of 20% after one year. A summary of activity for the year ended July 31, 1971 follows:

	Option price per share From	To	Shares
Options outstanding at July 31, 1970	$ 3.00	$16.50	399,300
New options granted	15.13	22.00	275,500
Less: Options exercised . .	3.00	12.00	(11,800)
Cancellations	3.00	19.25	(61,900)
Options outstanding at July 31, 1971	3.00	22.00	601,100
Options outstanding at July 31, 1971 which are currently exercisable . . .	3.00	16.50	58,360

No entries are recorded with respect to options until exercised at which time the excess of the option price over the par value of common stock issued is credited to additional paid-in capital.

(11) Commitments and Contingencies

An action has been brought to enjoin the use of the word "Homex" by the Company. In the opinion of legal counsel, the plaintiff will be unsuccessful in obtaining the relief which it seeks.

A former shareholder of restricted shares of Company com-

Exhibit 1. (continued)

Stirling Homex Corporation and Consolidated Subsidiaries

Notes to Consolidated Financial Statements (continued) July 31, 1971

(11) Commitments and Contingencies (continued)

mon stock has brought an action against the Company and another party, a broker. It is claimed that the Company refused, in concert with the other defendant, to permit the transfer of plaintiff's stock except at a price substantially below its alleged market price. Compensatory damages in the amount of $1,575,000 and treble damages are alleged. In the opinion of management, the suit can be successfully defended. In the opinion of counsel, the claim for treble damages is without merit.

The Company is engaged in other disputes involving claims which, in the aggregate, are insignificant compared to the Company's net worth.

Construction of a manufacturing plant in Mississippi is expected to be commenced in the latter part of 1971 at an approximate cost of $4,900,000. In a contract with the Company, Harrison County (where the plant site is located) has agreed to take the steps necessary to authorize the issuance and sale of tax exempt industrial revenue bonds in an amount necessary to meet the cost of constructing and equipping the plant. The contract also provides for a 30-year lease to the Company of the completed facility and the related land. Semi-annual payments in respect of the bonds will be based on principal and interest requirements; an additional $36,325 is due annually for the land. Options to purchase the plant and the land are provided for during and at the end of the lease term. If the bond offering is not consummated, the Company will arrange to finance the cost of the facility itself.

At July 31, 1971, the Company had leases on various equipment and office facilities with terms ranging from two to six years. Minimum annual rentals under such leases amount to approximately $404,000.

Notes payable consist of 90 day unsecured notes to eleven banks bearing interest at a rate ½% above the respective bank's best rate on the date of issue. The Company is required to maintain average annual compensating cash balances at each of these banks equal to approximately 15% to 20% of the outstanding indebtedness to such bank.

(12) Earnings Per Share

Earnings per common share are based upon the weighted average number of common shares outstanding during the periods presented after giving retroactive effect to the four for one stock split effected in February 1970. The preferred stock is not considered a common stock equivalent in accordance with Opinion 15 of the Accounting Principles Board of the American Institute of Certified Public Accountants. In addition, the effect of the preferred stock offering, for the fiscal year ended July 31, 1971 on a fully diluted earnings per share calculation is insignificant. Stock options outstanding have not been included in these computations since the effect of their inclusion would be insignificant.

Accountants' Report

The Board of Directors and Stockholders
Stirling Homex Corporation:

We have examined the consolidated balance sheet of Stirling Homex Corporation and consolidated subsidiaries as of July 31, 1971 and the related statements of income, additional paid-in capital and retained earnings and changes in financial position for the year then ended. Our examination was made in accordance with generally accepted auditing standards, and accordingly included such tests of the accounting records and such other auditing procedures as we considered necessary in the circumstances. The financial statements for the year ended July 31, 1970, included for comparative purposes, were examined by other accountants.

In our opinion, such financial statements present fairly the consolidated financial position of Stirling Homex Corporation and consolidated subsidiaries at July 31, 1971, and the results of their operations and changes in their financial position for the year then ended, in conformity with generally accepted accounting principles applied on a basis consistent with that of the preceding year.

Rochester, New York
September 15, 1971

Peat, Marwick, Mitchell & Co.
PEAT, MARWICK, MITCHELL & CO.

1. Does the method which Homex used to recognize revenue adhere in your opinion to generally accepted accounting principles, specifically in relation to (a) the timing of revenue recognition, (b) the allocation of profit, and (c) capitalizing expenses?

Fairmuir Instrument Corporation

Fairmuir Instrument Corporation sold a line of high-temperature measuring instruments (pyrometers). The principal users of the equipment were steel mills and various metal extraction companies, and Fairmuir's small sales force had concentrated almost exclusively on establishing good relations with these customers. Occasional inquiries and orders came from other sources, such as scientific laboratories, but the company had never actively solicited these markets.

The device in its present form had been developed and put into production in the early 1950s. Essentially it utilized principles that had been known for almost a hundred years, but until recently the accuracy attainable had fallen short of the requirements of modern industry. The company had introduced no new products until the last quarter of 1964. Effectively, the company had not faced any serious competition in its market area until 1960 and had maintained a stable sales level of around $3 million until that time.

During 1960 a competing product had been introduced to the market. Operating on completely different principles, this device performed substantially the same job as Fairmuir's product and gave similar levels of accuracy. The only major differences were in its useful life (5 years) and its purchase price, each of which were about half of those of the Fairmuir product. The lower purchase price was a telling sales advantage and Fairmuir's sales suffered accordingly. Exhibit 1 gives some of the financial data of Fairmuir Instrument Corporation from 1960 through 1964.

By 1961 the management of Fairmuir realized that without a new product to bolster its faltering sales volume, the company was facing a serious predicament. Management, therefore, began a search for an additional product that would complement the company's production facilities. In 1962 they approached an inventor who held patents for just such a product with a view to buying the patents. After some negotiation a mutually satisfactory price was reached, and, as part of the agreement, the inventor agreed to join the company and lead the additional development work that was required before a commercial product was ready for marketing.

On top of the cost of the patents and the development expenses, the company was faced with substantial start-up costs and investment in inventories. The company's financial resources, already adversely affected by the lagging sales of pyrometers, were inadequate without an injection of fresh capital. The company's capital stock was closely held by members of top management and a few of their friends and family members. None of these people was willing to contribute any further capital.

Management believed that the recent poor operating results made it unwise to seek fresh equity capital at that time and they, therefore, decided that a bank loan was the only feasible recourse. It did not prove an easy matter to find a bank willing to make the required loan, but eventually the capital was obtained from a bank. In extending the loan the bank imposed several restrictions upon the management of Fairmuir, one of these being that a minimum working capital level of $800,000 should be maintained. By the end of 1964, with the sales of pyrometers still falling and the new product only just introduced to the market, the company was close to defaulting on the requirements of the working capital covenant.

In the 1964 audit, the public accountant was satisfied with all the accounts except for the valuation of inventories related to pyrometers. Most of this inventory was in good condition, and had been carefully handled and stored. A few items of purchased parts had become obsolete and management had written them down. This represented an insignificant adjustment, however, and the bulk of the inventory was still reported on the company's books at cost. The auditor was not concerned about the physical condition of the inventory, but he had serious reservations as to the marketability of the product, and therefore the realization of the investment through profitable sales. In approaching management on this matter the auditor was aware that a large adjustment would throw the company into default on its loan covenant concerning working capital.

The auditor, Mr. Bill Adams, arranged a meeting with the President of Fairmuir Instrument Corporation, Mr. Tom Fairmuir, in order to discuss the 1964 financial statements. Part of the meeting is recorded below.

Mr. Adams   Everything seems to be in fine order except for your valuation of inventories relating to pyrometers, Tom. Now we discussed this matter briefly a few days ago and you expressed the opinion that there would be no material loss of value in the inventories and that you would in fact be able to sell it all in the normal course of business. Since then I have examined your record of sales orders, and at present you have only $58,000 worth of open orders on your books, compared with $65,000 worth at the beginning of the year. Your billings by quarters for the past year were fairly stable: $149,000 first quarter, $136,000 second quarter, $141,000 third quarter, and $157,000 in the final quarter.

I have also read several articles in trade publications, such as this one in *Steel Monthly,* which seem to indicate that your type of pyrometer is at a technical as well as an economic (in terms of purchase price) disadvantage.

Frankly, it appears to me that you are going to be left with a lot of inventory which will have to be marked down quite significantly to sell it.

Mr. Fairmuir   Now hold it, Bill, things are not so bleak as that. In fact, we have plans for our pyrometers which will return the sales volume to its previous level, or close to it. Look at these letters, Bill. These are inquiries concerning substantial orders, and we have been receiving such inquiries at a greatly increased rate recently. If this continues, and I have no doubt that it will, and even half of them become firm orders, we shall be selling pyrometers in 1965 at twice the 1964 level.

You know we hired a new sales manager this year? Well, he has reorganized our sales force and is beginning to get results. At the same time we have gone over our production process and reduced the manufacturing cost of our lines by some 10 percent. No doubt you noticed that our cost of goods figures, which have been stable at about 60 percent of selling price for several years, were lower for the past two or three months. We expect to improve on that further in 1965. Of course, this gives us some price flexibility when we are faced with a competitive situation. So you see, I have good reason to predict better results in the future

Mr. Adams   What exactly has the new sales manager done?

Mr. Fairmuir   He reorganized the sales territories and reassigned the salesmen so that we should get greater market penetration. He released a couple of the men who have clearly not been pulling their weight and hired a couple of bright young men to replace them. The main thing is that he has done wonders for the morale of the sales force.

In addition he has identified new markets and is helping the men to break into these markets.

Mr. Adams   Why don't we look at the prospects market by market, Tom? You had sales of only $62,000 to steel mills in 1964. It seems as if the steel mills market is almost defunct, wouldn't you agree?

Mr. Fairmuir   It has certainly declined. However, some of our men have built up a good relationship with their customers in the steel industry and we expect this to produce a certain loyalty. We should keep a small part of the business, say, billings of about $50,000 a year.

    Then in the other metal extraction industries we know that our product has some distinct competitive advantages, such as its ruggedness and lower maintenance costs. With the new emphasis on selling, we expect that our customers will be well aware of these advantages, and the downward sales trend should be reversed this year. On this basis we expect 1965's sales to this market to be at least $400,000 and to increase further in the future.

Mr. Adams   But look, Tom, that means an increase over this year's sales, bucking a strong downward trend. I can't base my opinion on your optimism, you know.

Mr. Fairmuir   Well, look at this market, which we think has great potential—scientific laboratories. We are going to place advertisements in some of the engineering journals and pay direct sales calls to many of the labs in our market areas, those which do a lot of high-temperature work. We anticipate a yearly volume of $200,000 to $300,000 in this market.

    And, finally, we have set up a contract with a representative in Washington to handle our line in government sales. He has already got some orders for us and he seems certain that we can build up a stable volume of some $300,000 a year. Several government agencies are testing our product at the moment, including the Atomic Energy Commission. If we get our equipment specified for installation into government nuclear plants, we shall have a large continuing market.

Mr. Adams   So you expect sales of about $1 million this year, twice 1964's sales?

Mr. Fairmuir   No, not right away. But we are confident of substantially reversing the trend of recent years and eventually, say in two years or so, building our sales up to at least $1.5 million for pyrometers. For 1965 we predict sales of about $800,000.

Mr. Adams   Well, look at this from my point of view. I have a professional responsibility to give an opinion on your company's financial statements and I cannot base my opinion on your predictions. I have to go on historic facts and reasonable expectations. The historic facts are that sales of pyrometers have been falling and you have only a small volume of open orders on your books.

    You have a substantial inventory, the value of which can only be realized through the sale of pyrometers. Any other representation of these facts would mislead the reader of the statements.

Mr. Fairmuir   I agree with you on that, and in my opinion, we *will* realize the value
of our inventory through normal sales. I could not contemplate a
write-down in the value of the inventory. For one thing, it would not
be right to do so, since it would be misleading in valuing our assets.
And for another, it could easily lead to a difficult situation with the
bank and, at worst, lead to liquidation of the company. True, we have
experienced a few bad years. But we are fighting back and I am confident we shall save our pyrometer line. And also our new line will start
to contribute to profits this coming year.

The discussion continued for some time and became fairly heated. Finally,
Mr. Adams terminated the discussion in order to consider the question further. He arranged a meeting with Mr. Fairmuir for three days later, at which
time the two men agreed they would come to a decision as to whether or not the
value of the inventory should be written down. Mr. Adams was concerned as to
what opinion he should issue on Fairmuir's financial statements of 1964.

QUESTIONS

1. What further steps should Mr. Adams take in preparing for the coming
   meeting with Mr. Fairmuir?
2. Putting yourself in Mr. Fairmuir's position, what steps would you take in
   preparing for the meeting? If Mr. Adams insists that the value of the inventory be written down, what would you do?
3. Do you think that the value of the inventory should be written down?
   If so, how should the adjustment be made?
4. If it were not written down, how would you, as auditor, phrase your
   opinion?

*Exhibit 1. Financial Data as of December 31, 1960–1964 (dollar figures in
thousands)*

	AUDITED RESULTS				UNAUDITED
	1960	*1961*	*1962*	*1963*	*1964*
Inventories related to pyrometers	791	806	909	805	627
Working capital	933	1,021	1,165	1,155	819
Net assets	1,889	1,965	1,995	1,926	1,549
Net sales of pyrometers	2,881	2,475	2,025	996	583
Other sales (net)	—	—	—	—	115
Net income (loss)	108	77	67	(91)	(376)

Reichman Pinball Machines, Inc. (A)

Early in February of 1973, Bill Lamprechter, a partner in the New York office of the "big eight" accounting firm of Kincaide, Cramer and McKee, sat back to reflect for a moment on a problem which had arisen in one of the audits for which he was responsible. The problem resulted from financial transactions between Reichman Pinball Machines, Inc. and Ridge Lending Corporation, a finance company which lent money to Reichman and other companies in the pinball machine business. Lamprechter asked Martha Hardcastle, the senior on the Reichman job, and Ted Hellman, the newly assigned manager on the job, to come into his office to review the problem and arrive at a final decision on the firm's position regarding the matter.

Lamprechter   We've dragged out this audit long enough. I'd certainly like to get it cleared up as quickly as possible because we're spending entirely too much of our time on a client who hasn't even paid for last year's audit. Martha, could you fill Ted in a little on the history of the account? Maybe we can find a solution to our problems.

Hardcastle   I've been following the Ridge situation rather closely since 1969, but it's been going on since 1966 when we first picked up the Reichman audit. The key to the problem is Arnold Ross, who is President, Chairman of the Board, and the major stockholder and supervisor of the day-to-day operations of Ridge. Ridge is even operated from an office on Reichman's premises. The way I see the situation, Reichman issues

This case was prepared by Laird H. Simons, III under the supervision of Associate Professor John K. Shank as the basis for class discussion rather than to illustrate either effective or ineffective handling of an administrative situation.

negotiable notes to Ridge, which endorses them and uses them as collateral for drawing on two lines of credit of $1 million each at the Exchange National Bank and the Nazarian National Bank. Ridge then transfers to Reichman the discounted amount of the notes, giving rise to the "Ridge payable" on Reichman's balance sheet. There is also a parallel and continuous series of loans by Reichman to Ridge, leading to the "Ridge receivable" account on Reichman's books. Most of these loans arise from Ross' custom of using Reichman and Ridge as sources of cash to cover his stock market endeavors. As soon as Ridge receives money from Reichman, Ross withdraws it for his own uses, leaving an Account Receivable from Ross on Ridge's books. As long as these borrowings and repayments substantially matched and the size was small, we did not feel it significant enough to press Ross for detail. Lately, however, it seems to be getting out of hand.

Lamprechter   That's certainly true! Reichman's cash payments to Ridge of $1,186,000 in 1969 apparently served no other purpose than to provide Ridge with cash, but by year's end the receivable stood at zero. The following year we noticed that the payments were becoming more frequent, were in round amounts, and were unaccompanied by written explanations. In fiscal 1970 the receivable ranged from $695,000 at the beginning of the year to $398,000 at year end, with a high during the year of $1,583,000 in April. The balance in the receivable account seemed, in some sense, seasonal, rising after the end of one fiscal year and falling prior to the end of the next. This sort of "window dressing" raised questions about the fairness of the year-end statements. Last year the amount got as high as $2 million so I telephoned Ross to discuss the situation. This "memo to the file" of mine summarizes our conversation. (*Lamprechter distributes copies of the following memo.*)

TELEPHONE CONVERSATION WITH ARNOLD ROSS, JANUARY 10, 1972

Lamprechter   *I've been going over this year's audit (1971) and everything seems to be in order. I'm a little worried, though, about the Ridge receivable account—it's more than double what it was last year.*

Ross   *Just because the amount is large doesn't mean there's a problem, does it? From what you've told me in the past, our treatment of the matter is well within the bounds of generally accepted accounting principles. I see no reason to make an issue of this item.*

Lamprechter   *Technically, you're probably right. Martha has confirmed the balance in writing and reconciled it to the amount appearing on Reichman's books. The computation of accrued interest was checked, Reichman's vouchers supporting disbursements to Ridge were ex-*

amined, and the cancelled checks representing the advances to Ridge were also examined, noting that they were received by Ridge and endorsed for deposit to Ridge's account at the Exchange National Bank.

At a minimum, we'll have to mention your position with the two companies on Reichman's financial statements. We won't comment in detail on the receivable, though, since we are only auditing Reichman, not Ridge. If this Ridge receivable account is as large next year as it is now, however, we'll have to take a look at Ridge's books as well.

Ross   *I guess I can live with that, but I don't like the implication that there is anything wrong with this account.*

Hellman   Well, what has happened to the Ridge receivable since then?

Hardcastle   Just before the end of the fiscal year, I talked with the Assistant Comptroller at Reichman. The receivable was slightly higher then and other problems had arisen. At that time I put this memo into our work paper file. (*Hardcastle distributes copies of the following memo.*)

CONVERSATION WITH DICK HARTMAN, SEPTEMBER 15, 1972

Hardcastle   *In working on this year's audit, we'll need more information on the Ridge receivable. What's it up to now?*

Hartman   *As of July 31, it was up to $3.6 million and I haven't posted any transactions since then. That's not the big problem, though. For several months, we've been operating a check float in excess of $500,000 a day—cash is really tighter than ever. I've been spending most of the summer just trying to juggle cash!*

Hardcastle   *Why does Ridge need so much money?*

Hartman   *Ross needed it to maintain his margin accounts on the Goren, Inc. stock and bonds and the Reichman stock he owns.*

Hardcastle   *I see. This could create an interesting reporting problem.*

Hardcastle   That was only the beginning. The October cash audit showed just how critical the shortage of funds had become. The $300,000 cash balance on September 30, resulted only from 30-day bank loans of $1.5 million. The Ridge receivable was still up around $3.5 million and the Ridge payable was $1 million, half of which is due within the coming year. I have copies here of the draft statements for 1972 (see Exhibit 2).

Lamprechter   We don't have any choice, do we? We'll have to look at Ridge's books. The receivable is completely out of line.

Hellman   I agree. From what the figures show and what you've told me, it looks like Reichman is in a very shaky financial position.

Hardcastle   You're right, of course; a full examination would be in order. But the Ridge financial statements just aren't available because their audit isn't completed. We've got to finish our audit right away—we're already a month late.

Hellman   Can't we protect ourselves with a "subject to" opinion and full disclosure in the footnotes? That would eliminate the need to look at Ridge's books and would still be in line with generally accepted accounting principles. We've established a pattern of disclosing the advances to Ridge on the balance sheet and Ridge's relationship to Ross. This extra step should get us off the hook with GAAP and with the client.

Lamprechter   Yes, I think the three of us could readily agree on this, but I doubt if Ross will go for it. He knows as well as we do that a "subject to" opinion is a real red flag. Breaking our pattern of disclosure on this issue clearly suggests we think something is wrong.

That afternoon, Lamprechter contacted Ross.

Lamprechter   There seem to be a few problems with this year's audit, Arnold, which I would like to clear up as quickly as possible.

Ross   Yes, I've looked over your preliminary audit and, to say the least, I'm very displeased. What we presented to you as a $109,000 profit has suddenly become a $900,000 loss. From the look of things, you're trying to ruin Reichman. What happened?

Lamprechter   That's not really what I called to discuss, but we might as well go over it since you mentioned it. You deferred R & D expenses this year which, as far as we can determine, should be written off, since there is no solid indication of future worth. There was also a lot of obsolete inventory which had to be written off.

Ross   What are you trying to do to us? Perhaps we should get new accountants. Our ideas are miles apart!

Lamprechter   I'm sorry, Arnold, but there really is no choice for us on these matters. It's always your prerogative to fire us, but if you were to start over with new accountants at this late date, there is no way the audit could be completed before summer. Since we're already flirting with violations of the SEC's 10K deadline, I think you'll have to go along with us for this year.

Ross   What the devil did you call for anyway? I hope you're not going to bother me about the Ridge receivable again! I thought we had that problem all straightened out last year—you haven't changed your mind, have you? Besides, if you back out now I guarantee that we'll sue for failure to get our reports out on time.

Lamprechter   Remember last year when I warned you that if the receivable was as large again this year we'd have to look at Ridge's books?

Ross   If Ridge's audit were completed, I'd happily make the statements available, but it's going to be a while. Isn't there some way we can clear up the problem? Ridge is solvent, but we're just not in a position right now to repay the $3.5 million debt to Reichman.

Lamprechter   Why not?

Ross   It's a personal matter. I've borrowed approximately the same amount from Ridge which I'm temporarily unable to repay. Perhaps we can work out some arrangement. I can personally secure this indebtedness with my equity in stocks, bonds, and other securities. I'll even put a mortgage on my home and personal assets if necessary as additional collateral, but I just can't come up with the cash now. What you do say?

Lamprechter   Would you go along with a footnote to the financial statements saying that the amount in the Ridge receivable is uncollectible, since Ridge has loaned approximately the same amount to you, but that you have pledged as security for the repayment of the obligation, securities in Reichman and other companies totaling approximately the same amount.

Ross   Not on your life. You're trying to make me look like a crook. You know as well as I do that generally accepted accounting principles don't require that kind of disclosure as long as the value of the receivables is assured.

Lamprechter   We'll have to see what we can do. We all want to finish up this audit as soon as possible.

The next day Lamprechter, Hellman, and Hardcastle meet once again.

Lamprechter   Ross is hopping mad. He'd like to find a new set of auditors, but for this year that's unrealistic. Nevertheless, if we miss the 10K deadline and the SEC goes after him for tardiness, we could well get sued. More to the point—Ross is a wealthy, solid citizen who has paid us substantial fees in the past and continues to use us for tax work, as well as year-end and special audit work. He's not about to go under. He may be "slow paying" this year but the problems with this year's audit have pushed the bills way up. He's in a cash bind but has always paid on time until the last 15 months. If we walk away now we'll have a tough time collecting the $63,000 in outstanding bills, and will have lost $50,000 a year in billings. I hope we can find a compromise position within generally accepted accounting principles which will satisfy him.

Hellman   I don't like it. We're asking for trouble if we permit personal loans of

	this size to go unchallenged. This company is on the verge of serious trouble.
Lamprechter	You may be right, Ted, but if we indicate that the loans are collateralized, doesn't that mean that we look not to Ross or Ridge but to the value of the collateral as the ultimate backing for Reichman's receivable?
Hardcastle	Even if that's true, don't we take a risk that the collateral, most of which would be Reichman and Goren securities, will fail to cover the receivable once this Annual Report showing a loss is made public. If we use this collateral, we'd better disclose fully in the footnotes what types of securities we're talking about—stock, letter stock, or bonds —from what companies they arise, and what liens or other encumbrances are outstanding against them.
Lamprechter	Ross will never go for that. He knows generally accepted accounting principles don't require it. All we are required to do is verify that the market value of the securities at date of certification is sufficient to make the receivable collectible. I don't see how we can insist that he disclose more. What right do we have to hold a client to a higher standard than the accounting profession requires? We've already forced him to show a big loss for this year when he thought it should be a profit. That should be sufficient to alert the stockholders that the situation requires careful review on their part.
Hellman	I hope you're not letting your desire to keep a client unduly influence your judgment, Bill.
Lamprechter	So do I, Ted.

QUESTIONS

1. What are the options open to Bill Lamprechter?
2. What would you do in his situation?

Exhibit 1. Consolidated Balance Sheet, September 30, 1971

ASSETS

Current Assets			
Cash			$ 1,500,000
Accounts and notes receivable			
Trade (Note 1)			
Ridge Lending Corp., affiliate	$ 7,900,000		
Others, including $671,460 from sales of pinball machines in operating locations and other capital assets	850,000		
	1,000,000		
	$ 9,750,000		
Less allowance for doubtful accounts	130,000		9,620,000
Inventories, at lower of cost (average or first-in, first-out) or market			3,800,000
Advance commissions			150,000
Prepaid expenses			680,000
Total Current Assets			$15,750,000
Mortgage receivable (noninterest-bearing, due 12/1/74			200,000
Investment, at cost			500,000
Noncurrent accounts and notes receivable, including $802,166 from sales of pinball machines in operating locations and other capital assets			1,350,000
Property, plant, and equipment (Note 2)*			
Pinball machines	3,400,000		
Other, principally buildings, machinery, and equipment	2,800,000		
	6,200,000		
Less reserve for depreciation	1,500,000		
	4,700,000		
Land	100,000		4,800,000

LIABILITIES

Current Liabilities			
Notes and loans payable (Note 3)			$ 5,000,000
Long-term debt, portion due within one year (Note 4)			
Ridge Lending Corp., affiliate		$ 500,000	
Other		3,000,000	3,500,000
Accounts payable			3,000,000
Accrued expenses and taxes:			
Federal income tax		700,000	
Other		800,000	1,500,000
Total Current Liabilities			13,000,000
Long-term debt (Note 4)			
Ridge Lending Corp., affiliate		300,000	
Other		3,200,000	3,500,000
Liabilities paid from proceeds of debenture issue (Note 5)			3,500,000
Deferred Federal income tax			100,000
Deferred income			150,000
Contingent liabilities (Note 6)			
CAPITAL			
Common stock, par value $.10 a share; 4,750,000 shares authorized, 4,000,000 shares issued and outstanding		400,000	
Capital surplus, as annexed		7,200,000	
Retained earnings, as annexed (Note 7)		1,400,000	9,000,000
			$29,250,000

Exhibit 1. *(continued)*

ASSETS				LIABILITIES
Property held for sale			100,000	
Excess of cost of companies or operating properties acquired over related net assets, less amortization			1,900,000	
Patents, at cost less amortization			1,500,000	
Deferred charges and other assets				
Research and development	1,500,000			
Advance commissions	400,000			
Other	1,250,000	3,150,000		
			$29,250,000	

*See Notes to Consolidated Financial Statements, 1971.

Consolidated Statement of Income and Retained Earnings For the Year Ended September 30, 1971

Sales and operating income		$29,200,000
Cost of sales		21,200,000
		8,000,000
Selling and administrative expenses		6,300,000
		$ 1,700,000
Depreciation and amortization		750,000
Other income, including net profits of $2,027,802 from sales of pinball machines in operating locations and other capital assets	$ 2,000,000	
Other deductions, principally interest	1,000,000	1,000,000
Income before provision for Federal income tax		$ 1,950,000
Provision for Federal income tax		700,000
Net income		1,250,000
Retained earnings, September 30, 1970	2,750,000	
Deficit, Pyramid Pinball Co., Inc., September 30, 1970	500,000	
	2,250,000	
Less, Adjustments in connection with pooling of interests	250,000	2,000,000
Retained earnings, September 30, 1970, as adjusted		3,250,000
Deduct, Amount based on market quotation for 252,698 shares of common stock issued as a 15% stock dividend		1,850,000
Retained earnings, September 30, 1971 (Note 5)		$ 1,400,000

Consolidated Statement of Capital Surplus For the Year Ended September 30, 1971

Balance, September 30, 1970	$ 3,600,000
Excess of capital stock account of Pyramid Pinball Co., Inc. over par value of 147,079 shares of the Company's common stock issued in connection with pooling of interests	200,000
Balance, September 30, 1970 as adjusted	3,800,000
Excess of market over par value of shares of common stock issued or to be issued	
252,698 shares issued as a 15% stock dividend, less expenses of issue, etc.	1,875,000
87,418 shares issued in exchange for capital stock of two companies and capital stock and debentures of another company	1,575,000
Balance, September 30, 1971	$ 7,200,000

379

1. Accounts and notes receivable in the approximate amount of $4,880,000 are pledged as collateral for notes and loans payable.
2. Property, plant, and equipment, with minor exceptions, is recorded at cost. Pinball machines include equipment which in effect is pledged as collateral security for certain notes payable, as well as equipment subject to chattel mortgages as collateral for unpaid purchase prices. Other properties are subject to mortgages payable. The aggregate recorded amount of property subject to such liens is approximately $2,800,000, and the aggregate of unpaid notes and mortgages is approximately $2,200,000.
3. Approximately $4,200,000 of the notes and loans payable is secured by collateral.
4. Long-term debt includes approximately $1,866,000, $1,317,000, $124,000, and $124,000 payable in the fiscal years ending September 30, 1973 through 1976, respectively, and $101,000 payable thereafter.

   Interest is payable at 6 percent per year discounted in advance on loans from Ridge Lending Corp. (an affiliate, of which company Mr. Arnold Ross is an officer, director, and stockholder). Interest on other long-term debt, including the portion due within one year, is payable currently at 6 percent a year on $2,595,000; at approximately 12 percent a year on $997,000; and at various other rates on $589,000. Interest is discounted or paid in advance, principally at 6 percent a year, on $1,949,000; approximately $150,000 is noninterest-bearing. Approximately $4,033,000 of these amounts was secured by collateral.
5. In December 1971 the Company sold $5,052,700 of 6 percent convertible subordinated debentures due September 1, 1986. The debentures are (a) convertible into the Company's common stock from June 1972 through August 1986 at $8 $1/3$ per share, subject to adjustment under certain conditions, (b) subordinated to all "senior indebtedness" of the Company, as defined in the indenture, and (c) redeemable at any time at the option of the Company as a whole or in part at prices ranging from 106 percent of principal amount in 1972 to par in 1975.

   The indenture provides, among other things, that the Company will make payments to a purchase or sinking fund on December 1, of each of the years 1972 through 1985, in the annual amount of $333,000 reduced by the amount of debentures converted into common stock and by the amount of debentures redeemed or purchased by the Company. The indenture places certain restrictions upon declaration of dividends (other than stock dividends) and upon the purchase or redemption by the Company of its capital stock. None of the September 30, 1971, balance of retained earnings is available for dividends or stock acquisitions.

   A portion of the proceeds of the sale of the convertible debentures was used to pay notes payable in the amount of $3,500,000. These notes are therefore shown in the consolidated balance sheet as noncurrent liabilities.
6. At September 30, 1971, the Company and its subsidiaries were contingently liable in the approximate amount of $13,000,000 in connection with notes discounted or guaranteed.

   In accordance with the terms of the agreement dated December 30, 1970, whereby the Company acquired all of the properties and assets of certain subsidiaries of Goren, Inc. called the "Apco Group" and assumed substantially all liabilities of such subsidiaries, 20 percent of the capital shares of a subsidiary is pledged as collateral for certain obligations owing by Goren, Inc. amounting to $300,000 at September 30, 1971. The remaining 80 percent of the stock of this subsidiary is pledged as collateral for notes payable by the Company to Goren, Inc. under the terms of the December 30, 1970, agreement. The aggregate balance of such notes at September 30, 1971, was $2,600,000, of which $800,000 was paid in December 1971 from the proceeds of the sale of convertible debentures. (See Note 5.)

   In January 1971 stockholders of Goren, Inc. instituted a derivative action to cancel and rescind the sale of the "Apco Group" to the Company. The Company is named in the action as a party defendant. It is the belief of counsel that there is no merit to this action.

   An annual rental of $107,125 is payable for a period of 25 years from November 1, 1967, on property leased by the Company at Westbury, New York. Under renewal options such annual rental is reduced to $53,562. The Company has a contingent liability of approximately $469,000 at September 30, 1971, as guarantor of a first mortgage on such property. Annual rentals of approximately $81,000 are payable on other leases expiring after three years from September 30, 1971.

7. There is an appeal pending against the Company for a breach of contract, and an action pending arising out of a counterclaim asserted in an action brought by the Company. It is the belief of management and of counsel that the appeal and counterclaim are without merit or substance and that there should be no recovery thereon.

In December 1971 the Company and two of its officers and directors were indicted on three counts alleging violation of the Taft-Hartley Act. In the opinion of counsel, the charges are without merit.

The Company has agreed to repurchase certain pinball equipment, sold to a leasing corporation by subsidiaries, in the event the operators of the equipment default under their rental agreements with such corporation. At September 30, 1971, the exposure of the Company amounted to approximately $2,000,000.

Exhibit 1. *(continued)*

```
ACCOUNTANTS' OPINION


To the Board of Directors
Reichman Pinball Machines, Inc.


We have examined the consolidated balance sheet of Reichman Pinball
Machines, Inc., and its subsidiaries as of September 30, 1971, and the
related consolidated statements of income and retained earnings and of
capital surplus for the year then ended.  Our examination was made in
accordance with generally accepted auditing standards, and accordingly
included such tests of the accounting records and such other auditing
procedures as we considered necessary in the circumstances.

In our opinion, the accompanying consolidated financial statements present
fairly the consolidated financial position of Reichman Pinball Machines,
Inc. and its subsidiaries at September 30, 1971, and the consolidated re-
sults of their operations for the year then ended, in conformity with
generally accepted accounting principles applied on a basis consistent with
that of the preceding year.
```

Kincaide, Cramer, and McKee

Kincaide, Cramer, and McKee

New York, February 1, 1972

Exhibit 2. Draft Financial Statements Consolidated Balance Sheet, September 30, 1972

ASSETS

Current Assets			
Cash			$ 300,000
Accounts and notes receivable:			
Trade	$6,200,000		
Others	700,000		
	6,900,000		
Less allowance for doubtful accounts	150,000		
	6,750,000		
Ridge Lending Corporation	3,500,000		
		10,250,000	
Inventories at lower of cost (average or first-in, first-out) or market		5,250,000	
Amounts receivable from purchasers of assets sold subsequent to September 30, 1972		3,300,000	
Prepaid expenses		1,000,000	
Total current assets		20,100,000	
Mortgage receivable (noninterest-bearing, due December 1, 1974)		200,000	
Noncurrent accounts and notes receivable			
Amounts receivable from purchase of assets sold subsequent to September 30, 1972	1,400,000		
Other	650,000		
		2,050,000	
Property, plant, and Equipment:			
Pinball machines	2,900,000		
Other, principally machinery and equipment	2,900,000		
	5,800,000		
Less accumulated depreciation	1,350,000		
	4,450,000		
Land	50,000		

LIABILITIES

Current Liabilities			
Notes and loans payable			$ 7,800,000
Long-term debt, portion due within one year			8,200,000
Accounts payable			2,300,000
Accrued expenses and taxes			700,000
Total Current Liabilities			19,000,000
Long-term debt			
6% convertible subordinated debentures	$4,700,000		
Ridge Lending Corp., affiliate	500,000		
Other	2,700,000		
			7,900,000
Deferred Federal income tax			100,000
Deferred income			450,000
CAPITAL			
Common stock, par value $.10 a share; 4,750,000 shares authorized, 4,080,701 shares issued and outstanding		400,000	
Capital surplus		7,200,000	
Retained deficit		(2,400,000)	
			5,200,000
			$32,650,000

Assets held for sale, at estimated net realizable value	4,500,000
Excess of cost of companies or operating properties acquired over related net assets	1,600,000
Patents, at cost less amortization	1,200,000
Deferred charges and other assets	1,500,000
	1,500,000
	$32,650,000

Consolidated Statement of Income (Loss) and Retained Earnings For the Year Ended September 30, 1972

Sales and operating income	$23,000,000
Cost of sales	15,300,000
	7,700,000
Selling and administrative expenses	6,800,000
	900,000
Depreciation and amortization	800,000
	100,000
Other income, principally interest	300,000
	400,000
Interest expense	1,600,000
Income (loss) before provision (credit) for Federal income tax and extraordinary items	(1,200,000)
Provision (credit) for Federal income tax	(300,000)
Net income (loss) before extraordinary items	(900,000)

EXTRAORDINARY ITEMS

Write-offs as of October 1, 1971

Deferred research and development expenses	$1,500,000	
Deferred expenses related to development of in-plant recreation program	500,000	
Write-down to estimated net realizable value as of September 30, 1972:		
Assets sold subsequent to September 30, 1972 and assets for sale	800,000	
Excess of cost of companies or operating properties acquired over related net assets	600,000	
	3,400,000	
Less Federal income tax adjustments	500,000	
		2,900,000
Net income (loss)		(3,800,000)
Retained earnings, September 30, 1971		1,400,000
Retained earnings (deficit), September 30, 1972		$(2,400,000)